Sherry

After leaving Cambridge, where he read Natural Sciences, Julian Jeffs got a job (by accident) in the sherry trade in Jerez de la Frontera, where he worked in a bodega and saw every stage in the production of wine. He was then called to the bar but took two years off to write the first edition of this book, and to pay other visits to Jerez before practising. As a barrister he became a QC, a Recorder of the Crown Court, Chairman of the Patent Bar Association and a bencher of Gray's Inn; he also wrote two more books on wine and others on law. He retired in 1991, in time to prepare this edition. He is President of the Circle of Wine Writers and general editor of the Faber Books on Wine.

FABER BOOKS ON WINE
General Editor: Julian Jeffs

Bordeaux (new edition) by David Peppercorn
Burgundy by Anthony Hanson
French Country Wines by Rosemary George
German Wines by Ian Jamieson
Italian Wines (new edition) by Philip Dallas
Port (new edition) by George Robertson
Sherry (new edition) by Julian Jeffs
Spirits and Liqueurs by Peter Hallgarten
The Wines of Australia (new edition) by Oliver Mayo
The Wines of Greece by Miles Lambert-Gócs
The Wines of Portugal (new edition) by Jan Read
The Wines of the Rhône (new edition) by John Livingstone-Learmonth

Drilling for Wine by Robin Yapp

SHERRY

JULIAN JEFFS

faber and faber
LONDON · BOSTON

First published in 1961
by Faber and Faber Limited
3 Queen Square London WC1N 3AU

Second edition published in 1970
Third edition published in 1982
Fourth edition published in 1992

Phototypeset by Intype Ltd, London
Printed in England by Clays Ltd, St Ives Plc

Julian Jeffs is hereby identified as author of this work
in accordance with section 77 of the Copyright, Designs and
Patents Act 1988

A CIP record for this book
is available from the British Library

ISBN 0–571–16445–5
0–571–16447–1 (Pbk)

2 4 6 8 10 9 7 5 3 1

This book
is humbly and affectionately dedicated
to the memory of
'DON GUIDO'
CAPTAIN GUY DINGWALL WILLIAMS, OBE, MC
British Vice-Consul at Jerez de la Frontera for forty years
Vintner

Charles: It's the cocktail-drinking does the harm:
   There's nothing on earth so bad for the young.
   All that a civilised person needs
   Is a glass of dry sherry or two before dinner.
   The modern young people don't know what they're drinking,
   Modern young people don't care what they're eating;
   They've lost their sense of taste and smell
   Because of their cocktails and cigarettes.

(*Enter Denman with sherry and whisky. Charles takes sherry and Gerald whisky.*)

   That's what it comes to.

(*Lights a cigarette.*)

From The Family Reunion by T. S. ELIOT

Contents

	Preface to the Fourth Edition	ix
	Acknowledgements	xii
1	The Sherry Country	1
2	Early History	4
3	Sherry Sack	17
4	The Growth of Trade	50
5	The Sherry Boom	77
6	The Recent Past	103
7	Vines and Vineyards	120
8	The Young Wine	175
9	The Wine Matures	202
10	Manzanilla	221
11	The Final Blend	231
12	Into the Glass	261

APPENDICES

I	Spanish Names	269
II	The Chemical Effects of Plastering	270
III	Baumé, Sikes and Gay-Lussac	272
IV	Selected Export Statistics	274
V	Marking of Casks in the Bodega	278
VI	Climatic Statistics	279
VII	Stocks of Maturing Sherry as at 1 September 1978	281

Glossary 282
Sources and Bibliography 289
Index 297

Preface to the Fourth Edition

So much has happened since the first edition of this book was published in 1961 that hardly a page remains as it then was. Between the publication in 1876 of Henry Vizetelly's *Facts about Sherry* and 1961 a great deal happened in the sherry country, but the trade remained extremely traditional and had Vizetelly returned he would have felt completely at home. Then things started to move; they moved rapidly and have done so continuously. Two things have brought this about: an understanding of science and increased labour costs. The changes resulting have nearly all been for the better. Wine merchants and drinkers thirty years ago were a very conservative lot, suspicious of any change. Now that is no longer so and a new generation has grown up which appreciates change. From the works of Chaptal and Pasteur to those of modern scientific oenologists there has been a steady progress throughout the world to eliminate disease and deficiency in wine – a progress that has a parallel in medicine. Nowadays a greater proportion of wines are fine wines than ever before.

Modern labour costs have rendered old techniques – such as treading the grapes and moving wine around a bodega by hand – utterly prohibitive. The new techniques that have replaced them give better wines. Conditions are much cleaner, and every stage in the production of wine is so carefully and knowledgeably regulated that things do not go wrong, as they used to do only too often in the past. Oxidation, for example, is now avoided.

The look of the place has changed, too. The sherry country is much busier and great modern buildings have sprung up, including bodegas of two and three storeys – at Gonzalez Byass, for instance, and Garvey. Happily most of the old buildings remain.

There are undoubtedly things to regret, though. The saddest is the demise of some of the old, small houses which used often to produce outstanding wine, and the amalgamation of others to form large companies. This has been brought about by the economics of trading. Too small a unit simply cannot survive: it cannot afford the new apparatus, it lacks the necessary capital and skill to make itself felt in the market-place and it finds itself overwhelmed by the paperwork of European bureaucracy.

One of the most fascinating stories that spans the four editions of this book, and which is by no means over yet, is that of the rise of the Ruiz-Mateos empire, which at one time controlled a high proportion of the sherry trade including such famous names as Williams & Humbert, Palomino & Vergara, Terry, Diez-Merito and Bodegas Internacionales. It was dispossessed by the government and the whole structure reformed; many of its smaller units disappeared or now exist only as names.

The advent of the EEC, of which Spain and many of its customers are members, has brought changes in regulations, trade practices and economics. When I worked in Jerez in 1956 the sherry shippers completely ran the place, and to my mind one of the most surprising developments is that they do so no longer. Important as the wine trade remains there, it is now just one of several – sugar beet, agricultural machinery and building materials, for example, though many other industries such as bottle making, carton making and printing still rely on the wine and spirit trade to a large degree.

Many of the people who gave me every possible help and good advice when I first wrote this book have, alas, died. However, I have not added 'the late' before their names in the Acknowledgements, which remain as printed in the first edition. Others who gave me great help in writing the second and third editions I thanked in the Introductions to those editions, and I hope they will forgive me for not listing their names again in this one. I must, however, mention one old friend: Manuel Gonzalez Gordon, Marqués de Bonanza, known to everyone in the trade as Uncle Manolo, who knew more about sherry and its history than anyone else who has ever lived and who was unstinting in imparting his wisdom to others, including myself. He was born so sickly a child that his life was despaired of. When he was four months old an eminent paediatrician declared that he could not last a week and that there was nothing to be done. However, as the butler passed by carrying a decanter of sherry with which to refresh the doctor, the baby gurgled and reached towards it. His mother took this as a sign and, as he was bound to die anyhow, gave him a teaspoonful. He kept up the diet ever afterwards and always had a glass of oloroso midmorning to prepare him for the copitas of fino before lunch. He did die, alas, but ninety-three years later.

Of those who have given me especial help with this edition, I owe much to Graham Hines of the Sherry Institute of Spain and to Luis Breton and Bartolomé Vergara of Exportadores de Sherry S.A., who were my hosts during a memorable visit to Jerez which they kindly and very efficiently arranged for me. I found the advice and scientific papers of Dr Alberto García de Lujan Gil de Bernabe of the Estacion de Viticultura y Enologia de Jerez invaluable in helping me to understand new viticultural methods, and I was also greatly assisted in technical and organizational matters by Beltrán Domecq Williams of Domecq; by Mauricio Gonzalez Gordon, Marqués de Bonanza and César Peman of Gonzalez Byass; by Rafael Balao of Emilio Lustau and by Manuel Dominguez of Harveys. Alexander Williams kindly made available a valuable archive assembled by his father, the late Charles Williams. Amongst others who were ever helpful and hospitable were (in alphabetical order): Antonio Barbadillo of Barbadillo, Alan Bell, Luis Caballero of Burdon, William Craven-Bartle of Williams & Humbert, José Ignacio Domecq of Domecq, José Esteve of Réal Tesoro, Nicholas Faith, Antonio Felipe and Diego Ferguson of Harveys, Jaime Gonzalez of Wisdom & Warter, Emilio Hidalgo of Emilio Martin Hidalgo, Javier Hidalgo of Vinicola Hidalgo, Professor Jocelyn Hillgarth, Arthur Humbert, John Lockwood, Ignacio Lopez de Carrizosa of Harveys, Jesus Medina of Medina, Jorge Mundt of Sandeman, George Ordish, Gabriel Osborne of Osborne, Pilar Pla of Maestro Sierra, Carlos del Rio of Garvey, Manuel Robles of Osborne, Alfonso Roldan of Williams & Humbert, David Trimby of Valdespino, Miguel Valdespino of Valdespino, Sergio Vazquez of Sanchez Romato, and Manuel Zarraluqui of Croft. All gave me every help they possibly could.

In addition, Alan Bell kindly read the proofs and made many helpful suggestions.

Julian Jeffs
East Ilsley, 1991

Acknowledgements

So many people have given help and encouragement in the writing of this book that it is impossible to mention all of them. They all gave every assistance they could, and if some did more than others, it was purely fortuitous. Despite all their efforts, there are doubtless many errors and omissions for which the author alone is responsible.

In particular I wish to acknowledge help received from: my father, A. W. Jeffs, for teaching me to enjoy wine; Mr Frederick Griffiths of Innes, Smith & Co., Ltd, for providing my first letters of introduction to sherry shippers; Captain Guy D. Williams, OBE, MC, Beltrán Domecq, and their co-directors of Williams & Humbert, Ltd, who provided every possible kind of help, including reading part of the manuscript; Joseph Craven-Bartle, of Williams & Humbert, Ltd, for invaluable technical advice; Hugh Ungricht and John Lockwood, of Sandeman's, who read part of the manuscript and provided information in connection with vineyards; Manuel Ma. Gonzalez Gordon, of Gonzalez Byass & Co., Ltd, who read part of the manuscript, supplied historical information, and whose classic work, *Jerez-Xerez-Scheris*, has been an invaluable guide; José de Soto y Molina, who very generously allowed me to use his unique library, without which much of this book could not have been written; José Antonio Delgado Orellana for genealogical information relating to the Domecq family; Duff Gordon & Co., Ltd, Garvey, S.A., and J. M. Rivero, S.A., for permitting me to copy ancient letters; André L. Simon, for supplying rare books from the library of the Wine and Food Society; David Peppercorn, of Morgan, Furze & Co., Ltd, for reading part of the manuscript; Antonio Osborne, of Duff Gordon & Co., Ltd, for historical information; José Pan, of Manuel Misa, S.A., for technical information; Luis Gordon, for books and old documents; Sir Osbert Sitwell, Bt, for information concerning George Sitwell; Professor G. M. Trevelyan, OM, for historical information; Arthur Robbins for information concerning the handling of wine; Dr J. N. Hillgarth for the use of his library; Miss Vera Ledger for transcribing ancient manuscripts; Dr E. J. Holmyard, Professor R. J. Forbes, Professor M. Plessner, Professor Millas Vallicrosa, and Professor H. E. Stapleton, for information relating to Arabic viticulture; the Rev. Dermot Moore, PH.D., for information concerning the history of the church of St George, Sanlucar; M. Pierre Maillet of the Laboratoire de Biologie Animale, Faculté des Sciences, Rennes, for his co-operation in supplying illustrations and technical information concerning the phylloxera; A. L. Kitching, MPS, for pharmaceutical information; the Director of the Royal Botanic Gardens, Kew, for information relating to ampelography and viticulture; Colman & Company, of Norwich, for copies of ancient documents; H.M. Foreign Office for consular information; Messrs. Fison's Pest Control, Ltd, for details of methods of combating the phylloxera; the staff of the British Museum (Natural History) for entomological assistance; the Secretary of the Wine Trade Club for permission to publish information concerning the club's portrait of Mr Van Horn; the staff of the British Museum Reading Room, the Public Record Office, Bristol Public Library, the Tettenhall branch of Staffordshire County Library, and the public library of Jerez de la Frontera; in addition I have received help from numerous people concerning the histories of individual shippers.

I wish to thank the following authors and publishers for permission to quote from published works: Don Manuel Barbadillo for his *Canción*; the executors of the late Professor George Saintsbury for a passage from his *Notes on a Cellar Book*; Faber & Faber Ltd for a passage from T. S. Eliot's *The Family Reunion*; the Hutchinson Publishing Group for a long passage by E. M. Nicholson in Guy Mountfort's *Portrait of a Wilderness*; Michael Joseph, Ltd for a passage from H. Warner Allen's *A Contemplation of Wine*; the editor of the *Daily Telegraph* for the passage quoted in the chapter on Manzanilla; Methuen & Co. Ltd and the executrix of the late G. K. Chesterton for verses from *The Flying Inn*; and Bowes and Bowes (Publishers) Ltd for an extract from Roy Campbell's translation of Garcia Lorca's *Romance of the Civil Guard*, taken from his study of the poet. The President of the Consejo Regulador kindly gave permission for an adaptation to be made from the official map of the sherry-producing zone.

J.J.
Wightwick, 1961

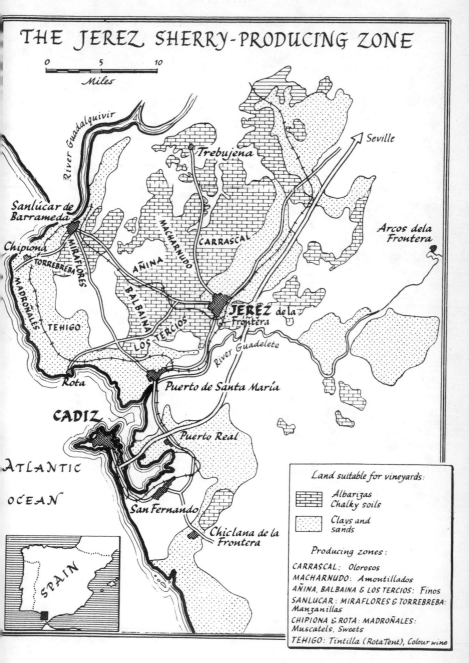

THE JEREZ SHERRY-PRODUCING ZONE

0   5   10

Miles

River Guadalquivir

Seville

Trebujena

Sanlúcar de Barrameda

Arcos de la Frontera

Chipiona

MIRAFLORES

TORREBREBA

MACHARNUDO

CARRASCAL

AÑINA

MADROÑALES

BALBAINA

TEHIGO

JEREZ de la Frontera

LOS TERCIOS

River Guadelete

Rota

Puerto de Santa María

CADIZ

Puerto Real

ATLANTIC

OCEAN

San Fernando

Chiclana de la Frontera

SPAIN

Land suitable for vineyards:

Albarizas
Chalky soils

Clays and
sands

Producing zones:

CARRASCAL: Olorosos
MACHARNUDO: Amontillados
AÑINA, BALBAINA & LOS TERCIOS: Finos
SANLUCAR: MIRAFLORES & TORREBREBA: Manzanillas
CHIPIONA & ROTA: MADROÑALES: Muscatels, Sweets
TEHIGO: Tintilla (Rota Tent), Colour wine

XV

VINEYARDS UNDER CULTIVATION 1979

River Guadalquivir

Trebujena

Sanlúcar de Barrameda

Chipiona

Arcos de la Frontera

JEREZ de la Frontera

River Guadalete

Rota

Puerto de Santa María

CADIZ

Puerto Real

Medina Sidonia

San Fernando

Chiclana de la Frontera

ATLANTIC

OCEAN

I

The Sherry Country

Jerez de la Frontera is a town in Andalusia nearly nine miles inland from the sea. It is on the old main road from Cadiz to Seville and it used to be cursed by travellers as it was a major obstacle. Few of them stopped there, which was a blessing. They drove along busy streets with clean modern shops and saw none of the Moorish remains or romantic ruins that people like to think are typically Spanish. There was nothing to make them suspect that wine was grown there except a surfeit of sherry and brandy advertisements. They could see no vineyards from the main road – only the salt flats near the sea and the fields of wheat and pasture further inland, vivid green after the spring rains and slowly baking to a golden ochre in the heat of the summer. The lack of vineyards surprised them and some asked suspiciously where sherry was grown.

Things are different now. The route of the old road to Cadiz has been changed; there is a bypass round the town and a new motorway to Seville. Unlike the old roads, the new ones pass in full sight of the vineyards, though to see the finest the traveller must turn off into the side roads that lead to Rota, or Trebujena, or Sanlucar de Barrameda, and travel to the north or west across the chalk downs on which the best sherry is grown.

Beyond Trebujena, the road stops and the country grows wild. Rare birds and animals, that are extinct in every other part of Europe, thrive there, and there are no towns or villages. It is the land of the Marismas and the Coto Doñana. Travel is difficult. Game birds abound, as few men ever go there. Those who do go are well rewarded: they may see an Indian sand lark, masked shrike, golden oriole or Spanish imperial eagle. A hundred and ninety-three species of birds have been counted on the Coto Doñana, and it is equally rich in animals and plants. At the beginning of February the storks fly in from South Africa and settle in high places such as church towers and the tops of disused chimneys. Here they breed and rear their young until they fly away at the end of June. To have a storks' nest on the premises is considered to be a sign of luck.

It is easy to see why the sherry country has never been a centre for tourists. The rolling downlands on which the vines grow are delightful but by no means dramatically beautiful. The towns have no world class architecture, yet they are full of good things: old churches, some palatial houses of real beauty, the more modest, mellowed houses of ancient families, and above all the fine bodega buildings. Yet when a traveller does stop in Jerez he can fall hopelessly in love with it and cannot draw himself away. It is a city of light and joy. I speak from experience; I first went there in 1956 for five days and stayed eight months. It became more enchanting every day. I used to wander for hours through streets of whitewashed houses and through the narrow alleyways of the old town, catching short, tantalizing glimpses of patios, and looking at the huge geraniums weaving in and out of the tracery of wrought-iron balconies. From the Alcazar I saw the sun setting radiantly on the tiled summit of the tower of San Miguel. Then at night, away from the bright lights of the Calle Larga, Jerez grew mysterious in the darkness, and isolated lamps threw irrelevant pools of light, making long shadows as the noise of the town became hushed.

Jerez (pronounced Hereth) is the principal of three sherry towns. The others are both on the coast: Puerto de Santa Maria, nine miles to the south-west, and Sanlucar de Barrameda, thirteen miles to the north-west at the mouth of the River Guadalquivir. Between them, they make all the genuine sherry that is sold throughout the world. Although they are only a few miles apart, even such a small distance is enough to cause some change in the climate and atmosphere, and any change, however slight, will be reflected in the wine: for wine is a living thing; it is never static but always changing; it will take its own course; it is often capricious and develops quite unexpectedly.

For those who love sunshine but can put up with an occasional torrential rainstorm, Jerez is an admirable place to live in. In summer the temperature sometimes rises for a few days to the uncomfortable height of 38°C in the shade and the maximum day temperature in winter is never much below 15°C; the average maximum is 23°C. It occasionally freezes at night in winter, but in the height of summer the minimum temperature may be as high as 19°C; the mean is

11°C. On the whole, the days are hot and sunny, while the nights are delightfully cool. It rains during seventy-five days each year, and when it is not raining, there is generally sunshine: grey, dull, inconclusive British weather is mercifully rare. The total rainfall is about 650 mm and the mean humidity is surprisingly high: 66 per cent.

There is not very much difference between the wines of Jerez and Puerto, though the latter is particularly noted for sherries of the fino and amontillado styles. The wines of Sanlucar, however, are entirely different: all the manzanilla is made there. It has a distinctive, very fresh flavour that cannot be reproduced anywhere else.

2

Early History

Jerez is a very ancient town whose origin is veiled in mystery. Most probably it was founded as a colony of the Phoenicians. They lived by commerce, manufacture and trade, and were attracted to Andalusia by rumours of fertility and by the mineral riches of the lost city of Tartessus. At one time or another this fabulous city has been identified with all the major towns of southern Andalusia, though some think its site has sunk beneath the sea. All one can say with certainty is that it stood near to the sherry area.

The Phoenicians founded Cadiz in 1100 BC and then moved inland to the town of Xera. There is a legend that they deserted Cadiz because of the Levante – the harsh east wind that blows for days on end and sends people mad. Those who know the Levante find the story easy to believe. No one knows exactly where Xera was, but many historians identify it with Jerez. Theopompos, the pupil of Isocrates, writing in the fourth century BC, refers to 'the town of Xera near the Columns of Hercules', and that could certainly apply to Jerez, but the identity is very doubtful. The prefix Xer- or Cer- is probably derived from the ancient Iberian word meaning a camp or fort on a river, and Xera could as easily be Vejer, or the deserted town of Cera, some nine miles from Jerez. Others have suggested that Jerez was founded by Greeks or Carthaginians.

If the origin of Jerez is doubtful, that of wine is even more obscure: no one knows who invented it. The Bible gives the honour to Noah: 'And God blessed Noah . . . And Noah began to be a husband-man, and he planted a vineyard: And he drank of the wine, and was drunken . . .' (Genesis 9:1, 20–21). Charles Tovey had another theory. Jam-Sheed, the founder of Persepolis, was immoderately fond of grapes and preserved them in great jars for eating out of season. Some of them got crushed, and the fermented juice tasted so unlike grape juice that he wrote 'poison' on the jar and set it aside to be thrown away. One of his favourite handmaidens was tired of life and drank the poison to do away with herself. The effect was not quite what she expected, and when she came round she drank some more, and so on, until there was none left. Then she confessed her crime. Thus was wine discovered, and it became known in Persia as *Teher-e-Kooshon* – 'the delightful poison'.

Grape wine is by no means the most senior potation: mead probably came first and then beer. The earliest fermented fruit juice recorded in history was date wine, and it was very popular. Xenophon described it as 'a pleasant drink causing headache'. The vine, however, was cultivated and grape wine was prepared as early as the prehistoric Djemdet-Nast period in Mesopotamia, and it was brought into Egypt before 3000 BC. These North African wines found little favour: Martial preferred vinegar, and Strabo claimed that Libyan wine tasted well when mixed with sea water. The Greeks, on the other hand, practised viticulture as an art, and the earliest detailed essays on the subject are by Theophrastus of Eresos (*c.* 372–286 BC), the pupil of Aristotle. An earlier treatise by Democritus of Abdera is unfortunately lost. Accounts of wine growing were also given by a number of Latin authors, notably Cato (234–149 BC), Varro (116–27 BC) and Columella (*fl.* 60 BC), who was born in Cadiz, though his treatise is based on grape growing in Italy.

The wild vine, in its various species, was widely distributed throughout the temperate regions of the world, and fossil remains have been found as far north as Iceland. It was first methodically cultivated in eastern Europe, in the regions of the Caucasus and the Caspian Sea. There is no reason to believe it was indigenous to Spain; nor do we know who brought it there. Although a bold historian has stated that the Phoenicians found better wine in Spain than they had ever known in Palestine or Cyprus, it is just as possible that they found none at all, and his assertion may be regarded as patriotic rather than historical. Others, indeed, have claimed that the Phoenicians actually introduced the vine, though it seems more probable that it was brought in by Greek settlers in the sixth or fifth century BC and, if so, it may well be that the name of Jerez is also Greek in origin. One of the greatest wines of history was malmsey, the Byzantine dessert wine produced in the Peloponnesus and exported from Monemvasia – the same wine in which the unfortunate Duke of Clarence was drowned. One of the centres of viticulture in those days was the Persian city of Shiraz, which was a probable source of any vines imported by the Greeks. What could be more reasonable than to name their new town after that city? And so, perhaps, Jerez was named by the same process as New York and New Orleans, not to mention Toledo, Ohio. Such a suggestion would have been scorned by Richard Ford. He condemned authors who 'to show their learning' derived the word sherry from the Greek θηρος and added 'to have done so from the Persian Shiraz would scarcely have been more far-fetched'. One can only speculate: the truth will never be known, though modern scholars are sure there is no connection.

The Phoenician rule was so disturbed by the hostility both of the natives and of the Greek settlers that they had to call to their allies the Carthaginians for help. Hamilcar came to the rescue, followed by Hasdrubal and Hannibal, but the plan miscarried: not content merely to give aid, the Carthaginians expelled the Phoenicians and took the colony as conquerors, only to lose it again to the power of Rome during the second Punic War. But even for Rome the conquest was not easy. Although the civilized Phoenicians and Carthaginians gave way easily, the native tribes offered terrible resistance and guerrilla warfare continued for two hundred years. Livy recorded, in his twenty-eighth book, that the population of Rome was alarmed by a series of most terrifying omens:

> In a state where the greatest anxiety prevailed . . . accounts of many prodigies were received; that Mater Matuta at Satricum had been struck by lightning. The people of Satricum were no less terrified by two snakes gliding into the temple of Jupiter by the very doors. A report was brought from Antium, that bloody ears of corn had been seen by the reapers. At Caere a pig with two heads had been littered, and a lamb weaned which was both male and female. Intelligence was brought that two suns had been seen at Alba, and that light had suddenly appeared during the night at Fregellae. An ox was reported to have spoken in the Roman territory. A copious perspiration was said to have exuded from the altar of Neptune, in the Flaminian circus; and the temples of Ceres, Safety, and Quirinius were said to have been struck by lightning . . . the extinction of the fire in the temple of

Vesta struck more terror upon the minds of men than all the prodigies which were reported from abroad, or seen at home; and the vestal, who had the guarding of it for that night, was scourged by the command of Publicius Licinius the pontiff.

When eventually the Romans captured Spain they found many vineyards, but the favourite drink of the Iberians was a kind of mead.

Jerez has been identified with the Roman city of Ceritium, and there are many Roman remains in the district, especially at Sanlucar. During the Roman domination, viticulture advanced very rapidly, and the area soon became renowned for its wine. in the archaeological museum at Jerez there is a fragment of Roman mosaic with a vine-leaf motif on the border, and Andalusian coins of the period were decorated with bunches of grapes. The wine was cheap, and it is not surprising that it became a favourite with the invader; it was exported from Puerto Real to Rome in great earthenware amphorae, of which there are many still intact. Some archaeologists believe the Arabic walls of Jerez were built on Roman foundations. Sections of these walls still exist and one of them passes straight through a row of private houses. Parts of them are incorporated into three of the bodegas, those of Domecq, Lustau and what was O'Neale; and the last-named includes a complete tower, from the top of which there is a wonderful view of the town.

Wine from the Roman provinces eventually became so good that the Italian growers could not face the competition, and in AD 92 the emperor Domitian ordered vineyards in Gaul and Spain to be cut down; but the order could not be enforced, and it was officially withdrawn by Probus in AD 282. By that time, the policy of *panem et circenses* had become so much a part of Roman life that large quantities of wine had to be imported from abroad to prevent a rebellion of the plebs.

Martial, like many other great Romans, was born in Spain during the first century AD. One of his more respectable epigrams is said to be about sherry, and has often been quoted:

> *Caeretana Nepos ponat, Setina putabis*
> *Non ponit turbae, cum tribus illa bibit.*
>   Book XIII, 124

(Let Nepos serve you with sherry; you will think it wine of Satia.

But he does not serve it to everyone – he drinks it only with a trio of friends.)

Whether this is in fact about sherry is doubtful: it could equally refer to the wine of Caere in Etruria.

The Roman supremacy ended with the invasion of the Vandals, a Teutonic tribe which was probably innocent of all the sacrilege suggested by its name. The Silingian Vandals occupied southern Spain in AD 409 and were soon virtually exterminated, but their fellow tribesmen, the Asdingian Vandals, marched down from the north and took possession of their country. They only stayed a few years – the whole nation set sail for Africa in AD 428 – but it was long enough for them to give a new name to the country they had conquered. They called it Vandalusia, and that name, except for its initial letter, has survived to this day.[1] Their descendants, the Berbers, were to return with a vengeance some hundred years later.

It was a period of perpetual wars and great turbulence. In AD 414 the Visigoths arrived. This tribe was the ally of Imperial Rome, and the Gothic power long survived the Roman in Iberia. The Goths embraced the Christian faith at the end of the sixth century, and a hundred years later, during the reign of Recceswinth, the law prohibiting a Goth from marrying a native was repealed. The rule of the Gothic aristocracy then ended and the two nations to some extent intermingled, creating the Romance Spanish language. Andalusia continued as a Gothic kingdom rather than a Roman province or a Spanish nation as we know it today, and documents of the period refer to Jerez as Scheres or Seritium.

In AD 711 the Visigoths were overthrown by the infidel Mussulmans, with their allies the Berbers, at the famous battle of Guadalete, fought not far from Jerez; current thinking is that it was fought by the Guadalete near Arcos de la Frontera. The battle was on a fantastic scale and raged for a week between Roderick, the last king of the Goths, and Tarik Ben Zeyad, leading the Saracens. It must have been a scene of the most abominable destruction and havoc. That the latter army was superior in quality is undoubted; that it was also superior in numbers, as sometimes suggested, is open to

1 This theory has been criticized, and R. P. Flores has suggested that the name is derived from the Arabic *andalos*, meaning 'end of light' – a word used when referring to the Occident.

question, as the Gothic civilization had become so decadent that it was no longer a formidable enemy.

With their comparatively small force the Moors swept over the Peninsula. Within the space of two or three years they had reached the Pyrenees, conquering every Christian army they encountered. At Cordova there was some fighting, but the other great cities of the Goths yielded without a blow. Even their capital, Toledo, fell without resistance, betrayed, it is said, by the persecuted Jews, who could be sure of more generous treatment from the infidels. The Christians only had time to gather up a box of relics: a tooth of Santiago, an arm of Eugenius, a sandal of Peter. Their worldly treasures were all left behind, and the invaders were vastly more satisfied with the gold than they would have been with the relics. The Moors indeed were enlightened conquerors, initially allowing the Christians to follow their own ways and even to celebrate mass in their churches – a liberalism of thought which was most emphatically lacking in the Christians when their turn came.

With the victory of the Moors, a period began in Andalusia that gave rise to one of the most astonishing civilizations in the whole history of Europe. From that time onwards, there is no need for conjecture: everything is well known and well documented. Moorish blood still flows through the veins of the people, and shadows of the past linger in their customs, music, art, and the habits of their minds. To trace the influence would be an enormous task; it is everywhere and it is indelible. Artistically, the era was unique; one has only to visit the mosque at Cordova or the Alhambra at Granada to see its beauty and artistry. There has never been anything like it before or since, and the preservation of such perfect remains is a wonderful tribute to Spain; had they been in England, they would have perished long ago. It is fascinating to try and reconstruct from old maps and records a view of Jerez as it was in those days, but such attempts must always end in sorrow. Granada remains more or less intact and we must be content with that. Nor can we complain too bitterly; the Moorish craftsmen applied themselves to Christian architecture and we have the great Giralda tower and the Alcazar at Seville to remember them by.

During the Moorish domination, Jerez grew and became wealthy. It was called Šeriš, a name that was later corrupted to Jerez by the Spanish and to Sherry by the English. In fact no other city in Spain has been given so many names: the only people who did not try to rename it were the Jews.[1] The ancient name of Puerto de Santa Maria (the second of the sherry towns) was Puerto de Menestheo, and it was the site of an old temple dedicated to the goddess Juno. When Alfonso the Sage wrested the town from the Moors in 1264, he dedicated it to the Virgin Mary.

The prosperity of Jerez followed naturally from its position, dominating fertile lands. In the twelfth century, El Idrisi or, to give him his full name, Abu Abdallah Ibn Mohammed Ibn Mohammed Ibn Abdallah Ibn Idrisi, the Geographer Royal to King Roger II of Sicily, published his *Mappa Mundi*, of which there is a copy in the Bodleian Library, and which clearly shows the position of Šerīš between *kadis* (Cadiz) and *išbilia* (Seville). Another ancient geographer, Ibn Abd al-Mun'im al Himyari, wrote in his *Ar-rawd al Mitar*: 'Xerez is a strong town of moderate size encircled by walls; the country around it is pleasant to the eye, consisting of vineyards, olive orchards and fig trees.'

The interesting thing is the mention of vineyards, as wine was strictly prohibited to the Mohammedans. But what nation can remain teetotal in the midst of the most productive vineyards in the world? The Moors certainly could not; and although the sale of wine was contrary to the law, it was subject to an excise tax. Al-Motamid, the Poet King, and last Moorish king of Seville, liked it so much that he publicly mocked at those who only drank water. And who can blame him? He was by no means alone; no one has written eulogies of wine greater than those of the Moorish poets:

How often the cup has clothed the wings of darkness with a mantle of shining light!

From the wine came forth the sun. The orient was the hand of the gracious cupbearer, and my loved one's lips were the occident.

---

1 Names listed by Parada y Barreto include: Asido, Asindium, Asidonia, Asidona, Asido Cesariana, Asta Regia, Asta Regia Cesariana, Anccis, Astasia, Carteya, Caesariana, Caesaris Castra, Cera, Ceret, Ceritium, Ciduena, Civita Regia, Esuris, Fera, Gerez, Gerencis Civita, Hasta Regia, Itucci, Jerez de la Frontera, Munda, Munda Cesariana, Medina Xerez, Reales de Cesar, Saduna, Siduena, Sidonia, Sera, Seriencis Civita, Seraciencis Civita, Sadormin, Tarteso, Turdeto, Tucci, Xarez, Xera, Xeracia, Xiraz, Xericio, Xereto, Xeris, Xerez Sidonia, Xerez Saduna, Xerez de la Frontera, Wandalia. Some of these, of course, are mere variants, and others are hotly disputed, while some probably relate to nearby towns rather than to Jerez itself, but the list is included for the sake of completeness.

*Between her white fingers the chalice of golden wine was a yellow
narcissus asleep in a silver cup.*

From the *Diwan* of Principe Marwan
(963–1009)

Even the most pious Muslims had no qualms about preparing
wine for the Christian and Jewish infidels. Grapes were also grown
for fruit, and viticulture was by no means neglected – a fact amply
demonstrated by the excellent article in Ebn-el-Awam's massive
work on agriculture.

It was not a peaceful time; the Moors were under frequent
pressure from the Catholic princes (when they were not too busy
fighting one another to bother about the heathen) and Jerez was
laid waste during the expedition of Alfonso VII against Cadiz in
1133, but it rose again and continued under Moorish rule until it
was finally reconquered by the Christians in 1264, or thereabouts;
the precise date is uncertain. There was a ding-dong battle between
the Christians and the Moors that lasted from Covadonga in 718 to
the final reconquest of Granada by the Catholic kings on 6 January
1492, with honours claimed repeatedly by both sides, often with
very little reason. One of the major battles was fought outside Jerez
in 1231, an occasion on which a miracle was said to have taken
place: the Muslims saw St James on a gigantic white horse, with a
white banner, waving a sword and leading a legion of knights. It is
difficult to say exactly when Jerez became Christian. It is recorded
that at various times (the years 1242, 1251 and 1255 being mentioned in old chronicles) the rulers of Jerez paid tribute to the King
of Castile and became his vassals without fighting but that the
Christians rose against the Moors and were expelled from the town
in 1261. The first of these dates at any rate does not appear to be
right: when Seville fell in 1248, many of the Muslim refugees fled to
Jerez. In Jerez it is generally accepted that the Christians under
Alfonso X took the town by surprise on 9 October 1264, the feast
of St Dionysius the Areopagite (of unfortunate literary memory).
They forced an entry, decked the walls with the sign of the Cross,
and made Jerez the principal Christian stronghold of the frontier
between the two warring kingdoms. It was never to fall again.

Five years later, King Alfonso granted arms to Jerez: 'Waves of
the sea in blue and white because they never rest from making blows
on the firm rocks, as you have waged continuous war on the enemy;

these surrounded by the lions and castles of our Royal Arms as the symbols of fortitude.'

The king was known as Alfonso the Sage, and was celebrated throughout the land for his learning. One of the wisest things he ever did was to encourage the cultivation of the vine and wine-making in his newly conquered territories. To some extent, at least, we owe the modern supremacy of sherry to his enthusiasm – the first of many royal patrons. He divided the lands between his supporters, and the story is told of how one of them was working in his vineyard, pruning the vines, when he noticed a figure walking behind him, picking up the branches. It was the king, content to be a labourer.

The continuous wars did not cease with the reconquest. For many years Jerez remained at the frontier of the Muslim kingdom, at the limit of the dominions of the Crown of Castile, and in 1285, very soon after the reconquest, it had to withstand a lengthy siege by the army of Jusuf, with his twenty thousand cavalrymen. It was one of the most glorious episodes in the history of Jerez. Unfortunately, Jusuf, like most soldiers, had no eye for the exquisite and saw fit to pitch his camp in the middle of the vineyards. All the battles and encounters were fought over the vines, and they were utterly laid waste. Well might Old Kaspar have mumbled, "twas a famous victory'; but what a price to pay!

It would appear that the vineyards in those days were principally to the east of the town, rather than in the directions most highly favoured today.

In 1380 King Juan I granted the privilege of adding to the town's name *de la Frontera* (which it shares with the other nearby frontier towns of Arcos, Castellar, Chiclana, Cortes, Jimena, Moron and Vejer) in honour of the part played by its people in the continuous struggle for power, and Enrique IV (1451–74) gave it the well-earned title, *Muy Noble y Muy Leal Ciudad*. But during the four-teenth century there was little mention of the vine; one can read only of typhus, plague and war. Even after the reconquest of Granada and the complete supremacy of Castile, the threat and terror of the raiders continued. As late as 1580, a dispatch from Roger Bodenham in Sanlucar reads: 'The Moriscos have risen again and done great harm . . . Sheris is in some doubt of them because they are many.' (The Moriscos were Muslims, mostly labourers, who found it convenient to be baptized but who never became loyal; they were finally expelled between 1609 and 1614.) But throughout its history Spain has been a land of political upheaval and unrest, living always at the edge of some terror: the Vandals; the Moors; the Holy Inquisition; English pirates; the Dutch; the Peninsular War; and, latterly, the ruin and devastation of the Civil War, in which the sherry country mercifully escaped very lightly.

At the beginning of the fifteenth century, times were bad: the population had been reduced by plagues, and the lands had been devastated by serious floods in 1402. On 5 April 1402 Enrique III issued a proclamation forbidding any man to destroy vines or olive trees. The penalty was a heavy fine, the money to be spent on repairing the city walls. But as the century progressed, there came a great resurgence of the vine, which soon spread from the inferior soil near the town to the present vineyard area. The books of *Actas Capitulares* of Jerez began to be kept in the first decade of the fifteenth century, and from then onwards there are repeated references to the export trade. In 1435 exports were forbidden owing to bad harvests and the high price of wine, but only in two years did the vintage fail completely: in 1479, when there was heavy rain in May followed by continuous Levantes and excessive heat, and in 1483, when the vines were damaged by hail. That trade with England and France was being conducted is further supported by a document of 1483 which states that Breton and English ships had ceased from calling owing to a war with Vizcaya.

These local events were taking place in the context of great changes which affected the whole of the Mediterranean region and which ultimately benefited Spain. The most important was the fall of Constantinople, taken by the Turks under Mahomet II in 1453. This ended the eastern Roman empire. From 1461 to 1477 there was war between the Turks and the all-powerful Venice; the Venetians lost many of their eastern possessions and their trade was further hurt by the discovery of America in 1492. Before its decline Venice had been the pivot of Mediterranean trade, which included the sweet wines exported to England. Spain was more than willing to fill the vacuum, and set to work at once.

In 1491 the local council declared that wines and other produce shipped abroad should be exempted from tax. The proclamation is important for two reasons: firstly, because it applied both to local and to foreign merchants, proving that these were living and trading in Jerez at the time, and secondly because it referred to the wines as *vinos de romania*, or rumney. Rumney, like malmsey, is a name that conjures up a glorious past. Originally it came from southern Greece, and the merchants of Jerez had no more right to ship a rumney than have the growers of South Africa to ship a sherry. Their intention was to take over the old Venetian trade. Rumney was not drunk locally, which suggests that it was too rich for the hot Andalusian climate and confirms that it was intended to replace the sweet wines of the eastern Mediterranean; it was avoided there as brown sherries are today, or like vintage port in Oporto. Nine years earlier, the governor of the new town of Regla de Santa Maria (now called Chipiona) had issued a proclamation that these export wines were to be made carefully, using good vines like those used for sherry, so that they would maintain their reputation.

The wine was evidently held in high esteem and fetched a very high price according to the standards of those days. Red wines were made as well as white, and continued to be made to a limited extent until well into the nineteenth century, but they were not very good.

In 1492 the Jews were expelled from Spain. It was one of the most controversial and far-reaching episodes in the whole history of Europe, and one which historians are still wrangling over. But it did not greatly affect Jerez. Thirty aranzadas of sherry vineyards were confiscated from the Jews and given to the Royal Convent of Santo Domingo. In Spain, as elsewhere, the religious houses were amongst the pioneers of viticulture. The great monastery of the Cartuja, or Charterhouse, was founded outside Jerez in 1475, and in 1658 it was reported as having flourishing vineyards that gave excellent wine. The street called Bodegas formerly led to the wine stores of the old monastery of Veracruz.

Before long, droves of foreigners came to fill the vacuum left by the expulsion of the Jews. They were, for the most part, Genoese, Bretons and English. Some acted as money changers, while the Genoese took over the tanneries and formed their own trade guild. The English were mostly merchants, and many of them were interested in wine. From the earliest days, the merchants trading in Jerez exported their goods from the quays of El Portal, on the River Guadalete, a mile or two from the town. This river port continued in use until the coming of the railway four hundred years later, and the goods were taken down to the sea on barges. There is still a street called Barqueros, where some of the barge masters had their offices, but the arrangement was never completely satisfactory: the quays were always falling into disrepair, and the river silted up.

The archives at Jerez contain many early references to wine being shipped abroad. As early as 1485 there is a record of wine shipped from Puerto de Santa Maria to 'Plemma, which is in the kingdom of England' – presumably Plymouth. By that date the vintage was already subject to strict control, and the greatest crime of all was to water down the wine. The size of a butt, for instance, following complaints from Flanders, was fixed at thirty arrobas – precisely as it is today; and the butts had to be branded by the cooper and by the council. The coopers were amongst the earliest of the recognized guilds, and in 1482 it was stipulated that wine casks must be made of good wood that was not tainted with any kind of fish, nor with oil. Any cask made of wood that could damage the wine was to be burnt and a fine imposed.

At the end of the fifteenth century there came to Andalusia the greatest excitement of all: nine months after the conquest of Granada, Columbus discovered America. All his efforts, his intrigues with the Church and the monarchy, his triumphs and disappointments, the elaborate preparations for his voyages, the voyages themselves, all were centred on Andalusia. From Andalusia he gathered his forces, and many of his men came from the sherry towns. He set forth from Sanlucar de Barrameda on his third journey, to discover the island of Trinidad in 1498, and Sanlucar was soon established as a major port for the new American trade; it was the port from which Pizarro set sail twenty-five years later on his way to conquer Peru. Alvar Nuñez Cabeza de Vaca, who discovered Florida, was the son of a Jerez wine grower.

The ships were well provisioned, and good supplies of wine were essential. Large quantities were bought from Jerez, and when Magellan set out to circumnavigate the world in 1519 he spent more on sherry than on armaments. It is safe to say that sherry was the first wine to enter the USA. It has been drunk there ever since. Not even the most fanatical prohibitionists could keep it out; they only succeeded in reducing the supplies of good wine and replacing them with poisonous pot-still liquors that blinded men.

The sherry trade with England was well established by the sixteenth century, but it originated much earlier, in the time of the Moorish domination. It may have begun during the reign of King Edward III, whose maritime policy encouraged such trade, and there is a record of Spanish wine being imported in 1340. Wine in those days was very properly regarded as a necessity, and the search for it provided one of the greatest incentives towards the development of the mercantile marine, which, in turn, ultimately led to Britain's immense sea power. One of the earliest trades with southern Spain, however, was in salt, prepared from the sea marshes near Cadiz, and it has been suggested that the local wines were first imported as a make-weight by merchants dealing in the salt and fruit trades.

In Chaucer's *Pardoner's Tale* there is an interesting reference to the wine of Lepe:

> *Now keep ye from the white and from the red,*
> *And namely from the white wine of Lepe,*
> *That is to sell in Fish Street or in Chepe.*
> *This wine of Spain creepeth subtilly*
> *In other wines, growing fast by,*
> *Of which there riseth such fumositee,*
> *That when a man hath drunken draughtes three,*
> *And weneth that he be at home in Chepe,*
> *He is in Spain, right at the town of Lepe,*
> *Not at the Rochelle, nor at Bordeaux town.*

'Fumositee' is a beautiful word; its meaning is so clear that no lexicographer would dare define it. Chaucer (1340?–1400) was the son of a vintner and was notoriously accurate in everything he mentioned, so it appears that wines from southern Spain were already fortified when he wrote his Tales, and this is borne out by the knowledge that the Moors distilled alcohol and used it for medicinal purposes. Elizabethan 'sack' was certainly fortified.

Lepe is a village between Ayamonte and Huelva, a few miles from the coast, and white wines from that district have been imported into Jerez for blending with sherry even during living memory. They are rather light but of a similar style. When Ford wrote his *Handbook to Spain* during the last century, he visited Lepe and found that 'much bad wine is made, which is sent to San Lucar, and converted for the English market into fine sherry . . .' In fact the wine is not at all bad, judged purely as a local *ordinaire*, was probably sent to Jerez and Puerto de Santa Maria in greater quantities than to Sanlucar, and could be used only for blending with mediocre sherry, but at least he was right in principle. Chaucer was writing of a wine very similar to sherry, if not of sherry itself.

3
Sherry Sack

The English are insatiable travellers and born shopkeepers; wherever good trade is to be found, there is sure to be an English colony, and there have certainly been English merchants in Andalusia since the Middle Ages. Their leading colony was established in Sanlucar, which was then an important port, thanks to its geographical position at the mouth of the estuary of the River Guadalquivir and to its political status as a suzerain of the powerful Dukes of Medina Sidonia. It had been awarded to Don Alonso Perez de Guzman, known as The Good, by the King of Castile in 1297 in gratitude for his services in the wars against the Moors. The sixth member of the family to enjoy the suzerainty was created Duke of Medina Sidonia in 1446. The principal commercial advantage lay in the fact that the Dukes exacted their own customs duties, which were lower than those of the Crown. The seat of the family is there to this day but the port was incorporated into Spain and the suzerainty ceased in 1645.

The Dukes did everything in their power to encourage foreign trade. It is not known when the English merchants first settled there but the earliest records that do exist clearly point to a long-established colony. In September 1491 the then Duke had issued a proclamation that Spanish and foreign merchants could export wine by sea without paying customs duty. Peace and steady trade do not make news and the sheer lack of records suggests that these admirable conditions obtained in the early days. Documents appear when things began to go wrong. In 1517 the regnant Duke became concerned that there were fewer English merchants in his port than formerly and issued a new charter of privileges which recited in its preamble that English merchants had been trading there since the grant to the first member of the family. The privileges they were granted included: a piece of land on which to build a church dedicated to St George[1] and to be used not only for worship but also as a meeting place; new rates of customs duty; speedier justice and the elimination of futile appeals that delayed the payment of debts due to them; the collection of debts owed by local merchants to the Duke to be delayed so that the debts due to foreign merchants could be paid promptly; improved lighterage and loading facilities; the right to carry weapons by day and by night; the provision of eight houses in the town to give them greater privacy and storage space; and the right of their consul to hear and settle disputes between them if they should so wish. Above all, the Duke put them under his own special protection. One matter deserves particular mention. There had been trouble with the customs officials when wine had been taken through the customs for shipment and then for some reason, such as lack of room on board ship, had had to be brought back for reloading later. He ruled that the cheaper wines such as 'bastardes' and 'cuytes' (vino de color, see below) could be landed without any formalities but that the landing of wines such as sacks and rumneys had to be reported; no more than ten butts could be brought back from any one ship and they had to be stored in premises having two locks, the key of one to be kept by an official and the other by the merchant, a system still used in bonds today.

Some of the merchants trading in Andalusia at that time had places of business both in England and in Spain. One of these was to play a particularly important part in the colony at this time: William Ostrych, who is recorded as living and trading at Sanlucar as early as 1523, when he described himself as a citizen of Bristol. His name had appeared for the first time in the Bristol customs records for the years 1517–18.

All the evidence is that the English merchants were rugged individualists and rivals. Trading together in one small town, they must have known one another, but during the days of prosperity there is no hint of any combination or organization. Only in adversity did they combine together and then not very effectively. They did so once in order to petition the Duke. To give coherence to their organization and standing in the eyes of the English government they petitioned King Henry VIII and in September 1530 he granted

1 For a detailed history of this church see *Publications of the Catholic Record Society*, Vol. XIV (1914).

them a constitution. It was then that the Andalusia Company – commonly known as the Brotherhood of St George – came into being. In the thirteen years since the Duke's charter, conditions between Spain, with its intense Catholicism, and England had deteriorated greatly. For a short period in 1528 the two countries had been at war. In 1529 the English merchants complained that they were the least favoured nation and that their privileges were not being observed.

At the beginning of his reign, Henry had been Defender of the Faith, most outspoken of all the European monarchs against the Lutheran heresy. By 1530, however, rumours were rife of his impending divorce from Catherine of Aragon and relations with Spain were extremely strained. With his eventual break from Rome and above all with his divorce and his marriage to Anne Boleyn in 1533, he became abominable to the Spaniards, and those English merchants who loyally tried to defend him stood in danger of the Inquisition if their defence extended to condoning his attitude to the Church. Their own position must have been very difficult, for some were undoubtedly good Catholics whilst others found it prudent to acknowledge one church when in Spain and another when in England. These difficulties and the apprehension of worse to follow brought the merchants together.

By the time of King Henry VIII's charter, the church of St George had been built – the first of three churches to be built on its site, one of which, though somewhat dilapidated, is still standing. Under the charter, the merchants were to assemble for the purpose of electing a consul, or governor, and twelve 'ancient and expert persons' to be assistants, with 'full power to levy such imposts as shall be thought necessary, and to make ordinances for their welfare'. Besides the London merchants, there were to be two each from Bristol and Southampton, though the evidence is that far more were trading from the former port. The imposts were inevitably to prove unpopular, yet without them it was impossible for the company to exist. Indeed, its life was short. Nothing is known of it immediately after its formation but on 24 April 1539, a meeting was held in St George's church which was attended by eighteen merchants who elected William Ostrych to be their governor.

Some years earlier, in 1530, an English merchant, who was described in the Spanish records as 'Juan Esvique', petitioned against an order that no one should buy sherry as agent for another. He stated that many other Englishmen living in the town were buying wine on behalf of 'rich English merchants who could not be everywhere at the same time and therefore have their agents in various parts', and that such an order would ruin their trade. He had apparently lived in Jerez for many years and thought of it as his home, but his identity remains a mystery: Warner Allen suggests his name was Weeks, but Rupert Croft-Cooke thinks it was possibly a corruption of Esquire, though the title of Esquire was not commonly used at that time and had a definite social significance. The only name of a known resident that is at all like it is that of James Wake, a merchant in Cadiz, and the mysterious Esvique could well have been another member of his family.

Apart from merchants, there were apparently English gentlemen of leisure living in Andalusia. When, in 1519, the mayor of Chipiona, Gonzalo Bernal de la Becerra, required a noble sponsor who would take him before the son of the Duke of Arcos to pay homage, he approached John Oste, of the same town – 'the English cavalier . . . known to be a nobleman'. It was common during the sixteenth and seventeenth centuries for the younger sons of noble and landed English families to go abroad and make a career for themselves in trade. They often grew rich and used their money to increase their families' estates – land being the most practical form of investment at that time. In 1664, for instance, George Sitwell, who had settled in the service of Alderman King, of London, as a merchant in Malaga, sent his father two barrels of Tent to Renishaw. He was a very generous man, for he was always sending presents home, including an emerald ring. Tent is a rather unusual wine made at Rota, a small seaside town between Sanlucar and Puerto de Santa Maria, well inside the sherry area.

In the early years trade may have been tranquil and profitable, but during the reigns of Henry VIII and Elizabeth it was full of perils and the English settlers were continually molested by the Inquisition. Thomas Pery, a wealthy cloth merchant who divided his time between London and Ayamonte, was tormented and imprisoned in the castle of Tryana in 1539.[1]

All English trading here are in fear of the fathers of the Inquisition.

1 For a detailed history of this affair and of Anglo-Spanish trade generally at this period see *Forerunners of Drake* by Gordon Connell-Smith (London, 1954), an invaluable book.

The people have little communication but to demand if the King has returned to the opinion of the Holy Church or is still a heretic and Lutheran; and if they reply that he is a Christian they are accused to the Inquisition, cruelly imprisoned, and their goods forfeited. Four or five Englishmen remained in prison. The Inquisition have made search in Cyville, Peres, Saint Lucar and elsewhere for divers English merchants. Some of them who are in England are afraid to return. Trade suffers in consequence. The Inquisition make those accuse others; and ask them whether they think the King a good Christian, and that he does well to pull down monasteries and put the religious to death.

> Signatures: Wm. Ostrych, governor.
> Thos. Harryson, John Swetyng, Wm. Folwode, John Fylde, John Bedyll, Geo. Maister, Edw. Lewys, Wm. Wylfort, Thos. Kingman, Thos. Wylson, Robt. Hunte, Thom. Rydley, John Lonnor, Water Fraunceis, Nicholas Saterley, Blase Saunders, Wm. Redstone, Ric. Hore, Nic. Skyres, W. Meryche, Nic. Lawforde, Chr. Southcarke.
>
> Dated 1540

The technique sounds only too familiar today. King Henry was so unpopular that a dispatch sent to him in 1545 relates how 'William Estridge . . . having suspecte acquayntaunce with dyverse naughtie freers in Seville, intendeth shortly to presente Your Majestie with dyverse costelye boxes of marmelado, given to him by the said freers, and suspected to have within theim thinges of danger and great perill . . .' Who was this Estridge? Could it have been William Ostrych, the governor, grown desperate? If so, one must have some sympathy with him. Another dispatch reported that 'all such Inglysshemen as wer in pryson . . . for the Bysshope of Romes mattars . . . have done open penance, and lost all their goodis to their utter undoing.' In the same year English merchants had their goods confiscated to compensate those whose treasure had been plundered by John Reneger, who had originally been a legitimate merchant in Southampton, where he imported large quantities of wine and exported wheat – sometimes illegally. But when trade got more difficult he became a pioneer free-booter, plundering the Spanish Main.

Despite these troubles and persecutions, trade continued to flourish. In 1548 Medina y Mesa put the total wine production at sixty thousand butts, of which forty thousand were exported to England and Flanders. Other exports included flour and olive oil.

The Andalusia Company continued in existence until 1585, by which time it owned a vineyard and some property in the nearby village of Chipiona. In this year ships on the Guadalquivir laden with the possessions of the English merchants who were taking them out of Andalusia were seized, while some of the merchants and sailors were handed over to the Inquisition. All that remained were a few Catholics, who met together on St George's Day, 1591, and, led by the sinister Jesuit Robert Parsons (or Persons), resolved that their lands and imposts should be devoted to a new seminary. Not unnaturally the exiled Protestants were furious.

There was an attempt to revive the Company on a much larger scale and it existed in a new form from 1604 to 1606, but neither in its latter years nor in its revival was it a very significant force in the wine trade.[1] The revived company may well have succeeded had not the disastrous choice been made to appoint Roger Bodenham as Consul at Sanlucar. No one knew Spain better: he was a Catholic with a Spanish wife who had lived for many years in Seville, where he had long acted as an English intelligence agent. He was, however, heartily disliked and was to prove useless as Consul. One of his kinsmen, Sir James Crofts, had been Controller of the Royal Household since 1570, but monarchs at this time were haphazard in their payments, to say the least, and the satisfaction of royal commands had long been a source of worry in the city. In 1586, for instance, there was a royal debt of £400 for sherry sack and the merchants offered to sell the best quality sack to Crofts at £3 per tun below the market price if the debt were paid promptly, but this offer was not taken up.

By Elizabeth's reign, sherry sack was established as a firm favourite, and more verses were written about it than about any other wine. Shakespeare, Ben Jonson, Marlowe, Raleigh and Spenser acclaimed it at much the same time; Middleton soon afterwards; Herrick, a century later; and Pasquil's *Palinodia* (attributed to Nicholas Breton) praised it at great length. It was enjoyed by lawyers as well as by poets, and the court of Star Chamber bought it by the hogshead, paying about 3s. 4d. a gallon.

1 For the latter period see *The Spanish Company* by Pauline Croft (London, 1973).

The word sack (there are several spellings) probably originated at the end of the fifteenth century, and is almost certainly derived from the Spanish verb *sacar* (to draw out). In the minutes of the Jerez town council for 1435 exports of wine were referred to as *sacas* – and were prohibited as there was a shortage. The term is still used for the withdrawal of wine from a solera. The word thus signifies any wine for export, and there are many references to Malaga sack and Canary sack, quite apart from sherry sack. Other derivations have been proposed, and many of them are most alarming: Dr Johnson informs us that Skinner, after Mandesto, derived the word from Xeque, a city of Morocco with which it had no connection whatsoever; and many other ingenious minds have been applied to the problem. The alternative spellings *sack* and *seck* appear at random in early documents, but it seems reasonable to say it has nothing to do with *seco*, meaning 'dry', despite the contrary view taken by the *Oxford English Dictionary*; indeed sack was always classified as a sweet wine. The idea, though, that sack meant 'dry' was firmly fixed in the minds of lexicographers; they stuck to their beliefs as a matter of faith, and apparently imagined sack to be somewhat similar to the popular 'amontillados' of today, which were not prepared, let alone imported, until the nineteenth century. It was even suggested that all Elizabethan 'sweet' wines were dry, but that is to enter the realms of fantasy and one can only assume they were drunk by a Jubjub under the Tumtum tree.

It is difficult to say exactly what Elizabethan sack wines were like; they were certainly fortified, and the methods of making *arrope* (which will be described in a later chapter) had long been known, but they were seldom matured in the wood for more than a year or two. Even the cheapest wines sold today are expected to show at least three years' maturation but perhaps the very cheapest olorosos are not so very far removed from sack. One famous shipper thought it would be interesting to market an old-fashioned sack, but would not associate his name with such an immature wine. In place of the rough, young olorosos originally used, he substituted a high quality, well-matured, light oloroso, and limited the quantity of sweet wine in the blend to produce a fairly dry, light-bodied sherry with a remarkably dry after-taste. It very rapidly, and very understandably, became one of the most popular sherries in the world. He called it 'Dry Sack', and the literally minded have complained from time to time that it is not 'dry' at all, but 'medium'; that is perfectly true, but although it may be a medium *sherry*, it is a very dry *sack*, and the name is absolutely accurate.

With the rising popularity of sack in England, and the Catholic orthodoxy of the reign of Bloody Mary, the English colony in Sanlucar might well have prospered, had not further conflict broken out between England and Spain in the reign of the heretic Elizabeth (1558–1603). The Spaniards can hardly be blamed for the animosity they felt against England for her naval activities and for supporting the rebels in the Spanish Netherlands; it must have been somewhat exasperating to have one's Main perpetually harried by knighted corsairs, one's chief seaport sacked, and one's beard singed. Trade between the two countries was, from time to time, banned, but the English government acted generously towards the merchants:

> Some English merchants sent from a town of Andalusia called Xeres de la Frontera at least 40,000 butts of wine annually besides eight or ten tons of fruit, which wine and fruit they are not able to consume themselves, whereby they are furnished of above 200,000 ducats annually to provide them for other necessaries, without which they could not live.
>
> Sir T. Chamberlain to the Queen concerning the 'common traffic lately forbidden', 27 Sept. 1561

The situation worsened. The continuous loss of men and treasure, captured on the filibustering expeditions of Hawkins and Drake, infuriated the Spaniards. By 1585 feelings had run so high that English merchants trading in Sanlucar were arrested and their goods sold. One of them, William Melson, took refuge in the church of St George for six or seven months. A dispatch of that date tells us that an officer was appointed to make inquiry throughout the country for Englishmen and their goods. But the people were less hostile than their government: when the officer approached, they hid their English friends, and as soon as he had gone away, the merchants went about their business just as before. They continued shipping wine to England in spite of all adversities, but they could not do it directly: it had to be sent in foreign ships or in English ships officially sailing for foreign ports, and it often entailed great risk.

The name of Drake became a byword of horror throughout the province of Cadiz, and it still is to this day. He is the local bogey man: when a mother wants to frighten her child into acquiescence, she says, '*El Draque* will get you if you're not good.' His most daring raid of all was in 1587. It was the time he 'singed the King of Spain's beard' by setting fire to the Spanish fleet as it lay at anchor in the bay. He remained in Cadiz for three days at considerable risk, and made off with 2,900 pipes[1] of wine, much of which was on board ships intended for the Armada. The figure comes from Spanish sources and may have been hysterically exaggerated, but Drake's spoils must have been appreciated in England, as wine imports from Spain had been greatly cut down in consequence of the war.

This superb malpractice helped to introduce sherry drinking on a large scale in England, and the publicity was cheap at the price; it has been repaid a million-fold. Drake's enthusiasm for sherry has given rise to another story. In a book called *Hombres Ilustres de Jerez de la Frontera* by Diego Ignacio Parada Barreto, published in 1875, there is a detailed account of how Francis Drake, known as Don Francisco Drake, worked as a sherry shipper in Jerez, but had a terrible quarrel with a man called Melgarejo; he took such strong offence that he left immediately for England and swore he would have his revenge. Earlier references occur in the histories of Bartolome Gutierrez (written in the middle of the eighteenth century), and of Portillo, written in 1839. The story is said to be based on evidence found in the Municipal Archives; it may be a legend or it may be true, but if the latter, it is very doubtful whether Francisco Drake was the English admiral. The name is quite common. The story could perhaps be a corruption of something that really did happen: one Juan Melgarejo was high sheriff of Santo Domingo and was blackmailed by Drake on one of his South American voyages in 1586 into giving a substantial sum to prevent his town from being destroyed.

Apart from the immediate material losses to Spain in wine, stores and ships, chaos was created in the Spanish naval and mercantile administration. While Drake was off the coast, not a single ship could be moved without risk of capture. In 1570, moreover, Pope Pius V outlawed Elizabeth by declaring her excommunicate and her subjects to be released from their allegiance. On the execution of Mary Queen of Scots in 1587, Sixtus V proclaimed a crusade, and Spain was ready to answer the call. All was ripe for the Armada.

1 Pipes were rather larger than butts, and were sometimes used by sherry shippers at that time. Port is shipped in pipes today, but the two measures may not have been identical.

Jerez had a new industry: the king built fifteen ovens in the town and they were kept working day and night making ship's biscuit. He also requisitioned five thousand butts of wine. The Spanish navy at that time was a perpetual burden to the people of Jerez. Some years earlier, in 1580, four thousand butts of wine were taken from Jerez as provisions for a fleet sailing against Portugal, and in 1582 the empty casks waiting for the harvest were requisitioned to provide water vessels for a fleet anchored at Puerto de Santa Maria. This resulted in the almost total loss of a vintage and the ruin of several growers. The combined efforts of the monarch and the pirate must have left Andalusia very short of wine – probably for the only time in history.

The Armada was commanded by the Duke of Medina Sidonia, a local man whose seat was at Sanlucar de Barrameda; many of his mariners and soldiers came from the sherry towns. Of the subsequent misfortunes of this ill-fated fleet, the less said the better. Alas, there was little wine left in the galleons that were washed up on the shores of Scotland and Ireland.

Amongst the many English recorded as being resident in Spain in 1591 was John Fletcher, who had a wine business in Jerez. He and his compatriots led a precarious life.

In 1595 the English sacked Cadiz again. Not unnaturally, in view of what their government was doing, the English merchants were put to some inconvenience at the hands of the Spaniards. They sent a list of their grievances to the Privy Council, to be used as the basis of an agreement with Spain, and some of their complaints show what conditions they were trading under. For instance, they demanded: that all English prisoners in the galleys, save those detained for debt, should be released; that sequestered property at Sanlucar should be returned; that they should not be compelled to write their accounts in Spanish; that they should be exempt from the Inquisition; and that if any 'vnkyndnes to fall out between his Majesty and the King of Spaine' they should be given six months' notice to remove their goods and themselves without fear of molestation.

When any Englishman died, his fellow-countrymen had little control over his affairs. Jefferye Harryson of Huelva and Peeter Edwards of Cadiz died without confessing or receiving the sacrament; their goods were seized and their bodies were refused Christian burial, the first being interred in a field and the second buried at sea. One of the merchants' demands, however, was hardly reasonable: they wanted exemption from all customs duties.

Nevertheless sherry continued to be exported to England on a large scale, and in 1598 received its most famous tribute. In *Henry IV*, Part 2 (IV: iii) Shakespeare wrote:

JOHN OF LANCASTER: Fare you well, Falstaff:
I in my condition,
Shall better speak of you than you deserve.
SIR JOHN FALSTAFF: I would you had but the wit: 'twere better than your dukedom. Good faith, this same young sober-blooded boy doth not love me; nor a man cannot make him laugh; but that's no marvel, he drinks no wine. There's never none of these demure boys come to any proof; for thin drink doth so over-cool their blood, and making many fish-meals, that they fall into a kind of male green-sickness; and then, when they marry, they get wenches. They are generally fools and cowards, which some of us should be too but for inflammation. A good sherris-sack hath a two-fold operation in it. It ascends me into the brain; dries me there all the foolish and dull and crudy vapours which environ it; makes it apprehensive, quick, forgetive, full of nimble fiery and delectable shapes; which deliver'd o'er to the voice, the tongue, which is the birth, becomes excellent wit. The second property of your excellent sherris is, the warming of the blood; which, before cold and settled, left the liver white and pale, which is the badge of pusillanimity and cowardice: but the sherris warms it and makes it course from the inwards to the parts extreme. It illumineth the face, which, as a beacon, gives warning to all the rest of this little kingdom, man, to arm; and then the vital commoners and inland petty spirits muster me all to their captain, the heart, who, great and puffed up with this retinue, doth any deed of courage; and this valour comes of sherris. So that skill in the weapon is nothing without sack, for that sets it a-work; and learning, a mere hoard of gold kept by a devil till sack commences it and sets it in act and use. Hereof comes it that Prince Harry is valiant; for the cold blood he did naturally inherit of his father, he hath, like lean, sterile, and bare land, manured, husbanded, and tilled, with excellent endeavour of drinking good and good store of fertile sherris, that he is

27

become very hot and valiant. If I had a thousand sons, the first human principle I would teach them should be, to forswear thin potations and to addict themselves to sack.

The real Sir John lived long before the days of sack. Be that as it may, sack was certainly a favourite of Shakespeare's, and what character could praise it more appropriately than Falstaff? When Marlowe was killed in a tavern brawl, he was probably drinking it, and I can think of many worse deaths.

After the reign of Elizabeth, trade was somewhat easier. England and Spain were soon at peace again, and sack became so popular in royal circles that on 17 July 1604 James I was obliged to issue an ordinance:

Whereas in times past Spanish wines, called Sacke, were little or no whit used in our Court . . . within these late years it is used as a common drinke and served at meales, as an ordinary . . . using it rather for wantonnesse and surfeitting, than for necessity, to a great wasteful expense; We, considering that . . . our nobility . . . may for their better health desire to have Sacke, our pleasure is, that there be allowed to the sergeant of our seller twelve gallons of Sacke a day, and no more.

Unfortunately the inevitable happened, and some of the less scrupulous merchants abused their prosperity by shipping very inferior wines. When Roos visited Jerez in 1610 he wrote that much of the sack sent to England was 'sophisticated', and 'of so Churlishe, and vnholsome a nature, that no man of honour . . . will drinke of it.' The Spaniards marvelled at the poor quality of the wines shipped to England, and described them as *vinos por borrachos* – wine for drunks. Roos had often heard Londoners boast of how their city was better served with wine than any other in Christendom. They certainly had variety, but in his travels through Spain, France and Italy, he continually heard the growers 'blesse themselves in wondering what Kinde of Creatures those be, which shall drincke those wynes'.

The English colony, meantime, was flourishing, and when a political exile died in Seville, a hundred of his countrymen attended his funeral. While some of these were undoubtedly in the wine trade, others traded in fish, olive oil, fruit, corn and minerals. There were also craftsmen in the sherry towns who were in no way connected with wine: when Peter Mundy visited Sanlucar in 1611 he stayed with an English weaver. British seafarers often went to southern Spain and lived there for some time. Some Englishmen were detained as galley slaves, including a number of genuine pirates, and others who had been accused of piracy on rather slender grounds. Once taken prisoner, they were beyond reach of the law, and there was no sure way of saving them: they were released or retained capriciously, as an act of the King's grace.

Merchantmen plied continuously between England and Andalusia. In 1620 one of them was diverted to America with a very different cargo; it is perhaps ironical that the *Mayflower* was a wine ship before she took her solemn load of Puritans across the Atlantic.

Even when they were not being pursued by the Inquisition, exciting things happened to the British merchants. In 1613 an Englishman who had married a Spanish lady, and who was living in Sanlucar, found his wife in bed with one of the King's commissaries, and murdered them both. After 'some trouble', he was acquitted and freed.

On only one occasion did the English attempt to emulate the successes of the Elizabethan sea-dogs, and that proved disastrous. In 1625, infuriated by the Catholic court's rejection of his suit for the hand of the Infanta of Spain, Charles I sent Sir Edward Cecil (later ennobled as Baron Cecil of Putney and Viscount Wimbledon) with ninety ships and ten thousand men on an expedition against Spain. Sir Edward's previous job, which was perhaps better suited to his talents, had been Warden of the Royal Preserve of the River Wandle. In every aspect of its planning, the expedition was ill-inspired, and Cecil, who had distinguished himself as a soldier in the Low Countries, proved a worthless commander in Spain. His ships were leaky and not fit to go to sea; there was no provision for the horses; the men were crying out for victuals, and some had nothing to drink save a 'beverage of cider that stinks worse than carrion'.

After landing on the coast of Andalusia, they marched against the fortress of El Puntal, just outside Cadiz, and besieged it with cannon. After two days it had to surrender. This rather futile victory gave the Spaniards time to prepare the city's defences, but all their work proved unnecessary: the British army was defeated by a bodega of sherry.

When the soldiers marched against the city, they had neither food nor drink. An ill-disciplined mob at the best of times, they were hungry, thirsty, and rebellious when they reached a house with a bodega of wine owned by Don Luis de Soto, the hereditary commander of Cadiz, whose descendants are today amongst the prominent citizens of Jerez. The British commander, thinking his troops would be appeased by a little refreshment, gave them permission to take some wine:

> Wee came . . . to a Gentlemans house; in which was 100 Tonnes of wine. Our Army quartered close by the house – Behind it on the side of a hill, on the Top whereof was another house with as much more wyne all in Iron bound caskes soe that I think it was appoynted for the Indies. The Generall gave to every Regiment a Tonne of Wyne, which with the liberty to Drinke that carried them to the house, where they forced a way into the Cellers, made them so Drunke that there was noe place for obedience to the officers, and the Generall Commaunded his guards to shoote at one vnruly company through the gate, whoe would have broken it open. I did never thinke myself to bee in soe much Daunger, for certainely the enemy with 300 men might have rowted vs and cutt our throates . . . since Sunday morning . . . the most part of the souldiers had not eaten any thing . . . Wee marched away and left soe many of our men vpon the place soe Drunke as they were not able to stirre. The wine in the house vpon the hill I thinke was not touched. The other wine was lett out, and wee left some souldiers tumbling in it. Many of our men with Drunkenes fell downe by the way, all which the enemy Killed. They followed vs with 2000 foote, but never came neere to skirmishe with vs . . .

There was no need for the Spaniards to fight: the British were utterly defeated. That expedition cost the Crown thirty ships and a thousand men, and it would have cost many more had there not been a muddle in the command of the Spanish army. One soldier, Richard Peecke, of Tavistock, was captured by the Spaniards, tried by battle and released. When he got back to England he wrote a book about his experiences, of which the frontispiece reads:

Three to One
Being, An Engliſh Spaniſh Combat,
Performed by a Weſterne Gentleman, of Tauyſtoke in
Deuonſhire,

with an Engliſh Quarter Staffe, againſt Three Spaniſh
Rapiers and Poniards, at Sherries in Spaine,
The fifteene day of Nouember, 1625.
In the preſence of Dukes, Condes, Marquiſses, and other Great
Dons of Spaine, being the Counſell of Warre.
The author of this Booke, and Actor in this Encounter, R. Peecke.

It is perhaps the earliest English document in which the town of
Jerez is spelt 'Sherries', though the wine had been referred to as
sherry many years earlier. In the text he refers to 'Sherrys, otherwise
called Xerez'. Peecke was a remarkable character, and the whole of
his narrative is well worth reading; it is reproduced by Edward
Hutton in his *Cities of Spain*, but the reader will be puzzled to
decide how much is truth and how much fiction. A contemporary
letter-writer, Dr Meddus, described him in a somewhat off-hand
way as: 'one Pyke, a common soldier, left behind the fleet at Cadiz'.

By the seventeenth century, sack was quite at home in England
and was popular with everyone. Moreover, of the many types of
sack, Sherris-Sack was thought the best. Thomas Randolph was
jovial in his praise, even if he showed little regard to historic truth;
but perhaps a hedonist was entitled to disregard it:

> Sacke is the life, soul and spirit of a man, the fire which Prome-
> theus stole, not from Jove's kitchen, but his wine-cellar, to en-
> crease the native heat and radicall moisture, without which we
> are but drousie dust or dead clay. This is nectar, the very Nepenthe
> the Gods were drunk with: 'tis this that gave Gannymede beauty,
> Hebe youth, to Jove his heaven and eternity. Doe you thinke
> Aristotle drank perry? or Plato Cyder? Doe you think Alexander
> had ever conquered the world if he had bin sober? He knew the
> force and value of Sacke; that it was the best armour, the best
> encouragement, and that none could be a Commander that was
> not double drunk with wine and ambition.
>
> Thomas Randolph, *Aristippus, the Jovial Philosopher*, 1630

During the regicide disgrace of the Protectorate, sherry suffered a
short-lived eclipse but this arose more as a result of matters in Spain
than from the change of government in England. During the civil
war and afterwards the nobility, who had been the greatest buyers
of wine, could no longer buy it on their accustomed scale. Some
were exiled and others impoverished. Although the Puritans detested

drunkenness and gluttony, they had no objection to drinking in moderation. The awful heresy of teetotalism was not to emerge for another three hundred years. The wine duties were increased considerably, but Cromwell himself bought wine on a substantial scale, and on his state visit to Bristol he accepted the gift of a pipe of sherry. In the later, more stable days of the Commonwealth the wine trade flourished. But the beginning of the Commonwealth coincided with the beginning of years of terrible plague in Jerez which resulted in the disruption of the wine trade for over two decades.

After the Restoration sherry was soon popular again. Sack is mentioned frequently in Pepys's *Diary*. On 20 January 1662 he and three friends bought two butts of sherry; his was 'put into a hogshead, and the vessel filled up with four gallons of Malaga wine, but what it will stand us in I know not: but it is the first great quantity of wine that I ever bought'. The mixture of malaga with sherry is not as odd as it may seem; the two districts are in the same province and the wines are not dissimilar. A hogshead is a large amount for a private person to buy, though, being equivalent to over three hundred bottles. But Pepys was a canny man, and in August he sold his hogshead to Sir W. Batten – 'and am glad of my money instead of wine'. Whether that were a reasonable attitude would depend largely on the wine. Pepys also drank 'raspberry sack', which was probably a kind of mead.

Six years later he was called to the bar of the House to defend the Navy Office against parliamentary critics of the ticket system, in which sailors were paid by means of negotiable bills instead of money. Now Pepys was a clever man and full of wit, but on that occasion a little Dutch courage was certainly necessary. His diary tells the rest:

> . . . to comfort myself did go to the Dog and drink half-a-pint of mulled sack, and in the Hall [Westminster] did drink a dram of brandy at Mrs. Howlett's; and with the warmth of this did find myself in better order as to courage, truly. . . . I began our defence most acceptably and smoothly, and continued at it without any hesitation or loss, but with full scope, and all my reason free about me, as if it had been at my own table, from that time [between 11 and 12 o'clock] till past three in the afternoon . . .

Needless to say, the Navy Office was exonerated.

It is surprising that Pepys could buy his sack so easily; as usual, there was trouble between England and Spain. Somewhat earlier, in 1655, the English had sailed in and captured Jamaica without any declaration of war; a year later Spain retaliated by declaring war against England and seizing all ships and goods belonging to English merchants in Spanish ports. After the war, trouble continued and the import of Spanish wines was hindered and bedevilled by excessive duties. In 1668 the vintners of Malaga were so furious that they dried all their grapes for sale as fruit and no sherry whatsoever was landed at Bristol during the autumn of that year. Nevertheless in the same year Thomas Thompson wrote in his play *The English Rogue*:

> *Come let us frolic, and call for our tipple,*
> *Our pockets we'll empty and our veins we will fill,*
> *For sack we'll not lack, nor will we be gripple,*
> *But carouse in despite of the two-toppéd hill.*
> CHORUS: *Parnassus shall pass us,*
>   *Nor will we inquire*
>   *For the font of the Muses:*
>   *'Tis sack we desire.*

'Gripple' meant mean or stingy and the two-toppéd hill was Parnassus. He wanted to banish Rhenish and English Metheglin (mead) and have 'brave Spanish liquor'.

In 1683 Pepys went on an expedition commanded by Lord Dartmouth with orders to evacuate Tangier, which was then a troublesome British possession, and to blow up the mole with a primitive mine. In December, their work completed, they called at Cadiz and Pepys visited the sherry country. He suffered various misfortunes including 'a mighty plague' of fleas and at one stage of his journey he found difficulty in getting a drink, which seems incredible. On the whole, however, the holiday was a success, and when he came to Sanlucar he found a flourishing colony of British merchants one of whom, a Mr Canham, supplied him with a cask of old sherry. But the old church of St George was beginning to fall into decay, and was rebuilt by one Francis Malbrank.

By the end of the seventeenth century the name *sack* was gradually being replaced by the modern *sherry*:

The next that stood up
With a countenance merry
Was a pert sort of wine
Which the moderns call sherry.

A rime from *Bacchanalian Sessions*, 1693

The word had been used earlier, and an entry in the Repertory to Decrees in Dublin Castle, dated 14 February 1561, reads: 'That Francis Tyrling shall pay to Thomas Fitzsymons . . . £28. 18. 8 for 3 butts of Sherry and for his costs, etc., 20/-.'

In 1695 there was a visitor to Spain who remained anonymous, but his *Account of Spain* was published by John Chantrey at the Pestle and Mortar without Temple Bar in 1705. The author held a high opinion of the fertility of Andalusian soil: 'At this day the Pasture is so rich, that the cattle will die of Fatness within 30 days, unless they be let Blood . . .' – an alarming phenomenon of which nothing is known today. He went to Jerez to visit an English nun, Phillipa Ward, who had been put into a convent during infancy and was famous for her beauty. All we know of her father is that he was a merchant in Puerto de Santa Maria and kept English servants.

At that time a great deal more of the sherry trade was centred in Sanlucar de Barrameda and Puerto de Santa Maria and rather less in Jerez. This followed from the unpredictable movement of shipping in those days: the boats sailed at the first favourable wind, and the wine had to be waiting at the port. The shipping bodegas of the principal houses, where mature wine was stored ready for export, were built in the coastal towns and they remained there until the middle of the nineteenth century, when the railway made transport quick and easy, and steam power made shipping less dependent on winds. By that time, the prosperity had steadily shifted from Sanlucar to Puerto de Santa Maria where some of the largest and finest bodegas were established. Shippers whose main bodegas were in Jerez had shipping bodegas there so as not to miss a favourable wind and even when this became unnecessary some of them kept their Puerto de Santa Maria bodegas and have them to this day, as the climate particularly favours the development of good fino wines.

Unfortunately the records that go this far back are sparse and any succession there may be between traders of those days and today cannot be traced; but one shipper can credibly claim to have a history stretching this far back and further: Valdespino. The

Valdespino family was active in the reconquest and believes that it has a continuous history of wine growing since those days. A similar claim to antiquity is made by the Palomino family, which later founded the house of Palomino & Vergara, now owned by Harveys.

Whatever the effect of wars may be in the history of mankind, they are almost bound to be disastrous for those international traders whose goods are far removed from munitions. The wars of the eighteenth century were disastrous for the sherry shippers. The War of the Spanish Succession, which began in 1702, lasted until 1713, and its first year saw a virtual repetition of the catastrophe which befell Cecil in 1625. An English force under Sir George Rooke set out to lay siege to Cadiz but landed at Puerto de Santa Maria, which had been abandoned by its inhabitants. Once again the bodegas were plundered, and this time there were many more of them. Then, not content with this outrage, they went on to plunder Rota. The result was again drunkenness, followed by unseemly disputes over the spoils. After a month, the English forces went away again, having achieved nothing but ignominy.

The sherry trade with Great Britain reached its lowest ebb during this century, when imports were fairly steady at above five thousand butts a year. The wine was still greatly praised and esteemed – it remained a favourite with the gentry and with sportsmen and was drunk regularly by cricketers at the Bat and Ball, Hambledon – but the trade went through a period of stagnation; the potential market was never broached, and the growers were far from prosperous. Sherry held its sway in Scotland, though. In his *Glasgow and its Clubs* Dr John Strong described how, in the middle of the eighteenth century, 'The liquor in common use was sherry, presented in mutchlin stoups, every mutchlin got being on the head of the stoup or measure. The quantity swallowed was ... almost incredible.' A mutchlin was a Scottish measure a little under a pint.

Philip V's ambassador to London was a Jerezano wine grower – Tomás Geraldino y Croquer – and he did his best to encourage sales, but even diplomatic aid was to no avail. There are many explanations. Unfortunately England and Spain were involved in a whole succession of wars that spanned the century and did little good to the trade between the two countries. Some of the Spanish wine trade was diverted to Portugal, and this tendency was encouraged by the preferential rates of duty arising from the Methuen Treaty of 1703. British merchants also began to trade extensively with the island of Madeira. This diversion of trade was used by supporters of the Gremio, or Wine Growers' Guild, of Jerez, to explain away the reduced demand for their wines, but these factors probably did less harm than did the many restrictive practices imposed by the Gremio itself. There had been earlier trade restrictions, but these had only affected the local market. For instance, the Dukes of Medina Sidonia had stipulated in 1448, in 1469 and again in 1621, that if any merchant brought wine from other provinces into the area of the Duke's vineyards, it was to be poured away, and the offender's boat or wagon was to be burnt. Such restrictions had little effect on the export trade; if anything, they helped, by preventing adulteration, and they have modern counterparts in the regulations of all the reputable viticultural districts. But the restrictions imposed by the eighteenth-century Guild went much further.

The Guild was governed by a council of six: two ecclesiastics, two municipal representatives, and two wine-growers. These met before and after the vintage to fix the price of grapes and that of the new must; as far as it is possible to calculate such things, based on the relative cost of living then and now, these prices were more than double those of today. When the West Indies fleet was provisioned with wine, this was arranged by a quota system, rather than by free competition. A grower could not also be a merchant. Worst of all, merchants were forbidden to accumulate large stocks; wine was therefore not matured long enough, and trade was lost because lack of stock caused delay in preparing the blends for shipment. The idea behind this extraordinary regulation was that such wine stores would divert profits from the hands of the growers into those of merchants, and that it would encourage speculation. The only large stores of old wine were in the possession of the Church and in a few private cellars.

These restrictions aimed at making the trade easy and profitable with a minimum of effort and competition, but in fact they had the opposite effect, and sherry shippers were unable to compete with wines grown elsewhere. Malaga, for instance, exported a rich, dessert wine not unlike sherry, and it became popular in Britain under the name of 'Mountain'. This captured much of the available market for Spanish wines, and exports from Malaga were greater than those from either Cadiz or Sanlucar.

The restrictions of the Gremio were opposed by a number of

merchants, notably by Juan Haurie. There was a lawsuit, and much acrimonious wrangling, not all of which was concerned with wine: the deputies were accused of spending too much on fireworks for the annual feast of San Gines de la Jara – the patron saint of the vintage, a very exclusive, not to say obscure, saint, not to be confused with the martyr of Arles – and on presents of chocolate. But despite all the efforts of its opponents, the Guild continued until it was dissolved by Royal proclamation in 1834, after 101 years of disastrous existence.

While the efforts of the Guild reduced the trade in sherry to a fraction of what it might have been, it was certainly not extinguished. It was popular in the Highlands of Scotland and it is recorded that in 1746, not long before the fateful battle of Culloden, the Young Pretender ordered three dozen claret, half a dozen Lisbon and half a dozen sherry to be sent to his lodgings. At this time in Scotland it was often called 'Zerrie' or 'Zerrey'.

By 1754, owing to the poor state of trade, there were only nine sherry shippers left in Jerez, and it is doubtful whether more than one of them was English. The solitary Englishman was John Brickdale, who was known to be a Freemason, in spite of which he was apparently on good terms with the local ecclesiastics. He was also a supporter of the church of St George at Sanlucar, though this does not necessarily mean he was a Catholic: perhaps he supported it simply because he was English. Other English merchants, however, were trading in Cadiz and one of them at least – Henry Pickering – was also interested in exporting wine. At a date which is not exactly known, possibly in 1756, Arthur Gordon came from Scotland and traded as a general merchant in Cadiz. He was the younger brother of the Laird of Beldorney. In 1774 he bought a bodega in Jerez and by the turn of the century had become prominent in the trade. He died in 1815 and left a legacy to the Scots College in Valladolid. His only son died in infancy but he was succeeded by his kinsman Charles Peter Gordon, whose descendants are still prominent in the trade to this day, not least in the blood of the Gonzalez family, which has changed its name to Gonzalez-Gordon.

Juan Haurie, who had a number of British assistants, was a refugee from France, and he was joined by kinsmen and fellow-countrymen such as Pemartin, Domecq and Lacoste, whose work was to do much to revive the sherry trade. Other families of French origin include Lustau, Lacave and Delage. There was also an influx of capital from the Indies, brought back to Andalusia owing to political turmoil in the colonies.

Such English merchants as there were lived at Sanlucar, and the most prominent of these was Henry Stonor. As a younger son, he could expect no inheritance and, as a Catholic, no great career lay open to him in Britain. Like many other cadets of his family he chose to seek his fortune in a Catholic country. After finishing his schooling at Douai in 1760, he settled in Cadiz, carrying with him an official copy of his pedigree and arms, obtained from the College of Heralds. After a few years, he married an English wife, Elizabeth Gardiner-Brown, and they settled in Sanlucar where Stonor built up an extensive business as a general merchant. He exported orange and lemon trees to stock the fashionable orangeries, together with broods of Spanish partridges and, of course, sherry. In return he imported British saddlery and sporting dogs, specializing in greyhounds. One of his four sons took a temporary commission in the Spanish army and created a sensation by visiting his English relations resplendent in his striking uniform.

Other English residents in Sanlucar at that time included a Captain David Ferrier, whose precise occupation (if any) is uncertain, but he had a clerk named Gaspar Muclek and a butler named Joseph Colisons. In 1754 thirty-two English residents signed a petition to the Pope, concerning the appointment of a visitor to the church of St George. Probably only a few of these were connected with the wine trade.

Prior to the eighteenth century the wine trade was in the hands of small individual merchants, and establishments on the scale of modern bodegas were entirely unknown; there was no continuity of name and no records of individual merchants have survived. Only one modern firm – J. M. Rivero – could trace its direct ancestry to an earlier period. This house had been trading at least since 1653. Its trade mark was CZ – the initials stood for Cabeza y Zarco, the family name of Don Pedro Alonso Cabeza de Aranda y Zarco, who was its founder. One of his descendants, Don Antonio Cabeza de Aranda (who was created Marques de Montana by Royal Decree in 1775) took Don Francisco Antonio de la Fixera into partnership. Don Francisco's granddaughter married Don Pedro Agustin Rivero, whose descendants owned the business until it ceased trading in 1990. Its loss is a very sad one. The firm had many valuable archives, including letter books dating from 1734 and account books from

1802, which recorded the names of many British merchants trading in Andalusia. Commercial records dating back to this period are rare, as much of the business was done by word of mouth, to avoid the royal taxes.

Another recent casualty was the oldest established of the many bodegas founded by immigrants from the British Isles: Rafael O'Neale. The O'Neale family fled from persecution in troubled Ireland during the seventeenth century, and entered the armies of France and Spain, to follow the only profession that was open to them. In 1724 Timothy O'Neale, who had married into one of the best local families, established his bodega in Jerez.

Of the large bodegas, that which has the longest documented history is undoubtedly Pedro Domecq. The Domecq family originated in the Basses-Pyrénées, and their history has been traced in great detail by a private investigator, apparently to satisfy his own curiosity, as it remains in his possession and is unpublished. It is, however, a remarkable document and makes fascinating reading. Inevitably there are elements of comedy, as when a noble lady's dowry included two cows (with bells) and a feather bed. But essentially it is the record of a great aristocratic family who had the rare privilege of doing obeisance to each successive king of France and presenting him with a pair of white gloves. Like many other French aristocrats, some members of the family found it prudent to leave their native country during the eighteenth century, and their arrival in Andalusia had a profound effect on the history of the sherry trade. But the Domecq bodegas trace their origin to the year 1730, when the Domecq family was still in France, busy presenting white gloves to French sovereigns.

The house of Domecq was founded neither by a Frenchman nor by a Spaniard, but by an Irish farmer and wine-grower called Patrick Murphy. He came to Spain some time prior to 1730, and although he soon became prosperous, he cared little for his business, as he was a bachelor and was in poor health. His great friend was Juan Haurie, who lived next door in Plaza de Plateros, where he had a bakery and traded as a general merchant, particularly in cloth. In 1745 Haurie began to help his friend in the management of his vineyards and when Murphy died on 21 July 1762, Haurie was his heir. He inherited all his properties, including vineyards in the finest areas of Macharnudo and Carrascal; and the wine business so suited him that he entirely abandoned his other interests.

Haurie was a man whose intense ambition was not confined to acquiring fame and fortune: he also wanted to make his wine as good as it could possibly be made. But his efforts were continually frustrated by the restrictions of the Gremio, which prevented sherry shippers from accumulating the necessary stocks of old wine. In 1772 the prolonged conflict was taken to the courts, and Haurie was eventually permitted to take part in all three branches of the trade, becoming a grower, storekeeper and shipper. He bought extensive bodegas and had his own cooperage. Like his Irish friend, he was a bachelor; with his brothers and nephews, he went to live in a magnificent house where there was also room for his offices. To develop the business, he founded a new company with his five nephews: called Juan Haurie y Sobrinos, it included not only the wine business but also several farms and shops. His principal interest, however, remained in the wine, and he steadily acquired new vineyards.

Juan Haurie died in 1794. Under the terms of his will, all his capital remained in the business and was kept undivided, as a central trust fund for the benefit of his five nephews equally. One of these was Pedro Lembeye, the son of Haurie's sister Doña Maria. Lembeye's sister had married a Domecq, and their son was named Pedro. But Pedro Domecq's story – like that of another nephew Juan Carlos Haurie – belongs to the next century, and so to the next chapter.

A number of shippers can trace their histories back to the latter half of the eighteenth century. The Vergara family started their business in 1765 in Puerto de Santa Maria. They later merged with an English firm, becoming Vergara & Dickinson, and in the early years of the twentieth century merged with the Palomino family in Jerez to become Palomino & Vergara, now owned by Harveys. The Palomino family was amongst the oldest established as wine growers, said to have been active since the tenth century, and the principal vine grown today is said to take its name from them. Another of the larger existing shippers, Sanchez Romate, was founded in 1781.

Sir James Duff was British Consul at Cadiz in the latter half of the eighteenth century. The exact date when he started business as a sherry shipper is unknown, but correspondence has been found in England that proves he was shipping sherry prior to 1767. He was born in Ayrshire and died, aged eighty-one, in 1815, after living just long enough to see the French defeated at the battle of Waterloo. Even allowing for the lapidary optimism of executors, he must have been a very fine and much-loved man, for his tomb in Gibraltar speaks of his hospitality, generosity, friendship, goodness and loyalty. It describes, too, how he inspired the Spanish when they were 'enslaved by the powerful French Emperor', and he was created a baronet for his services. But all his achievements save the one are now forgotten. He bought his first wines from Haurie. By 1818 his successors' wines were commanding the highest prices in the market. Customers included the Prince Regent, the Marquis of Hertford and Lord Cholmondeley.

At the end of the eighteenth century, Thomas Osborne arrived in Cadiz from Devon to join Lonergan & White, a firm of merchants and bankers. He soon became a close friend of the consul, and before long he, too, was exporting wine, mostly to America, and storing it in his friend's bodega. In the next century the two firms merged and moved to Puerto de Santa Maria, becoming one of the most important houses in the trade; they still use both names – Osborne and Duff Gordon.

Yet another British house was founded during the same period – that of Garvey. William Garvey originally came from New Ross, County Waterford, in 1780, and in 1794 he married a Spanish girl in Cadiz. Soon afterwards he moved to Sanlucar, where he traded as a general merchant, though his principal interest was in wine. He was the second son of Patrick Garvey of Castle Annagh and, through the House of Ormonde, traced his descent from Edward I, King of England. The earliest letter-book at the Garvey bodegas dates back to 1798, and reveals that Garvey bought much of his wine from Gordon & Co. He also had dealings with members of the Irish family of Shiel, who had become prosperous wine growers in Jerez. While the greater part of his business was in wine, his other interests as a merchant were not neglected. In 1801, for instance, he received fifteen kegs of snuff from New Hampshire and sent two quarter-casks of sherry in part exchange. For a short time, during the nineteenth century, he was a member of a partnership, but he is primarily remembered as the founder of the great Garvey bodegas. Being Irish, his patron saint was Patrick; he gave the same name to his only son; his bodega was the bodega of San Patricio; and his descendants' most famous wine? *Fino San Patricio*, naturally.

William Garvey was a man of great business acumen and never

did anything by halves. When he built his bodega it had to be on the grandest scale and, until recently, there was none other to compare with it – 558 feet long by 126 feet, and completely full of wine. It is a wonderful sight, a sight to stir the soul. When it was built it was unique, but now there are several larger bodegas, the largest single building at the moment being that of Bodegas Internacionales just outside the town on the road to Puerto de Santa Maria.

Garvey became almost as famous for his horses as for his wine; the Garvey family has won races all over Europe and at one time had stud farms in Jerez and in Pau. Perhaps thanks to them, it is often said that a Jerezano has three loves: horses, wine and women. Some put one first and some another, but only three are considered.

The name has often been confused with Harvey. The story is told of a naïve Englishman visiting Jerez who had only heard of one make of sherry and that, of course, was Harvey's. He asked a native to direct him to Harvey's bodegas and, as Harvey's had no bodegas whatsoever in Jerez at the time, he was sent round to Garvey's, which was the nearest his adviser could get to it. The hospitality of sherry shippers is proverbial; it knows no bounds and nothing is too good for the visitor. He was so pleased by it all that he wrote to the British Consul in Cadiz telling him how very hospitable Harvey's had been – 'but how odd they should spell it with a "G" in Spain!'

Three important Spanish houses can also trace their histories from the latter part of the eighteenth century: de la Riva and Misa in Jerez and Vinicola Hidalgo in Sanlucar. The de la Rivas have no idea when their ancestors first began making wine, but they were certainly in the trade as far back as anyone can trace. Documents and accounts survive from 1776. Until the end of the nineteenth century they ignored the lucrative export markets entirely and concentrated on the Peninsular trade, but they are now well known throughout the world. They have become a subsidiary of Domecq's.

Of the early days of Misa, alas, very little is known. The Misa family was certainly in business in the eighteenth century but many of the early records are said to have been destroyed by an English manager who, like Henry Ford, thought that history was bunk. Perhaps, though, he has been maligned, as some of the earliest account books have recently turned up (but have not yet been examined). The earliest known document is a letter dated 7 April 1802 from Don Mariano Gisper of Vera Cruz, Mexico, saying he would send 4,000 pesos of gold (some £800) by the master of the frigate *La Nueva Liebre*, to be invested in wine or Spanish brandy at Misa's discretion; and such confidence could only be placed in a man of the highest standing. Manuel Misa was Marques de Misa, Conde de Bayona, and a grandee of Spain. He had a high commercial reputation both in London and in Jerez, where he was noted for his charity; he was also an accomplished scholar, and held a doctorate of the University of Santiago. Misa became part of the Ruiz-Mateos empire and is now part of Bodegas Internacionales, but the bodega buildings have been bought by Harveys.

Vinicola Hidalgo, which dates from 1792, happily retains its independence and flourishes as a privately owned company run by Javier Hidalgo, a descendant of the founder.

Ever since the early days of mead and cider, Englishmen have been amongst the heaviest drinkers in the world, and have been none the worse for that. In the old Wine Trade Club in London there was a portrait of a Mr Van Horn, who was a Hambone merchant in the middle of the eighteenth century and who belonged for twenty-two years to a club called the Amicable Society, that met at the Bull Inn, Bishopsgate Street. During that time he drank 35,680 bottles of wine, averaging nearly four and a half bottles per day. He only missed two days – the day his wife was buried, and the day his daughter was married – and he lived to be ninety. We do not know who supplied the Bull Inn with the wine that Mr Van Horn drank, which is a pity; for a knowledge of those who sell wine sometimes leads us back to those who grow it.

It is perhaps, therefore, not so very surprising that in this period things were happening in the United Kingdom that were to have a lasting influence on the history of the sherry trade.

In the last decade of the eighteenth century the first of the great importers set up his office in the City of London. George Sandeman was a member of an old and prominent Scottish family. In May 1790 he had written to his sister in Perth:

> I can scarcely bring myself to think seriously of leaving London . . . When a person has left his native place for a long time, he wishes to show some sort of splendour when he returns: therefore I shall remain where I am, till I have made a moderate fortune to retire with, which I expect will be in the course of nine

years; which to be sure is a long time, but some lucky stroke may possibly reduce it to five or six.

His father lent him three hundred pounds, and he hired a wine cellar. At the beginning he conducted his business from Tom's Coffee House in Birchin Lane, Cornhill, and he specialized in port and sherry. Until 1805 he was agent for Sir James Duff's sherries, then for a while he bought from Lacosta & Lagarde. In April 1809 James Gooden, who had become a partner in the firm, was sent to Cadiz, where he was responsible for buying and shipping Sandeman sherries. By 1818 Sandeman was again selling Duff Gordon's wines (as the name had become, following the death of Sir James Duff in 1815), and he obtained the Pemartin agency in 1823.

From 1796 to 1798 he had his brother David as partner, but David Sandeman was more interested in banking than in wine, and the partnership was dissolved amicably so that he could devote the whole of his attention to founding the Commercial Bank of Scotland. George Sandeman continued alone, and in 1805 he took the lease of offices and vaults at 20 St Swithin's Lane. At the same time he moved into a private house at 13 Sherborne Lane, which backed on to his offices, and George G. Sandeman Sons & Co. Ltd occupied the same buildings until 1969. The boundary of the two parishes of St Swithin and St Mary Abchurch met in the cellars, and every year until the Second World War the parish clergy, beadles, and choristers used to go there on one of the Rogation Days to 'Beat the Bounds' between the two parishes with long willow sticks; the ceremony was probably pre-Christian in origin, and in the cellar of a vintner it certainly had some of the atmosphere of a Bacchanal.

The original inventory of fittings and fixtures included: 'A Capital Patent Crane with three iron wheels, Jib Roller, Rope, Pulleys and Jigger.' It has been dated as made in 1795 and they have it yet, still serviceable though no longer in use.

When not working at his offices in the City, George Sandeman, undeterred by the Peninsular War, travelled extensively in Spain and Portugal. His experiences in the wine countries enabled him to select and recommend his ports and sherries with real knowledge and authority. While abroad, he also made many valuable friends, amongst whom was the Duke of Wellington. He was the last man to go on 'Change' in breeches and top boots, long after everyone else had given them up, and he wore a white wig, which caused him to be known affectionately as 'Old Cauliflower'. He died in Brussels in 1841 and was succeeded by his nephew George Glas Sandeman (1792–1868), who widened the Company's scope to include insurance and trade in linen and cotton goods, but not to the detriment of the wine business. He was followed by his sons, and his great-grandsons continued to be directors until 1991. Between 1879 and 1923 the Jerez house traded as Sandeman, Buck & Co. A few years ago David Sandeman married the daughter of the late Antonio Valdespino, forming the last link in the great family tree that now joins all the major sherry shippers. The company was bought by Seagrams in 1980.

Today the name of Sandeman is associated with the striking and mysterious silhouette of a black-cloaked Spaniard, which was drawn as a speculative poster design by George Massiot-Brown; it has been the company's trade mark since 1928.

To many wine drinkers, sherry is synonymous with the name of Harvey, and John Harvey & Sons Ltd, of Bristol, have built up a world-wide demand for their wines. It is rather surprising that two Bristol wine merchants – Harveys and Avery's – have two of the most comprehensive lists of sherries in the country; these lists, and those of several other leading provincial merchants, are far more interesting than anything I have yet found in London. Of the two firms, Avery's are slightly the elder; they were founded in 1793 by Mr James Russell, and the present managing director, Mr John Avery, is one of his direct descendants. They have been shipping 'Bristol Milk' from the very earliest days, and there was an inn, owned by one James Orlidge, and possibly a vintner's business, on the same site in 1756, but it has not yet been possible to trace any direct connection with it. Most of the old records have unfortunately been destroyed.

Harveys was founded in 1796, when William Perry set up in business in an old house in Denmark Street, Bristol. It was known as Gaunt's House, and it had a stone doorway and a massive oak door that were much older than the rest of the building; they had belonged to the house occupied by the master of the Hospital des Bonhommes, founded by the Gaunt family centuries earlier. The site of the original hospital is now occupied by Colston Hall, but the chapel (dating from 1220) still stands; known as the Lord Mayor's Chapel, it is just behind Harveys' offices. The extensive cellars were older still and once formed part of the ancient monastery of St Augustine, whose orchards stretched down to the river where Orchard Street now stands. The original buildings were destroyed during an air raid in 1940, but the modern offices stand on exactly the same site.

Bristol is one of the most ancient and historic ports in England; it was already important by the time of the Norman Conquest, and wine was landed in considerable quantities during the twelfth century. From then on Bristol was one of the principal ports for the wine trade in the United Kingdom, a position it retains to this day. The centre of the city is built over a maze of cellars. 'Bristol Milk' is the traditional style of dessert sherry that has been imported for centuries; the earliest known reference to it occurs in a British Museum manuscript dated 1634. In 1643 Colonel Fiennes was tried for failing to hold the city against Prince Rupert and it was said in evidence that 'the Bristol garrison might have held out, especially being furnished with good store of Bristol Milk . . .' Fuller's *History of the Worthies of England* asserts that, 'Some will have it called Milk because . . . such Wine is the first moisture, given Infants in this City.' If that were so, there can be no wonder that it bred great mariners.

'Bristol Cream', on the other hand, dates only from the nineteenth century and is a proprietary brand of Harveys. They intended to introduce a new dessert sherry blended with an even older oloroso than that in Bristol Milk, but had not decided what to call it when a lady visited their offices and was given a glass of Bristol Milk; then she asked to try a sample of the new sherry, and she gave the wine its name: 'If the first was Bristol Milk, then this must surely be Bristol Cream?' There are stories behind the names of several other sherries which are, or were for many years, on Harveys' list – for instance, *Reina Victoria* was the favourite sherry of Queen Victoria Eugenia of Spain; 'Bank' was served in the board room of Harveys' bankers in Bristol; while 'Anita' was named after the daughter of a former partner.

From the very beginning William Perry concentrated on selling sherry and port, though he also dealt in spirits, madeira, and other Peninsular wines such as Lisbon, bucellas, calcavella and mountain; he imported small quantities of claret, hock and canary wine; but he did no business in burgundy, nor in the Italian wines. He also dealt in leather.

A few years later Perry took Thomas Urch into partnership, and Urch's sister Ann was the second wife of Thomas Harvey, a renowned sea captain. His father had also been named Thomas Harvey, and was a seaman of outstanding character. Many stories are told of him and one of them has particular significance in view of the future of his family. One night he was sitting with a friend enjoying a bottle or two of wine; late in the evening he rang the bell and when the servant came he pointed to a recumbent figure on the floor, saying: 'Kindly remove Mr Prothero and bring me another bottle of port.' His ship was eventually lost in an Atlantic hurricane, and he died, with his wife and the whole of his ship's company.

Although less of a 'character', his son, the second Thomas Harvey, became one of the most respected Bristol sea captains of his day, and amongst the Harvey heirlooms there is a watch, presented to him by grateful passengers when his skilled seamanship saved them from shipwreck in a storm. Perhaps it is not surprising that his eldest son, John Harvey, had a 'horror of the sea'; in fact he so detested it that he would not go on his father's ship even for the short journey to Avonmouth. His inhibitions might have been overcome by the firm efforts of a determined parent, but Bristol shipping was no longer what it had been; other ports were gaining ascendancy, and it was agreed that he should enter his uncle's business. He did so in 1822, when he was sixteen years old. William Perry was already dead. In 1829 he became a partner in an associated company at Kidderminster, marrying at about the time of the move, and living over the shop, his place in Bristol being taken by his younger brother, Charles. By 1840, however, John was back in Bristol and Charles became manager at Kidderminster. The company was owned and managed by successive generations of the family, who built up a world-wide demand for their wines. Sherry was always prominent in their lists, and that for 1867 included nineteen sherries at prices ranging from thirty shillings to a hundred and twenty shillings per dozen.

Just after the last war there was a ludicrous episode of bureaucratic farce. It was a period of muddled government and preposterous restrictions, when Mr John Strachey was enjoying distinguished office as Minister of Food with Dr Edith Summerskill as his parliamentary secretary. A literal-minded hack in the 'Food Standards and Labelling Division' of this thankless ministry was suddenly inspired with the thought that the name Bristol Milk contravened

Regulation 1 of the Defence (Sale of Food) Regulations and misled the gullible public 'as to the nature, substance, or quality of a food or in particular as to its nutritional or dietary value', as it had no connection whatsoever with a cow, even though, no doubt, it could be used for making a syllabub. But that had not occurred to him. There came into the bureaucratic mind the horrific image of an inept nanny filling her charge's little bottle with an alcoholic beverage from distant Spain – not even a decent British sherry. When, with unkind logic, Harveys suggested that if Bristol Milk were illegal, then so, surely, was Bristol Cream, and if so there would have to be a general and widespread purge of shaving creams, hair creams, face creams, vanishing creams, boot creams, perhaps even Cream of Magnesia, and certainly all the lesser creams, the literal mind of the ministry could only reply that it was 'discussing regulations pertaining to the sale of food only'. The answer opens up an endless realm of speculation: what, for instance, of the unfortunate child who asks for a taurine optic and is given a mere peppermint confection? Warner Allen was moved to poetry:

> *A Book of Verses underneath the Bough,*
> *A Jug of Wine milk'd from the Sherry Cow –*
> *And Thou beside me in the Wilderness . . .*

Who could that mysterious *Thou* be, *the fair, the chaste, and unexpressive she*? The unnamed Milkmaid of the Sherry Cow? Surely not the then reigning Ministress of Food? No, the rhyme of my delirium went off the lines.

> *Our National Dairy-Maid Summersilk*
> *Was skimming the Cream off the Bristol Milk.*

Doubtless she made it into honest mousetrap cheese or churned it into better-than-butter margarine.

After further correspondence, the matter was disposed of behind a curtain of public laughter. The clerk responsible was officially described as 'over-zealous'.

The last director with the name of Harvey was Jack Harvey, who resigned from the board a few years before his death in 1958. In the same year, John Harvey & Sons, Ltd, became a public company and later a subsidiary of Showerings, the makers of Babycham, who in turn were bought by Allied Breweries. Jack's son John is now also working for the company.

4

The Growth of Trade

The Peninsular War left Jerez in a state of utter ruin and desolation. Andalusia was a battleground, occupied alternately by the French and allied soldiers. The armies were relentless in their demands for wine, particularly the French. William Garvey had no time for them at all, and moved with his whole family to Cadiz, which was occupied by Spanish and British garrisons. His account books contain a vivid entry: 'Wine robbed by the French soldiers, 30 arrobas.' Such conduct was enough to make any vintner cross. Sir Francis Darwin described how stores of the finer wines were bricked up, but the French bribed undesirables to show them where these were.

Several others of the wine shippers besides Garvey abandoned the town of Jerez for the safety of Cadiz, or went abroad, and during their absence the vineyards were left untended, trampled by warring armies and spoilt through lack of cultivation. Moreover, wine was perpetually being plundered, stolen or requisitioned for thirsty troops, and when the merchants set about re-establishing their trade after the war, they found stocks of old wines disastrously depleted. To the officers and ratings of the Royal Navy, Cadiz was notable as a centre of bullion smuggling; the headquarters of this illicit trade was a hotel kept by a Mr and Mrs Young.

Even before fighting broke out in the Peninsular War, when England was still busy destroying the sea power of Napoleon, wine shipping had become difficult and hazardous owing to Spanish hostility. The vicissitudes of war brought their own problems; the sherry country had to endure a period of trial, excitement, disaster and even starvation.

Legend has it that the guns fighting the Battle of Trafalgar could be heard in the streets of Jerez, though it seems incredible; and the ancient house of Cabeza y Zarco had a consignment of wine on a ship which was captured by the French. When the cargo was brought ashore at Tarifa and auctioned off, they knew how good the wine was and bought it all back.

At the beginning of the nineteenth century, one of the most important merchants was the Scot, Mr C. P. Gordon, whose son later became British vice-consul in Jerez. His bodega was the natural rendezvous for all British visitors, and his hospitality was described with gratitude in many books written by travellers and soldiers. Whenever war was in the air, Byron could be expected within pistol shot, and surely enough he arrived at Jerez in 1809. To his mother:

> At Xeres, where the sherry we drink is made, I met a great merchant – a Mr. Gordon of Scotland – who was extremely polite, and favoured me with the inspection of his vaults and cellars, so that I quaffed at the fountain head.
>
> Gibraltar,
> August 11th, 1809

Five days earlier he had written to Francis Hodgson:

> I have seen Sir John Carr at Seville and Cadiz, and, like Swift's barber, have been down on my knees to beg he would not put me into black and white.
>
> I shall return to Spain before I see England, for I am enamoured of the country.

Sir John Carr, known as 'Jaunting Carr', made a fortune out of travelogue. He later published an account of his travels in Spain, describing how he was entertained at Puerto de Santa Maria by a Mr Fleetwood, an English merchant 'of great respectability' who had a 'hospitable country house (for so it was considered although in a town)'. In Jerez he was entertained by the inevitable Mr Gordon.

Byron's visit almost exactly coincided with the French invasion of Andalusia; and they remained there until Marshal Soult's evacuation in 1812 after the battle of Salamanca. Eighteen months after Byron's visit, on 5 March 1811, a bloody if indecisive battle in the Peninsular War was to be fought on the edge of the sherry country: the battle of Barrosa, near Chiclana.

We must thank merchants such as Gordon for maintaining the sherry trade during an intensely difficult period, and we owe a great deal to their efforts. In the aftermath of war it was easier to export than to trade internally, for there were many brigands, often soldiers in hiding after the Peninsular and Carlist wars. The Civil Guard was not formed until 1844. After the devastations of the Peninsular War it needed a man of genius to set the sherry trade on its feet again and fortunately such a man was already there, awaiting his opportunity: the great Pedro Domecq Lembeye.

The history of the house of Domecq during the early years of the nineteenth century is a tragedy centred around the figure of Juan Carlos Haurie, who was by far the most important sherry shipper in Jerez. He was a nephew of the original Juan Haurie and a cousin of Pedro Domecq Lembeye, whose mother Catalina was the daughter of Juan Haurie's sister. Although Haurie had lived all his life in Spain, he was proud of his French ancestry, and during the Peninsular War he supported the French invaders. His name soon became the anathema of the Jerezanos. On 2 June 1808 the mob rose against him. The priests did their best to restore peace and to preach forgiveness, but the people would not listen, and the mayor had to let bulls loose upon the crowds – a remedy far more drastic than tear gas.

In the name of the Emperor Napoleon, Marshal Soult gave Haurie the contract to provision the French army, and he was empowered to sequester any wines and foodstuffs he needed. Worst of all, he collected taxes levied upon the local people to pay for the war. For some time there was a state of anarchy in Spain, and Haurie was particularly vulnerable to patriotic robbers, but during the years of French ascendancy he was still highly prosperous. From February 1810 till August 1812 the French occupied Jerez, and in 1811 Joseph Bonaparte celebrated his saint's day while staying in Calle Francos. The year 1812, when the French power was on the wane, was known as 'the year of hunger'. Crops were fed to the French horses while the people who had grown them died of starvation in the streets. Their hatred of collaborators can well be understood.

When the French were finally expelled. Haurie was utterly ruined. Although there were no more riots, he had to pay a vast sum in compensation, and despite efforts extending over decades, none of the debt owed by the French government for his services was ever paid. He was left friendless and penniless. One creditor seized his young wine at the time of the vintage. He was unable to meet his bills and had to pay his chief clerk with brandy, aniseed, wine and casks.

Although Jerez would no longer tolerate Haurie, there was no suggestion of animosity against his kinsman Pedro Domecq. Domecq was born in Jerez, but his childhood, like the rest of his life, was cosmopolitan. He was educated in France and England, and then took a post as a clerk in London with Gordon, Murphy & Co., who were Haurie's agents. He apparently wanted to learn the foreign side of the business rather than to settle permanently, as he was subject to none of the rules and discipline of a merchant's office.

At this point another of the great personalities of the sherry trade enters the picture and, to understand what Domecq was planning for the promotion of his wines, it is necessary to move the picture to England. John James Ruskin was serving a hard-working and ill-paid apprenticeship to the City of London; then, in 1808, he joined Gordon, Murphy & Co. His new employers were prosperous merchants in a very large way of business, chiefly with Spain and the West Indies. There were three 'Princely Partners' – Sir William Duff Gordon, Colonel Murphy and James Farrell – and they employed Ruskin as cashier and customs clerk. He was paid only £150 a year, but the partners were so pleased with him that they increased this to £200 almost immediately; before long he was getting £300 and was given rooms in the junior partner's house. All was apparently going well, but Ruskin was dissatisfied. The 'Princely Partners' were just a little too princely, and vast sums were lost on bold but utterly rash enterprises. Sir William was the Member for Worcester and spent money with a glorious abandon: £25,000 for contested elections, £20,000 for a house and furniture in Portland Place, £10,000 for jewels when he married Lady Duff Gordon. And that was not all: on one occasion they sent abroad goods worth £150,000 and received nothing in return, as Colonel Murphy's brother had gambled it all away. Ruskin saw that such a state of affairs could not last, and he was looking for a chance to break away and start a business of his own. The chance came in 1813.

Owing to the calamitous state of Haurie's finances in Jerez following the Peninsular War, his sherry business was very much on the wane, and his decline may well have been made all the worse by his agents' inability to sell what wine he had. At the time when he quarrelled with his agents, Pedro Domecq was given the task of finding a new agent. Without hesitation he approached Ruskin, who later wrote:

Domecq associated only with the Foreign Clerks – of whom there were Six or Seven. He had not exchanged ten words with me in as many months when he called me aside one day & asked if I would join him & be agent to his Uncle if he could get the appointment for me, – I said only on Condition of Gordon Murphy Co. giving me leave – When I named it to Sir W. D. Gordon he said he had plans of his own for me – but I was determined to avoid connexion with such extravagance.

Ruskin had worked all this time for Gordon, Murphy & Co. without a single break, and he decided to take a holiday in Scotland, but he caught typhus fever on the way, and almost a year passed before he could rejoin Domecq in London, towards the end of 1814. The two partners had only £1,500 between them, but fortunately they were introduced to Henry Telford, a wealthy and amiable bachelor who lived in the country with his unmarried sisters. He was very fond of horses and never pretended to be a businessman. He supplied the necessary capital, however, and the new firm of Ruskin, Telford & Domecq started business in 1815 at 11 Billiter Street, in premises which he owned; but he never took any part in the business at all save when Ruskin was away on holiday; then he would go into the office and supervise the routine matters until his partner came back. In fact he was just the man Ruskin and Domecq were looking for, and they all got on very well together: Ruskin had the brains, Telford had the money and Domecq had the sherry. It was such a success that before long Ruskin and Domecq were even richer than Telford. Thanks to the energy of the new partners, Haurie's shipments soon rose from twenty butts a year to three thousand. When Haurie's establishment eventually collapsed, Ruskin continued as agent for Domecq.

In 1815 old Sir James Duff died in Cadiz and left his sherry business to his kinsman, Sir William Duff Gordon, who promptly (and rather improperly) approached Ruskin and asked him to sell Duff Gordon sherries as well as those of Haurie. More improperly still, Ruskin consented, but he realized that such a state of affairs could not last, and he soon gave up Sir William, 'as I could not well keep both'. Gordon Murphy & Co. retained the agency, and their eventual failure in 1820 severely embarrassed their Spanish house. Fortunately, however, it was strong enough to weather the storm and it soon achieved the high position which it still firmly occupies.

In the meantime it had also built up a considerable business with Sandeman – a reliable connection that greatly helped matters. A letter from Duff Gordon's Spanish bodegas, dated 12 June 1818, suggests that Ruskin was no longer very popular:

> Your antagonists Ruskins are cunning hands, and Juan Carlos (Haurie) is wholly led by them. They of course, pursue the system most profitable to themselves, and care but little for the real interest and credit of their employers. They have tricked Granstone and John Gordon, and fairly cut them out of several orders from Leith and London in defiance of Haurie's solemn pledge to act in concord regarding the new prices.
>
> | Haurie | 37 | 40 | 45 | 52 | 60 |
> | Gordon | 37 | 43 | 48 | 54 | 60 |
>
> The object Ruskins have had in view is evidently to persuade the trade that they can ship as low and as high as Gordon in the first and last qualities for which but few orders are generally sent. But in the intermediate numbers they are about £3 cheaper than their neighbours. Let us resolutely follow up our own plan in a fair and open way, and ship Super wines at such prices as may yield us a competent profit for our labour and risk, leaving them to enjoy and benefit if they can such pitiful manoeuvres, which may turn out much against them in the end.

Both methods of salesmanship proved equally successful, and both houses prospered: as for the quality of the rival wines, it is probably safe to say that there was very little to choose between them, as they were all excellent.

The name of John James Ruskin is found in many reference books simply because he was the father of John Ruskin, the Victorian aesthete and socialist. Such reflected fame is an indignity for Ruskin senior, who was the greatest English sherry shipper of his time. Although his career was less spectacular than his son's, he was a man of vision, character and intelligence. In this psychoanalytical age we should probably label him with some complex: it was his whim to employ inferior clerks. The mistakes they made while he was away pleased his vanity, and he enjoyed putting things right when he came back. He could not stay in the office and leave them to do the travelling, as he knew they would have done more harm than good. Inquisitive biographers can find something ludicrous in almost any man's life, and it is enough that Ruskin, by his industry and intelligence, did much to raise the house of Domecq to the high position it enjoys today. His energies in business were honoured and admired by his son:

> ... the letters to customers were brief in their assurance that if they found fault with their wine, they did not understand it, and if they wanted an extension of credit, they could not have it. These Spartan brevities of epistle were, however, always supported by the utmost care in executing his correspondents' orders ... His domiciliary visits ... were productive of the more confidence between him and the country merchant, that he was perfectly just and candid in appraisement of the wine of rival houses, while his fine palate enabled him always to sustain triumphantly any and every ordeal of blindfold question which the suspicious customer might put him to. Also, when correspondents of importance came up to town, my father would put himself so far out of his way as to ask them to dine at Herne Hill, and try the contents of his own cellar.

All the time he was an agent his list included sherries of every possible style and age, including one venerable wine that was more of a curiosity than a commercial proposition – it cost a thousand pounds a butt. Amongst many interesting relics there is a letter sent to Thomas Phillips, of Birmingham, in 1856, with a present of rare sherry when his daughter got married. This included a pint drawn 'out of a cask from which Lord Nelson was supplied from our stores before the battle of Trafalgar 51 years ago'.

His business was not unprofitable, and he died worth some £200,000 – a fortune that was to play a larger part than he could ever have imagined in the history of English culture.

John Ruskin's interests in architecture and landscape were aroused during his childhood when he travelled around England with his father visiting wine merchants, and thanks to the sound lessons his father gave him he became one of the most valuable wine propagandists of his time. His prestige was enormous, and his enthusiasm and respect for wine were infectious in an age that was so often dominated by puritanical teetotallers. When his father died, John Ruskin left as his epitaph: 'He was an entirely honest merchant, and his memory is to all who keep it dear and helpful. His son, whom he loved, to the uttermost, and taught to speak truth, says this of him.'

After the bankruptcy in 1815 of Juan Carlos Haurie – who, by 1814, was the only survivor of the original five nephews of Juan Haurie – it was left to Pedro Domecq to restore the fortunes of his house. For some years Domecq had helped with the management, and from 1816 onwards it was he who principally directed the affairs of the company, but it was an uphill path: as the French debts proved irrecoverable, he was continually beset by pressing creditors. The affairs of Juan Carlos were getting steadily worse, and were further bedevilled by the speculations of his brother Enrique. The firm's only profitable activities were entirely the work of Pedro Domecq, and in 1818 Juan Carlos granted him the right to ship wines under the Haurie mark. From then onwards, the sherry business was his own property and sole responsibility. Haurie was left to his own devices. In 1821 he did not have enough money to pay for the vintaging of his grapes and in the following year he was declared fraudulently bankrupt and sent to gaol. Most of his vineyards, bodegas and wine eventually went to Domecq, and the remainder were bought by Duff Gordon. Domecq now traded under his own name. His reputation already stood so high that when King Fernando VII visited Jerez in 1823 he was given the royal warrant and appointed *Gentilhombre de Camara*, or Gentleman of the Bedchamber.

When John Ruskin wrote his *Praeterita*, he remembered Domecq clearly:

> Mr. Peter Domecq was . . . a man of strictest honour and kindly disposition . . . My father saw that he could fully trust Mr. Domecq's honour and feeling; but not so fully either his sense or his industry, and insisted, though taking only his Agent's commission, on being, both nominally and practically the Head Partner of the firm.
>
> Mr. Domecq lived chiefly in Paris, rarely visiting his Spanish Estate, but having perfect knowledge of the proper processes of its cultivation, and authority over its labourers almost like a chief's over his clan. He kept the wines at the highest possible standard, and allowed my father to manage all matters concerning their sale.

Ruskin's father had not been altogether fair in assessing either

Domecq's sense or his industry, for both were soon to become by-words. But Ruskin was more interested in Adela Domecq, Don Pedro's second daughter. In 1814, while still working in London, Pedro Domecq had married Diana Lancaster of Bermondsey and they had five beautiful daughters, all of whom were to marry into the French nobility. John Ruskin fell in love with Adela and remained devoted to her memory, but she refused him; indeed, she laughed at him. Perhaps she acted wisely, but Ruskin was broken-hearted. He said that it took him four years to recover, but it is doubtful whether he ever did.

Soon after forming the partnership, John James Ruskin went to Jerez and saw all the desolation of the war-scarred country. He apparently gave his son a vivid description of the journey and some of John Ruskin's enchantingly immature schoolboy verses describe the Macharnudo vineyards as they were at that time:

> Alas, and it filled me with grief
> To see there no promise of fruit
> For the insect was eating the leaf
> And the worm was at work on the root.
>
> Neglected for many a year,
> Unpruned and untended they hung.
> The leafage was withered and sere,
> And the vineyards looked sad in the sun.
>
> No wine had attained to old age here,
> It was new, it was sour, it was dead.
> Oh, here was no voice of the gauger:
> Nor sound of the cellarman's tread . . .

But Pedro Domecq filled him with confidence:

> He cometh, to be the erecter,
> Of vaults upon vaults by a wink.
> He comes, to make wine into nectar
> He comes, that the nations may drink.

Ruskin's youthful enthusiasm was not unjustified: Domecq's vigour and resource led the way in restoring the trade to its former prosperity. In all his work, he was indefatigable, and he bought every available vineyard, restoring them from dereliction to fertile prosperity.

Anyone looking through lists of shippers published at about this time will be confused by the numbers of Domecqs and Hauries who were exporting wine. There were two more Pedro Domecqs, also of French origin and probably related, who shipped sherry from Cadiz at the turn of the century, and with whom Pedro Domecq Lembeye was for a time associated. Another family of Domecqs had extensive bodegas in Jerez, where they traded under the name of *Juan Domecq y Hijos*. This business was later absorbed by Pedro Domecq's successors.

Juan Carlos Haurie was obviously an out-and-out bounder. Despite his agreement with Domecq, he decided to found a new firm to exploit the goodwill of his name. Whether he was entitled to do so, having already given it to Domecq, is at least doubtful, but he purported to revoke his grant, and a new partnership was formed in 1824 between Juan Haurie (his nephew), James Wilson and William Garvey. Such a procedure was immoral if not illegal and the result was chaos. In the same year the new partnership wrote a letter to Colonel Warburton, of the 85th Regiment, stationed in Malta, in which they referred to their 'antient establishment', that had apparently been shipping sherry to the 'Royal Family, Nobility and Gentry of Great Britain and Ireland' since 1740. By 1827 they were claiming to be the largest exporters, with 3,095 butts (made up by 1,865 from Wilson and 1,230 from Garvey) compared with Pedro Domecq's 1,944.

Haurie's creditors claimed, rather half-heartedly, that it was they who had the right to his mark, but nothing further is heard of their contention. Domecq, however, was a man of action, and on at least one occasion he seized a shipment of their wine as infringing his trade mark. There followed a series of fantastic machinations culminating in the inevitably inconclusive lawsuit, but Domecq was no longer really interested, and he stood to lose nothing. It was he who had built the business up after it had collapsed; he was already shipping most of his wine under his own name; the trade knew the facts, and the genuine goodwill was his own; above all, he controlled Ruskin, Telford & Domecq of London, with whom no new agent could effectively compete. He had also enlisted the help of a brilliant assistant, Juan Sanchez, who came of a prominent family in Santander and was the greatest sherry expert of his day. He had formerly collaborated with Juan Carlos Haurie, and also had bodegas of his own, where he stored first-class wines for sale to the shippers; but he was not a shipper himself. He was the most famous *capataz*, or bodega foreman, there has ever been; he was so good that he could dictate his own terms and he worked as a freelance. Besides helping Domecq, he also blended wine for Duff Gordon, and one of their early letters complained wryly that a blend he had prepared regardless of cost was so good that they would have been ruined had they shipped much of it.

From this point, the story of Domecq is one of steady prosperity, but that of the rival partnership is the very opposite. Juan Carlos Haurie, his debts still unpaid, died in 1828 aged sixty-six. In 1830 Patrick Garvey decided he had seen quite enough of his father's associates and left them, to resume business under the family name and brand – one that was soon to be numbered amongst the most honoured in the trade. The new firm of Haurie went bankrupt in 1841, and their creditors took most of their assets, but did leave some wine, and Haurie's went laboriously on until they became bankrupt again in 1855. In 1856 all the remaining assets were sold by public auction. Like a phoenix, the house of Haurie again rose from its ashes, only to suffer a final eclipse at the end of the century. The Haurie family, however, did manage to add a new word to the Spanish language: a pack of hounds is still known as a *jauría*.

Born a cosmopolitan, Pedro Domecq did not stay in Jerez a moment longer than he had to. As soon as he could, he left all his commercial interests in the able hands of his younger brother, Don Juan Pedro, and went to Paris, where he had a house in the fashionable Rue de la Madeleine. When he was not in Paris, he occasionally went to stay with the Ruskins in London and travelled around the country visiting his British customers. He died in his native Jerez, though, in tragic and rather ludicrous circumstances. He suffered severely from rheumatism and gout, and his doctors advised him to take steam baths. He was suspended by a system of ropes over a cauldron of boiling water, and one day, in February 1839, the whole crazy structure collapsed. He was badly scalded and died a few days later. He was only fifty-seven and his death cast the whole town in mourning. Eight thousand followed his funeral.

Soon afterwards, the full extent of his success became apparent: his estate was valued at more than a million pounds – an incalculable fortune in terms of modern money. As he himself grew rich, others made a little on the side, and Richard Ford, writing in 1861, tells us that:

Juan Sanchez, the Capataz of the late Pedro Domecq, died recently worth £300,000. Towards his latter end, having been visited by his confessor and some qualms of conscience, he bequeathed his fortune to pious and charitable uses, but the bulk was forthwith secured by his attorneys and priests, whose charity began at home.

Pedro Domecq once claimed to have made his fortune in two years of hard work, and with conditions as they were, it might well have been true. His great success was continued by his brother Juan Pedro, who also became a legend in Jerez. To Garcia Lorca (Andalusia's greatest modern poet) he was a hero, and he was almost a god in the eyes of the gypsies:

> Saint Joseph moves his arms
> In a silken cloak entwined
> And with three Persian sultans
> Pedro Domecq comes behind
> The crescent in the ecstasy
> Of a white stork is dreaming
> And over the flat roof-tops
> Come flags and torches streaming.

> from Romance de la Guardia Civil Española,
> translated by Roy Campbell

The present directors of the Domecq company are descended from Pedro's elder brother Pedro Pascual (1785–1884).

The recovery in the sherry trade was rapid, thanks partly to the First Gentleman of Europe, who roundly damned Madeira and swore – by God – he would drink nothing but sherry. In 1823 1,074 gallons of wine were imported free of duty by the Spanish ambassador; his official allowance was 252 gallons. Sherry had 'arrived', and soon a decanter was found on every English sideboard. Jerez had never heard of such wealth. Rich sherry shippers had mansions with gardens planned after the English taste; sweeping lawns of green turf and boxwood hedges, watered continuously by deep wells. Julian Pemartin went one better and built himself a palace in the style of the Paris Opéra; it still stands, a splendid folly, next to the great Sandeman bodegas.

The foreign colony grew steadily in strength, the most prosperous shippers being English, Scottish, Irish and French. Things foreign and elegant were all the rage. As the century progressed and the boom showed no sign of dwindling, Jerezanos, dressed in Lock's hats and Savile Row suits, travelled in English carriages to banquets prepared by French chefs. Everyone was gay and carefree. Money was no object. It has been said that labourers went to the vineyards wearing patent leather shoes; presumably they benefited from their masters' cast-offs.

The early years of the nineteenth century clearly provided a propitious time to found a bodega, and one of the largest – Barbadillo of Sanlucar – dates from this time. It was founded by a family from the north of Spain which had acquired wealth in Mexico. Its real burgeoning, however, is later history.

In the year 1825 there was a little tragedy: the Sad History of the Thirsty Thunderbolt. A certain Señor Estevez, who was passing along on his lawful occasions, was alarmed by the sight of dense black clouds suddenly gathering in the sky. He ran at once to a friend's house to take shelter, but no sooner was he there than there came a clap of thunder and a blazing thunderbolt fell neatly down the chimney. It raced across the whole house without causing a trace of damage until it was finally halted in the cellar. Then the calamity occurred. It completely consumed four whole butts of sherry before it faded out. Many words were spoken, and Vulcan was made to understand that Jerezanos do not spend years growing sherry just to satisfy the whim of a thunderbolt.

Jerez was gay and prosperous, but what was it like to live there? George W. Suter, who went there in 1831 and was British vice-consul from 1869 to 1887, has left us a graphic description of the town as he first knew it. Before the fine carriages were imported, there were only three private coaches, and there was none for hire. One of them, a huge and ancient vehicle drawn by mules with rope harness, was owned by a local Marquis. It was so high and cumbersome that a footman had to carry a three-legged stool to help his master in and out. The streets were neither drained, paved nor lighted, and there were stepping stones in the main road so that people could cross without having to wade through mud and water. When a family went out in the evening to the theatre or to a party, a servant carrying a lighted torch in one hand and a stout cudgel in the other walked in front, while the young men (who were the only people who could safely go out alone at night) had small lanterns, lit by pieces of wax candle, attached to their high-peaked hats. By moving their heads, they could aim the light into dark places or suspicious doorways. They armed themselves with swords, or occasionally with pistols.

Writing in 1838, Captain C. Rochfort Scott gave another interesting description, but he was not entirely comfortable: 'It is needful to walk in the streets with nose in air, and eyes fixed on things above . . .' He also wrote of the 'endemic fever, generated in its pestiferous gutters'.

In the same year yet another notable British house was founded. Fletcher Ivison started his business in Puerto Real, on the coast beyond Puerto de Santa Maria, whence it was later moved to Jerez. It continued under family ownership until 1964, when it was acquired by Wisdom & Warter.

During 1834 there was an outbreak of cholera. The fever had come to nearby towns earlier, and the town council devised absurd quarantine regulations, but these proved useless. By June fifty people were dying every day and a third of the population had fled into the country, where they were safe from attack. The bodies were taken away in covered carts to the cemetery and buried in a common grave without any pretence of Christian rites. Four thousand people are said to have died in three months. Only four people made any effort to keep the plague under control, and all of them were foreigners: Dr Wilson, a native of Dunbar (whose brother was Haurie's partner); George Suter; Bernard Shiel, who was of Irish descent; and a Frenchman, Adolf Capdepon. Between them, they did manage to mitigate the terror, but the real tower of strength was Dr Wilson, who had been in charge of the Civil Hospital in Gibraltar during the yellow fever epidemic of 1828, and who did a great deal of good by visiting the fever-ridden houses in the poor quarter of the town, preaching cleanliness and the benefits of ventilation.

Jerez recovered from the plague and its prosperity increased day by day. Lists of exporters included many British names that have long since vanished: the widow of R. Shiel, Widow Harmony, Campbell & Co., F. W. Cosens, F. G. Cosens, nephews of P. Harmony, F. Morgan & Co., W. Rudolph, Gorman & Co., W. Oldham and several others, apart from a number that are still flourishing in Jerez or Puerto de Santa Maria. It is fascinating trying to trace the history of houses that have gone out of business. Sometimes their wines were sold and divided; sometimes merely the name was changed. In the library of the late Don José de Soto y Molina, now owned by the municipality, there are many records of those old firms, but their connections are impossibly intricate and complicated: to trace them would be a life's work.

Notable people have always visited the sherry country; they come every year, and the list is endless, but one arrived in 1828 who deserves special mention, as his stories of Andalusia have helped to make him immortal – Washington Irving. He came to Puerto de Santa Maria to live quietly while finishing his *Tales of the Alhambra*, and he became a friend of Böhl, a German who was manager of the Duff Gordon bodegas at that time. Irving left his mark in a wholly unexpected direction. One of Böhl's daughters, Cecilia, was intent on becoming a writer, and he encouraged her; later she became a famous Spanish novelist, using the pen name Fernan Caballero, and when her father wrote to Irving in later years, she used to send messages telling him how she was getting on. After leaving Andalusia, Irving wrote to Böhl ordering wine for the American legation in London. His order was an unusual one:

> I have pledged myself to Mr. McLane [the minister] through your aid, to procure him a cask of old sherry, that should carry sound argument in every glass – some such liquor as that with which Lady Macbeth undertook to *convince* the pages of King Duncan. Will you enable me to redeem my pledge by shipping a cask of choice, generous old wine? I know you to have an admirable taste in this as well as in other things of high practical nature.

His abilities in affairs of a 'high practical nature' were Herr Böhl's greatest blessing, but Irving's order was rather a tall one for a man who was notorious for his lack of imagination. However, he fulfilled it, apparently with every satisfaction, by sending them a butt of 'our most superior old Sherry'. Irving remained a customer and wrote again in 1833:

> I am hoping to find a great revolution taking place among our wine drinkers and that Sherry is completely superceding Madeira: a change particularly favourable to my stomach. I wish you would have the kindness to send me two *half butts*, or whatever else you may call them each of about 60 Gallons, of the *very best* Brown Sherry. I wish them to be of the same quality as wine that I may brag about – and I mean to make some of it procure you ample

orders from Boston. Ship it to me at New York and draw upon Peter Ramsey & Co for the money. Recollect I ask this as from a friend, and a loving brother of the poor; so send me the best your vineyards can produce.

The bodegas expanded under Böhl's management and continued to do so under that of Thomas Osborne. Osborne had been advising Böhl and the Duff Gordons for years, and to all intents and purposes he was a partner. In 1825, at the age of forty-four, he had married Böhl's daughter Aurora, who was much younger. In 1833 he signed a partnership deed with Cosmo Duff Gordon and, after fifty-two years' residence in Spain, he became a partner in law as well as in fact. When Böhl died in 1836 he was not replaced, and Osborne was left in full command – a position he retained until his death in 1845. Ever since then, the bodegas have been owned by his descendants, who finally took control after Cosmo Duff Gordon retired in 1848, and they bought the Duff Gordon family interests in 1872. The present head of the family, which has become entirely Spanish, is the Conde de Osborne.

All wines were still sold under the name of Duff Gordon until 1890, when the Osbornes, who had formerly concentrated on the export markets, decided to sell wine in Spain and also to enter the highly profitable local market for brandy. 'Duff Gordon' is an impossible name to pronounce in Spanish, but the name 'Osborne' sounds equally natural in either language.

The Osborne family is also responsible for the vast bullring at Puerto, one of the very best and the third largest in Spain. Whether it was originally erected through altruism or as a business venture remains obscure, but whatever its origin, it turned out a complete white elephant. Behind the Spanish *toreros* there lurks a sinister troupe of agents, organizers and managers; many of them are gypsies, as are many matadors, and their morals are those of the race-track and of the horse-dealer. Their sharp practices were entirely beyond the sound business understanding of the Osbornes, and the proprietor, in sheer desperation, managed to sell it to a politically-minded *almacenista*. It is the scene of many of the best fights in Andalusia.

Many of the great sherry shippers began as clerks who left their employers to start their own businesses. John William Burdon originally worked for Duff Gordon; when he left, he built up a highly successful business that absorbed the old Harmony bodegas. His house and his beautiful bodega buildings, the stonework decorated with his monogram, still survive, though they are bodegas no longer: they are the stables for the Terry family's famous horses. He had a valuable personal connection and spent a great deal of time travelling in Britain. In 1854 he was the leading shipper, followed by Garvey. He married a Señora Carmen Berges, but they had no children and the business was sold to Luis de la Cuesta, who in turn sold out, in 1932, to Don Luis Caballero; he preserves the complete accounts and many of Burdon's letters dating back to the early years of the nineteenth century, together with his equestrian portrait, his clock by Smith of Clerkenwell, his chair and his desk. The Caballeros were in the wine trade at Chipiona in 1795, and their business as shippers dates back to 1830. Amongst its many interests it owns the Moorish castle in Puerto de Santa Maria, which has been carefully restored; it was once the seat of the Medinaceli family. Caballero is currently one of the most vigorous houses in the trade and in 1991 bought a controlling interest in the well-known house of Emilio Lustau in Jerez.

Gonzalez, Byass & Co. was founded in 1835, but the story really begins much earlier, in 1783, when twenty-five-year-old Don José Antonio Gonzalez y Rodriguez, a member of the king's bodyguard, was appointed administrator of the Royal Salt Marshes at Sanlucar de Barrameda. The post was an extremely important one, as the marshes were a great source of revenue, and it was a high honour for so young a man; but Don José was clever, handsome and one of the royal favourites. He had an enviable reputation – '*el terror de las damas guapas de la Corte*' – and what could be better than that? It was even whispered that Carlos III wanted to keep his friend at a safe distance; that certain ladies of high degree . . .

Soon after arriving at Sanlucar he married María del Rosario Angel; they lived happily together, and María del Rosario gave birth to seven children, five of them boys. Then, quite suddenly, Don José died.

María del Rosario was left in poor circumstances, but she was a woman of great character and would not give way easily. She was determined to see that all her sons had every chance to succeed in life, and she moved to Seville, where four of them were educated at the university. They were all excellent scholars and had distinguished careers as doctors and lawyers. The fifth, however, was a problem, and it was he, needless to say, who ended by having the greatest career of all: he founded Gonzalez Byass. His name was Manuel María Gonzalez Angel and he was the weakling of the family; he was so delicate that he could not study like his brothers. For the sake of his health his doctors advised he should live by the sea, and his mother found him a job as clerk to a firm of bankers and merchants in Cadiz. Although he was not expected to live many years, he worked hard and prospered. Soon he had branched out as a shipper and merchant on his own account, and the story is told of how he nearly met with disaster at the very beginning of his career. He was shipping a cargo of potatoes from Huelva to Cadiz when his boat sank just before it reached home. All his capital (and a little more) was tied up in the venture and things looked very bad, but his mother was a woman of great determination: she was not one to be defeated by such a trifle as a shipwreck. She applied herself to the problem at once: all she asked for was a bucket of sea-water and a few samples of his potatoes. They floated. Mother and son dashed out and chartered a fishing boat. Within a few hours three-quarters of the potatoes had been caught in the nets, and his mother had saved the day. Is it apocryphal? Almost certainly, but it is no more extraordinary than a hundred and one other tales of the great men of Andalusia.

In his love affairs Don Manuel was equally enterprising and, at the beginning, just as unfortunate. He fell in love with Victorina de Soto, daughter of the richest man in Cadiz. Victorina's father was furious and ordered his servants to douse young Gonzalez with water as he stood outside the house, but he was unmoved by the flood. Then another expedient was tried: he was bitten by fierce dogs. Weakling or no, he would not surrender, and it was de Soto who eventually gave way. They were married in 1833 and moved to Jerez, where Gonzalez had sensed the fortune to be made out of wine. Some years before, he had bought a little bodega near the market place, but had done nothing more about it; now he was to begin in earnest. He was helped by the fact that the old Gremio had been dissolved so that at last the trade was open to enterprise. Industrious as he was, he did not make his first shipment to England until two years later, and then it was only ten butts. The price was probably about fifty pounds a butt – hardly enough for a young man and his wife to live on but not a bad start. The cholera plague of 1834 would hardly have helped. In 1836 he did rather better and shipped sixty-two butts. He could have shipped more; he was a man of knowledge and enterprise, and a great worker, but he lacked one thing: capital. Soon, however, he became friendly with a rich man, Señor Aguera, who had money to invest and every confidence in his ability. With the capital Aguera provided, Gonzalez bought a large stretch of land next to the Collegiate Church (now the cathedral) on the edge of the town, the site of an old and mediocre vineyard called La Sacristia, and built his first large bodega, which was given the same name. He looked far ahead, laying down good wine and building up the soleras that were to be the foundation of his future prosperity. Meanwhile his export trade was rapidly increasing; by 1839 the figure had risen to 819 butts and he had to employ a clerk, John Barlow, to handle the English correspondence. That was business on a sensible scale.

In a few years Señor Aguera took fright. Trade was too good to be true; it could not last; the end was in sight; what was the use of buying all that wine which would give no return for years? Why lay store for the future when there was no future? He wanted his money back. And he got it. Gonzalez continued alone, but he could not go on indefinitely without a partner. He could manage the business in Jerez easily but had no time to visit his customers, of whom there were already many in England. Moreover, he was determined to open up trade connections throughout the world, including Germany and Russia. In Juan Dubosc, the son of a French Catalan who lived in southern Spain, he found just the partner he needed. Gonzalez stayed in Jerez while Dubosc travelled the world. The company, now called Gonzalez & Dubosc, continued to expand, and in 1853 they started to build the great Constancia bodega. By 1855, when the new bodega was completed, exports to England alone were more than 3,000 butts, and were to rise still higher: in 1873 the export figure reached the peak of 10,409 butts – not far short of seven million bottles.

By 1855 the English trade had become so important that the London agent, Robert Blake Byass, was taken into partnrship, and the name of the company became Gonzalez, Dubosc & Co. When Dubosc died in 1859 the name was continued unchanged, by arrangement with his widow, until 1863, when it was changed to Gonzalez & Byass. Seven years later it was changed again, this time to Gonzalez, Byass & Co. All the present directors are lineal descendants of Manuel Ma. Gonzalez.

Manuel Gonzalez was a bold businessman and was not at all afraid of a bold investment. In 1864 he bought the stock of Simeon Sierra for £45,000 and the whole Moseley establishment in Puerto de Santa Maria for £73,000. He was fully supported by his partner Byass. Walter Gilbey wrote in his Travelling Journal of 1874: 'If ever Mr. Gonzalez wrote and consulted Byass about a purchase he would immediately wire back to close with it and if necessary draw on London at sight.' But the most complete speculation came some time later when the Marques del Castillo de San Felipe died, and it was well known that he had left wines of the very highest class in his private bodega, but no one knew quite how good they were, nor did they know the quantity. His widow knew nothing of wine and wanted to get rid of it as quickly as possible; she had no time at all for delay or argument, and would not let anyone into the bodega to inspect the stock. But she did know her price: £10,000 cash down (in gold). It was a bold risk, but Don Manuel took it. He paid the money and was given the key. Inside the bodega he found a hundred butts of very old wine, worth far more than he had paid. Twenty-seven of them, in the form of a small solera, remain to this day in the Bodega Constancia and are named the *Parte Arroyo Solera*, in memory of the widow who sold them. Such private cellars were as common a hundred years ago as they are rare today. Wine lovers with only two or three casks could afford to let them go on maturing for many years and their wines included some of the greatest amontillado and oloroso sherries. One enthusiast went so far as to keep his best wines in his bedroom and firmly locked the door throughout the day so that no one could get near them.

One of the highlights in the nineteenth-century history of Jerez was the visit of Queen Isabella II to the Gonzalez bodegas in 1862. The Queen was interested in wine and her host was told that she wanted to see exactly how sherry was made. There were no railways, and she had to travel the whole way in easy stages by coach. Unfortunately Her Majesty's royal caprice had taken her to Jerez long after the vintage was over. So trifling a difficulty, however, did not daunt Don Manuel. Then, as today, peasants used to buy grapes cheaply at the time of the vintage and hang them from the rafters of their houses for eating at Christmas. He let it be known that he would buy all the grapes they had at a very generous price, and he managed to get hold of a large quantity. He pressed them on two successive days, the first half on the day before the Queen was due and the second half in her presence, so that she could see everything in one day. She could even taste the young must – though I doubt whether she wanted to drink any.

To hold the wine of this extraordinary vintage, Don Manuel brought a gargantuan cask from Heidelberg with a capacity of no less than 3,500 gallons, compared with the mere 108 gallons of an ordinary sherry butt – and that is no mean vessel. Somewhat irreverently perhaps (because it holds thirty-three butts and Christ was thirty-three years old), the giant cask was called *El Cristo* – Christ – and the must inside it developed as a wine of truly outstanding quality, fully worthy of the cask. Perhaps the present generation is more wary of blasphemy than was its predecessor, for *El Cristo* is now called *El Maestro*, as the apostles used to call Jesus. It now has twelve apostles, each filled with the best possible example of the different styles of sherry. They are each named and are placed as the apostles were at the Last Supper according to the picture of Leonardo da Vinci. Judas does not appear: he is in the vinegar store.

The Queen was pleased, as she should have been, in view of the fact that she had only been there a few hours and her entertainment had cost Gonzalez no less that £6,000. As a reward she offered him a dukedom, but he declined and would only accept the Grand Cross of Isabella the Catholic. His work was enough; he wanted no more and felt himself so unworthy that he never wore the insignia of his order.

In spite of himself, however, he was dragged into politics and became member of parliament for Jerez, but resigned after a very short time, and one can hardly blame him for finding politics distasteful. On another occasion, in 1877, he had the misfortune to be elected mayor of Sanlucar unopposed and by acclamation without even knowing he was a candidate. It was a great compliment, of course, but he had to flee from his house in the middle of the night to avoid being taken by main force to fill the mayoral chair. Life must have been very difficult, but rather entertaining. In January 1887 he died, after confounding all the prophecies of his doctors and living to the ripe age of seventy-five. During his years by the sea in Cadiz, his health was not one whit improved, but after coming to Jerez, living amongst his sherry casks, breathing the atmosphere of the wine and spending hours on end in his tasting-room, his health soon became excellent. He was mourned by all his work-people and is still remembered for his generosity. Amongst many benefactions he built and endowed a free school for his employees' children. In the Gonzalez Byass bodegas, his tasting-room has been preserved as a memorial and has not been touched since he died; amongst the dust and cobwebs, his bottles still stand, their labels faded, their corks decayed and their contents wasted away, but all of them are just as he left them.

For all his qualities, however, Don Manuel will never be as famous as his Uncle Joe. A friend of mine once overheard two old gentlemen talking to one another in a dining-car on British Railways:

'Will you have a glass of sherry?'

'Yes, I think I will. What sherry are you drinking?'

'Tio Pepe.'

'Is that a dry sherry?'

'Yes, it's very dry. "Tio" means "very" and "Pepe" means "dry".'

The fellow was a humbug! 'Tio Pepe' means 'Uncle Joe'. Uncle Joe was a maternal uncle of Don Manuel, José Angel de la Peña, who was in the wine business at Sanlucar. Sanlucar is the home of those light, fresh, delicate wines known as manzanilla, and Uncle Joe was accustomed to drink them; he had no time for the heavier amontillados and olorosos of Jerez. So his nephew took two butts of his most delicate fino, marked them 'Tio Pepe' and kept them in a special room where Uncle Joe could go and entertain his friends. The friends liked the wine as much as the uncle did. Vizetelly, rather alarmingly, likened it to one of the rarer growths of the Rhine. Soon people were asking for it, and a solera was started. At first it was known only to a few *cognoscenti*. It got its name in 1849 but sales in the nineteenth century were small. It rose to become popular between the two world wars. It is now the most popular fino in the world.

In the days when foreigners were rare in England, and everything foreign was regarded as erotic and wicked, Don Manuel's son visited Liverpool selling his father's wines. One of the wine merchants had some vague knowledge of these dreadful aliens and thought he would put his visitor at ease with a few polite inquiries:

'Are you married, Mr Gonzalez?'

'Yes, I am.'

'Ah! At your tender age I suppose you have only one wife?'

He explained that monogamy was an old Spanish custom.

Anyone going to the Gonzalez Byass bodegas today will see something quite unusual: a family of inebriate mice. They are kept by an old foreman who spends half his time looking out for cats. He thoroughly enjoys showing his dissolute vermin to visitors, and they are well worth looking at; they drink quite neatly out of a sherry glass but do not always know when to stop, and get up to all sorts of antics.

Another important British firm, Mackenzie & Co., was founded in the middle of the nineteenth century: Kenneth Mackenzie came to Jerez in about 1842. He was succeeded by his nephew, Peter Mackenzie, who was perhaps the most British of all the British residents: although he lived in Jerez for many years, he never learnt to speak Spanish properly, and he used to delight the Jerezanos with his odd phrases. Unfortunately little more is known of the history of Mackenzie & Co., as all the old documents are lost. In 1970 the company was bought by John Harvey & Sons, Limited, the great British wine merchants, and the name is no longer used; but that story belongs to a later chapter.

By 1840 the fog of Victorian respectability was beginning to descend upon England: everything had to be done properly; there was a new beatitude of bourgeois conventions, and one dictum at least was to benefit the sherry trade for many years before ultimately leading to disaster – it was considered 'correct' to entertain with wine, but the quality did not matter much. Even in quite humble houses there was a decanter of sherry with a few biscuits waiting for whomsoever might call.

The demand rose steadily. In the early years of the century, the total export was about eight thousand butts; by 1840 the figure was 17,001 butts; by 1850, 21,457; by 1860, 30,725; by 1870, 49,597; and in 1873 sales reached the record of 68,467 butts. In 1864 43.41 per cent of the total wine imports to Great Britain were sherry. And by the middle of the century sherry had begun to reach a more widespread range of customers: a Mr Short, giving evidence before a Select Committee in 1852, said that in his wine house 'we have a great many cabmen and omnibus men, and that class of men who used to drink gin. Now, five or six of them together, they come to drink sherry which costs twice as much.' It cost 4d. a glass when porter cost 1½d.

With sales soaring, the shippers might well have been sitting back and taking life easily, and some of them doubtless were, but there were many anxious faces: all was not well in the vineyards. In 1855 there was an attack of oidium (*Uncinula Necator*), known locally as *cenizo*, or ash-coloured, owing to the dark stain that occurs on the stem of the vine and the powdery matter on the grape. A fungoid parasite, it arrived from France and was a terrible blow to the growers. There was not another good harvest until 1861. Not surprisingly, the price of wine doubled.

As if that were not enough, there was an attack of *pulgón*, a repulsive insect that feeds on the vine and finally destroys it. It had periodically devastated the vineyards ever since the Middle Ages and it returned in 1867. It was eventually exterminated, but there was not another good harvest until 1870.

These successive calamities, occurring in the vineyards at a time when the demand for wine had reached an unprecedented peak, had to be overcome as best they could. There was only one way: must was imported in ever-increasing quantities from the outlying districts of Lebrija, Trebujena and Chiclana – districts which were only on the border of the sherry area. Considerable quantities of wine were also brought from Huelva, clearly outside it. The result was inevitable and rapid: the poorer grades of sherry decreased in quality and increased greatly in price, so that a wine which had only cost £25 per butt in 1850 sold for £43 in 1862, while the cost of a good quality wine selling for £70 in 1850 only increased to £74.

In 1864 the consul at Cadiz, Alexander Graham-Dunlop, reported that there were four classes of sherry:

1. Low and spurious compounds, at from £10 to £20 per butt; say, one-fifth of the whole;
2. Common, ordinary and middling sherry, from £25 to £45 per butt; say, two-fifths;
3. Good sherry, from £45 to £70 per butt; say, three-tenths;
4. Superior sherry, from £70 to £200 per butt, one-tenth.

There were also special wines quoted at £500 or even more, but the average price was £36. First quality wines were sold at £120 and not more than a hundred butts per year were sold at higher prices.

The greatest problem for the reputation of sherry lay in the 'low and spurious compounds' which contained little if any of the genuine wine and which were sometimes fortified with British or German spirits distilled from grain or potatoes. A year later the consul reported that the lowest class of sherry went to America, Hamburg and France 'where the worthy Parisian drinks it under the name of

"Vins de Madère" '. The best wines were bought principally by Great Britain and Russia.

The situation was made worse by the less reputable British merchants who were determined to maintain the demand by keeping the price steady, and preferred to lower the quality of their wines rather than to add a few pence to the cost of a bottle. In the short term their policy was probably commercially sound, but nothing could have been more surely calculated to get the wine a bad name.

On 22 June 1854 there was great excitement: a new railway line was opened from Jerez to the Trocadero mole near Puerto de Santa Maria. There had been talk of a railway much earlier and Stephenson had visited the town in 1827, but nothing came of the plans until a group of good Jerezanos got together and decided to finance the venture, for the glory of Jerez and for the benefit of the wine trade. It was the first railway in Andalusia and the third in Spain: work was started in 1852, only four years after the first Spanish railway had been opened in Barcelona. The new line was solemnly inaugurated with all possible pomp and ceremony, and the Cardinal Archbishop of Seville came down specially to give his blessing. Afterwards there was a bullfight and everyone made merry.

The new railway was a great help to the wine trade: it reduced transport costs considerably and eliminated the long delay in carrying wine from Jerez to Puerto de Santa Maria by bullock cart. Merchants no longer needed shipping bodegas on the coast and they used them instead for maturing fino wines, which develop especially well in the sea air. The situation was further improved in 1870 when an urban railway was laid through the streets of Jerez, passing the doors of all the major bodegas, so that wine could be taken from the shipping bodegas in Jerez to the quay in a few hours. It was still occasionally used until 1969, to the horror and alarm of visiting motorists, whom it charged like a bull and who came off a bad second after contact with its century-old rolling stock.

The Trocadero mole was used until 1922, when it had to be abandoned. The authorities, anxious to capture trade for Cadiz, had let it fall into decay; shipping companies were reluctant to use it; there was no adequate storage space for wine; thefts were the rule rather than the exception; finally, to make victory certain, the shippers were offered the use of a private mole in the modern harbour of Cadiz, and the Trocadero mole fell into disuse.

The railway arrived at a most opportune moment, for in the year it was opened the French vineyards were devastated by oidium, and the sherry shippers were happy to help to fill the gap.

In the same year the new railway was opened, Joseph Warter left the Haurie bodegas, where he had been working for two years, and set up in business in his own, taking a Mr Wisdom into partnership. Warter became a well-known local character; he was an art collector as well as a noted horseman and a fine shot. Mr Wisdom is a most elusive person: no one knows anything about him at all, save that he lived in London where he conducted the English side of the business. The partnership prospered, and by 1860 they were already tenth on the shipping list. The name 'Wisdom & Warter' could have been coined by Gilbert, and *Punch* suggested unkindly that, 'Wisdom sells the wine, Warter makes it'; if one repeats it often enough, it sends one mad. Warter bought his first supplies of wine from the ancient Ysasi bodegas.

At about this time the British colony was sent into frenzies of rage by the conduct of its consul, Mr C. P. Gordon, whose father had been such a prominent merchant at the turn of the century. He was a Roman Catholic and ardent in his faith if not bigoted. He would have no truck with Protestant priests and disliked his heretical fellow-countrymen. As consul, he was expected to provide a room where British Protestants could worship when any itinerant clergyman was visiting the district, and Gordon flatly refused to do this. It was the nineteenth century and feelings ran high. In 1861 Gordon was dismissed and Charles Harman Furlong was appointed vice-consul in his stead. But Gordon was an obstinate man and could not be got rid of that easily: he retained the British arms over his doorway, would not part with the official seal, and kept all the consular archives. His successor wrote to the Foreign Office: 'It is patent in Jerez, that Mr. Gordon is using all his influence – which is not inconsiderable – with the Spanish Court, to frustrate the present intentions of the British Government.' These observations were confirmed by an ominous letter on black-edged paper addressed from the consulate and bearing an illegible signature. Brackenbury, the British consul in Cadiz, was sent by the Foreign Office to Jerez with orders that Gordon was to be relieved of his duties forthwith.

Gordon's machinations were aimed at discrediting Furlong with the Spanish Government. He accused his successor of being a liberal, a propagandist and paid agent of a secret religious society, and a distributor of Protestant Bibles and tracts, adding that he had allowed 'persons of the Protestant faith' who were not British subjects to assemble for divine service under his roof. All of this would have been very serious in Spanish eyes and was hotly denied by Furlong. Gordon, however, was eventually dismissed and Furlong was accepted, so the British colony's main source of entertainment was destroyed. He remained vice-consul until 1868, but his subsequent history must be left until a later page.

5

The Sherry Boom

During the 1870s the sherry trade reached its climax. In one month alone – October 1873 – Manuel Misa shipped 1,400 butts of wine and all the other bodegas spoke of similar prosperity. Meanwhile, another drink was being introduced to the market that was to bring even greater fortunes to its makers – Spanish brandy, distilled, in those days, in Jerez and Puerto. At much the same time, sherry shippers began to bottle their wines and sell them direct to the public. Previously they had all been bottled and sold by merchants. At first the new trade was confined to the Peninsula but soon it was extended to England.

The boom produced a mushroom growth of small bodegas, although few had any merit. Most of them, together with some very reputable firms, were subsequently wiped out by the combined effects of the phylloxera and the trade depression, but some of them, such as Emilio Martin Hidalgo, founded in about 1867, are still flourishing and two grew to be amongst the largest: Diez Hermanos was founded by a local family of bankers in 1876, and Williams & Humbert was founded by Alexander Williams one year later. The latter's is a supreme success story. Alexander Williams was a discontented clerk working for Wisdom & Warter. He was a man of ability, drive and character, who was determined to make a fine career for himself. For some years he worked contentedly, all the time learning the trade. Then Amy Humbert, whose father was a great friend of old Joseph Warter, came to visit Jerez. They fell in love and married. Soon Williams found he could hardly manage on his meagre salary and suggested that a young man of his drive and industry might be rewarded with a partnership. But the answer was – No. Perhaps some time in the future? But again the answer was No, and a very emphatic No, at that. Not then, nor at any other time, would Warter part with the smallest share of his business. Unfortunately, Warter was downright rude about it. Williams could stomach him no longer, and left. There was some dispute about the manner of his going, Williams claiming to have been summarily dismissed without notice and Warter that he walked out without giving any. Williams had a friend in Jerez called Edward Engelbach, who had been sent out by Coutts' bank as their agent to take charge of the Seville and Sanlucar properties of the Duque de Montpensier who had been banished from Spain following the abdication of Queen Isabella. Like Williams, Engelbach was a man of imagination and he urged his friend to start up on his own. With a young wife, and no private fortune, it was a bold move, but Williams made it. His father-in-law, C. F. Humbert, advanced £1,000 (which was a large sum in those days) and stipulated that his son, Arthur Humbert (who was himself learning the sherry trade with Wisdom & Warter), should enter the partnership when he came of age. This is the letter he wrote to his son:

Little Nascott, Watford, Herts.

My dear Arthur,

    This is very sudden, but Mr. Warter wrote him a letter in reply to his application for a partnership or a better position, which no man having any self-respect could in my opinion tolerate.

    I was simply astounded at it. He told Williams he might leave immediately, and he has taken him at his word. He will try to establish a shipping business with Engelbach and me, for you . . .

    I have written to Mr. Warter to ask him what under the circumstances he wishes you to do: – to leave or to stay with him for a time. He will probably say to leave, but I wish to be very careful to do him no injustices, and no unkindnesses.

Which was very generous, under the circumstances. Subsequently he became more explicit:

Little Nascott, Watford, Herts.
October 16th, 1877

My dear Arthur,

    . . .

    I wrote to Mr. Warter by this post to tell him that his wishes shall be carried out, that Williams will take charge of you as soon as your successor arrives from England to supply your place, and you will be from that day, clerk to Williams, Engelbach & Co., at a salary of £100 per annum.

. . .

. . . if the firm fails I shall lose my £1,000 and as to Williams and Amy all will be destruction.

You must, therefore, succeed, and I am sure that the way to do it is to sell good wine at a reasonable rate of profit, at less profit in fact than has usually been taken, and to do the business honourably, and as well as it can be done.

. . .

You must take care to discharge your duty faithfully, to the last, and there is no occasion for any quarrelling or unpleasantness. You must remember that all you know of the business has been obtained through Mr. Warter himself: – that no-one else would have so taken you to teach you.

Kind love from all,

Yours affectionately,

C. F. HUMBERT

'You must succeed.' I like that 'must': it is a splendid attitude, and very Victorian.

Williams looked after the Spanish side of the business and Engelbach set up an office in London. To begin with, they rented a corner of a bodega and bought a solera as a going concern. It produced a fresh, delicate fino-amontillado – one of the wines just then being pioneered on the British market. They called it *Pando*,[1] and first shipped it on 23 June 1878. It has been shipped ever since. Their first order, however, was not for wine at all but for six hundred boxes of raisins, and during their first year they only succeeded in shipping eleven butts and twenty-four dozen bottles of sherry. A certain amount of general merchanting continued for a long time: as late as 1915 the company was selling hams to Fortnum & Mason. But Mr Humbert need not have worried about his thousand pounds: the new firm survived the phylloxera, weathered the depression and soon became prosperous. Being new to the trade, Williams and Humbert could supply the great stores which, thanks to Gladstone's

1 The name was derived from that of a vineyard proprietor in Montilla, J. P. Panadero, who supplied the first wine to form the solera. It has nothing to do with the P. & O. Line, as has sometimes been alleged.

policy,[1] were able to form their own wine departments. With unlimited enthusiasm and capital, these stores could compete with anyone, both in quality and value, but, not unnaturally, they were abominated by the old-established wine merchants, and many sherry shippers refused to supply them for fear of offending their old customers. A new shipper had no old customers to lose and could make the most of these markets.

Then, as now, there was great friendliness between the rival bodegas; they may compete furiously for the markets of the world, but they do so without any ill feeling. In fact they will go out of their way to help one another. When Alexander Williams started in business he was short of capital and made ready use of negotiable bills, which was usual at the time and is still far more common in Spain than in England. Unfortunately one of the local bill brokers was the very epitome of tactlessness: he took one of Williams's bills and tried to discount it to Joseph Warter. By that time Williams, the upstart clerk, the pushing young man, was the anathema of Warter: he was beginning far too well. Warter would have nothing to do with the bill and said so in no uncertain terms. The broker was dismayed. Warter, above all, should have known whether Williams's credit was good. So he took the bill to William Garvey, who was reputed to be the toughest businessman in Jerez. Garvey took it at once and said he would take as many more as the broker could give him. That did the trick: Williams's credit soared, and has been impeccable ever since. Garvey was justified, and lived to see the new firm well established. In 1887 Mr. Engelbach retired to pastures new – in fact into theatrical management, where he had a distinguished career as co-lessee of the Lyric and other famous theatres – and the company took on its present name. He remained a friend of the Williams and Humbert families, however, and there was always a box for them at the Lyric if they wanted one. It remained a family business until bought up by Ruiz-Mateos in 1972.

At about this time Sandeman acquired the Pemartin bodegas. Their founder, Julian Pemartin, had died in 1853, leaving his business to his three sons Julián, José and Francisco. Julián was enormously extravagant and by 1864 his firm was drawing large, unauthorized credits from Sandeman. At the same time the quality of the

1 Gladstone's budget of 1860 reduced duty on French wines and removed the old Empire preference, and his 'Single Bottle' Act of 1861 brought off-licences into being and opened the wine trade to grocers.

wines seriously deteriorated. In 1866 he dissolved partnership with his brothers and ran the business himself. The excesses and extravagances of Julián Pemartin, culminating in his Garnier-designed Paris Opéra House-style palace in Jerez – completed in 1870, five years before the Opéra itself – led to his ruin. While the good days lasted, he lived on a magnificent scale; there was no end to the splendour of his hospitality or to the excellence of his board, and his guests included famous men of every nationality. On one occasion a young and innocent English virgin went to stay at his house. While she was there she wanted to learn Spanish, and the job of teaching her was given to the butler. He was apparently a roguish man with a perverse sense of humour, and he taught her not the Spanish she was expected to learn but a very different language adapted to suit his tastes. It included strange exclamations and unwholesome adjectives which, in his own special dictionary, corresponded to the most innocent English words. Many of his words, indeed, would not have been included in normal dictionaries at all. After some weeks of lessons, the girl dared to try out her newly acquired knowledge on a dinner party of very proper gentlemen and strait-laced ladies. She opened her mouth to utter some pleasantry, and the company was aghast. She made some polite inquiry, and things became infinitely worse. The butler was summoned. Now the butler was an old friend as well as a servant of the family and he was greatly loved. There was a move to fire him on the spot but he was repentant and friendship prevailed. He was given the unenviable task of unteaching all the Spanish he had taught and beginning again.

After such high living, the crash had to come, and when it did, it came dramatically. Pemartin entertained the King to a magnificent ball in the palace. In the middle of the festivities he went up to him and asked:

'Is there anything Your Majesty finds wanting?'

The King replied that there was everything a king could desire.

'Your Majesty is mistaken. One thing is missing: a rope to hang myself with, for I am a ruined man.'

And he was: in 1879 Pemartin went bankrupt. There was considerable political unrest in Spain at that time. Eight years earlier the peasants had risen in rebellion, and to add to his troubles a mob collected in his vineyard, intending to attack Jerez. But there were not enough men to storm the town, so they sent to Trebujena for reinforcements. While they were waiting for news, they broke into the bodega and took a draught of wine; still no news came, and they took another; then, another, and yet another, until they forgot about all their other felonious intentions. They set fire to the bodega, as a gesture, and then went away; so the town was saved at Pemartin's expense.

The business had been founded in 1818, and ever since 1822 Sandeman & Co. had been the British agents. By the time he went bankrupt Pemartin owed Sandeman £10,000. Sandeman acquired most of his assets, including his soleras, bodegas, vineyards and, of course, the palace, which they were later delighted to sell for a song to a wealthy Spanish duke. Sandeman did not, however, acquire the Pemartin trade marks and paid royalties for their use until they were eventually bought from Pemartin's heirs in 1889. All did not go smoothly: the Pemartin bodegas were re-started by his creditors and there was much acrimonious correspondence between the two houses as to who was entitled to use the name. There was also an exchange of pamphlets. In the end they reached an amicable settlement and the Pemartin bodegas are now flourishing again separately. Sandeman, however, retained the trade marks and still use one of them, *Imperial Pemartin*, for one of their greatest wines – a rich dessert oloroso of considerable age. It is very good indeed, and so it should be: their soleras of old oloroso are second to none.

The first manager of the Sandeman bodegas was John Carey Foster. He was a man of great intelligence but was cursed with an ungovernable temper; he eventually lost it irrevocably and had to return to England. He was succeeded by Walter J. Buck, who came from the old firm of Matthiesen, Furlong & Co. and was later famous not only as a sherry shipper but also as a naturalist; with Abel Chapman, he wrote two of the very best books ever written about the Spanish natural history: *Wild Spain* and *Unexplored Spain*. There is another now – Guy Mountfort's *Portrait of a Wilderness* – but for nearly fifty years there was no book to compare with those of Chapman and Buck.

Matthiesen, Furlong & Co. was once an extremely important bodega and was unique in one respect: it flourished in an abandoned Jesuit monastery, vacated by the expulsion of the Order at the beginning of the century. C. H. Furlong was British vice-consul in Jerez from 1861 to 1868; by 1870, however, sad rumours reached London that he was guilty of malpractice and shady business dealings, and it was obvious that the wine was not being made properly. Walter Buck was sent out from England ostensibly to learn the trade but in fact to investigate the rumours. We do not know what he found, but soon afterwards Furlong retired to England and Buck took his place. He married and had two daughters, both of whom are now dead, but until 1957 they lived near Jerez and I came to know them quite well. They could claim one very rare distinction: they were born in a Jesuit monastery. Both Buck and his wife became well known and well loved in Jerez. When Leon Diaz wrote his *Siluetas Jerezanas* in 1897, the first portrait was that of 'Mistress Buck' who, although she was not a Catholic, was admitted as being a Christian, while Walter Buck struck the author as being free and independent 'like Defoe's Robinson Crusoe'. Apart from being an able naturalist, he was also a musician. Juan Haurie wrote lyrics and Buck set them to music.

When Walter Buck went to Sandeman's his place at Matthiesen, Furlong & Co. was taken by Enrique Coll, a Catalan who created a precedent by abandoning wine for the call of the Church. Usually the traffic is in the opposite direction. In 1884 the Jesuits returned and the bodega was disbanded, the name passing to José Ma. Fernandez y Gonzalez and subsequently to his successors Fernandez Gao Hermanos, which eventually was amalgamated with Mackenzie's and which is now part of Harveys. It is all very complicated but Jerez is like that: there is perfect continuity of interests despite a change of name, and people turn up in the most unexpected places. To make matters worse, everyone is related to everyone else, at least by marriage, and the family tree of Jerez would look like a maze if anyone had the perseverance to work it out.

Alexander Williams and Walter Buck lived practically their whole lives in Jerez and established great bodegas. Other young Englishmen came during the boom, left during the slump, and their names are forgotten. One shipper dating from this time is Fernando A. de Terry, founded in 1865 by the descendants of an Irish family that had come to Puerto de Santa Maria in the seventeeth century and had had connections with the wine trade for many years.

By the latter half of the nineteenth century the prosperity of the wine trade had turned Jerez into a clean, safe and comfortable town with a modern water supply installed by British engineers and no more plagues. In fact British influence was to be found everywhere and the British sherry shippers joined with their Spanish rivals in promoting a Grand National Club, which continues today as the Casino Nacional. In 1873 the new club held a special dinner to celebrate the vintage and one of the guests was Charles Tovey, the most accident-prone traveller who ever lived. His hoodoo followed him to the feast and the catastrophe is best described in his own words:

> The Grand National Club expended nearly £2,000 on a large pavilion, with a ball-room, reception-rooms, and a large dining saloon. On the day preceding the opening of the pleasure fair I had visited this pavilion, which was beautifully decorated with much artistic taste, expensive hangings, crystal chandeliers, and mirrors; altogether fit for the reception of Imperial guests. In the night came the Levante, and in the morning the whole of the ball-room was a wreck. The force of the wind had shivered the huge masts, which were of immense strength; and as these supported the frame-work, the whole fabric gave way, destroying all the mirrors, chandeliers, and elegant furniture. The dining and cooking saloon, and the lower common dining-room, were, although much damaged, still habitable, and a sumptuous dinner had been ordered . . . After the races . . . we returned to the fair. The cold was intense, and the elegantly, but thinly, attired ladies were unprepared for such an inclement wind. Several carriages were overturned by its force, and an adjournment soon took place to get shelter in what remained of the tents and pavilions. The dinner was an excellent one, but partaken under great difficulty; and many expressed a doubt as to whether the whole fabric would not come down, and share the fate of the adjoining ball-room. The wind came in at all quarters; occasionally a stanchion of iron would fall amongst the glass and crockery on the table; the suspended lights were soon blown out, and candles innumerable were flickering; still good-humoured merriment, speeches, and songs went on, until it became hazardous to remain longer in such a tottering fabric. Without the scene was fearful, and the return to Xerez was an adventure that I shall long remember.

The Levante is still rather a menace but it has never blown like that in recent years. And anyhow it is a hot wind.

When trade is booming it is rather too easy to live in a fool's paradise. Even when orders reach new heights, corruption starts to eat away at the foundations of the structure and it is soon ready to

'The Sincerest Form of Flattery'
(from *Sherryana* by F. W. C., London, 1886)

collapse. The sherry slump at the turn of the century was brought
about by five factors working together: the dreadful imitation
sherries or 'horrible mixings' from Hamburg and other places; the
very inferior wines made in Jerez itself during the boom years; the
ignorant attacks of certain doctors who claimed that the wine was
'plastered', 'gouty', 'full of added spirit', and 'acid to the stomach';
the caprice of fashion; and, lastly, the plague of the phylloxera
which for several years made wine-making difficult, unprofitable
and heart-breaking.

Imitation may be a subtle form of flattery, but the spate of ghastly,
and sometimes chemical, liquids that flooded England during the
boom and which were passed off as sherry on ignorant customers
by disreputable wine merchants, ultimately did great harm to the
trade. In 1866 a terrible advertisement appeared in *The Times*:
'Partner wanted – A practical distiller, having been experimenting
for the last seventeen years, can now produce a fair port and sherry,
by fermentation, without a drop of grape juice, and wishes a party
with £2,000 to £3,000 to establish a house in Hamburg for the
manufacture of wines. Has already a good connection in business.'

In a little book called *Sherryana*, by F. W. C., which was published in 1886, there is a drawing of an Andalusian girl carrying oloroso, followed by a fräulein with Hamburg 'sherry', a negress with Cape 'sherry', a French girl with 'sherry' from Perpignan and Cette, and a kangaroo with Australian 'sherry'. All of which is a splendid joke except to the honest man who bought such wines knowing no better and came to dislike sherry as a result. I have never come across the German version and have mercifully only once tasted French 'sherry'. For the French, above all people, to foist off such stuff would seem a mortal sin. The South African and Australian versions were, until the names were abolished by an EEC directive, readily available, together with a nauseating fluid from California. I well remember the first time I tasted South African 'sherry', and I have never lived it down. I was a callow youth and had not been to many grown-up parties, when a charming and elderly gentleman who knew my girl friend gave a cocktail party and asked her to bring me along, or else she persuaded him to let her bring me, I am not sure which. At any rate, I went and was given some wine in an ominous green glass. I quite liked it, but could make neither head nor tail of it; in fact I spent some moments speculating on what he had made it of and decided it must have a sherry base. I was familiar with most styles of sherry at home, but my father (who was one of the most sincere and knowledgeable wine lovers I have ever known) would never let the imitation sort cross his doorstep.

'Will you have another glass of sherry?' my host inquired.

I held out my glass.

'I'll have the same again,' I said. 'I don't know what it was, though, but it certainly wasn't sherry.'

Unfortunately he persisted, and so did I, but he filled my glass from the anonymous decanter and took it all in very good part. I suspect it appealed to his sense of humour, and it was not until months later that I identified his wine. The astonishing thing is how closely the flavour of South African sherry approximated to that of the poorer Spanish wines; in fact many members of the wine trade have identified them wrongly in blind tastings. On the other hand, the finer Spanish wines are in a class on their own. If anyone prefers a wine from elsewhere, their choice deserves every respect, and they are very welcome to it, but let them call it by its proper name. To offer sherry and then to pour out a fake is at least ignorant. To many it seems mean and nasty.

Charles Dickens described these bogus wines beautifully: 'Cloudy fluid, served up by shabby waiters in vinegar cruets to disconsolate bachelors at second-rate restaurants and miscalled sherry.' Dickens was an *aficionado* of sherry and when he died there was a large stock of it in his cellar. He actually visited Jerez in 1858 and wrote up his visit in the 13 November issue of *Household Words*. Unfortunately he disguised the name of his host, but there was no doubt about what he thought of the wine:

> . . . we are away on the wings of the wind to the region of your nutty, full flavoured, unbrandied Amontillado sherry, the golden juice I have so often held up to the light with ridiculous affectation of knowingness; the stuff, to use Binn's the wine merchant's affectional phrase, that Falstaff grew witty and racy on, and called his sherris sack . . .

Unfortunately the shippers did not concentrate on doing the one thing that would have put them above the competition of bogus sherries: to concentrate on wines that were so good as to be inimitable.

The shippers did complain about the usurpation of their geographical name, but the position in law was not clear; moreover, there was no organization that could finance an action or co-ordinate the efforts of the shippers. So spoof sherries became commonplace, usually sold with geographical qualifications. Successful prosecutions were eventually brought against bogus wines sold simply as sherry – the first in 1924 and there were many others – but action against the geographically qualified wines came too late. In 1967, when the British wine manufacturers Vine Products brought an action against the sherry shippers, claiming *inter alia* a declaration that they were entitled to call their product British sherry, the judge, Mr Justice Cross, held that sherry by itself meant the Spanish wine, but the terms 'British sherry', 'English sherry', 'South African sherry', 'Australian sherry' and 'Cyprus sherry' had been used for so long that the doctrine of laches was invoked, and Vine Products got their declaration. However, the door was barred against newcomers like 'Canadian sherry', and in 1976 Mr Justice Whitford made an order prohibiting some English wine merchants from using the words 'amontillado', 'oloroso' or 'fino' on wine other than sherry. They had in fact been using them on Montilla-Moriles wines, which had actually been the origin of the word amontillado.

By the end of the nineteeth century the labels of the lesser merchants had become notoriously inaccurate, but it was only history repeating itself: the same thing had happened a hundred years earlier. When a popular singer and composer set up shop in the Haymarket and wrote on his door, 'Michael Kelly, Composer of Music and Importer of Wine', Sheridan suggested that 'Importer of Music and Composer of Wine' would have been better, 'for none of his music is original and all his wine is, since he makes it himself.' Charles Tovey told of a man who had bought what he thought was excellent sherry. When he went to order some more he was astonished to hear his wine merchant say: 'Ah, sir, you cannot get it anywhere else, for I made it myself.' What a terrifying thought!

Just what these forgeries consisted of is obscure, but several formulae have been suggested. One that sounds quite interesting is: 'French brandy, Sicilian marsala, Cape wine, Devonshire cider, and Thames water.' The composition of a butt of Elbe sherry was said to be: '40 proof gallons of fine potato spirit, 56 gallons pure Elbe water, 4 gallons Capellaire, and, to be liberal, 10 gallons of luscious grape wine.' As early as 1692 Charleton described how merchants transformed 'the Laggs of Sacks and Malmsies into Muskadels', and how 'they sell decayed Xeres, vulgarly Sherry, for Lusenna wine.' In 1839 Joseph Hartley gave an elaborate recipe in his *Wholesale and Retail Wine and Spirit Merchant's Companion and Complete Instructor to the Trade*. His imitation sack was made of water, rue, fennel roots and honey. Whatever the usual may have been, it was certainly a theme with variations.

These strange fluids did a great deal of harm in the nineteenth century, though they were little worse than some of the wines shipped from Jerez itself. The trade was hideously easy; anything labelled 'sherry' could be sold, and there was a large market for cut-price wines to compete with the imitators. These, like most very young wines, were thoroughly indigestible. Perhaps a typical reaction of a traditional sherry drinker of the time was that of George Waddington, Dean of Durham, who in 1861 told Augustus Hare 'What with *diner à la Russe*, crinoline, and pale sherry, England is fast going to the dogs.' The sherry he was drinking that time was one of 1815 for which he had paid £12 a dozen.

In 1864 the British consul at Cadiz, A. Graham-Dunlop, sent a complete report on the sherry trade to the Foreign Office, and his revelations betokened inevitable disaster:

During the past year large quantities of wines have been introduced into the district from Malaga and Alicante; but these wines
have not proved serviceable or usable, their peculiar, earthy and
tarry character, being impossible to overcome; as altho' mixed
with other wines in but small quantities, the unpleasant flavour
and 'smell', is always distinguishable to a judge of wine.

The low spurious compounds are made up with molasses,
German potato-spirit, and water; to which some colouring
matter, and a small quantity of wine, are added; much in the same
manner that the 'Hamburg-Sherries' have been manufactured to
which of late the London Custom-House has, very properly,
refused admittance. Of course, no known respectable wine-mer-
chant would lend himself to ship such low and adulterated compounds, but that it *is* done, and moreover with the cognizance of
the consignees in London, is well known here; because such wines
are usually sold by auction on their arrival, at extraordinarily
low prices . . .

At least one-half of the English shippers at Jerez are supposed
to be shippers of low wines, and some of them are not considered
to possess so large a Capital as the business done by them would
argue . . .

There can be little doubt that this report was even more damning
than the truth warranted. However bad the wine, it is most doubtful
whether it was ever diluted with water, as this would have called
for further fortification[1] and would not have been an economic
proposition. Sherry still formed the basis of the blend, but it was
hopelessly young – perhaps not more than a year old. The German
potato spirit (and in another part of the report he also refers to
Scottish grain spirit) was not as bad as it sounds: it was merely
industrial alcohol imported into Spain from Scotland and Germany.
It was harmless, but at that time contained impurities which tainted
and ruined any good sherry which it fortified. Sherry blended in
such a way would have been abominably bad.

By the late 1870s merchants all over England were telling the
same story: their customers were giving up sherry because 'It is not
what it was.' And their customers were quite justified. Wines that
were previously 'Shipped off to the leathern-tongued customers of
Hamburg or Quebec at £15 per butt' were being sold in England at

---

1 i.e. strengthening with alcohol.

far higher prices. Members of the wine trade were well aware of the declining quality. The *Wine Trade Review* put the complaint very clearly and begged that 'the goose which has laid so many golden eggs in the past should not be sacrificed at the shrine of profit'. Giving evidence to a House of Lords Select Committee on wine duties in 1878, a Mr Gordon Park said: 'Take the article sherry, which used to be one of the most popular wines in the country . . . whether at hotels, wine bars, or even private houses people rather shudder now at a glass of sherry. It is a very different article to what it used to be, and I attribute a great deal of that to their being imported so as to arrive as cheaply as they possibly can. The shippers and preparers are sending over young wines with a large amount of spirit added.' But the shippers took no heed of the warning. Perhaps it was too late.

To make matters worse, the wine trade got into bad hands. German touts were touring the country trying to pass off very odd wines on unsuspecting customers, and Gladstone's policy had opened the trade to the grocers. Chesterton knew all about them:

> The wicked Grocer groces
> In spirits and in wine
> Not frankly and in fellowship
> As men in inns do dine:
> But packed with soap and sardines
> And carried off by grooms
> For to be snatched by Duchesses
> And drunk in dressing-rooms.

Whatever their virtues and knowledge, grocers certainly knew nothing of wine, and one catalogue even contained the glorious entry:

	per doz.
Sherry, Château d'Yquem	40s.
Ditto, Finest Sauterne	34s.

It is not surprising that the trade was put into chaos.

Nor was life very comfortable in Jerez at this time. Following the short and disastrous reign of King Amadeo from 1870 to 1873 and until the proclamation of King Alfonso XII in 1874, the country descended into a state of anarchy complicated by Carlist risings. There was a revolution, and things looked so unpleasant in Jerez in

1873 that the Gonzalez family spent a time at the safer haven of their house in Puerto de Santa Maria.

The medical attack on sherry was launched on 27 November 1873, when Dr J. L. W. Thudichum, of 3 Pembroke Road, Kensington, wrote a letter to *The Times*. He was a popular and successful doctor, but his letter was one of vain humbug, composed of truths, half-truths and downright lies. It charged sherry with containing unfermented grape juice, and announced that the grapes to yield a single butt were:

> . . . dusted with 30–40 lb. of burnt plaster of Paris (sulphate of lime). The effect of this practice, of which my enquiries amongst sherry makers have not taught me the object, is to precipitate all tartaric and malic acid of the must and substitute in their place sulphuric acid . . . in consequence all sherry contains nearly the whole of the potash of the must as sulphate, amounting to from 1½ kgs–7 kgs per butt . . . not only plastered but impregnated with the fumes by combustion of about 5 oz. of sulphur per butt, which adds about a pound of sulphuric acid to that brought in by the plaster.

There is, of course, some element of truth in all this; gypsum *is* used in the pressing of the grapes, sulphur *is* used to fumigate the casks, and both processes will be described in the relevant chapters of this book; but the doctor's chemistry was extremely doubtful and his quantitative analysis was so ludicrously inaccurate that one can only charitably suppose it was guesswork.

Johann Ludwig Wilhelm Thudichum was born in Germany in 1829. After studying at the universities of Giessen and Heidelberg, he came to London. In 1864 he was engaged on behalf of the Privy Council to undertake chemical research in the field of diagnostic medicine. That his work was not an unqualified success may be gathered from his obituary in the *British Medical Journal*:

> It is possible that Thudichum attempted in these researches too much – more, that is to say, than the then state of physiological chemistry had rendered it possible to achieve; at any rate, the results were not generally considered to correspond adequately to the time and money which they cost, and his views have not, we believe, been generally accepted by other workers in this field of chemistry.

Of his medical researches I know nothing, but his work on sherry was truly appalling and appeared in a book published in 1872: *A Treatise on the Origin, Nature and Varieties of Wine, being a complete manual of Viticulture and Oenology*, by J. L. W. Thudichum, M.D. and August Dupré, Ph.D. It was a portentous book containing many *ex cathedra* pronouncements that could not be supported. His experimental methods, looked at critically, failed to establish anything. For instance his experiments on plastering were carried out with musts produced in London from imported Lisbon grapes and using 'plaster' in vastly greater quantities than ever used in the vineyards. But the Victorians listened to the voice of medicine with awe and reverence and thus, wholly unjustly, he was able to condemn sherry. His analysis of some sherry made for the Pure Wine Association Ltd is full of brave observations:

They all have the sherry flavour due to the Pedro Ximenes grapes, and the finesse which is only met with in true Amontillados . . . But it is clear, from the amount of sulphuric acid present in wines (as potassium sulphate), that they have been plastered. The practice has the object of removing from wine its natural acidity, and making it smooth to the taste.

He was careful to omit details of experiments he had previously performed at Jerez, but Henry Vizetelly, in his excellent book *Facts About Sherry*, told all about them:

In common candour the author of this incredible misrepresentation ought not to have withheld from the public his qualifications to speak so confidently on the subject. He should have told them that he had visited Jerez under the auspices of certain shipping houses to whom he offered, if not to repeat the miracle of Cana, at any rate to produce amontillado by purely chemical agency – that he was provided with considerable funds for the purchase of scientific instruments which he was incompetent to use, and that he resided at Jerez in style for a period of three months at the expense of his principal patron, during which time he lost him half his vineyard's produce through the so-called amontillado which he professed to fabricate turning out such vile stuff that it could only be employed for rinsing casks with, while a further experiment which he made in the bodega of a second shipper resulted in transforming the wine into vinegar.

The public, knowing nothing of the motive which prompted these attacks upon sherry, naturally grew alarmed, and for a time the subject formed a common topic of conversation at all dinner-tables, where by the lady at your side you found sherry generally declined with thanks. Middle-aged gentlemen, too, perfectly hale and hearty on their daily pint of sherry, fancied that perhaps for them a day of reckoning might be near.

Local reports of his activities suggest that he danced round the wine press muttering incantations and sprinkling powder from his waistcoat pocket over the grapes. When *The Times* reviewed his book, they made their opinion quite clear:

> We have heard with pleasure that a recent attempt to chymicalize the making of wine in Spain, although undertaken with much confidence, and carried on under conditions favourable to success, has resulted in a failure which was indeed signal, but which, in the interests of the public, we cannot bring ourselves to call disastrous.

So much for Thudichum! To his credit, though, he eventually saw the light and in 1893 published a very valuable book: *A Treatise on Wines, their Origin, Nature and Varieties with practical directions for Viticulture and Vinification*. It is still well worth reading.

The wine merchants, to preserve their trade in the face of such attacks, started importing odd wines which they advertised as free from these defects. It is strange to think of a vintner actually attacking sherry, but James L. Denman did so in a series of pamphlets, and tried to substitute Greek wines 'which have neither been plastered nor fortified'; one of which was alarmingly described as 'resembling Amontillado with a dash of hock'. Perhaps that was how he made it. He was also an importer of 'Aragonese Sherry'. In his favour, it should be said that his attacks were largely the results of an ill-informed but perfectly honourable preoccupation with 'purity'. Others advertised wines that were 'free from spirit'; just how free was not stated. One of these was a Mr W. J. Trafford, the importer of Haurie sherries, who in 1880 advertised them as 'free from all impurities, unnatural heat or acidity, containing about 30 or 32 proof spirit' – equal to 17° to 18° Gay-Lussac, the strength at which sherry is commonly imported today and about 3° lower than was the current practice, which would indicate that they were not unfortified.

Nevertheless, the leaders of the trade continued to list complete ranges of sherries at sensible prices. For instance in 1880 Victoria Wine listed sixteen sherries, the cheapest of which cost fourteen shillings per dozen, with a fino at thirty-six shillings and an amontillado pasado at sixty-four shillings. And, to counter the critics, sherry had its champions. The most notable, by far, was Ruskin. Praise from such a worthy and utterly respectable source was very valuable, and he wrote in no uncertain terms. In his *Praeterita*, for instance:

> If the painters . . . chose rather to talk of sherry, my father could, and would with delight, tell them more about it than any other person knew in either England or Spain; and when the candles came, and the good jests, over the nuts and olives, there was 'frolic wine' in the flask at every right hand, such as that never Prince Hal nor Jack Falstaff tasted cup of brighter or mightier.

There were two other voluble and knowledgeable champions: 'Don Pedro Verdad' (Walter Mallock Gee) and Henry Vizetelly. Don Pedro wrote a little book called *From Vineyard to Decanter*. In it, he most effectively routed the detractors of sherry, and his scorn burnt fierce against the analysts: 'My belief is, that if a sample of wine were given to an analyst, marked "poison" so that he would neither smell nor taste it, he could by no test yet known in chemistry affirm that it was wine at all.'

Don Pedro was quite right: there is still no chemical test that will establish whether a given solution of alcohol in water with sugars, esters, aldehydes, and so on is a natural wine or a chemical mixture. In the nineteenth century, long before the days of such useful tools as gas and liquid chromatography, analysis was even more worthless. That chemists should have produced such extraordinary reports is not surprising: doubtless they made analyses that were perfectly accurate as far as they went, but which were notable principally for their omissions. That qualified doctors should have been dupes to the same ignorance seems incredible.

The other champion of sherry, Henry Vizetelly, was a man of many parts. Although at one time very famous, he suffered a breakdown in health after being imprisoned for publishing the works of Zola, which were too strong for nineteenth-century tastes. He lived his last few years in comparative obscurity, so that his brief obituary notice in *The Times* of 2 January 1894 was sandwiched between that of the author of a book about frogs and a colonel 'who will be remembered as the officer who was shot through the head . . . at Kambula.' Before he fell ill, though, he had founded two illustrated papers, acted as Paris correspondent of the *Illustrated London News*, published Zola, written an enormous work on champagne and another work on wines in general with the optimistic title *The Wines of the World Characterized and Classed*, acted as wine juror for Great Britain at the Vienna Exhibition, and published a fascinating autobiography. He also planned a history of sherry, but unfortunately never lived to write it.

Eventually the medical profession itself came to the rescue. Doctors were perpetually badgered for information by patients who had read the quasi-scientific attacks on sherry in the press, and they were unable to tell them anything. The *Lancet*, as the leading professional paper, sent a Mr Vasey as their commissioner to Jerez, and charged him with investigating all the complaints. Many stories are still told of the antics he got up to. He was given a free run of all the bodegas and nothing was hidden from him. He would crop up from anywhere, pouncing when least expected from behind a butt of fermenting must, or watching from a concealed place to see the exact amount of plaster added to the grapes. His conclusions were triumphant:

> In defining sherry we may very properly call it a wine which is peculiar to Spain and essentially Spanish. There is no genuine wine like it produced in other countries. Of course, as with all good and genuine things, there is the counterpart in fictitious substances . . .
>
> There is no point in any single particular in the foregoing analyses[1] which may fairly be regarded as evidence of adulteration. Nor does an inspection of the entire methods concerned in the production of sherry from the vineyards to the bodegas give any suspicion of anything being carried on that is not honest and publicly open to view . . . It follows as the outcome of our inquiry that it cannot be correctly said that sherry in any particular contains a single ingredient foreign to its composition. We again lay stress on the fact that in coming to these conclusions we are speaking of vinum Xericum, the vino de Jerez, or the wine

1 See Appendix 2.

produced in Spain generally known as sherry, and not of those fictitious wines which are produced, or rather concocted, only too freely elsewhere.

Sherry was exonerated and all the charges of the medical profession were proved false. At a later date Thudichum's findings were directly contradicted by F. W. Tunnicliffe, M.D. But the damage had been done; the prejudice was already rooted in the public mind and there was no gainsaying it.

Both the repulsive flavour of the imitation wines and the medical attacks on sherry were factors that led to the slump, but even without them trade would have suffered to some extent. Fashions are always changing. In the earlier years of the nineteenth century, lunch consisted merely of a snack chosen from dishes on the sideboard and eaten standing up; wine was also provided and invariably it was sherry. Readers of Anthony Trollope will remember how Mr Harding in *The Warden* during his miserable 'long day in London' suddenly felt the pangs of hunger about four o'clock in the afternoon and made a meal of a mutton chop, potatoes and a pint of sherry, the sherry costing him half-a-crown. At the height of the boom 40 per cent of the wine imported into England was sherry and the custom was to drink it throughout meals. The principal meal of the day was dinner, which began at about six o'clock. Towards the end of the century, meals began to fall into the modern pattern, and were washed down with 'Gladstone claret' that was subject to a lower rate of duty. The rich sherries shipped in those days were hardly suitable for use as aperitif wines; nor was there any demand for aperitif wines, as the idea of the drink before dinner only came in with this century and the invention of the cocktail. Nineteenth-century guests had to be content with polite conversation, which notoriously began to flag without the stimulus of alcohol, especially if someone was late.

It would appear that the shippers had closed their eyes to the change in fashion, for in 1884 consul Joel, of Cadiz, wrote:

The shippers at both Jerez and Port St. Mary appear to be oblivious to the change which has taken place in the English taste during the past decade, as they adhere to a fixed idea that wine for the English market should be an alcoholised sweetened wine, which no longer meets the requirements of that market. Sherry in its natural state is a light, dry wine, thoroughly wholesome, and to convert this by the addition of factitious spirits and saccharine matters into a wine that would certainly have a deleterious effect on weak digestions appears to me to be a great mistake, and the sooner the shippers recognise this fact the better it will be for their trade, which is now labouring under a serious depression.

A year later he wrote:

The depression in the wine trade, which set in about 10 years ago, has each succeeding year continued to deepen, and not only has the quantity exported diminished year by year, but a serious fall in price has also occurred. The cause was primarily the suicidal policy pursued by some shippers more than 10 years ago, who, in order to undersell the old-established firms shipping genuine wines, commenced to ship under the name of sherry highly-fortified immature wines of inferior quality, the product of the vineyards of Chiclana, Moguer, &c., and the introduction of this spurious wine into the English market, where it was freely advertised and as freely purchased as 'sound sherry' soon began to discredit the high reputation which sherry had up to that time enjoyed. The use of any particular wine is, in a great measure, a matter of fashion, and it is highly probable that the discredit which the sale of these inferior wines brought upon sherry generally was the cause of its decline as a fashion at the dinner table.

Another factor which contributed to the falling demand was the changing moral attitude towards drink. By the 1880s Victorian smugness and philistinism were reaching their peak; the Salvation Army had been beating its drums for years and saving souls from the torments of alcohol; Dick Turner had long since coined the word 'teetotal' and the exponents of that ghastly creed were preaching misery throughout the land; pious faces could be seen every Sunday leaving tin tabernacles to threaten publicans with eternal damnation. There were, of course, a few of the enlightened, but Saintsbury's influence lay still in the future and G. K. Chesterton was far too young to compose the rimes of *The Flying Inn*. The naughty nineties were hardly in sight, and even when they did come the gay young things thought only of champagne. To make matters worse, when Queen Victoria died in 1901, Edward VII sold all the surplus wines in the royal cellars and these included no less than sixty thousand bottles of sherry, accumulated through some oversight of the royal bureaucracy, which continued placing orders for wine at the old level although entertaining had virtually ceased with the death of the Prince Consort. Some irreverent journalists also suggested that the state of His Majesty's liver was at least partly responsible for the sales.

The market became glutted with sherry and the press wrote of it condescendingly as an outmoded survival, only to be pitied. In 1937, however, when some of the despised wine was sold for the second time, at Christie's, in favour of Queen Charlotte's Hospital, the story was very different. Three bottles of an 1875 dessert sherry, bought by Messrs Hedges & Butler at the royal sale and bearing the private seal of Buckingham Palace, were sold for five guineas, or thirty-five shillings a bottle, at a time when a good oloroso could be bought for seven-and-six. Another interesting lot, some 1815 'Waterloo' amontillado, presented by Lord Howard de Walden, fetched a pound a bottle. But in 1901 sherry had no champions amongst the young, and was drunk indiscriminately with mediocre meals by elderly ladies up for the day from the country. There can be no wonder that sales slumped.

To some extent, it is as well they did. In 1894 the devastating plague of the phylloxera struck the vineyards of Jerez. It was caused by an aphid, a form of louse brought over in vines sent from the USA to France in 1863; these insects bred rapidly and lived on the vines, eventually destroying them. In the 1880s the phylloxera destroyed nearly all of the great French vineyards, and it came to Malaga at much the same time, on vines sent by French horticulturalists. It was brought to Jerez from Malaga by itinerant labourers, and it soon laid waste all the vineyards. All the old vines had to be replaced with American stocks which were immune to the pest. It is a blessing that there were vast quantities of wine in the bodegas to tide over the lean years.

Two years before the phylloxera hit the vineyards, there was a peasant rebellion in Jerez that was an aftermath of the Black Hand Movement. It has been described vividly (with fictional adornments) by Blasco Ibañez in his book *La Bodega*.

At the turn of the century the great boom in sherry had entirely gone and the trade was in its nadir. Wine growers were hungry and many emigrated. Some of the soleras in the hands of the *almacenistas* – sherry wholesalers, or store-keepers – went out of condition because the scales were not being run. The Marqués de

Casa-Domecq addressed his fellow shippers and he had no doubt about the cause of the trouble: it was shipping inferior wines at low prices, wines that were no better than their imitators. And he equally had no doubt what the answer was: to ship top quality wines at higher prices to exploit the unique individuality of the styles of sherry. His successors would do well to heed his message.

Even when sherry had reached the rock bottom of popularity, happily it still had some old-fashioned admirers to support it. When John Galsworthy wrote *The White Monkey* in 1924 he included a conversation between the crotchety Soames Forsyte and his son-in-law Michael Mont:

'. . . Will you have a sherry?'

'Sherry!' repeated Soames. 'You young people think you've invented sherry; when I was a boy no one dreamed of dining without a glass of dry sherry with his soup, and a glass of fine old sherry with his sweet. Sherry!'

'I quite believe you, sir. There really is nothing new. Venin, for instance – wasn't that the fashion, too; and knitting, and royal ties? It's all cyclic . . .'

The life of the British colony went on from year to year in the sherry towns much as before, and the merchants were united in friendship. The great wine merchant Ian Maxwell Campbell went out as a student in 1889 and he described it as 'a small, very united, group of about seven families who seemed to vie with each other in making the stranger in their midst feel at home.' In 1897 they placed a stone tablet in the garden of the Sandeman palace. It later hung in the office of the British vice-consul, and read:

En Commemoracion del 60	(To commemorate the Sixtieth
Aniversario del Reinado	Anniversary of the Reign of
de S.M.I. La Reina Victoria	Her Imperial Majesty Queen Victoria
de Inglaterra, la Colonia	of England, the English
Inglesa de esta Ciudad	Colony in this Town
de Jerez y sus amigos	of Jerez and their Spanish
Españoles, Acordaron Grabar	Friends, Join Together to Erect
esta Inscripcion de 21	this Memorial on the 21st
de Junio de 1897	of June, 1897)

Following the lunatic closure of the British vice-consulate by the government in 1979, in the wholly mistaken belief that it would save money, the tablet has unfortunately disappeared.

For many years, and at least as far back as 1873, a clergyman of the Church of England, recommended by the Bishop of London and approved by the senior British resident, had been appointed chaplain to the British colony. The little church was then also in the garden of the Sandeman palace. He lived in Jerez only during the 'Winter Season', which lasted from November till May, as so many of the colony visited England with their children in the summer that there were not sufficient left to form a congregation. This system continued until 1916, and only in three seasons (1894–5, 1899–1900 and 1912–13) was the colony without a chaplain, who stayed successively as the guest of four or five of the leading British families.

In the Preachers' Book of the old Anglican Chapel there was a dangerous column headed 'Remarks'. Usually these concerned the numbers present and the weather, but sometimes other things were said:

Sunday, April 15th, 1894.	Seven only (Jerez Races).
Sunday, December 29th, 1895.	16 present. Masculine element gone shooting.
Sunday, January 5th, 1896.	Church unfit for use, drain broken. No services.
Sunday, March 24th.	21 present. Mr. Gandell read lessons. No sermon. Voice gone.

At the end of each term of office, the chaplain wrote a farewell message to his congregation, usually of thanks for hospitality, kindness and Christian enthusiasm. Only once was there a note of discord: 'The only remarks the Chaplain of 1910 can make, are to express surprise at the amazing and continued inferiority of the harmonium and the conspicuous inelegance of the arrangement of the altar flowers.'

The inferior harmonium that so vexed the chaplain was replaced but the chapel, alas, is no more. In 1967 a law was passed which purported to be a law of religious liberty. If the chapel was to remain open there had to be an official register of worshipping Protestants, a committee had to be formed, and government inspectors had to be given access to the financial records. There were few

Anglicans left and fewer still who were prepared to have their faith officially recorded, so the chapel was closed and its furnishings passed over to a local Spanish Protestant group.

Prosperity had brought new blood and virility, and when the slump came the sherry shippers were not easily defeated. As soon as the vineyards were producing efficiently again, they made every effort to stage a comeback. It was hard going, but in the end they were triumphant. The wines they introduced were altogether better than the majority of those that had been on the market previously and were a delight to the connoisseurs who had affected to scorn sherry; the shippers found, too, that it paid to advertise, and the Spanish houses were also helped by the profitable brandy trade they were building up, principally in the Peninsula and South America.

King Alfonso XIII was friendly with several sherry shippers, one of whom, Joaquin Ma. Rivero, was acting as a steward at the royal palace. When the king made his state visit to London in 1906 he did everything he could to help his friends. The virtues of sherry were whispered to King Edward and cases of wine were given as presents to his courtiers. Better still, fine sherries were served at all the royal banquets: Jerez 1849, Jerez Macharnudo Seco 1780, Moscatel Victoria Eugenia, Jerez 1847, Jerez Amontillado Alfonso XIII, Jerez Macharnudo 1780, Moscatel Viejo España. They were in good company, the principal table wine being Mouton Rothschild 1878.

To revive the sale of sherry in England, a number of the leading shippers came together in 1910 to found the Sherry Shippers' Association. They pooled their funds and launched an advertising campaign to publicize sherry as a wine, rather than the products of individual shippers. It was a pioneer scheme of its kind, and proved by its success that however good a wine may be, it still needs a bush.

A period of consolidation and retrenchment is never as exciting as one of rapid expansion and development, and the early years of the present century were no exception. Many things happened in Jerez, but only one of them had any real bearing on the history of sherry: in 1912 Sandeman's Bodega Grande caught fire. It contained some very old oloroso, and the fire was terrible: the wine got so hot that the alcohol distilled off and burnt. It was a tragedy but, as in so many tragedies, there was an element of comedy. The whole town turned out with pots and pans, jugs and mugs, to scoop up the wine as it ran flaming down the gutters, and when the fire was put out, they all settled down to an orgy of mulled sherry. Sandeman's managed to replace the old wine they had lost, and they soon rebuilt the bodega in the traditional style. Now it looks just the same as all the others.

Perhaps the greatest fillip of all to the revival of sherry was a whim of Carl Williams: he gave the first sherry party and the idea caught on. The craze for cocktail parties was just beginning, but the more discriminating began to take sherry instead. Eventually the whole ethos that had produced the cocktail perished, but the taste for sherry remained and went from strength to strength.

Since 1933 the preparation of sherry has been controlled by the Consejo Regulador de la Denominación de Origin Jerez-Xérès-Sherry. This authority corresponds to those that control the various regions of the French *Appellation Contrôlée*, and all casks and bottles exported from the sherry area bear the seal of the Consejo Regulador as a guarantee of authenticity. Over the years it has promulgated a series of orders governing the viticulture and oenological techniques that may be used by the wine growers and shippers. The aim has been to achieve complete authenticity in a strictly controlled geographical area. There are now two separate denominations: Jerez-Xérès-Sherry, as before, and Manzanilla-Sanlucar de Barrameda. The methods to be employed in growing and producing both classes of wine are laid down in great detail, including such matters as the vines that may be used, the method of pruning, the places in which the wines may be matured, the proportion of his stock that a shipper may sell every year, and so on. The principal provisions will be referred to in the relevant chapters which follow. In the event of there being any breach of the regulations, sanctions can be imposed, ranging from a small fine to the suspension of the shipper's right to export any wine for five years.

6

The Recent Past

History is continuous, in a trade as in a nation, and with either the future grows out of the past. Dates signify little. Changes come not from single events but from a concatenation of events and attitudes, some of which may seem remote indeed from the changes that they help to bring about. In 1956, when I was living and working in Jerez, the sherry trade was set firm in its traditions and looked as if it would go on in the same way for ever. Yet in that year two quite unrelated things happened which did much to revolutionize the pattern of the trade: an *almacenista* (a store-keeper or sherry whole-saler) in quite a small way of business called Zoilo Ruiz-Mateos began to export wine; and there was a massive wage rise – one that by modern standards may not appear significant but was such that the workers themselves thought it would fire inflation. And they were right.

The trade of an almacenista in those days was an important one. Many shippers, even some of the largest like Williams & Humbert, preferred to work with modest stocks of wine and to own no vineyards, relying on contracts with wine growers and the avail-ability of plentiful supplies of almost every kind of wine from the almacenistas to supply their needs. Most of the big firms had been founded in the nineteenth century, when the costs of wine, casks, taxation and buildings were very much lower, and when enterprising men could expect to build up great businesses from small beginnings. By the mid-1950s, the initial outlay to start a business had become so large, and the returns so small, that the shippers were smugly asserting that no new bodega could be founded as a commercial proposition. José Maria Ruiz-Mateos, one of Zoilo's sons, thought otherwise; and it was he who was right.

For over 150 years John Harvey and Sons Ltd, the Bristol wine merchants, had been buying sherry in large quantities from several bodegas in Jerez and Puerto de Santa Maria, and they had built up one of the largest connections in the trade; but they owned no bodegas of their own. This led to difficulties, especially in the export markets, so in 1958 they formed an association with Zoilo Ruiz-Mateos and in 1964 entered into a hundred years' contract for him to supply them with all their needs. Within a year he had been able to accumulate stocks that astonished his competitors and was building luxurious new premises.

The Ruiz-Mateos business could trace its history back to 1857, when Zoilo Ruiz-Mateos Rodicio established a small business at Rota, growing the local red wine *Rota tent*. In 1930 his son, Zoilo Ruiz-Mateos Camacho, set up business in Jerez. He died in 1962, and a few years later, shortly after John Harvey and Sons Ltd were taken over by Showerings, the Somerset cider and perry firm (which in turn merged with Allied Breweries), the contract was rescinded and Zoilo Ruiz-Mateos, S.A. ceased from supplying the whole of Harvey's needs. Harvey's resumed their former practice of buying on the open market with Ruiz-Mateos as a major supplier.

Zoilo Ruiz-Mateos, S.A., continued under the management of Don Zoilo's two sons. The elder, also called Zoilo, concentrated on the wine side and looked after the vast interests in Jerez. The younger brother, José-Maria, was the financier and moved his headquarters to Madrid. He formed a group of companies that became a veritable empire: Rumasa. The companies absorbed included a number of banks so that the group became one of the most important bankers in Spain with branches in many other countries. It also included insurance, shipping, building, hotels, chemicals, farming, food products, engineering, property development and a host of other interests.

It did legendary things in the world of business. Once it bought three banks in a day. It began with wine, though, and wine remained a very major part of its activities. The first independent shipper it absorbed was the old-established A. R. Ruiz Hermanos. It went on to control the following companies, most of which were wholly owned: Zoilo Ruiz-Mateos, S.A.; Union de Exportadores de Jerez; Williams and Humbert; Palomino and Vergara; Misa; Pemartin; Varela; Bertola; Otaolaurruchi; Diestro; Lacave; Diaz Morales; Valderrama; Vergara and Gordon; Bodegas Internacionales; Garvey; and finally Diez-Merito. In addition the group had very large interests in Rioja table wines (which included Paternina and Bodegas Franco Españolas), in brandy, liqueurs, sparkling wines, beers, wine-importing companies and wine retailing companies, which included the Augustus Barnett chain in England and Skjold Burne in Denmark. It had as its symbol a bee, the tireless insect that produces sweet things. And its symbol was to be seen all over the sherry country. Its Jerez headquarters, *La Atalaya* – formerly the mansion of the Vergara family – had one of the most beautiful gardens in Andalusia, adorned with black swans, peacocks and all manner of exotic things, and also included a superb museum of clocks.

The impact of the Ruiz-Mateos empire was enormous. The whole atmosphere of the sherry towns changed utterly. When the first edition of this book was written, the vineyards, the pressing of the grape, the bodegas, and the offices were all much as they had been a hundred years before. Labour was cheap and machinery was dear so that many men did the work that could have been done by few, and the emphasis was on men. Men controlled the bottling lines and male clerks kept the books. Now all that was changed. It would no doubt have changed even without the catalyst that Ruiz-Mateos provided; wage inflation and the availability of cheaper and better machinery would have seen to that. But it would have happened more slowly. As it was, once the revolution had begun, it progressed at a breathtaking pace. Old names in the wine trade, like Croft's and Harvey's, appeared suddenly for the first time in Jerez. The other great houses were not to be left behind: Domecq, Gonzalez Byass, Sandeman, Osborne, all moved rapidly into the space age, and the smaller shippers manfully tried to keep pace. A new class of executives emerged, as it had throughout Europe. Computers replaced the traditional great ledgers and penholders. Women moved into the offices and bottling lines.

It was in 1970 that both Harvey's and Croft's, by coincidence, decided to set up in Jerez. Although Croft's are the older, their interest in sherry is much more recent, so the activities of Harvey's in Jerez will be described first.

After the contract with Ruiz-Mateos was terminated in 1967, Harvey's clearly needed a presence in the sherry country. Their label was the most popular on sherry bottles throughout the world, especially in the United Kingdom and in the United States of America. They bought vast quantities of wine and credibility demanded that they should have bodegas of their own which they could show to their agents and customers. More important, Harvey's had a growing market on the continent of Europe and some countries insisted that the wine should come direct from the country of origin. There was no shortage of capital, especially after the takeover by Showerings: the Showering brothers had shown that the cider orchards of the West Country can nurture tycoons as powerful and efficient as any who have sprung from more likely places. In 1970 they got exactly the foothold they needed when they bought Mackenzie and Co., an old-established firm with a fine stock of wine, which had long been amongst their suppliers. Another major supplier was Antonio Barbadillo of Sanlucar de Barrameda, a firm with magnificent stocks of old wine which remains independent but in which Harvey's acquired a small shareholding. In 1979 Harvey's were able to expand greatly when they bought the Misa bodega buildings (but not the name or wine) from Ruiz-Mateos. The Misa bodegas lay next to Harvey's and were notable for their beautiful gardens. They made the perfect setting into which Harvey's could expand.

At the time of the acquisition, Mackenzie's had some vineyards of their own, but Harvey's wanted far more, so that in 1973 they formed two joint vineyard companies, one – Viñarvey – with Garvey and the other – Gibalbin – with Barbadillo. The grapes from the Viñarvey vineyards were divided betwen the two owners, each making its own wine, while all the grapes from Gibalbin were vinified on the spot in the most modern and revolutionary press houses in the whole of the sherry country; but a description will be left to a later chapter. The partnership with Garveys came to an end in 1985, when Harvey's bought Garvey's share. Gibalbin is a massive operation that presses ten million kilos of grapes, half of which are bought from nearby vineyards.

Croft and Co. Ltd is one of the oldest companies in the wine trade. It was founded in 1678 as Phayre and Bradley in Oporto, and the name of Croft did not appear until 1736, when it was called Tilden, Thompson and Croft. John Croft (1732–1820) was a fascinating partner who somehow combined his activities in Oporto with the trade of a merchant in York, of which he became sheriff. His work as an antiquary was important enough to earn him a place in the *Dictionary of National Biography*, but historians of wine know him best for his very valuable, if occasionally unreliable little book *A Treatise on the Wines of Portugal; and what can be gathered on the Subject and Nature of the wines etc., Since the Establishment of the English Factory at Oporto Anno 1727.* Early in this century Croft and Co. Ltd was bought by Walter and Alfred Gilbey who, in the sherry trade, had very close links with the Gonzalez family. In 1962 W. and A. Gilbey Ltd merged with two other companies to form International Distillers and Vintners (I.D.V.), which itself succumbed to a takeover bid in 1968 to become a subsidiary of Watneys, the brewers, which in turn became a subsidiary of Grand Metropolitan. The merger resulted in a group with very large sherry sales and sales that were potentially larger still if a leading brand could be established. The brand was already there, in the form of Croft, and the sensible step was to expand it into sherry. This was done in 1970, with the formation of Croft Jerez, S.A., which originally also had Spanish shareholders but which is now a wholly owned subsidiary.

The new company started in some bodegas near the bull ring but, new as it was, it did not start from scratch. It had the benefit of the established soleras that Gilbeys already owned in the Gonzalez Byass bodegas and of the instant demand for wine from I.D.V. It soon embarked on building Rancho Croft in an ideal position, a huge complex of very traditional bodegas beside the vineyards on the outskirts of the town. It very soon came into the big league and, like Ruiz-Mateos, it shows how very wrong the traditionalists were in 1956 when they were certain that no new major house could be founded.

The balloon went up very suddenly in February 1983. The Rumasa empire was expropriated by the state. At the time the press announced that the government had anticipated a run on the banks which had failed to submit to the Bank of Spain's requirement for an independent audit, and that the whole of the Spanish economy might collapse. There had been, however, no such run, and although the affairs of the group were very complicated and have taken a long time to untangle, nothing has been published to suggest that it was insolvent. Assets sold in a winding-up notoriously fetch less than they are really worth and it may well be that the true value of the group can never now be established. Another suggestion was that the expropriation was the political move of a socialist government bent on nationalizing a major enterprise, but this can hardly have been so as its various parts were sold off to private buyers as soon as these could be found. Inquiries of the government elicit nothing: there is an exasperating silence.

Whatever the reason may have been, the results are clear enough. When the government sold the businesses there were bargains to be had. John Harvey bought two of the major companies in 1985: Palomino & Vergara and Terry. The former had large stocks of wine and a renowned fino, Tio Mateo. The latter gave Harveys an important place in the Spanish brandy trade. Bodegas Internacionales – which carried with it many famous names including Duke of Wellington, Bertola, Pemartin, Misa, Don Zoilo, Diez Hermanos, Varela, Diestro and Otaolaurruchi – was bought by Marcos Equizabal, an entrepreneur from the north who made a large fortune in property and who also invested heavily in the Rioja. He keeps a very low profile and leaves the management of the bodegas to executives, but has happily made it well known that he is looking for quality in his wines. Garvey, which includes Valderrama and Vergara & Gordon, was sold initially to a German co-operative which got into financial difficulties and sold the business to the United Dutch, a publicly quoted company which bought it as an investment. A substantial development of its town-centre properties seems likely. They have a huge new bodega on the outskirts of the town and bought large quantities of sherry from Bobadilla when it was sold. Williams & Humbert, which incorporates Lacave, was the last to go and ended several years of rudderless state management while the sale was delayed by litigation about who owned the Dry Sack trade marks. These were claimed by the Ruiz-Mateos family as its own property but the dispute was resolved in favour of the company, which was promptly put up for sale. At first it was rumoured that it had been bought by a company controlled by a Venezuelan bank, but this came to nothing, and eventually, after having been rather disastrously run by civil servants for several years, it was quietly bought by Bobadillo in 1988. It required a further input, however, in the form of marketing know-how and muscle, so in 1991 substantial interests were sold: 45 per cent to Bols and 10 per cent to Luis Paez, a small sherry house in Jerez owned 50 per cent by Medina and 50 per cent by Ahold, a Dutch group which owns the retail chain Albert Heijn.

The Rumasa empire, after having dominated the sherry trade for many years, was no more. But perhaps there will be a comeback, for in 1991 the family acquired the reputable and old-established house of de Soto.

The sherry country after Rumasa will never be the same as it was before, when there were a large number of relatively prosperous houses, each steeped in its own traditions, run by members of a small number of inter-related families which had formed themselves into an aristocracy and employed generation after generation of workers who themselves belonged to the tradition. Rumasa brought the rule of executives whose eyes were firmly fixed on the accounts. Moreover the empire was, quite rightly, run as such, not as a number of separate individualistic houses. Soleras were simplified and moved about to provide larger and more economical supplies of fewer wines. Old houses that have become independent again or which have been absorbed by other groups cannot turn the clock back. They simply do not have the soleras to produce the speciality wines, with their low sales, that were once their pride. Not only the wines but also the executives were moved about. Visiting some of the bodegas in the Rumasa days I mentioned managers who had been renowned in the trade twenty or thirty years before and no one had heard of them. *Sic transit gloria.*

Most of the houses who sold out to Rumasa did so through sheer economic necessity. They could not survive standing alone, usually because they had overstretched themselves by planting vineyards which had rapidly become redundant when demand fell, and by buying expensive new plant, particularly press houses and stainless steel fermentation vessels. Others, the smaller ones, were simply uneconomic and were also weighed down by an ever increasing load of paperwork, much of it generated by the regulatory bureaucracy.

There have been changes not directly related to Rumasa, though it can be said that the consequences of its rise and fall have been all-embracing. Osborne, which went through a difficult period, has resurged under new management. In 1991 it bought Bobadilla and has also bought some fine vineyards. It is still family owned but members of the family play no part in day to day management.

Gonzalez Byass remains family controlled but the Gonzalez family bought out the Byass family in 1988 and subsequently sold a 15 per cent stake to the Italian fashion company, Benetton. They then sold 2 per cent to the Mercian Corporation of Japan and 1 per cent to Haecky Holding of Switzerland. For many years Gonzalez Byass have owned Wisdom & Warter, which trades independently under its own name, and also Ivison.

Emilio Lustau changed hands partly as a management buy-out and partly as a takeover. The Lustau family retained ownership of the real property but the business and stocks passed from their hands. Rafael Balao, who had been running it for many years, acquired a minority share and the controlling interest passed to Luis Caballero of Puerto de Santa Maria, who also injected a large vineyard in the Montegilillo district. It incorporates Abad and Alexander Gordon.

There have been losses, though, and many of these have been very sad. They include such old-established concerns as Rivero and O'Neale. Amongst the largest, and one that used to be numbered amongst the best, was Cuvillo. Others include: Guerrero, Delage, Parra Guerrero, and Carlos & Javier de Terry. Some of the remaining concerns survive just tenuously or have degenerated into subsidiary names used by the big shippers. One of the old names which has disappeared from the market is Mackenzie. Harveys do not find sales of small brands to be commercially attractive, and it has gone in a process of rationalization.

It is at present a very difficult period for the small shippers. There are no longer the multitude of independent wine merchants and local brewers who used to buy most of their wine in bulk and bottle it themselves. The market is changed, with the emphasis now on national brands and supermarkets. In the United Kingdom in 1989, buyers' own brands accounted for 29.1 per cent of the market; of this, Sainsbury had 12.1 per cent, Tesco 8.7, Marks & Spencer 4 and the rest 4.3 between them. In the Netherlands Heijn had 18 per cent of the market. These companies gave large orders and the wines were bottled in Spain, as nearly all sherry is now, and it will all have to be by 1993. The cost of a modern bottling plant alone is an enormous burden to a small shipper; a large plant can cost £2 million.

On the other hand several new houses have been built up. In Jerez, José Estivez, who made a fortune out of sand for making bottles, has risen into prominence and controls the old-established house of Réal Tesoro. In Sanlucar there is a new empire, not on the Rumasa scale but nevertheless now of major importance – that of Medina, which has been built up since 1970 by an ex-employee of Rumasa and which includes José Medina and controlling interests in Perez Megia of Sanlucar, Luis Paez, J. V. Vergara (which broke off from Palomino & Vergara when Rumasa took it over), B. M. Lagos and Dos Mercedes of Jerez together with wine interests in Huelva, agricultural products and real estate. It is now in the big league of sherry shippers, with large exports to the Netherlands.

The position in 1990 was that ten companies – Harveys, Gonzalez Byass, Barbadillo/Williams & Humbert, Sandeman, Bodegas Internacionales, Medina, Domecq, Croft, Garvey and Osborne – controlled 88 per cent of the production of sherry.

Arising from all these changes there is a tangled web of shareholdings, almost as complicated as the family tree of the families who used to command. Harveys have 12 per cent of Barbadillo, which in turn has 45 per cent of Williams & Humbert; Allied-Lyons, which owns Harveys, has a half share in Hiram Walker Europe, the other half of which is owned by a member of the Domecq family, while Hiram Walker Europe in turn owns 56 per cent of Domecq, so that Harveys effectively own 28 per cent. Domecq in turn controls Blazquez and de la Riva. However, there is no suggestion that these interlocking shareholdings are used to direct the trade or to influence the management in any way. They are just there, often for reasons which now appear historical.

The fluctuations of the trade within living memory are remarkable. The Spanish Civil War had surprisingly little effect. In Jerez a major who had forty troops at his disposal bluffed the local mayor into believing that he had 500 and took over control of the town. It is said that in the local communist headquarters a hit list of 800 of the most prominent citizens was found: all the employers of labour. The town remained in the hands of the Nationalists throughout and the slaughter that occurred in most Spanish towns, whoever was in power, did not happen there. None of the battles was fought in the sherry country and the Falangists needed the foreign currency that the exports brought, so that the sherry trade continued as before. With the shipping difficulties of the Second World War, however, trade collapsed and little wine was exported in the years 1941, 1942 and 1943. The almacenistas and the proprietors at Sanlucar suffered the most at this time as the big shippers in Jerez and Puerto could not sell their own wine and certainly did not want to buy anyone else's, so that men with stocks normally worth fortunes were penniless. By 1950 things had got back to normal and by the second half of the decade exports were growing fairly steadily. In round figures, exports (in hectolitres) were 183,000 in 1950, 246,000 in 1955, and 332,000 in 1960. Then there was a dramatic increase. The figure for 1965 was 494,000 and for 1970 was 726,000. From then onwards the figures are shown on the graph. A peak was reached in 1972 and the figure for 1973 was little lower but in 1974 and 1975 there was a very serious decline. Then the graph did indeed go up again but only to decline in the 1980s, to a new low in 1989, though the figure for that year was distorted by the fact that several of the big shippers stopped bottling in England and used up their stocks before starting the Spanish bottling. One of the main troubles had been over-production.

The graph, besides showing the past, explains the present and provides a pointer to the future. In retrospect 1973 was the year in which everything went wrong. The graph had been moving steadily and had been extrapolated ever upwards. To meet the anticipated demand vast new vineyards were planted, using borrowed money, with Rumasa in the lead. When the world depression brought about by the energy crisis came and sales fell, panic set in. More wine was grown than sold and much that was sold went for wholly uneconomic prices. This particular rot was started in the Rumasa days, when that magic phrase 'cash flow' began to be muttered and when the executives demanded a fast turnover of the wine. There was an official minimum price (no longer possible in the EEC) but it was largely avoided by giving hidden discounts. One result was that when Rumasa was expropriated it was found to have vast stores of unsaleable sherry in England (amounting to 1,125,000 litres, with further quantities in the Netherlands) that the Spanish government had to get rid of. The cash-flow criterion is still with us: in 1991 I was in the office of a reputable shipper when he received a telephone call from Germany asking him if he could supply a large quantity of wine at a given, very low price. No sample was asked for and no style even was stipulated. All that mattered were the price, and the fact that the wine could legally be sold as sherry. Asked individually, each shipper would deny doing this trade and would insist that his focus is on the highest quality end of the market; but most do it.

The rise of the Netherlands as a market was a phenomenon. In the past it had been small and steady. Then it suddenly began to take off: in 1963 it was 36,881 hectolitres, it rose to 107,585 in 1967 and went on rising to a dramatic peak in 1972. This was brought about by the caprice of fashion. Dutch housewives enjoy

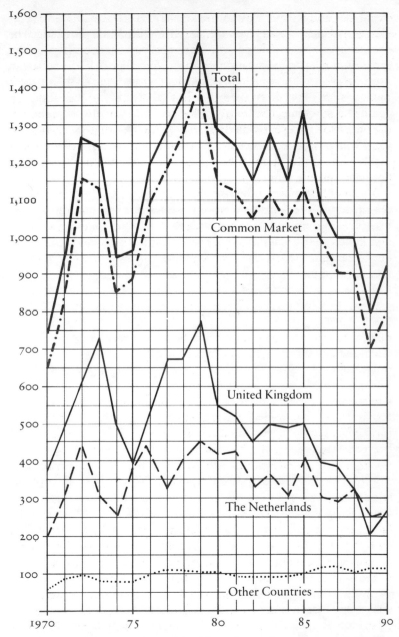

Total

Common Market

United Kingdom

The Netherlands

Other Countries

Exports in thousands of hectolitres, 1970–90

social gatherings, and they found that a glass – or perhaps several glasses – of cheap sherry was the ideal thing to drink with a piece of cake. Sometimes this happens in the morning, more often in the afternoon; it is drunk as an aperitif too, but the largest quantity is drunk after dinner. Some of the shippers wisely refused to compete at the very lowest end of the range but others took any orders they could get and many stories have been told about the horrible happenings in that particular market – stories which always concern some other shipper, of course. But even discounting malice, there can be little doubt that some of the wine exported there was very poor stuff. Too young, too weak and too sweet, it even gave rise to problems of secondary fermentation. Lots of other things went wrong, too. And there are credible stories of horrible mixings having been made by merchants who imported container loads which they bottled in bond. Such things did much harm. The lesson appears to have been learned, though. The market is now steadying and the leaders are those who kept their standards up.

To counter the crisis of over-production there was a four-year plan starting in 1983, with the dramatic distillation of 31 million litres of surplus must and the institution of shipping quotas. No new vineyards were to be planted and some of the existing ones were grubbed up. In the first year of the plan the vineyard area was reduced by over 2,300 hectares; but although it helped, it was not enough. In 1970 the vineyard area was 11,600 hectares; by 1982 it had risen to 21,700. And those who did grub them up as part of the four-year plan are now very angry as they did not get anything like the compensation they would get today if they pulled them up under the plan's successor.

By 1989 it was clear that something radical had to be done to save the trade, and the shippers, who had come together with striking unity in the days of the four-year plan, once again joined forces to find a solution. The provincial government engaged Price Waterhouse to prepare a report. This, which was published in the following year, proved to be very long and detailed. It contained few surprises, for the root cause of the trouble, that supply greatly exceeded demand, was obvious to everyone. To put it all into writing was a very expensive exercise, but it needed the authority of an acknowledged independent expert to bring change about; and advice that is paid for is more readily followed than that which is gratuitous. The report contained some interesting statistics. Between

1980 and 1988 the vineyards had produced 27.5 per cent more must than was necessary to support the sales of wine, and the price of grapes had gone down by 38.8 per cent; nor were the grapes paid for on the nail, so the independent growers were under great pressure. All of this particularly affected the small growers in the co-operatives. The sherry vineyards were the only major ones in Spain where the price of grapes had gone down in real terms between 1985 and 1989. The price of sherry in real terms also had been falling steadily. It had fallen in the United Kingdom from a level of 100 in 1985 to 82.3 in 1982 and in the Netherlands to 86.4; but the Netherlands bought cheaper sherry to begin with. Between 1980 and 1988 sales had decreased by 27.2 per cent but stocks had risen by 1.8 per cent. The only success story had been manzanilla on the domestic market, which had raised its share between 1985 and 1989 from 2.3 per cent to 10.8 per cent. The prospects were not bright. It was doubtful whether the popularity of sherry in the United Kingdom had reached its nadir; indeed the graph was pessimistically projected downwards. And in the Netherlands there were signs that it had begun to lose out to port.

Something clearly had to be done. The measures proposed were essentially those that had been discussed among the more enlightened shippers for some time. The principal one was to balance supply and demand by the removal of 10,900 aranzadas (approximately 5,200 hectares) of vineyard. Compensation had to be provided, of course. Either the vineyards could be declassified and used for producing the newly created table wines or vinegar, for which there was a limited market; or they could be grubbed up entirely and turned over to the alternative crops of sugar beet, sunflowers (for making oil) or cereals, in which case a contribution could be obtained from the EEC. The recommended resolution is to be implemented, but on a rather reduced scale of 4,000 hectares. There is also to be a temporarily limited yield of 56.3 hectolitres per hectare, to be increased for smaller growers to 69.3 if they pay a levy. Not all the new vineyards had been planted on very good sites and it was hoped that those on the poorer soils would be the first to go. This hope has to a large extent been fulfilled, as growers with several vineyards would obviously prefer to lose the poorer ones; and richer soils which are less good for wine are often better for alternative crops. Nevertheless there are sadly bare patches in some of the best albariza districts. If demand should rise again there will be plenty of soil to supply it.

There were also to be quotas for the sale of wines, based on demand and not on production. The reduction of stocks will perhaps be the most difficult to achieve as the must to replace them in due course will be more expensive; but this aspect of the matter is the least important and there are arguments against reducing stocks at all, particularly in the context of a quest for quality. The new system will take four years to implement.

Instead of official plans the whole situation could, of course, have been left to market forces, which no doubt would have sorted everything out in the end, as they did at the turn of the century. But market forces often act in a very painful way. There can be little doubt that the problem was best tackled by a rational plan, and happily it has been.

Mention should also be made of Spain's accession to the EEC in 1986, which will have far-reaching consequences. The equalization of taxes on beverages has increased prices in Spain itself and will inevitably have an effect on the market. Sherry is now subject to EEC Regulation 4252/88 which has, amongst other things, banished the use of sugar for sweetening and has enforced the use of concentrated rectified must (see page 237) instead. It does, however, permit the use of Pedro Ximenez from Montilla-Moriles. The rules for Spanish brandy are laid down in EEC Regulation 1576/89.

Although Spain's presence in the EEC is no doubt necessary for its future prosperity, the immediate effect on the sherry trade has mostly been negative. One result has been duty and VAT on spirit used for fortifying, which has greatly increased its price and which has to be paid at least two and a half years before the wine can be sold.

Another advantage just failed to materialize. It was hoped that following Spain's accession to the EEC wine from elsewhere which usurped the name of sherry would no longer be able to do so. This has not happened. South African and Australian wines are now no longer allowed to call themselves sherry but British, Irish and Cyprus sherries remain as permitted designations at least until 1995. British sherry enjoys a totally unfair fiscal advantage amounting to about £1 per bottle. It is hard to see how the British government could have come to insist on such exceptions save by the pressure of vested interests.

The markets that really last are those that are founded on quality and value. The low quality of the wines shipped at the height of the sherry boom in the nineteenth century killed off the trade. The poor quality of some of the wines shipped in the 1960s and 1970s may well have put some people off sherry and no lasting market is likely to be founded on the basis of the very cheap wines being shipped to customers on the Continent. Happily the United Kingdom super-market chains are highly quality conscious.

One of the recommendations of the Price Waterhouse report has given teeth to the quality-control function of the Consejo Regulador. It is to be hoped that inferior wines will finally be stopped. In addition to this, the shippers are inevitably affected by the swings of the pendulum of fashion – at present in their favour in the Nether-lands and against them in the United Kingdom. And there is always the hope, indeed the likelihood, that new markets will be opened up. One of the difficulties that sherry has – just as it had a hundred years ago – is that of being associated with the fuddy-duddies of the older generation. My experience has been when young people are introduced to good sherries, they are won over at once. The problem is to get them to try. This will probably be helped by the new popularity of tapas bars and with the realization that sherry is so good when taken with food. There is one important way, though, in which the current picture differs from that of a hundred years ago: the leading shippers have never lost sight of the lasting demand for high quality wines. The best have never been better. This was demonstrated by Lustau's introduction of its sherries from the almacenistas in 1982. Supplies were, and are, very limited but they are all taken up. The big shippers such as Gonzalez Byass, Domecq, Harveys and Sandeman have all introduced premium ranges aimed at the connoisseur market. These can never form more than a minority of total sales but they must help to sell the very excellent wines that can be produced in larger quantities. The knowledge that sherry is one of the world's truly great wines that offers value that is second to none will surely spread.

In 1990 *Harpers Wine & Spirit Gazette* pointed out that sherry is seen on the shelves of supermarkets at a wide range of prices and there is no easy way that ordinary shoppers can distinguish what they are getting. Many ports and madeiras are given ages: five-year-old, ten-year-old, and so on. This would not be easy with sherry because of the solera system, though an easy calculation can give the age of the bulk of the wine in a solera. The solution that *Harpers* proposed was to introduce categories such as *solera* sherry (three-year-old minimum), *reserva* (five-year-old minimum) and *gran reserva* sherry (seven-year-old or more). Such an idea is at least worth considering.

In 1986 there was a pleasing diversion: the poet laureate, Ted Hughes, was presented with a butt of sack. It was an old custom revived. Chaucer was given a daily pitcher of wine. In 1619, when King James I appointed Ben Jonson poet laureate, he was given a 'Butt of Sherry Sack' and so were his successors until that most obscure of laureates, Henry James Pye, a political appointment of 1790, commuted it to a payment of £27 to pay off some of his many debts. When John Betjeman was appointed in 1972 the good custom was partially revived; he was given an annual present of wine of his own choice. But the legend of the butt of sack lingered on and was given reality by the gift to Ted Hughes.

In 1991 there was a tragic strike. It was all concerned with pensions and retirement. The Montepío de San Gines, which administered pensions, was to be closed down and new arrangements substituted. A perfectly reasonable plan was put to the workers in May, but they were not having it. The diehard trade union leaders called a strike which lasted for fifty-nine days. Unfortunately it was bitter and violent. Picket lines at the pressing stations in the sherry towns prevented any grapes from coming in and desperate growers brought mothballed press houses in the vineyards back into use; one even used presses that were arranged as a museum. It may well be that not all the must attained the highest modern standards but as it came in a period of serious over-production there is no quality crisis. However, despite all these efforts, some 40 per cent of the production was lost. At the end of it all faces were saved but the strikers had gained little that they could not have had in May, and they had lost two months' wages. Those now aged forty-eight or more will be able to retire on full pay at sixty, which was already agreed, and the only difference appears to be a participation in the scheme by the regional government. But the atmosphere was charged and labour relations, which are not easy at the best of times, are likely to be very difficult for quite a while. Another unfortunate consequence of the strike was that for two months no sherry could be shipped, with the inevitable loss of some of the valuable Christmas market in 1991.

A development that lies outside the scope of this book is the use of surplus grapes to make good table wines, a market pioneered by Barbadillo. It is a much better solution than distillation or the grubbing up of vineyards. There is also a substantial production of good wine vinegar. The fact remains, however, that some of the large shippers owe their prosperity almost entirely to their profitable sales of excellent brandy.

7

Vines and Vineyards

There is something immensely satisfying about a vineyard. On the undulating slopes between Jerez and the sea one can sit for hours without hearing a sound or seeing a soul, and on every slope as far as the horizon there are green vines laden with heavy bunches of grapes. Perhaps it is the anticipation of what the grapes will become that gives half the pleasure. Even in the winter, when the vines are nothing more than gnarled and twisted stumps, the sight is scarcely less pleasing, for the great vineyards of Jerez grow on *albariza* soil that reflects the bright sunshine radiantly from its clean, white surface.

At the time of the Moorish domination, and during the continuous wars between the Christians and Moors, the vine was grown immediately outside the walls of the town. In the fifteenth century, when Jerez was at last under the undisputed control of the Catholic monarchs, it became safe to work throughout the day beyond the range of the town's protection, and the vineyards gradually spread to the area where they are today.

The sherry vineyards are cultivated on three principal types of soil. Listed in order of quality, these are: *albariza*, *barro* and *arena*. Albariza soil, although very high in calcium, can be quite good for agriculture, but the only serious rival to the vine in the past has been the olive; as the wine trade has suffered its ups and downs, so have the olive trees encroached and receded. In the 1980s sunflowers suddenly became popular, while sugar beet and cereals can also be grown. The grapes in the vineyards around Jerez are quite good to eat, but they hardly compare with big, luscious hothouse grapes, nor with vineyard grapes grown specially for the table, while fine table grapes seldom make good wine. It is the small, uninspiring grapes that make the finest wines – grapes that have struggled for existence in waste places, or in hot, parched climates, like that of Jerez, where the fruit grows slowly and absorbs all the natural goodness of the soil. The grapes of the wine countries are like human beings: they do their best work after a tough upbringing. Anyone digging a well in the sherry area will find black streakers of dead vines descending vertically through loam, lime and rock to a depth of 10 metres in their search for water. Emilio Lustau has an old vine root 7.5 metres long and even that is not its full length for its end is broken off. Most of the root system, however, is at a higher level and spreads out all round the vine at a depth of 50 to 60 centimetres. It follows that vineyards which look the most luxuriant are often the worst. The nature of the soil, together with the climate, ultimately decides the quality of wine that can be produced. Vines from Jerez grown in the soils of Galicia or Zamora give entirely different wines.

Unfortunately I am no geologist, but the origin of the district has been described very clearly by E. M. Nicholson, who wrote the chapter on ecology in Guy Mountfort's superb *Portrait of a Wilderness*:

Before and during the Tertiary epoch, which began some seventy million years ago, the Betic Massif became buckled up between the continental pressure of shifting Africa to the south and the rigid line of what is now the Sierra Morena to the north. The great squeeze thrust up a mountain dome whose remains now dominate both sides of the Strait of Gibraltar, and left a corresponding deep depression submerged beneath the sea following the course of the present Guadalquivir valley down to the Coto.

As it is the fate of mountains over the millennia to be eroded away and carried down in particles to the sea, the Betic Depression over long ages became filled with sediment until eventually, helped by uplifting, it rose above the sea in the form of the delta of the Guadalquivir, opening out just below Sevilla, and advancing to fill the gap between the higher ground behind Huelva and behind Jerez de la Frontera. This delta, it so happened, faced south-west out on to the Atlantic and was thus exposed to much the same south-westerly gales as the British Isles, while the coastal current, running from north-west to south-east towards the Strait, caught it with full force once the Sevilla-Huelva-Jerez triangle was filled up.

The combined effect seems to have been to arrest the further outward growth of the delta along roughly its present line, and to begin throwing back on the beach in the form of sand much of the fine sediment which had formerly been gradually deposited to build the delta farther out to sea. This ample material, now surplus and literally rejected by the Atlantic, was transformed and piled up to build first a long finger of temporary sand bars and eventually a more permanent line of sand dunes, pointing south-east from near Huelva towards Jerez and Cadiz.

This no doubt helps to explain why marine fossils are often found in vineyards. Other large shells appear to have originated in fresh-water lakes as the soil is far from being rich in minerals.

In appearance the vineyard landscape is of gentle rolling hills, not unlike English downland. The height of the best vineyards varies between about 100 and 150 metres. Vines are planted on all the slopes, and in the hot climate of Andalusia all get enough sun and heat to ripen thoroughly, but those are considered to be most favoured that are planted on the south-east slopes, as they are protected from cold winds and frosts in winter and they get the most of the sunshine in summer.

The albariza soil on which the finest vineyards are grown is also called *tierra de anafas*, *tierra blanca* or *tosca*, and is found principally to the north and west of Jerez with outcrops in more distant places, notably in Montilla. It also occurs in the immediate subsoil of the vineyards to the south of the town and is there known as *albero*. The name 'albariza' is derived from *albo*, meaning snow-white, and from a distance it does look as white as snow, but when examined closely it is seen to contain many earth-coloured particles. If a handful is dropped into a glass of water, it falls to the bottom, releasing bubbles of air on the way, and then gradually separates into a distinct layer of pasty mud. This mud is so slippery that crossing an albariza vineyard during the rainy season is a very perilous undertaking. When the soil dries out again, though, it turns back into a fine powder; it does not coagulate and there is little trace of the cracks that appear when ordinary mud is dried by the sun. This even texture is extremely important in the climate of Jerez. In February, March and April there are heavy rains which the earth absorbs as if it were a sponge, and when the hot sunshine follows in May, the surface of the soil is baked into a homogeneous and hard layer without many cracks or irregularities. Cool air and water are trapped beneath it to feed the roots of the vines throughout the semi-tropical summer. James Howell, in his book *Familiar Letters*, described wine as 'water sublimed', which is entirely accurate, as it is the moisture from the ground, absorbed by the roots of the vine, that eventually fills the grape with juice. Howell told how an Italian wine-grower complained during a drought: 'For want of Water, I am forced to drink Water; if I had Water, I would drink Wine.' But thanks to the remarkable character of the soil in the sherry vineyards, a drought can only cause much damage if it is very severe. Albariza soil can absorb as much as 34 per cent, by weight of water.

According to the analyses of Don Gonzalo Fernandez de Bobadilla of the Estacion de Viticultura de Jerez, the chief chemical constituent of albariza soil is calcium carbonate, or chalk, of which it contains from 30 to 60 or even 80 per cent, the remainder consisting for the most part of sand and clay in widely varying quantities. But although a chemist regards calcium carbonate and chalk as being the same thing, a geologist does not. The albariza soils are of the Oligocene age – thirty million years too young to be referred to properly as chalk. To a geologist the soil is simply lime-rich. Perhaps because of its comparative youth, the soil has not been greatly eroded. It is therefore very deep and the vines can penetrate without obstruction.

Albariza soil can be subdivided into a number of distinct types. *Tajón* has the highest proportion of limestone: rising to 80 per cent. There are not many vineyards on these soils and they are not very satisfactory, as this soil is too hard and the lack of balance tends to make the vines suffer from a disease called chlorosis. They are very white in colour. *Barrosa* contains a certain amount of clay so that it tends to crack superficially in dry weather and the moisture in the soil then evaporates. Very little of this soil is planted with vines, though occasionally islands of the soil are found in proper albariza vineyards. *Lantejuela* is softer than *tajón* and is only about half calcium carbonate; it is sometimes mixed with barro. *Barrajuela* has about the same amount of calcium carbonate and is slightly yellowish. *Tosca* has slightly less limestone but at least 40 per cent. *Lustrillo* is slightly reddish to look at owing to the presence of iron oxide and is found particularly around Trebujena, along the road to Seville, and to a very small extent by Sanlucar, where the soil is called *polvillejo*. Vineyards are planted where there is a good albariza subsoil and not too much iron. There are further variants and subdivisions that have been classified by viticulturalists and geologists. In the finest albariza soil, the composition varies somewhat with depth. At the surface it has 25 per cent or more limestone, 40 per cent at about sixty centimetres down and 60 per cent at about eighty centimetres down.

It is the existence of the sand and clays, especially in the thin layer of topsoil, that give such a varied appearance to the vineyards when they are looked at closely. From a distance, especially in bright sunlight, they look almost as white as snow; but when you are walking through them you see many colours – shades of grey, brown, ochre and even red – while some, with hardly any topsoil at all, really *are* white. Often there are several colours in a single vineyard. What matters most, though, is the subsoil from which the roots of the vines get their nourishment. This soil gives wines of the very highest quality, but the yield is small: once only about three butts per acre though now increased to eight or ten, thanks to vine selection and disease control, but falling to half that quantity in bad vintages, as in 1945 and 1958, when there had been persistent drought in the three previous years. The Levante (see below) can also reduce the yield by drying the grapes if it blows for a long time while they are ripening.

Barro soil is darker in colour and gives a rather coarser wine, but the yield is greater – about 20 per cent more than albariza. This soil occurs in the valleys between the hills of albariza and also along the coast from Sanlucar practically to Gibraltar, though only a proportion of this stretch of country is suitable for vines. Like albariza soil, barro is slippery and treacherous when wet and intensely hard when dry, but it contains a lower proportion of calcium carbonate. Iron oxide often gives it a red or yellowish tinge, though the overall colour is brown, and it also contains many fossil shells. Apart from the somewhat inferior quality of the wine produced, viticulture is made difficult in the barro regions by wide gaps in the soil which are filled with almost pure sand, and after heavy rain the clay and chalk tend to be washed beneath the surface, leaving a layer of pebbles and sand on top, which makes it hard to see what is good and what is not. Moreover the high fertility causes a prolific growth of weeds, while the heat of the sun dries it unevenly, producing wide cracks or fissures.

Arena soil, sometimes known as *barro-arena*, is very inferior and consists almost entirely of sand with a more marked yellowish-red tinge caused by iron. There is comparatively little of this soil, but it is easy to work and there is little trouble from weeds. The yield is higher – about half as much again as that of albariza – but the quality of the wine is so inferior that the price it fetches is less than half. These vineyards were most popular at the end of the last century, as the phylloxera did not make much headway in the sandy soil. There are still some Moscatel vines planted ungrafted in this soil. The demand these days, however, is almost entirely for quality wines and the arena vineyards are practically extinct.

The vineyard areas are divided into *pagos*, that may be anything in size from an acre to the two thousand acres of the great Macharnudo district. The most important pagos on albariza soil are Macharnudo,[1] Carrascal, Balbaina, Añina and Los Tercios, lying to the north and west of Jerez; but Diego Parada y Barreto, writing in 1868, listed 134 pagos in all, each of which he carefully classified. Today there are probably 150, and a detailed description of each is beyond the scope of this book. Smaller albariza areas include St Julián and Carrahola, while Montealegre is the most highly regarded on arena soils. The most noted areas for manzanillas around Sanlucar, are Miraflores and Torrebreba.

At the southern extremity of the sherry area lies the village of Chiclana. Owing to its richer soil, the vineyards give very large yields, and the wine is therefore cheap, but it is not of the highest quality. Chiclana is particularly noted for cheap finos, which have a distinctive, but by no means unpleasant flavour; some of these are matured in bodegas on the spot while others are brought into Jerez and Puerto de Santa Maria.

The style of a wine naturally depends to a significant extent on where it is grown. Balbaina is especially noted for finos, and other fine finos are grown in Añina and Los Tercios. Macharnudo is especially noted for finos that develop into amontillados, while Carrascal provides olorosos.

Although the hills are planted with vines all over, this does not mean that the climate is the same throughout the vineyards. Manifestly it is not. People feeling baked in the summer heat of Jerez drive, if they can, to Sanlucar, where it is noticeably cooler. These differences affect the development of the grapes so that vineyards near the coast give grapes with about one degree less

1 The name is derived from the Arabic meaning 'The farm of Ibn Dawd'.

sugar (and therefore wines with one degree less alcohol) than those that are inland. It is these vineyards that produce the best fino. Further inland, too, the grapes tend to pick up more minerals and extract from the soils, giving bigger wines, especially olorosos.

The health and development of the grapes is also affected by the two prevailing winds: the Poniente and the Levante. Happily the former is more common than the latter. The Poniente is cool, humid and not very strong. When it is blowing the humidity is usually about 90 per cent, but the breeze makes it rather agreeable to sit out in the sun and the humidity increases the yield of the vines. The only snag is that it also tends to bring mildew. The Levante, on the other hand, is a horrible wind. Blowing from the south-east, it is dry, hot and strong – the enemy of the wine growers and hated by all those who live in the sherry country. It can blow for days on end. The relative humidity is normally about 50 per cent in the middle of the day and 75 by night. When the Levante blows, it rapidly goes down to 30 per cent: a hot, dry wind, that puts tempers on edge and which is even said to drive men mad. In the vineyards it dries out the grapes and reduces the yield, breaks the tendrils of the vines and knocks over the props that, in the traditional methods of viticulture, were used to hold the heavy bunches of ripe grapes off the ground. It also brings with it swarms of insects.

Although it can be rather damp in winter and distinctly too hot for comfort at the height of summer, the sherry country has a very pleasant climate to live in. More important, it is a very good climate for wine growing, not least in its consistency. The nearness of the sea has a major influence both on maintaining humidity and in moderating temperatures. Some detailed climatic statistics are to be found in Appendix 6. An analysis over a number of years has shown that the average temperature is 17°C, with a maximum rising to 44°C and a minimum as low as −5°C. These extremes are rare, though. In 1963 the lowest temperature recorded was 0.7°C and the highest was 37°C. The average rainfall is 640 litres per square metre, nearly all of which occurs in the winter and early spring. This is a good deal higher than, for instance, in Castile, and it is not beyond the reach of Atlantic storms.

A storm at vintage time is only too common, sometimes with flash floods and occasionally, as in 1979, with hail. In the months of July and August there is a very heavy dew. Irrigation is totally forbidden, which is perhaps a pity as the yield can be very depressed in years of low rainfall, while quantity and quality go together in the circumstances prevailing in the sherry country. Australia has shown how very good wines can be grown with the aid of carefully controlled irrigation in a hot climate. The danger of course is that too much would be used, simply to increase yield, and that would certainly reduce quality.

The sherry area is strictly delimited by the Consejo Regulador and no wine from outside this area may be used for blending with sherry, save for a very limited importation of sweet wine from Montilla. The area may be divided into two parts: Jerez Superior, which includes the great albariza pagos and Zona. In aranzadas planted, the figures at 1 September 1990 were as follows:

	Jerez Superior	Rest of the Zona	Total
Jerez	9,645.59	828.20	10,473.79
Puerto Sta Maria	1,164.09	123.91	1,288.00
Sanlucar	1,410.05	470.83	1,880.88
Chiclana	–	1,445.55	1,445.55
Chipiona	64.30	479.10	543.40
Lebrija	–	212.69	212.69
Puerto Real	–	908.48	908.48
Rota	133.40	240.93	374.33
Trebujena	–	767.42	767.42
Total	12,417.43	5,477.11	17,894.54

Jerez Superior gives the finest wines. In contrast, wines from Chiclana, as has been mentioned, tend to taste rather coarse, while those from Trebujena are darker in colour, lack fragrance and are very fat, big-bodied wines. This is not to condemn them. In every wine-growing area some parts are better than others. They are still good wines but by no means the best. The emphasis, though, is on quality, and it is the unplanted areas within Jerez Superior that are principally being developed. This makes good economic sense as well as being good for the consumer. A vineyard in a second-class area costs as much to plant and to cultivate as does one of the best and, not unnaturally, the wine sells for less. This is demonstrated by what has actually happened. In 1960 not more than 50 per cent of the vineyards were in the Jerez Superior. In 1980 this had increased to 85 per cent. The vineyards on the sandy soil of Chipiona have virtually disappeared and tomatoes are grown there instead.

To make sure that the shippers as a whole keep up the quality of their wines, the Consejo Regulador insists that each, before 1 February each year, buys a minimum quota of must from the Jerez Superior proportional to his previous year's production; but this, of course, takes into account the shipper's own production if he has vineyards of his own.

The Consejo Regulador's regulations are being rigorously enforced and wines from outlying districts that used to supplement the supplies of sherry are no longer available. Fortunately there is no foreseeable shortage. There is in fact serious over-production. In the 1970s exports were rising steadily and the graph was extrapolated ever upwards. As it takes five years for a vineyard to produce a useful yield and another three years for the wine to be mature enough for sale, there is minimum delay of eight years between planting and production, and at least twice as long for fine wines. Panic set in and everyone started planting new vineyards, with Rumasa in the lead. Not all of them were planted in the best places.

When the phylloxera struck Jerez at the end of the last century, many growers thought that the good days would never come again. They planted olive groves and corn where vineyards had been. In 1991, as has been related, a plan was agreed for vineyards to be grubbed up and the olive trees will be back. Despite that great new vineyards have been planted in the last few years, but there are still a very large number of peasant proprietors, especially around Sanlucar, as the figures opposite show (the chart shows total areas in aranzadas comprised by vineyards of from 0 to 1 aranzada, and so on, as at 1990). In 1991 there were a total of 4,200 hectares shared among 800 proprietors.

Much of the harvest is vinified by co-operatives, of which there are one in Jerez, two in Sanlucar, one in Chipiona, two in Trebujena and one in Chiclana.

In the early days vineyards were separated by crude hedges, as they often still are, and there were no buildings. The labourers had to travel from town every day. When the grapes were ripening, the growers put up rough and rickety shelters made of wooden poles and draped with esparto grass matting for protection from the sun. These were manned day and night by armed watchmen, and they are still seen in the remoter places. They are called *bienteveos*,

Total Areas (in Aranzadas) of Vineyards by Locality in 1990

	from 0 to 1	from 1 to 2	from 2 to 5	from 5 to 10	from 10 to 20	from 20 to 30	from 30 to 50	from 50 to 100	from more than 100	Total
Jerez	49.77	161.22	769.30	1,695.64	1,968.95	2,060.96	2,972.14	3,751.19	10,035.82	23,464.99
Puerto Sta Maria	29.68	52.87	198.93	311.62	509.58	371.65	537.58	596.25	286.39	2,894.65
Sanlucar	660.77	1,027.00	1,010.59	552.61	437.30	311.97	169.72	60.34	0.00	4,230.30
Chiclana	967.59	870.05	737.03	239.23	240.84	98.34	151.68	239.34	0.00	3,544.10
Chipiona	326.73	260.35	224.69	114.73	103.51	22.65	139.39	51.84	0.00	1,243.89
Lebrija	80.01	76.82	130.83	138.63	53.23	0.00	0.00	0.00	0.00	479.52
Puerto Real	106.39	104.83	150.54	50.66	83.11	66.00	153.29	267.87	1,319.71	2,302.40
Rota	95.55	147.44	187.40	144.28	133.59	49.46	82.98	0.00	0.00	840.70
Trebujena	625.57	446.61	356.80	133.12	81.23	99.55	0.00	0.00	0.00	1,742.88
Total	2,942.06	3,147.19	3,766.11	3,380.52	3,611.44	3,080.58	4,206.78	4,966.83	11,641.92	40,743.43

meaning, 'I can see you well'. The system is ages old; it dates back even to the time of Isaiah: 'My well-beloved hath a vineyard in a very fruitful hill: And he fenced it, and gathered out the stones thereof, and planted it with the choicest vine, and built a tower in the midst of it, and also made a winepress therein.' There is an old proverb in Jerez – '*Las niñas y las viñas difíciles son de guardar*'[1] – and it has been known for thieves to be shot and killed during the vintage. No one minds a man pausing by the roadside and helping himself to a bunch of grapes, but the growers get very cross when anyone tries to get away with a cartload. During the Middle Ages, they also had to wage continuous war against wild pigs and ferocious scavenger dogs that roamed the countryside.

At the beginning of the nineteenth century the countryside, which until then had been noted for its brigands, became safer, and the wealthier wine growers began to build large houses in the middle of their vineyards; they went to live in them during the vintage and sometimes spent part of the summer there. In each vineyard there was also a house for the foreman and a big pressing room. In the early years it was quite usual to have a bodega there, where the must was stored until it finished fermenting, but this idea was dropped, and the must was taken into the towns immediately after the grapes were pressed. In the last few years it has been revived again. The new houses were built in all styles of architecture, from the pseudo-Moorish castle of Viña Tula (described delightfully by Vizetelly as a 'costly whim') to the austere and humble buildings of the smaller vineyards. Several of them had one feature in common: a tower tall enough to give a view over the whole vineyard. Nearly all the early buildings have survived, and very charming they are.

It is a pity they were only occupied for a few weeks every year, but the Spaniards have always been city dwellers, and quite apart from that, it was still not safe to live in the vineyards. Until early in the twentieth century, any wealthy man who ventured there alone and unarmed ran the risk of being kidnapped. His captors would take him to a hideout in the Sierra and keep him imprisoned, quite courteously and with every comfort they could provide, until an enormous ransom was paid. While they treated their victims very well if there was any chance of getting the ransom, they had little compunction about killing them if it were not forthcoming. Rather

1 'Girls and vineyards are hard to guard.'

surprisingly, the countryside has only been completely free from bandits in fairly recent years, as there was a new generation of outlaws following the Spanish Civil War. Even now, when it is safe to live there, the houses in the vineyards are nearly all left empty, and one must admit they are not very convenient. In the winter they are unprotected and cold; in the summer there is not a trace of shade to mitigate the shimmering heat; and they are very isolated. Even so, a few of them are occupied during the summer.

At the beginning of the nineteenth century a wide variety of vines were grown in the vineyards around Jerez; perhaps there were a hundred species in all, and in 1868 Diego Parada y Barreto listed forty-two. For many years, however, the Palomino, Moscatel and Pedro Ximenez vines had been the acknowledged leaders, and growers were known to deny that there were others in their vine-yards, though any observant visitor could see them growing there. Scientific viticulture, with the abandonment of the less satisfactory varieties, was pioneered by Pedro Domecq and went ahead rapidly throughout the nineteenth century but, owing to the long life of the vines, the replanting could not be completed until after the phyl-loxera had wiped out the vineyards in the 1890s.

The classic sherry vine is the Palomino, said to take its name from one of Alfonso X's knights – Fernán Yáñez Palomino – from whom a well-known Jerez family, still active in the wine trade, claims descent. But there are in fact two Palominos, related but different. Historically the Jerez vineyards were planted with the Palomino de Jerez, now known as the Palomino Basto, which is still found growing in the older vineyards. It was mentioned in a document of 1483 and was described by Alonso de Herrera in 1513. By 1807 it already occupied 95 per cent of the vineyards near Sanlucar. It has now, however, been supplanted by the Palomino Fino, originally found growing in vineyards near Sanlucar. The latter is clearly the better of the two in the quality of the wine it provides and it gives a similar yield, flourishing particularly well on albariza soil. It is a sub-variety with different flowers and grapes, and is pollinated more easily. Also known as Listan, Horgazuela, Gencibel, Seminario, Xerez, Palomina, Temprana and Alban, its grapes are medium size, tasty and quite sweet, though by no means as good as table grapes; they are pale green in colour but ripen to a translucent golden ochre under the sun, and are generally ready for picking during the first three weeks in September.

Nowadays the sherry growers, like most wine growers, practise clonal selection, selecting the finest vines and propagating them. Of course this has led to a better yield, but (unlike, for instance, Burgundy) the yield has been incidental, the main object being to select healthy vines: a matter of consistency rather than quantity. Individual vines are examined to eliminate those with too high a yield and those with too low a yield. Apart from the two well established clones already mentioned, several others are recognized: Palomino Pelusón, Palomino Macho, Palomino Negro, Palomino Fino (clone 84) and Palomino Fino (clone Davis). The two latter were respectively the work of Fernández de Bobadilla and the University of Davis, California.

The experience of one grower, which was probably typical, was that the Basto gave five butts per aranzada, which cultivation with tractors increased to seven. His yield now, with the Palomino Fino and modern cultivation, is nine to ten butts. This is mainly thanks to the healthier vines and the improved cultivation, as the Palomino Fino appears to give a slightly lower yield when grown in the same conditions.

The main object of clonal selection is to eliminate disease, principally the various virus diseases. The most serious is that causing fanleaf (entre-nudo corto, court-noué), which has swept through the European vineyards and has been a particular nuisance in France. Others include those causing leafroll (enrollado, enroulement), stem pitting (la leña rizada, bois strié), fleck (jaspeado, marbrure) and corky bark (acouchado de la corteza). These diseases have been present for centuries. In 1807 Boutelou described a condition of the vine that is now thought to be court-noué – but they have only recently come to be studied scientifically. From the earliest days, even as far back as Columella – who wrote a treatise in vine-growing in the first century AD – the practice has been to select the healthiest and most vigorous plants, and this is now done systematically in a programme started in 1970. Healthy vines may be expected to give good wine, but if the yield is increased too much the concentration and hence the quality of the wine can be reduced, so that clones have to be studied very carefully before they can be accepted.

A recent direct comparison of the principal varieties in an experimental vineyard has yielded the following results:

	Kilograms per vine	degrees Beaumé of must
Palomino Davis	6.07	13.23
Palomino 84	5.85	11.32
Palomino Pelusón	5.77	11.65
Palomino de Jerez	5.33	11.48
Palomino Fino	4.59	11.81

The famous Pedro Ximenez vine is next in order of importance, though it does not do particularly well in the sherry vineyards and is very much on the decline. It is grown on the lower slopes of the albariza vineyards and produces medium-sized bunches of golden, transparent and intensely sweet grapes that ripen during the first half of September. It is particularly noted for making superb sweet wines, but it can also be used for preparing dry sherries of the highest quality, depending on the way the grapes are treated, though for this purpose it is less satisfactory than the Palomino. It is also harder to cultivate, more prone to disease and gives a lower yield, so it is now rarely planted and only forms a very small proportion of the whole, being much more common in Montilla-Moriles where it grows particularly well. It is likely to decline even more in the future as it has been found that excellent sweetening wine can be vinified from Palomino Fino grapes.

The Pedro Ximenez vine is the subject of legend. There is an old tradition that it originally grew in the Canary Isles and from thence it was somehow taken to the Rhine. Cuttings were brought from the Rhine to Spain by Peter Siemens, a soldier of Charles V, who came to Castilleja de la Cuesta to recuperate after waging war in Flanders. From Castilleja it was taken to Los Palacios and eventually reached Jerez, where it still bears the name of the soldier who brought it with him into Spain. However, there is no documentary evidence to support the story and one has doubts. It may appear strange that a vine which flourishes in Spain, and especially in the hot climate of Montilla-Moriles, would also grow in Germany; but vines are strange plants, adapting themselves to very varied conditions and changing subtly in the process. This helps to make ampelography an inexact science, faced with puzzles as hard to sort out as the racial origins of humanity. The identification of the Pedro Ximenez with the Verdelho of Madeira was once generally accepted but is not confirmed by modern research. H. Goethe, in his *Handbuch der Ampelographia* (Berlin, 1887) described the Pedro Ximenez as being grown only in Spain, and knew nothing of the legend, which appears to have originated in P. J. Sachs's *Ampelographia* (Leipzig, 1661). It has been quoted by nearly all subsequent writers, some of whom warmed to their subject and supplied fascinating details. It was even quoted by Roxas Clemente. But if the story were accepted in principle, the legend of the soldier of Charles V would have to be rejected, as Sachs claimed that the vine was imported in the thirteenth century and quoted as his reference the *Cosmographia* of Georgius Merula, written at the end of the fifteenth century. Sachs, moreover, made no mention of the Canary Isles, and it seems likely that the story really is a mixture of two entirely separate legends.

There has been a family named Jimenez in Andalusia from time immemorial, and a far more plausible theory, suggested by José de las Cuevas, is that the vine was named after a Don Pedro Jimenez who lived in Arcos during the eighteenth century and was a great wine grower, being particularly famous for his sweet wines. Unfortunately, however, this theory must also be rejected, as a vine mentioned in the seventeenth century could hardly have been named after a man who lived in the eighteenth. There appears to be no other source of information and the origin of the name remains obscure.

These vines account for by far the greatest part of the production, and these, together with the Moscatel, are the only varieties which may now be planted. When Palomino and Pedro Ximenez vines grow in the same vineyard, the difference in their appearance is striking, the former tending to spread horizontally while the latter grows upright. The remaining varieties are unimportant, but nevertheless they still exist in old vineyards and and are likely to for some years yet. The Cañocazo, or Mollar Blanco, combines to some extent the properties both of the Palomino and of the Pedro Ximenez; it is a useful compromise between the two, but is gradually falling into disuse, as it is hard to fertilize and there is a danger of the crop failing. It is also very easily attacked by mildew. The Albillo Castellano, or Calgalon, is also sometimes found on albariza soils; its grapes, which are sweet and juicy, ripen in the second half of September and give quite a good wine, but it is rather vulnerable to insects. It may well be identical with the vine that Columella referred to as *albuelis*. Columella was a practical wine grower born in Cadiz and anyone reading his *De Re Rustica* (*c.* AD 64) will see that wine growing has not changed all that much over two millennia.

All the above vines are also found in barro soil, together with the Moscatel Gordo Blanco, Mantuo Castellano, Perruno and Beba. The Moscatel is by far the most important of these, and is one of the few vines that can be identified with certainty in the writings of the ancients, including those of Pliny; its name is derived from the Latin *musca*, a fly, because flies are greatly attracted by its sweet grapes. It gives a good crop of large grapes with a very characteristic flavour, rather as if they contained honey instead of sugar; they ripen during the first half of September. The Moscatel is grown extensively, particularly around Chipiona, and provides a good sweet wine that is used, for the most part, for blending with drier wines to make rich sherries for export. The Mantuo Castellano ripens very late – often not until the end of October; it used to be quite popular and gives a passable wine on mediocre soil, but the grapes are apt to go rotten and the crop is far from safe. The Perruno is far less common now than it was at the beginning of the nineteenth century; it gives satisfactory wine and an excellent crop, but does not ripen until well into November, and is therefore very vulnerable to the weather. Both the Mantuo and the Perruno are also occasionally found growing on albariza soil. The Beba gives a rather dark and delicious grape that is, however, unsatisfactory for wine. It ripens in the second half of October and the first half of November, and the grapes are used for eating and for turning into raisins. They keep a long time and are often seen at Christmas hanging from the rafters of Andalusian peasants' houses. These are known as *uvas de cuelga* (hanging grapes), and one of them is eaten for luck with every stroke of the bell as midnight chimes on New Year's Eve.

Palomino and Beba vines are also grown on arena soils, together with Mollar Negro, which is of the same family as the Cañocazo, and Mantuo de Pila, otherwise known as Mantuo de Rey, or Gabriela. The Mantuo de Pila gives big grapes that do not ripen until late in November; they are used partly for wine and partly for eating.

Now that scientists are employed in making crosses, throughout the world there is a quest for new and improved grape varieties. In the sherry country one promising new variety has been created:

Corredera, which is a cross between Palomino Fino and Cardinal Number 4. However, it has not yet been planted commercially.

To compare the features of the principal vines, the following table has been prepared from figures published in *Variedades de Vid en Andalusia* by Alberto Garcia de Luján, Belén Puertas García and Miguel Benitez:

	Palomino Fino	Palomino de Jerez	Pedro Ximenez	Cañocazo	Moscatel
Budding	24 March	27 March	20 March	22 March	22 March
Flowering	20 May	24 May	21 May	25 May	24 May
Veraison (colouring)	19 July	27 July	23 July	10 July	20 July
Ripening	13 Sept	17 Sept	13 Sept	17 Sept	6 Sept
Yield (kilogram per vine)	5.08	5.47	3.31	2.74	2.25

Jerez enjoys the finest climate imaginable for growing vines: plenty of rain in winter and spring with hot, continuous sunshine throughout the summer to ripen the grapes. There is no such thing as a vintage year as the French know it; practically every vintage is good both in quality and quantity, though some years, of course, are better than others. Only very rarely does it fail completely. It failed in 1708 when the rainfall was so great that the streets of Jerez became mud and carts could not get through them; twenty years later it failed again when the summer was so hot that the grapes burnt and withered on the vines; in 1842 the vintage was very poor owing to frosts in the spring, and in 1844 it was reduced through excessive heat in July, which happened again in 1915; as recently as 1979 there was a long and heavy storm with severe hail during the vintage, which badly damaged a few vineyards and stopped the harvesting altogether for two or three days as the vineyards became too muddy to work in. In fact, very occasionally there is a calamity, but the trials and tribulations of the Jerez wine growers are nothing compared to those of almost any other area where wine is grown. Moreover, the diseases which attacked the vines from time to time until the end of the nineteenth century have been practically eliminated by modern methods of viticulture and pest control.

Vineyards are peaceful places, remote and undisturbed, but there is never any peace for the men who tend them; from the day the vines are planted to the day they are uprooted at the end of their useful lives, the vineyards are scenes of quiet, unending work. The wine grower can never have the pleasure of standing idle by his fields and watching his crops ripen; there is always something to be done. Even the hard life of a British farmer seems simple in comparison, and vineyard workers are amongst the most highly paid in Spain.

In general terms, the many labours of the vineyard are directed at loosening the ground to absorb the rainfall, killing weeds, grafting and pruning the vines so that they grow in the right way, removing suckers, and destroying harmful insects or fungoid parasites. First of all, the earth must be prepared to receive the young vines. This is done in late July or early August and the task is called the *agosta*. Weeds grow profusely at that time of the year and their roots often go a long way down, spreading out under the ground to break forth again at a distance. All the weeds have to be pulled out, and the soil is broken up and crumbled with an adze. The rest of the work is then done by the scorching August sun which desiccates any roots that are left. The earth is hard and the heat of the sun intense; the temperature often rises to over a hundred degrees in the shade, and there is often no shade to be found at all. The labour used to be herculean but nowadays only the most modest of the peasant growers have to face it, as all the larger vineyards are mechanized, and the agosta can be done more efficiently with a tractor. Caterpillar tractors are used as tyres do not give enough grip on the very slippery soil.

This assumes that the ground has never before been planted with vines. When old vines are grubbed out and the vineyard replanted, the ground needs to be disinfected and rested for a while. The principal trouble arises where the vines previously planted have been infected with viruses, such as those causing fanleaf. Although every effort is made to pull out all the old roots, some always get left behind and act as focuses for reinfection. It is necessary to wait for seven years for the vineyard to be clear. The viruses are transmitted by nematodes (threadworms), in particular Xiphinema. These can be destroyed by nematicides, which drastically cut down the length of the fallow period needed. The first year after the vines have been uprooted, the ground is planted with a cereal crop, usually barley. In the second year it is deep-ploughed and disinfected.

Then it is ready to be replanted. If it is not replanted within seven years the right to replant is lost.

In the following January, after the broken ground has been soaked by the first rains of winter, it is levelled off with a harrow. The soil is analysed to find the most suitable vine stock and is then manured and marked out ready for planting the new shoots at the end of the month. There are traditionally two alternative patterns for planting out a vineyard: *marco real* and *tresbolillo*. Both have advantages and disadvantages. The former is a pattern of squares, while the latter consists of equilateral triangles. The tresbolillo accommodates about 15 per cent more vines, while the marco real leaves more room for cultivation. The tresbolillo pattern, however, has the further advantage that it gives a uniform distance between adjacent vines and it is therefore generally used, though vineyards planted in fairly recent years have wider gaps between the rows than previously to allow for tilling by special tractors. This has now been carried a stage further. By about 1960 it became clear that vineyards would have to be cultivated mechanically, and the traditional method of planting was modified so that the vines are now closer together within the rows, but the rows are further apart. This gives 10 per cent less stocking, but yields are actually superior owing to the better cultivation of the land. In the marco real pattern, the distance between vines is approximately 1.57 metres, in the tresbolillo it is 2.10 metres, while in more modern plantings there are gaps of 1.1 to 1.15 metres between the vines in a row and 2.25 to 2.4 metres between rows. The maximum density of planting allowed by the regulations of the Consejo Regulador is 4,100 vines per hectare.

Nowadays all new vineyards are planted so that the vines can be cultivated up wires – *espalderas* – which stretch horizontally along the rows of vines. I first saw it in 1958 in an experimental vineyard of Gonzalez Byass. It was found to be so effective that it has now become almost universal, reducing work a lot and allowing for more mechanization, perhaps even eventually for mechanical harvesting.

In February comes the second main task, the *cavabien*, when the earth is hoed, though nowadays this is also done mechanically with tractors; this is repeated at the same time each year throughout the lives of the vines. It follows the heavy winter rains and is really the conclusion of the *deserpia*, which takes place in October and is the first big task after the vintage; it will be described later, as it is only done in the second and subsequent years.

The *Marco Real* or square system   The *Tresbolillo* or diagonal system
Patterns for planting vines

At the end of April and the beginning of May comes the *golpe lleno*, when the earth is broken up to a depth of about 18 centimetres to keep the weeds down. This is done every year and is a continuation of the cavabien.

The fourth main task takes place in July; it is called the *bina* and consists of another digging similar to the golpe lleno, but apart from killing weeds it protects the soil from the heat of the summer sun and frees the moisture that the vine must live on during the months of drought. The soil is broken up and settled several times until it becomes compact without being hard, as hardness would damage the plants. New shoots are also cut away to give strength to the roots. The bina is one of the most important tasks and has to be done very carefully.

In October, after the vintage has been gathered from the mature vines, a new year begins in the life of the vineyard. First there is the *repaso*, when all the vines are examined to see whether any have failed. The proportion to be replaced may be as many as 15 per cent, particularly in the first year or two. After that, the routine starts again with the *deserpia*, when a pit about a metre square is dug to a depth of 15 to 20 centimetres with the vine in the middle and a ridge of earth on every side so that the vine is boxed in. This catches the rain and diverts it to the point where it does the most good. A light rainfall at this time is considered advantageous. On the other hand, when the rainfall has been excessive, channels have to be made in the lower parts of the hills to take away the waters and prevent soil erosion. This is called *alomado*.

In December and January there is the annual task of the *desbraga*, when any unnecessary shoots are cut off, together with the superficial roots that grow within 15 centimetres of the ground. Immediately this has been done, vines that have failed or died are replaced and work in the vineyard then goes on much as before until August, when there comes a task that is unique to the second year: the *injerta*, or grafting. Ever since the great plague of the phylloxera in the last century, the ground has been permeated by those destructive aphids, and it is still quite impossible to grow the old-style vines. American vines, however, are resistant to the phylloxera, though the wine produced from their grapes is very inferior. To get the best of both worlds, American stocks (*riparia*) – or, more frequently, hybrid stocks bred by crossing American with native vines – are planted and when they are established the native vines are grafted on to them. A great deal of work has been done in the Instituto Nacional de Investigaciones Agrarias (INAO) of Jerez and in the Estación de Viticultura y Enología de Xerez (EVEX) on establishing the best stocks compatible with a soil that is so high in calcium. In albariza soils the demands on the root stocks are particularly high. The most commonly used stock is 13–5 Evex, which dates from 1940, and which is a descendant of Berlandieri Resseguir No. 2. Other prominent stocks include 13–1, 13–44, 41B, 161–49 and 333EM (Escuela Montpelier) together with some use of Berlandieri – X Colombard 1 and 19–62. In lower and damper soils 99–R may be used.

One of the problems has been to get root stocks that are virus free, and Gonzalez Byass have established their own 83ha nurseries to produce them. In 1975 they got in touch with the University of California at Davis, which co-operated in research and provided indicator vines that are very sensitive to viruses. One, for example, is Cabernet Sauvignon, which responds rapidly to the leaf-roll virus. The indicator vine is planted in a pot and the vine to be tested is grafted on to the top of it. There are only three nurseries in Spain producing virus-free stocks.

The grafts are made at ground level, and are protected by heaping earth up around the plants. Big growers, however, now use bench grafting, planting cuttings that are already grafted in nurseries. The graft is very carefully made and is covered with molten wax containing a healing hormone and a fungicide.

Undoubtedly when grafted vines were introduced into some districts the quality of the wine may have suffered; one hears this particularly of claret and port. On the other hand, this does not appear to be true in Jerez. The results depend on a great many different factors, and it is clearly wrong to suppose that grafted vines are necessarily inferior, or that what is true of one district will be true of another. There is one particularly attractive style of sherry called *palo cortado*, which will be described in Chapter 9, and which has been more difficult to prepare since the phylloxera, but that is the exception: the general opinion of sherry shippers who lived through the critical years was that wines from the grafted vines are slightly better.

If the first grafts do not succeed, the vines are grafted again in the period between December and February; this is known as *injerta de yema*, but it is never as satisfactory as the first grafting. For one thing, the graft is higher up, and there is more trouble from suckers coming out lower down.

Rain is welcomed during the winter months as it soaks the soil and prepares it for the hot, dry summer. In March, when the vines begin to grow leaves, a heavy rainfall is essential for an abundant harvest; but afterwards, the less rain the better.

In February comes the *abonado*, when the ground is manured. The traditional method of manuring was to use only horse dung and to empty a spadeful into a hole between every four vines, doing it in rotation so that each vine benefited from fertilizer once every three years. There was a legend that a good taster could tell the difference in the wine when cow dung had been used. Nowadays there are fewer animals, particularly horses, so compost and peat are used and there is also an increasing use of mineral fertilizers. In the interests of mechanization, the fertilizer is laid in a ditch dug between alternate rows of vines or in a hole dug with an attachment carried by the plough. Usually a quarter of the vineyard is manured each year. A master at my preparatory school, who was a keen amateur botanist, told me that a dead cat was incomparably the best manure for vines, but I have not been able to find any confirmation for this dictum, while according to Conrad Heresbachius the best manure is 'pisse, old stale urine'. With that I would emphatically disagree. Sir Hugh Platt, in his *Garden of Eden*, rather alarmingly prescribes two quarts of ox-blood with a 'hatful' of pigeon dung.

This is followed in April by the *castra*, when the vines are lightly pruned and tied up. During the next three months of every year, following the golpe lleno, the vines are sprayed to prevent mildew and similar diseases caused by fungoid parasites; this is done about once a fortnight in small vineyards, or more often if it rains (as humidity encourages harmful fungi). It used to be done by workers who carried petrol-driven pumps on their backs. In the 1960s helicopters were used to speed things up, but although quick they were not thorough; by the 1980s the vineyards had become fully mechanized and tractor-driven sprayers were found to do the job better. An advantage of helicopters was that they could be used when the vineyard workers were on strike, which happened quite often at that time. One of them crashed in a Gonzalez Byass vineyard after hitting a well head. The pilot was uninjured but required an instant glass of sherry.

Speed is extremely valuable in particularly dangerous weather conditions: when there has been a day of heavy rain in summer, followed by hot sunshine, for instance. Otherwise, one half of the vineyard could be attacked while the other half was being treated. The traditional solution used for spraying was called Bordeaux Mixture and consisted of copper sulphate and slaked lime dissolved in water, beginning with two kilograms of each per hundred litres of water for the first two sprayings and increasing the strength by 50 per cent for the remainder. Nowadays, however, it is more usual to use one of the proprietary spraying mixtures, such as Cuprosan. The vines used also to be fumigated with finely divided sulphur to prevent a disease called oidium, but nowadays a systemic fungicide is used instead.

The blossom comes in May and grapes appear early in June. With any luck, a vine may yield a small crop in its third year and should give a useful one in its fourth. During all this time, the work described above is repeated month by month, but there is an additional task that calls for a different approach every year, and that is the most important of all: the *poda*, or pruning. If this were done badly, the life of the vine would be futile and short. The traditional method of pruning Palomino vines, which is virtually unique to the sherry vineyards, is called *de vara y pulgar*. The *vara*, or stick, is left with seven or eight 'eyes', or knots, which produce the year's grapes, while the *pulgar*, or thumb, is a small shoot waiting to become the vara of the following year. But this arrangement takes some time to achieve. In the third and fourth years the stem is generally cut off to a height of 30 to 40 centimetres from the ground, leaving only one knot above the stock, although it may be pruned further back to encourage growth if the vine looks weak. In the fifth year the upper shoot is cut off, leaving two shoots growing from the stock. In the sixth year these shoots are pruned so that one is left with several knots and the other is cut off to leave only two knots. In the seventh or eighth year, when the vine is strong enough, it is left with four shoots, which are then pruned alternately, so that one is always available to bear fruit while the other three are kept short to wait their turn. The number of 'eyes' left on the vara influences the style of wine produced; if the grower wants wines with plenty of body, he prunes the vines well back, but if he wants light and delicate wines, he leaves a longer vara, particularly in the vineyards producing manzanilla sherry in Sanlucar. The usual figure is ten buds on the vara and one or two on the pulgar. After very dry years the vines are pruned back to give them strength and to help them recover; the yield is then smaller but the life of the vines is prolonged.

In selecting the shoots to leave, the foreman must distinguish between the dry side of a vine and the green side. The dry side becomes dry because the pruning knots interfere with the flow of sap, so the new shoots are taken from the green side. Since the new shoots are always taken from the same side, it follows that after a number of years the vine assumes a corkscrew shape, which helps to account for the gnarled, grim and twisted appearance of old vines when they are bare of leaves and fruit in the winter.

After pruning, the ends of the shoots are painted with a 30 per cent solution of iron sulphate to prevent invasion by insects and fungi. One of the reasons for pruning in a way that keeps the grapes close to the ground is the old belief that they would benefit from the reflected heat of the soil by night, though it is doubtful whether this really matters in the hot Andalusian climate. There has recently been quite a lot of experiment with pruning, stimulated by the modern practice of cultivating the vines on wires and by the possibility of mechanical harvesting. Pruning systems used in other major vineyards have been tried, such as Guyot and cordon, but none has been adopted. A widespread practice, however, has been to increase the height from 30 to 60 centimetres. This results in a slightly lower yield and a slight increase in alcoholic degree, but also a slight decrease in acidity. The vines are easier to work and the bunches of grapes are cleaner – as they do not touch the ground – and more easily harvested, possibly in the future by machinery. Another form of traditional pruning which may become more widespread is to leave four buds on the thumb, which gives small increases in yield and alcohol but slightly less acid.

When the vines are mature and heavy with fruit, there is, in traditional vineyards, yet another job to be done: the *levantar varas*. From June onwards, the fragile branches have to be propped up with wooden sticks to keep them horizontal, so that the grapes do not go rotten through lying on the ground. In October, the sticks have to be gathered in again, and this is called the *recogida*. The whole of this labour is, however, extremely tedious and expensive because it takes so long, and the method of support is not particularly satisfactory – the sticks can easily fall over, especially in a strong wind. With the increasing shortage of labour, it has sometimes been impossible to do. To avoid it entirely, the vines are now trained along wires. As the vines grow – and the method of pruning leads to a compact growth – not much support is required. The wires are thus relatively flimsy compared with some of the structures that are needed elsewhere, but they provide all the necessary support and have rendered the levantar varas obsolete. They enable another task to be done much more speedily and easily, too. Two wires are arranged close to the top of the structure and these can be raised by machinery late in the season so that the leaves are swept upwards to expose the ripening grapes fully to the sun. Previously some of the leaves were cut off in a summer pruning; this had the disadvantage of increasing acidity; although this can actually be an advantage when growing grapes for table wine.

That is an outline of the work, but it is nothing more than an outline: there is no end to the labour. Cultivation of the earth to control weeds goes on throughout the spring and early summer, but it stops on 20 July and is strictly forbidden during August, as cultivation during this period increases the yield but at the cost of quality. At the end of the fourth year of planting, the owner has to apply for a formal declaration that his vineyard is entitled to be classified as Jerez Superior. It is then inspected by the officials of the Consejo Regulador to check that it has been properly planted – that the density of planting is not too high, for instance. The pruning must also be right. If it does not qualify, then it is simply classified as Zona and the grapes are worth much less. If authorized varieties are not used, or if the density is too great, it is not even classified as

Zona and the grapes cannot be used for sherry at all. So far, however, no grower has been so foolish as to fall into this trap.

A newly accepted vineyard is, however, by no means ready to produce good wine. Any wine produced in the first year is used for distillation, that of the second and third years for making mistela sweetening wines, that of the fourth year (a small crop) for cheap sherries, and then serious production begins in the fifth year. But few would find the quality acceptable until the vines are at least five years old and Gonzalez Byass, for instance, will not use any wine for their brands that comes from vines less than eight years old.

Throughout the blazing heat of summer and the torrential rain of early spring the vineyards must continue to be tended, and the return is very small in relation to the capital and work involved. When the vintage is poor, the landowners lose money; when it is good, they make only a small profit. It has always been the same, though it is now worse than ever, owing to the phylloxera, as the grafted vines need replanting much sooner than the old ones. The economics of viticulture are very complicated, but as far back as 1886 the vineyard owners had to pass a resolution to raise the price of their grapes; they also started using manure and what they termed 'terrible machines' in order to scrape a living. Mercifully, neither the manure nor the elementary mechanization did any harm to the wine. Bankruptcy was staved off for a few years, but when the phylloxera came many were ruined. It is only thanks to the increasing use of machinery that the cost of cultivation is still bearable.

Nowadays all the work in a vineyard of any size is done by machinery, but the quest for machinery began many years ago. In May 1884 a steam plough made by John Fowler & Co. of Leeds specially for use in vineyards was tried in Chiclana, but it never caught on. It was only after the Second World War that suitable machinery became readily available.

The traditional method of cultivating a vineyard is obviously extremely labour intensive. Much of it is directed to eliminating weeds, which compete with the vines for minerals and water, provide focuses for fungi and homes for harmful insects. They would completely take over a vineyard if left to their own devices. Some, like bindweed, thistle, couch grass, mallows and trefoil, are perennial; others, like hedge mustard and sow-thistle, are annual. The most objectionable is bindweed, which can spread all over a vine and envelop the bunches of grapes. All of these can now be controlled by herbicides, but bindweed requires the use of several. It is usual to use pre-emergent herbicides in October, after the vintage, to inhibit the growth of autumn weeds; but these need to be used with care to prevent a toxic accumulation in the soil. Some weeds, such as the beautiful but awful bindweed, call for systemic herbicides, absorbing them through their leaves, but care has to be taken to prevent these from getting on to the leaves of the vines. Specific herbicides are used in the spring and summer. Weedkillers are generally used in conjunction with the traditional methods of cultivation.

An extreme solution is to eliminate cultivation altogether: the method of *no cultivo* or *no labreo*. Cultivation has advantages: it loosens the soil to allow rainfall to penetrate during the rainy season and then further cultivation in the summer eliminates cracks in the surface of the ground and so conserves water. It also works to increase the nitrogen in the soil and makes manuring easy. On the other hand, mechanical cultivation has disadvantages. The tractors compact the soil, especially if it is damp; a relatively deep working destroys the higher roots which grow in the richest level of the soil; the machinery can injure the vines, sometimes actully killing them, while lighter injuries make entry points for infection. Following the path of *no cultivo* greatly reduces the labour required but increases the expenditure on herbicides and on fuel. The economics are not altogether straightforward. So far this technique has only been used experimentally but results over fifteen years have shown little difference in yield and a cost saving of 19 per cent. There has been less soil erosion but manuring is more difficult; surface fertilizers are being used, but if these are not sufficient the long-term fertility of the soil may be harmed. On the whole it is thought that non-cultivated vineyards look less healthy and the cautious have perceived degeneration after six or seven years. So far no differences have been reported in the quality of the wine. It is early years yet but this is a development to watch closely. It could be of real value in other vineyard areas where the terrain makes cultivation difficult. It is quite possible that experiment will lead to a compromise, some tasks being done and others omitted. It has been suggested, for example, that the deserpia should be done (it can be done mechanically) and the vineyard then left to itself. Or it could be followed by one ploughing in the spring to avoid the cracks which appear in the hollowed-out areas.

Another technique being experimented with is aleopathy: keeping down weeds by cultivating their parasites.

Traditionally a good albariza vineyard was reckoned to yield eight butts of must per aranzada. The yield has now gone up to about nine butts per aranzada. There is no single reason for this increase; nor indeed is it a particularly dramatic one. Vineyards throughout the world are yielding larger crops than they used to; and so, for that matter, are cornfields. So it is as well to put this into perspective, because wine-lovers are very apt to panic at any wind of change. One of the reasons for this improvement is clonal selection of vines; but this is effected largely to select strains that are more resistant to disease, particularly the virus diseases, and the potential yield when healthy is of secondary importance. The increase in yield through the absence of disease is far more significant and this is brought about not only by selecting the vines for new vineyards but also by careful viticulture in all the vineyards, sure diagnosis and effective treatment. Fertilization also plays a part but a very marginal one indeed. By far the most significant change lies in much more regular cultivation to eliminate weeds – cultivation that is made much easier in vineyards planted in such a way that tractors can easily pass between the rows. But there is a limit to what any vine, however healthy, can give; and the increased yield has brought with it a decrease in strength, so that musts which developed 12 to 12.5 degrees of alcohol are now producing a degree less. Knowledge that this was happening made me extremely suspicious and I have tasted young añada wines whenever I have had the chance (which has been quite often) over the years to see if I could see any lowering of quality. I could not. If anything the reverse was true. Alcohol is only one aspect of the wine, and one that can quite easily be corrected by the way in which sherry is elaborated. What matter most are flavour and balance. These are not lacking at all and the modern wines seem, if anything, to have more finesse.

Throughout the year, the vines are watched carefully for disease, which may break out at any moment, particularly when the weather has been damp or sunless. Diseases are of four types and may be caused by deficiencies in the soil, fungus growths, insects or viruses.

There is only one disease in the first category: chlorosis. This is usually caused by an excess of calcium in the soil, which makes the leaves turn yellow and wither, but it is very rare in the sherry area despite the nature of the soil. When leaves go yellow in the spring it is not necessarily anything to worry about. It rarely persists if the right root stock is used, but if it does it can be cured by injecting iron chelates into the soil or by painting them on to the leaves of the vine.

Any condition affecting the leaves of the vine is inevitably serious: the sugar which eventually accumulates in the berries is first formed in the leaves; the plant breathes through them; they protect the grapes against sunburn; and evaporation of water from the leaves cools the vine at the height of summer.

There are only two diseases of any importance caused by fungi: oidium (*Uncinula necator*, *Uncinula americana* or *Uncinula spiralis*, formerly known as *Oidium tuckeri*); and mildew (*Plasmopara viticola*, formerly called *Peronospora viticola*). These, however, are very serious indeed unless spotted and checked at once. Oidium is indigenous to North America, and was first observed in Europe by one Tucker, who found it in a hothouse at Margate in 1845. A London gardener named Kyle found the remedy a year later. The vineyards at Chiclana were attacked in 1852, and the disease spread rapidly, reaching Jerez in 1855; it was not fully checked until 1858, and there was not another good vintage until 1861. In the meantime, the yield of the sherry vineyards was drastically reduced, and the French vineyards were devastated at much the same time. The old-established shippers sold less wine at higher prices, but there were upstarts of no integrity who were only too willing to satisfy the demand by importing inferior, though not dissimilar, wines from other parts of Andalusia.

When a vine is attacked, the first symptom of oidium is a dark stain on the stem, and it is known locally as *cenizo*, or ash, owing to a fine ash-like powder that covers the grapes soon afterwards, turning them sour and rotten. The fungus requires a minimum temperature of about 10°C and generally starts growing in damp weather, so it is likely to appear after rain at any time between the flowering of the vine and the vintage, though strong and well-pruned vines are less susceptible to attack than others. Spraying helps to keep it under control, but the only real remedy, as discovered by Kyle, is powdered sulphur.

Mildew grows under similar conditions, though it fails to germinate if the temperature approaches 37°C. When it attacks vines, white stains like icing sugar appear, often at the edges of the leaves, and gradually spread inwards. It also affects the grapes; when it infects young fruit it is known as 'grey rot', but when it attacks fruit that is almost ripe a different colour is produced and it is known as 'brown rot'. Unfortunately there is no sign of infection until it has taken a firm hold of the grapes, and by that time it is incurable. It is very rare today, though, as it is prevented by spraying with some such spray as Cuprosan or with the old Bordeaux Mixture during the dangerous summer months, or by the use of a systemic fungicide, which also can be sprayed on. Unfortunately, just as bacteria develop resistance to antibiotics, fungi can develop resistance to fungicides, and new fungicides have to be developed.

Many insects are found on vines, and most of them are harmless, but a considerable number can cause disease, of which the twelve most notable are: *sámago, pajuela, pulgón, Pseudococcus vinis, Polychrosis botrana, Sparganothis pilleriana, Eriophyes vitis, mosquito verde, Cryptoblabes gnidiella, Iobesia botrana, Tetranychus urticae*, and worst of all phylloxera. Palomino grapes are thin skinned and are therefore easily attacked.

Sámago causes the stem of the vine to become spongy; it stops bearing fruit and eventually dies. This disease was recorded several times during the last century but apparently only when the vine was replanted on tired soil which had not been given time to recover after the old vines had been uprooted. Pajuela is caused by a tiny insect that weaves its nest round the petals of the vine, gnaws the tender shoots and destroys young branches. Both these insect diseases, and also pulgón, have been eliminated by careful viticulture and insecticide sprays. But until spraying became universal during the nineteenth century, pulgón was a very serious menace, and it was the scourge of wine growers during the sixteenth and seventeenth centuries. In 1566 the people of Beaune petitioned the curé of Autun to excommunicate the pest, and in the chapter meeting of 10 April 1603, in Jerez, a prominent landowner, Don Diego Caballero de los Olivos, who was tired of waging war against a noxious yellow-green coleoptera, again clamoured for its excommunication, saying there was a learned and godly friar called Francisco de Porras who had successfully excommunicated it elsewhere and was prepared to do so again. Whether or not the anathema of the Church worked as a deterrent is not recorded, but everyone faced ruin, and the mayor ordered a procession of the whole town to the convent of Our Lady of Mercy. The scientists of that time scorned the remedies of religion

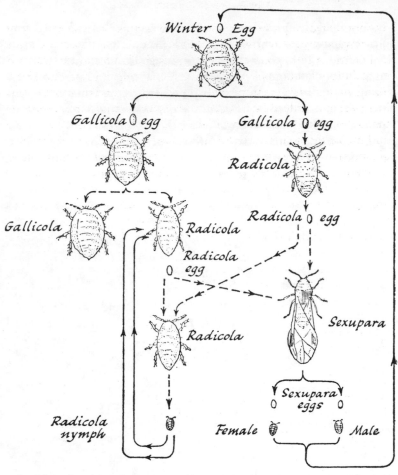

The life cycle of the Phylloxera on the American vine Vitis spp. On vinifera
the insects over-winter as resting radicolae.

(following Vidal-Barraquer Marfâ and Cañizo)

and ordered the vines to be painted with the blood of a bull. Pulgón
was last recorded in Jerez in 1867.

Pulgón, or *cuquillo*, is a species of coleoptera known to entomol-
ogists as *Haltica lythri* Aubé, sub-species *ampelophaga*. These oval,
yellow-green insects, measuring about four millimetres long by two
millimetres wide, used to appear in early spring after spending the
winter concealed beneath the bark of the root of the vine, or in the
crevices of brickwork, or in any similar sheltered hiding place. By

the summer their eggs had hatched out and a vast swarm of tiny yellow grubs attacked the vines, eating the leaves and the tender shoots. They lived on the leaves and bred at a prodigious rate. Every vine had to be examined and the infected leaves burnt, but that was never more than a partial remedy. It was a terrible plague, and even after it was exterminated the vines took two or three years to recover.

Pseudococcus in its variety of *vinis* is a comparative newcomer amongst the pests. Its origin is unknown, but it is completely at home in the Mediterranean climate and was first observed attacking fruit trees. It is a dirty-yellow insect about four millimetres long and has a white, woolly protection that makes it difficult to destroy. The only successful insecticide is a mineral oil emulsion used in conjunction with a high-pressure direct spray. Like the pulgón, this insect also hibernates beneath the bark of the vine, and its spread is prevented by scraping the vine in December, when it is exposed and dies of the cold.

Polychrosis botrana, known as eudemis, is a moth of the tortricidae family, known in English as the grape berry moth, whose larvae attack the grapes. *Sparganothis pilleriana* is a moth of the same family whose caterpillars, known in English as the vine pyramid caterpillar, attack young shoots and sometimes grapes. Both have been a considerable nuisance of late and are kept under control by the use of insecticides. *Eriophyes vitis*, or *acaro de yema*, known in English as the bud mite, attacks the buds and aborts the flowering, causing a condition known as erinosis. It is a serious problem and one that has to be lived with as the mite is hard to kill.

The latest insect nuisance to appear is the *mosquito verde* (green mosquito) which was unknown until about 1970 and which first became a nuisance in the cotton fields. Each year sees the arrival of a new pest and a new insecticide. The problem has been to maintain the balance of nature: insecticides can kill off the predators of some insects, leaving the situation worse then before. Insects, too, become immune to insecticides. Finding the right time to apply insecticides also poses a problem. One technique is to put pots of diluted molasses in the vineyards to catch the insects and to prepare a graph of infestation which enables the critical moment to be predicted. This method has now largely been superseded by the use of hormones as the attractive force. Insecticides having a long persistence are best but the choice is limited as some can taint the wine and none is used within twenty days of the vintage.

Of all the plagues, by far the worst was phylloxera, not only in Jerez but in every wine-growing district of any note throughout the world. In 1863 Westwood found it in hothouses at Hammersmith and there is a detailed description in the 1871 edition of Thomson's *Practical Treatise on the Grape Vine*, quoting an article by M. J. E. Planchon in the *Comptes-Rendus de l'Institut* of 1868. Pasteur claimed that it originated in vines imported from America owing to their high resistance to the previous plague of oidium. It spread rapidly through the great vineyards of France. By 1863 it had already reached Spain; by 1875 it had ravaged the vineyards of Malaga; and on 21 July 1894 it was found in Jerez, carried there on the clothes of itinerant vineyard labourers from Malaga. In the following years, one great vineyard after another was laid waste and by 1898 most of them were irreparably damaged. The last Spanish vineyards to be attacked were those at Cuenca, in 1918. The old prosperity vanished; the smaller growers were bankrupt; even the iron-nailed, cowhide pressing boots were pawned. Mercifully French experience had already shown the remedy and the larger Spanish growers had long been prepared for battle. All the old vines were uprooted and replaced with American stocks. But those were the most troubled years Jerez has known within recent memory.

The plague of the phylloxera is caused by an aphid known as *Viteus vitifolii, Aphis phylloxera, Phylloxera vastatrix, Pemphigus vitifolii, Xerampelus vitifolii, Peritimbia visitana* – or simply as the 'vine louse'. It was first described in the USA by Dr Asa Fitch in his *Noxious Insects of New York* (1856), and subsequently by a number of modern authorities, the most valuable recent accounts being those of Professor José Ma. Vidal-Barraquer Marfa, Professor Pierre Muillet, and George Ordish in his complete book on the subject, *The Great Wine Blight*.

It is yellow-brown in colour and horrible to look at through a magnifying glass, but it cannot be seen very clearly otherwise as it is only a half to one millimetre long. Its life cycle is extremely complicated and varies according to the conditions under which it lives, but it breeds and multiplies at a prodigious rate. The female lays a single egg in the stem of the vine during the autumn; this hatches out in the spring to give a fundatrix, which may lay anything up to thirty eggs. These in turn hatch out and multiply, so that it has been estimated that one fundatrix born in April could give rise to twenty or thirty million insects by November.

The *Phylloxera vastatrix* exists in five different forms, each occurring at a separate point in the life cycle. The winter egg is laid under the bark of the vine and hatches in the spring to give a phylloxera of the *gallicola* form. The winter egg, however, has never been found in vinifera shoots, where the creature over-winters as a *radicola*. The *gallicola* lives on the vine leaves, on which it forms galls. It is self-fertilizing and lays eggs which produce larvae of two kinds; one half become gallicolae and continue to live on the leaves, while the other half pass down into the roots as *radicolae*. This form also multiplies indefinitely by parthenogenesis and can hibernate as nymphs during the winter, but some of its larvae hatch out to give a third form of phylloxera: *sexuparae*. These have wings and fly to the higher parts of the vines where they lay eggs of two kinds, the larger hatching out as females and the smaller as males. The two then mate and the female lays a single large over-wintering egg which hatches during the following spring to give a fundatrix, thus completing the life cycle.

Gallicolae are rarely seen on European or grafted vines, and for that reason the full cycle of the phylloxera is seldom completed. On the other hand, the radicolae can perpetuate themselves indefinitely, causing debility, and ultimately the death of such vines as are vulnerable to them. They produce lesions which result in abnormal growth of the part attacked and also allow other parasites to get in, such as fungi and bacteria. Eventually the whole of the root beneath the lesion is separated from the remainder of the vine and dies.

The gallicolae, if they should appear, are relatively harmless, though they cause some damage through feeding on the sap.

When phylloxera attacks a vine, for the first year or two there is no sign at all of its existence; if anything the yield increases slightly. The debility is only noticed after the phylloxera has got a firm hold of the vine. This may happen in two or three years, or it can take as many as eight. Then the damage begins to take effect: the tendrils are less well-developed, the shoots are thin and short, and bunches of grapes are small. Even so, the contrast is not great, but the phylloxera has taken hold and the vine is doomed. The next year, the same symptoms are seen, but they are more marked. By the following year the vine is clearly drying up and preparing to die.

Phylloxerae travel from vine to vine through the ground or over its surface, particularly when helped by wind or rain; the sexuparae, in particular, can be blown to quite distant vineyards. They can also be spread by vineyard tools, machinery and clothing. Although many attempts have been made to exterminate them, none has been successful. The most drastic and dramatic remedy was to flood the vineyards during the winter, but this could only be done in suitable geographical areas and was quite out of the question in Jerez. Viala proposed a remedy involving human urine, but this proved worse than the phylloxera. Eloy Martinez attempted to electrocute the pests, but his experiments were equally futile. Fumigation of the roots and soil with carbon disulphide, organic acids and arsenic compounds has been tried with limited success, but it has been found impossible to control phylloxera on a large scale. The problem has been to find some form of soil insecticide that does not cause more mischief than it cures, by leaving undesirable residues in the vine. Moreover, it is doubtful whether any systemic insecticide (which is absorbed into the plant sap to attack the pest from within) could operate successfully against phylloxera, as the parasite produces galls which deaden the plant tissues and reduce sap flow just where it would be required. In fact there is no known remedy, and the only solution is to pull up all the vines and replant with American stocks that resist attack. This, however, does not cure the plague, but merely renders it innocuous.

A healthy vine grown to bear fruit for eating can undoubtedly live for several hundred years. Pliny wrote of vines 600 years old; and in the patio of a school in Jerez that was formerly part of the Rivero bodegas, there was until the middle of this century a Beba vine said to be over 300 years old; its trunk was 43 centimetres wide and it was 3 metres high. The doors of Ravenna Cathedral are made of wood from a giant vine, and vines planted at Santa Barbara by the first Californian settlers grew to have a base circumference of 2.5 metres; in 1895 one of them yielded nine tons of fruit. There were certainly vines over a hundred years old at Sanlucar until the time of the phylloxera, and the great Black Hamburg at Hampton Court, which was planted in 1768, is still giving a full yield of fruit. In fact, if carefully tended, a vine goes on almost for ever and old vines give excellent wines, although the yield drops and eventually becomes uneconomic. Before the phylloxera, the useful life of vines in the sherry area varied between fifty and eighty years, and they

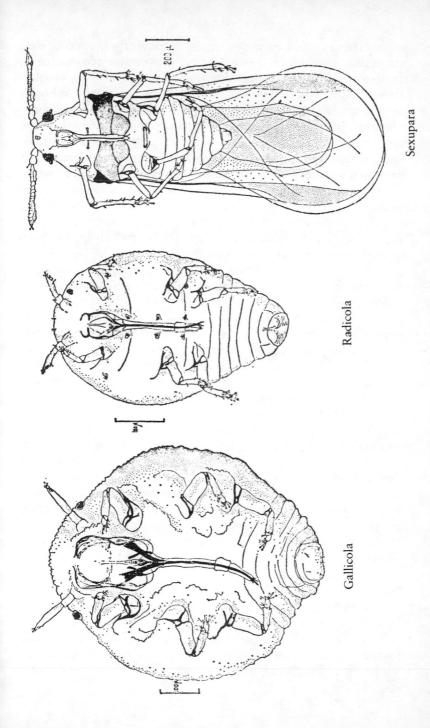

Gallicola

Radicola

Sexupara

SHERRY

never gave first-class wine until they were twenty or twenty-five
years old; but the grafted vines have really productive lives of only
twenty-five to thirty years, though some growers do not uproot the
vines until they are as much as forty-five years old, giving a much
reduced yield of top-quality must. To offset this a little they give up
to 20 per cent more must,[1] and produce good wine when they are
only five years old. However, now there is over-production and
some shippers do not find it worth while to replant. For instance,
Javier Hidalgo has vines that are eighty years old.

Many vineyards are owned by shippers, who gain on the round-
abouts what they lose on the swings, but some of the large vineyards
are still controlled by landowners, who sell their produce by any of
three methods: *compra de uvas, a la piquera* or *al deslio*. The first
method, as a rule, is used by small growers, who sell their grapes as
fruit delivered to the buyer's press-house. In the second method, the
shipper buys the must as soon as it is prepared and gambles on its
quality, trusting that the grower will not water it down, though
some growers deliberately add a little water to must pressed from
grapes that are very over-ripe; he may also gamble on the quantity
and buy the whole output of a vineyard early in the year, though
this method is less usual. In the third, he buys the must when it has
been racked off the lees (see page 190) after fermentation has ceased.
The more important shippers generally buy what they need by a
combination of the latter two methods.

When the grapes are first formed, they are small, hard and acid.
Chemically, they consist of tannin, chlorophyll, malic acid and
tartaric acid, with the merest trace of glucose; in fact at this time
there is often more sugar in the leaves than in the fruit. As the berry
grows, it draws nourishment from the roots and leaves of the vine,
and gradually eliminates the chlorophyll and starch; it then becomes
soft and is the centre of many chemical reactions, most of which are
brought about by photosynthesis. Pectin and sugars accumulate
while the acids are gradually eliminated: the first sugar to appear is
dextrose, and then laevulose, while practically all the tartaric acid is
converted into cream of tartar, and the malic acid is mostly destroyed
by oxidation, though some of it reacts with bases derived from the

1 Must, derived from the Latin *mustum*, is the name given to fresh grape juice; it is
retained in Jerez for longer than in most other wine districts, and the fermented
juice is not referred to as wine until it has been racked off the lees, some six months
after the vintage. The Spanish is *mosto*.

156

soil. If it should rain for a few days while the grapes are nearly ripe, the sugar content stops rising and may even fall slightly, while the acids decrease substantially during the rain, then increase, and then begin to fall again. Eventually the berries grow to their full size and receive nothing more from the leaves, but the process of oxidation continues until they are ripe, when the fruit consists essentially of sugar (in the form of both laevulose and dextrose) and tartaric acid, with vitally important traces of other organic compounds. There are also live yeasts, especially on the skin. It is these additional compounds that give each type of grape its characteristic flavour and it is the yeasts in the 'bloom' of the grapes that start the fermentation when the fruit is crushed.

The Jerez wine growers, like all others, have their legends and omens for telling whether the vintage will be good. For instance, there is a crested bird that has a taste for small lizards and mole crickets, and rejoices in the name 'hoopoe'.[1] If it sings before the vine buds, it is supposed to be a sure sign of a good vintage.

The vintage is hard work, but it is good fun as well. I remember how it was in 1956. The ragged labourers sat talking together and eating their gazpacho; many of them were gypsies, and suddenly the *gitanos* started singing and dancing flamenco in the patios. It was all so natural: that was the beauty of it. Lovely, lithe gypsy girls in hand-worked shawls turned and twirled in their dances just for the fun of it while newly picked grapes lay outside, covered with esparto grass to protect them from the morning dew. The gypsies have nothing to worry them, but the grower lives in suspense. Once the grapes are ripe for picking, it does not matter if the weather is hot or cold, but there is one danger: rain. Continuous rain during the vintage can be disastrous. The must from rain-sodden grapes is feeble in strength and dreadful in quality; it is often only fit for the still. A short, sharp storm, on the other hand, does not matter much.

In most wine growing districts of Spain the vintage begins on the feast of St Matthew, 21 September; in Jerez the official day is 8 September, the feast of the Nativity of Our Lady. But nature is a bad timekeeper. Sometimes, when the weather has been very sunny and dry, the first grapes are picked a little earlier. More often the

---

1 Between 1865 and 1875 Sandeman had an 86-ton ship called *Hoopoe* to carry their wines to England.

vintage is a week late, which seems very Spanish. Once it has begun, it lasts about a month.

The vintage is carefully timed. If the grapes are picked before they are ripe, the wine will be weak and will probably be acid. Moreover, when the grapes are fully ripe, the pips are separated more easily from the stamens and the pulp from the skin. If they are picked too late, the grapes shrivel, giving a reduced yield, and the must lacks natural acidity; and every day of delay increases the danger of damage from rain. Sometimes, when wet weather is prophesied, the vintage is hurried on and the grapes are picked before they are quite ready, but it is generally considered better to wait for the rain to stop and let the sun dry them while they are still on the vines. Vines of different species, of course, ripen at different times, and vines of the same species often ripen at different times in different parts of the same vineyard, depending on the aspect of the slope on which they are grown. In the old days, the grower used to taste the grapes to see whether they were ripe, and he chose the date of the vintage according to his skill and judgement. The next development was to crush one or two bunches in a small wooden press and test the specific gravity of the juice with a hydrometer, or to use an instrument to check the refractive index. Both methods give remarkably accurate indications of sweetness and hence of ripeness. Instruments designed for this specific purpose are known as glucometers. Nowadays, though, a large grower will normally rely on laboratory analysis rather than vineyard tests.

The grapes are picked for the most part by men, though some growers also employ women. They work throughout the day, cutting the bunches from the vines with clasp knives and filling wooden carriers (*tinetas*) or cane baskets (*canastas*) that hold about thirty pounds of fruit. These are fitted with shoulder straps, but when they are full, the harvesters carry them on their heads, which somehow looks '*muy tipico*'.

Labour, though, is getting increasingly expensive and hard to get. When I was staying in a vineyard in 1970 the pickers went on strike for higher wages and there seemed, for a while, doubt whether the vintage would happen at all. One old rogue with a twinkle in his eye, who employed only women, thought he was safe, but he was not: they came out too. Happily a settlement was reached, but only just in time and the pickers got most of what they wanted. But now that they are very well paid for their work, perversely the gaiety seems to have been sapped away. The spontaneous flamenco which I have described and which I saw often when I was living in Jerez in 1956 was conspicuously absent in 1970, and I would not expect to see it again save in the small, family-run vineyards. And as the price of labour rises, those who employ it have inevitably to try and find ways of either using less, or to quote the modern catch-phrase, improving productivity.

In 1979 experiments began with grape-harvesting machinery developed in California. The modern method of planting vines would enable such machinery to be used and no doubt one day it will be. It is already commonplace in the classic wine growing areas of France. But the sherry growers are conservatives and still have doubts as to whether the machines will affect quality, particularly of finos. But quite apart from that the sherry district has two quite different snags of its own. The first is the combination of the weather and the nature of the soil. There is very often a short heavy storm at vintage time, which does no harm but which makes the albariza soil very slippery indeed, so that control of the machines becomes very difficult. The second is the labour situation. Spain is a country of strong trade unions and of very high unemployment, so the introduction of machinery is being strongly resisted. The Luddites live on. But the new plantings lend themselves to mechanical harvesting and no doubt it will come, especially bearing in mind that harvesting accounts for about 30 per cent of vineyard costs.

Right through the 1960s a visitor from the nineteenth century, or a good deal earlier, coming through time to the vintage would have seen little to wonder at. But since then the sherry growers have moved into a new technological age. In remote vineyards, or for publicity, perhaps, pressing by foot may be seen; but in the course of a decade it became obsolete and practically disappeared. This is recent history, though, and without an appreciation of the past it is difficult to understand the present.

After the grapes have been picked, rotten fruit is thrown away and the larger stalks are removed; traditionally, the grapes were then put on esparto grass mats on the *almijar* (a piece of open ground in front of the press-house) to dry in the sun. This process, known as *soleo*, reduced the amount of moisture and hence increased the proportion of sugar, though the actual quantity of sugar was very slightly reduced; it also lessened the amount of malic acid and tannin to some extent. Sunning the grapes was a very old

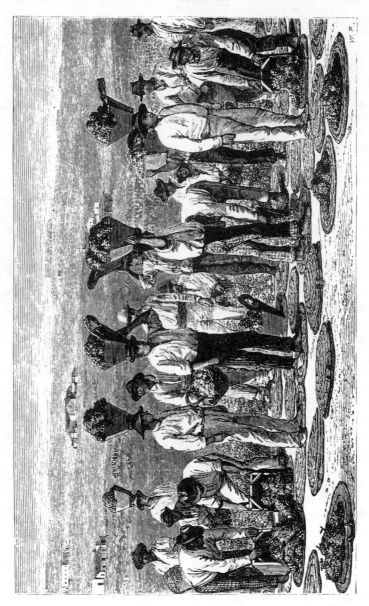

Villagers arriving with grapes at a nineteenth-century almijar
(from *Facts about Sherry* by Henry Vizetelly, London, 1876)

practice and no one knows quite when it began, but it was certainly used by all the sherry growers at the beginning of the nineteenth century. It probably dated back to the beginning of Spanish viticulture and originated in classical Greece, where it was described by Hesiod in the eighth century BC in his *Works and Days*:

> *. . . when Orion and the Dog Star move*
> *Into the mid-sky and Arcturus sees*
> *The rosy-fingered Dawn, then Perses, pluck*
> *The clustered grapes, and bring your harvest home.*
> *Expose them to the sun ten days and nights*
> *Then shadow them for five, and on the sixth*
> *Pour into jars glad Dionysus' gift*

How long the grapes were left in the sun depended partly on the weather and partly on the type of wine that was required. Palomino grapes, for making dry sherry, were left out for twelve to twenty-four hours; if a grower wished to make a high proportion of light fino wines, he would sun his grapes for a shorter time or not at all; but Pedro Ximenez and Moscatel grapes, used for making sweet wines, were sunned for anything from ten days to three weeks, until they looked rather like raisins and contained a very high proportion of sugar. At night they were covered with esparto grass mats to protect them from the dew, and they were brought in as soon as possible if there was any sign of rain, as they should be completely dry when they are pressed. Some vineyards were equipped with protective awnings that could be drawn across cane frameworks.

Such labour-intensive work is now no longer possible, though, and it is rare indeed to see any sunning except when sweet wines are being made. To some extent this is offset by the increasing practice of training on wires, which results in greater ripening, and by careful timing of the vintage by use of the glucometer, so that it tends to start now a week or more later than it used to. But this is perhaps one of the reasons why the musts tend to be weaker now than they were twenty years ago, though not all that much, and weakness is to be avoided for purely economic reasons: the alcohol of fermentation is not taxed but the alcohol of fortification is. Sunning is still, however, used when making sweet wines; and as this is more important in Jerez than it used to be, following the ban on sweet wines other than Pedro Ximenez being brought in from elsewhere, some work has been done to find the best way. Grapes were experimentally dried on corrugated asbestos but this was found unsatisfactory. The best way found so far is to have a long strip of esparto grass which is covered with a sheet of transparent plastic if bad weather is predicted. A free flow of air around the grapes has been found to be essential.

The traditional method of pressing was unique and delightful to watch; since it can still sometimes be seen, I shall describe it in the present tense. When the grapes are ready for pressing, they are carried indoors and put in a *lagar*, or wine press. This is a wooden trough some five metres square and 0.6 metres deep. It stands on trestles that raise it half a metre off the ground and is slightly tilted so that the juice runs towards the outlet. It holds enough grapes to make a butt of must – about 1,500 pounds – and it could hold more, but some room has to be left to prevent the juice from overflowing. There used to be a row of these lagars – perhaps half a dozen or more – in the press-house at each of the large vineyards. The grapes from each vineyard are thus pressed separately, though two varieties of grape grown in the same vineyard may occasionally be pressed in the same lagar; this applies particularly to Pedro Ximenez and Cañocazo grapes, which are sometimes deliberately mixed. In districts farmed by small growers, on the other hand, such as the areas around Chipiona and Sanlucar, the grapes are brought in great panniers on the backs of donkeys to central pressing stations in the towns. These are owned by shippers, merchants or co-operatives, and grapes from various vineyards are often mixed to produce a uniform quality of must.

Four labourers, known as *pisadores*, work in each lagar. They are dressed in short trousers and are not barefoot, as in the Douro, but wear special cowhide boots, or *zapatos de pisar*, whose soles are heavily nailed with large-headed tacks driven into the leather at an acute angle. This method of nailing is very important and gives results similar to bare feet but with far less discomfort. The pips and stalks are trapped undamaged between the nails and a soft layer of grapeskins forms over the soles so that the hard pips and stalks of the other grapes cannot be broken. The weight of a man is just right for the work.

The pips and stalks must be left intact for two reasons. In the first place they contain a lot of tannin which gives a harsh flavour to white wine, although a certain amount is essential if the wine is to be clear and bright, and enough is normally obtained without

Treading the grapes in the nineteenth century
(from the *Illustrated London News*, 14 October 1876)

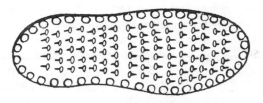

Sole of pressing boot showing nails

difficulty. To make sure, the must is analysed and tannin is added when necessary, though it seldom is. If there is only a very slight excess of tannin, it is used up as the wine matures and is not important. But the stalks and particularly the pips also contain strongly flavoured essential oils which can never be got rid of and, for this reason rather than for any other, they must not be crushed.

The pressing begins in the middle of the night and finishes at about noon the following day, so that the labourers can rest during the hottest hours. Working at night, they are also less troubled by wasps, which find freshly crushed grapes almost as attractive as jam. Quite apart from comfort, pressing the grapes in the cool hours delays the start and speed of fermentation, which is a great advantage, as it should be kept slow if a first-class wine is to be made.

Before treading is started, the grapes are sprinkled with three to four and a half pounds of gypsum, or *yeso*, for 1,500 pounds of grapes. This harmless practice considerably improves the quality of the must, but it was strongly and ignorantly attacked during the nineteenth century and its use will be explained at length later.

Unlike the merry labourers of the Douro, the pisadores are solemn and dignified people. They mark time slowly throughout the night becoming bespattered with juice and wading in a frothy, green-brown, muddy-looking liquid pulp of half-crushed grapes, juice and stalks, which scrapes and irritates their legs until their skin gets hardened after a day or two's work. They march solemnly from side to side of the lagar, pressing first one half of the grapes and then the other, while they support themselves with their right hands on short wooden spades; hardly a word passes between them; only occasionally do they sing. The must looks most uninviting and smells even worse than it looks; it gives no hint of the glory to follow as it flows steadily from the lagar and is filtered first by an open-mesh basket to take out the larger foreign bodies, such as stalks, and then through a sieve to get rid of the skins and pips, on its way to the waiting cask.

The grapes are pressed by foot until they form a pulp, which is then stacked up around a 2-metre-high steel screw that is fixed permanently in the centre of the lagar. While this is being done, the larger stalks are removed and a little more plaster is added. The pulp is tapped into place with wooden spades, forming a cylinder with the screw in the middle; this is known as the *pie*, and it has to be very even in shape if the second pressing is to be a success. It is wrapped round tightly with a strong band of plaited esparto grass, 12 centimetres wide and 24 metres long, both ends of which are fastened to wooden blocks. One block is attached to the lagar at the bottom of the pie; the other, at the top of the pie, dovetails with a further piece of wood to fit round the screw, the pair being known as *marranos* or hogs. These are separated by a metal washer from the big nut which rotates on the screw; this nut is called the *marrana*, or sow, on account of the grunting noise it makes when it is turned. It is fixed to a massive steel handle, about 2 metres long from end to end. As this is turned, the pie is compressed and juice squeezes out through the mesh of the esparto grass band and through the orifice formed by the wooden block at the bottom.

The screw turns quite easily at first, and it is light work for two men, called *tiradores*. It gets harder and harder, though, and after a few turns it has to be worked by four tiradores, two on either end of the handle. When the screw is about half-way down it gets so stiff that it cannot be turned continuously, and they press it round in jerks; they even have to tie their hands to the handle, as every muscle is tensed for work and they would probably break a bone or rupture themselves if they slipped and lost their support. Any irregularity in the shape of the pie at this stage produces strong lateral forces on the esparto grass band, and the whole flimsy structure shatters, fragments of pulp flying all over the place.

The must produced by the first pie is known as *de yema* (the bud) and is of first-class quality. It is combined with the foot pressing, and together they account for about 85 per cent of the total.

After the first pie the residue is broken up with the wooden spades and as many more of the stalks are removed as possible, often by riddling. A second pie is then built up. In the olden days, the must from this pressing was mixed with water to dilute the tannin and acid, and it is still known as the *aguapie*, although the dilution process has not been used for years. The aguapie is of inferior quality and only accounts for about 5 per cent of the total.

In the smaller vineyards there is sometimes a third pie pressing, known as *espirraque*, but in the larger vineyards the second pie is followed by a hydraulic pressing, known as the *prensa*. The residues from the second pie are shovelled into shallow esparto grass baskets which are placed one on top of another between the fixed and moving platforms of the press. Most of the presses are primitive machines made in the nineteenth century: water is driven into a cylinder by means of a hand pump and the cylinder contains a tight-fitting piston that forces together the two platforms of the press. As triumphs of engineering, the ancient presses may lack finesse, but they work very well – so well, in fact, that the marc which comes out of them looks completely dry and is blown about like chaff in the wind. It is generally used as fertilizer, but occasionally as pig food. The wine obtained from the prensa is very inferior indeed and only fit for rinsing casks, distilling for alcohol or turning into vinegar. During the last century some fermenting grape residues are said to have been distilled without having been pressed at all, but this process is no longer used. In France it is used principally with the marc from black grapes, and was probably abandoned in Jerez when black grapes ceased being grown there.

That is the traditional way of pressing the grapes, but nowadays practically every vineyard uses mechanical methods. The quest for the perfect press to replace the human foot has been going on from time immemorial. A simple mechanical wine press was illustrated as early as the Third Dynasty in Egypt, but it seems that it was only approved for making the poorer qualities of wine. The lagar is exactly like the Egyptian foot presses, and the esparto grass pie had a predecessor in the bag press, known in Egypt 3000 BC. Pliny, who died in the catastrophe of AD 79 at Pompeii, described four presses. In the Madrid wine exhibition of 1877 Lorenzo Bernal y Ponce, of Jerez, exhibited a press worked by horses, but it was never heard of again. The real urge to mechanization came with the growing technology of the nineteenth century, and the machines illustrated in Thudichum's *Treatise on Wines* (1894) are practically the same as some of those that were still used during the 1960s.

One of these, formerly known as Lomeni's Crusher, consists of two elongated gear wheels, about a metre long, with their axes so far apart that the teeth never completely mesh. The grapes fall down a shoot, pass between the wheels, and come out the other end looking just like the grapes that have been trodden by foot. From there they generally pass into a rotating sieve that removes the stalks. After the sieve, the residue is put into vertical cylinders 0.75 metres in diameter and 1.5 metres high, made of wooden staves bound round with iron hoops; there is a small gap between adjacent staves big enough to let the juice out but small enough to keep the skins behind. They look just like a row of pulpits and are, in fact, known in Spanish as *pulpitos*. Similar machines are often seen in France. The grapes are crushed by a wooden platform, and gypsum is added just as before. After the pulpitos, the residues are passed to the hydraulic presses.

When mechanization was started, at round about the turn of the century, some growers used all these machines and others, such as the Domecqs, in their great vineyard at Macharnudo, passed the grapes from the stalking machine, or mill-hopper, into lagars, where the subsequent pressing was done by the traditional pie method. Perhaps this compromise was the most sensible of all, as the lengthy and arduous foot pressing was avoided with no danger to the wine.

There are many pitfalls and dangers when mechanical presses are used. The first vital precaution is to reduce contact with iron parts to an absolute minimum, and some growers rub all metal fittings with rags soaked in paraffin, leaving a tenacious film that does not come off and mix with the must, while more modern machines are made of chemically inactive metals, such as stainless steel, that are not attacked by the acids in the fruit. There are many other difficulties; for instance a lagar contains 1,500 pounds of grapes, but the cement tank that feeds a mechanical press may contain as many as 66,000. Those at the bottom are crushed by the weight of those on top, and fermentation often starts prematurely at the bottom, where there is practically no oxygen. This results in a very poor must. The old method had the further advantage that the must was prepared one cask at a time and it was possible to keep a close check on that produced by different parts of the vineyard.

What I have described above was picturesque, but now it is almost entirely historical. The old ways may still be used by an occasional small grower making wine for himself. The commercial growers of necessity have moved into a new age.

Until the 1960s the treading was done in the vineyards; but some growers were better at it than were others. The must was then delivered to the shippers. Then the shippers began to see the advantage of doing their own pressing under careful supervision and in the best conditions. Some still kept to the vineyards and built modern press houses there, for instance the Harvey/Barbadillo Gibalbin. Most, however, moved their pressing into the towns and huge plants were constructed in Jerez by Gonzalez Byass, Domecq, Croft and Sandeman. The grapes are delivered in awe-inspiring quantities from the vineyards in plastic boxes, each containing 13 to 15 kilograms, by relays of enormous lorries. How different from the days of the bullock cart! The shippers use different coloured plastic to avoid confusion and also perhaps to advertise the great scale on which they operate. The move from the vineyards to the great press-houses has been painful for the traditionalists; but it has worked.

By the 1960s, and only just in time, in view of the steadily mounting cost of labour, the deficiencies of the mechanical press were overcome. Modern stalking machines work on a centrifugal principle which does the work very quickly and efficiently. An additional process used, for instance, in Domecq's and Gonzalez Byass's great press-houses, is to break the grapes under very low pressure by passing them between rubber rollers spaced about one centimetre apart. A substantial amount of must is released at this stage before the grapes reach the press. From these machines the grape pulp is passed to one or other form of horizontal press. The simpler form consists of a stainless steel cylinder, perforated to allow the must to run out, in which a piston is gradually moved by means of a screw thread to crush the grapes at a carefully controlled pressure. This form of press, known as the Vaslin press, has proved satisfactory in the sherry district as it has throughout the table wine districts of Europe. Even the most conservative growers agree that the results are in no way inferior to those given by foot pressing. There is a more sophisticated machine, however, which some consider gives marginally better results: the German pneumatic press, known as the Willmes press. This consists of a horizontal stainless-steel cylinder in the centre of which is a strong rubber bag. The cylinder is filled with grapes and then the bag is blown up by air pressure, squeezing the grapes against the side. The pressure is then released and the cylinder is rotated rapidly, which rearranges the fruit so that a further pressing can be performed. This process is repeated several times, until no juice is left, and the soft, resilient nature of the rubber bag prevents any pips or remaining stalks from being accidentally crushed.

As an indication of the sheer scale of the operation, Gonzalez Byass, in their enormous press-house at Las Copas, process 1.5 million kilograms of grapes a day, working two shifts. They use both Willmes and Vaslin presses but prefer the former for their best wines, and they monitor the pressure of each in a central office. The duration of each pressing is timed with a device like an egg-timer. The aim is to get the maximum extraction with the minimum pressure and as quickly as possible to avoid oxidation. The best technique appears to be to use several very light pressings. The residues are then passed down to a high-pressure continuous hydraulic press. With either kind of press there can be separate pressings without removing the grapes from the press but using successively higher pressures; the must from the heavier pressing is kept apart as it will produce inferior wine. A very important advantage provided by the new presses is sheer speed, which reduces oxidation and the risk of contamination. In Gonzalez Byass's press-house at Las Copas the work is carried out in three storeys: at the top, the presses produce the yema; one storey down the aguapie is pressed; then the pomace is taken by conveyor to the lowest storey for final processing. These devices have proved completely satisfac-tory, but one precaution has to be meticulously observed: absolute cleanliness. The new methods are so easy that in the early days of their use one or two growers went cheerfully ahead regardless, and the result, in one instance, was disaster. The must became infected with practically every known disease and half of it was worthless. But the lesson has now been learnt, and the musts produced today by these methods are of the very highest quality.

In the 1970s at Gibalbin, Harveys pioneered a new concept in pressing. The principal designer was Diego Ferguson. Although he was born a Jerezano and worked all his life in the Mackenzie bodegas which Harveys bought, he is anything but a hide-bound traditionalist, and before designing the new plant he went to study wine-making in South Africa and Australia, where a great deal of valuable experimental work has been done. He found there that the horizontal presses were regarded as obsolescent and that pressing was carried out by a continuous process which he brought to Jerez, though modifying the machines to a design of his own, aimed at giving the highest possible quality. The grapes are first put into a pre-dejuicer, which is effectively a tank in which the juice is extracted by the weight of the grapes alone. About 70 per cent comes out at this stage. The process, however, is continuous and this is its principal difference from what has gone before. The grapes are moved by screws through inclined, perforated, stainless-steel tubes, the screws turning slowly to avoid crushing the grapes. At first there is no pressure at all. This free-run juice is best and is known as super yema. Then the pressure is gradually increased by adjusting counter-pressure in the latter stages of the machine. Juice is extracted in several stages depending on the pressure applied. It is interesting to note that the must extracted at higher pressures has more colour as more is extracted from the grape skins. After the final stage the grape residue is no more than damp. It is sold for the production of alcohol, as is the must from the heavier stages of pressing. The must is passed into a large tank where the solids can settle and are taken out from the bottom by a screw and passed to a crusher. The must for fermentation from the tank is then centrifuged and passed through stainless-steel pipes to stainless-steel fermentation tanks of 200, 400 and 800 butts capacity, the must prepared at different pressures being separated. Refrigerated water is passed down the outside of the tanks and the temperature is carefully controlled by means of a thermostat. Plants of a similar kind are now used by Crofts and by Sandeman. In the Sandeman plant 50 to 55 per cent of the juice is extracted in a mill without any pressure at all. Then there are two stages at a pressure of 20 kg/cm^2, producing a total of 15 per cent for second quality wine, followed by a third stage at a similar pressure which produces a further 15 per cent for third quality wine. Finally there is a high-pressure stage at 18/100 kg/cm^2, producing 20 to 25 per cent for distillation.

A modern press-house, with its controls, expensive centrifuges and so on, represents a very substantial capital investment, and if it is to be economic, full use has to be made of it. Even now it is worthwhile to have a small press-house in a substantial vineyard, especially if it is in a rather remote place. The modern tendency, however, is to build giant press-houses, either in the vineyards or on the edge of the town. These operate continuously at vintage time, pressing the grapes from one vineyard after another, which makes very good sense, as there is a substantial variation in the time the grapes reach full ripeness from place to place. There are the disadvantages, though, that far more transport is required, owing to the greater bulk of the grapes as compared with the must, and land used for this purpose in the towns costs more; on the other hand, the pressing can be supervised far more closely and conducted under less hot conditions. The grapes are brought in by the lorry-load, usually in palletized plastic boxes, filled at the vineyard with about eighteen kilograms of grapes. Tipper lorries with an appropriate installation can also be used.

The first light pressings, whatever method is used, yield about 72.5 litres of must per 100 kilograms of grapes. This is used for making sherry. Subsequent pressings provide wine for distillation.

From the very earliest days, *yeso*, or plaster, has been sprinkled over the grapes before they are pressed. It was mentioned by Pliny as an African practice; it was discussed in the Cortes of Castile in 1570; generation after generation of Spanish and French wine-growers used it; Walter Charleton knew all about it in 1692; all acknowledged its value. The earliest clear reference to it I have come across in English occurs in *Pasquil's Palinodia* (1634), in a passage where the jocular author is discussing all the indignities suffered by 'that true good-fellow, Sherry Sack':

> *And lest all these base wrongs should not provoke him,*
> *With* Yesso *they him Purge, with Lime they choak him.*

It has been said that Shakespeare condemned it:

> FALSTAFF: Give me a cup of sack, rogue. – Is there no virtue extant? . . . You rogue, here's lime in this sack too.

But it is doubtful whether Shakespeare was referring to yeso. At that time, and for some centuries afterwards, vintners and taverners reduced the acidity of badly made wines, or wines that were turning into vinegar, by adding lime. Charleton described exactly how it was done, but he was not at all enthusiastic:

> To correct Rankness, Eagerness and pricking of Sacks and other sweet Wines, they take 20 or 30 of the whitest Limestones, and slack them in a Gallon of the Wine; and then they add more Wine, and stir them together in a half-tubb, with a Parelling staff; next they pour this mixture into the Hogshead, and having again used the Parelling Instrument, leave the wine to settle, and then rack it. This wine I should guess to be no ill drink for gross Bodies and Rheumatick Brains; but hurtful to good fellows of hot and dry constitutions and meagre habits.

In the middle of the nineteenth-century sherry boom, alas, a bunch of very odd doctors came to hear of it (see Chapter 5). The age of scientific medicine had only just been born, but the brilliant light of discovery had so blinded the doctors that they could no longer see the great wasteland of their own ignorance. They were not used to scientific reasoning and many of their dicta were founded on inadequate knowledge unsupported by experiment. Their opinions on almost every aspect of dietetics, for instance, were absurd. In fact the arguments they used to condemn yeso would sound hilariously funny today if the laughter were not damped down by the knowledge of the disaster that their campaign brought to the sherry country. There was, of course, as there usually is on such occasions, some element of truth in their attack, for it is undeniable that some of the less reputable wine growers used more yeso in those days than is thought proper today. But used moderately, there is no vice in it at all, and first-class sherries can seldom be made without it. Early writers have suggested that the quality of wine was found to be improved when it was matured in alabaster or marble vessels, but that does not sound very probable. When the *Lancet* commissioner visited Jerez in 1898 to investigate sherry-making, he put forward a new theory: the soil around Jerez is rich in chalk, and when the wind blows soil is scattered and adheres to the ripe fruit. Perhaps the growers noticed the fruit covered with soil made better wine, and chalky albariza soil could, in fact, be used in place of gypsum with much the same effect, but it is clearly wiser to use the mineral, which is obtained locally and consists of almost pure calcium sulphate.

Not very much is used: at most four and a half pounds for 1,500 pounds of grapes when the vintage is poor, and three pounds when it is good – just one-tenth of the amount reported by Thudichum. The account given by D. J. Portillo in 1839 suggests that even smaller quantities were used in those days, and it would be interesting to know how Thudichum obtained his figures. To refute the charges, the wine growers asked Don Francisco Revueltas Carrillo y Montel, an eminent Spanish doctor who was a native of Jerez, to carry out an investigation. He discovered that the most terrible compound produced by plastering is potassium sulphate; even when taken in large doses it is only a very mild laxative, comparable with Epsom salts, and there is so little in a bottle of sherry that it could not even have that effect. Both he and the *Lancet* commissioner were unanimous in giving the principal chemical reaction as:

$$2KHC_4H_4O_6 \ + \ CaSO_4 \ \rightarrow \ K_2SO_4 \ + \ Ca_4H_4O_6 \ + \ C_4H_6O_6$$

cream of tartar	+	plaster	→	potassium sulphate	+	calcium tartrate	+	tartaric acid

All this means is that the potassium hydrogen tartrate (or cream of tartar) in the must is converted into a harmless salt and two important organic compounds: calcium tartrate and tartaric acid. The former is insoluble and falls into the lees of the wine, helping the clarification, while the latter augments the acidity of the must and helps fermentation. In fact growers in some wine districts have for years been adding pure tartaric acid to the must as a matter of course, instead of using plaster, and this is now being done by some of the growers in Jerez. Even without the use of plaster there is less cream of tartar in the fermented wine than in the must from which it is derived, as the solubility is less when alcohol is present, and the tartrate is precipitated in the lees. For this reason, wine is inevitably less acid than the must from which it is derived.

Carried away by their apparent abhorrence of potassium sulphate, two enthusiastic scientists, Dr A. H. Hassall (who had made a reputation for himself by detecting by microscopy the adulteration of foods) and O. Hehner, both of whom were resident in the Isle of Wight, evolved a method of eliminating this noxious substance from wine and applied for letters patent, which were granted in 1875. Their process was to add a calculated quantity of finely powdered barium tartrate, after which 'the wine is agitated'; a few days later they separated barium sulphate by decantation, leaving potassium tartrate in solution. According to the inventors this improved the flavour, but unfortunately barium tartrate is a highly poisonous substance and, as a miscalculation could result in an agonizing death. I have never been moved to attempt the experiment.[1] The barium sulphate would be an amusing by-product: it could be administered as a barium meal.

Further work has recently been done on the subject by José Ma. Quiros Carrasco and by José R. Garcia de Angulo. They show that the total effect produced by yeso is somewhat more complex than suggested by the simple formula given above: it increases the acidity of the must, which improves fermentation; it increases the total acidity of the wine, which preserves it and helps it to mature; it reduces the amount of cream of tartar present, which can cause the wine to go muddy by precipitation if its limit of solubility is passed; it reduces the phosphoric acid content and so helps to avoid the disease of *casse blanca*; it assists the formation of volatile organic compounds which give the wine its fine aroma; it augments the natural defences of the wine against hostile micro-organisms; and it has a purely physical effect in making the pie easier to construct. In addition or alternatively some growers, as has been mentioned, add tartaric acid if analysis shows that the must is too low in acid. They aim for a pH of about 3.3.

It has now, however, been discovered that it is not necessary to use yeso at all. The essence of its use was to correct the acidity of must produced from very ripe grapes that were further ripened by sunning. With modern equipment the ripeness can be assessed more

---

1 Should anyone be brave enough to try it, the antidote is atropine.

accurately than in the past, and if the grapes are picked early enough the must has the right balance of acid and needs no correction. Thus Harveys and Sandeman, for example, use no yeso.

It has already been mentioned that clonal selection and improved cultivation considerably increased the yield of the vineyards in the 1970s. The yield of must was further increased by the new pressing methods which extracted a higher proportion of the available juice from the grapes. These factors alone would no doubt have resulted in a lowering of the concentration and consequent alcoholic degree of the musts, but there is the further influence of the abandonment of sunning. The combined result of all these things is that musts nowadays are about a degree weaker than they used to be, though extensive tasting sessions have persuaded me that the mature wines (which grow in strength as they mature) are as good as ever. The typical strength of a newly fermented wine would be 11°–12°. Another factor that has played a part in this is that the average age of the vineyards is lower than before owing to expansion and replanting.

The maximum yield allowable per hectare is 80 hectolitres for Jerez Superior and 100 hectolitres for the rest, though from 1991 these are being reduced to meet an over-production crisis. The Consejo Regulador has a representative permanently by each press to check the amount of must made. In some years of immensely high yield, a grower may apply for his extra yield to be classified and when this happens a decision is made about an individual vineyard, taking into consideration the yield in the area as a whole. Usually these applications come from small, peasant growers who have cultivated their plots intensively. If over-production is found, however, the whole output of the vineyard is condemned and may not be used for sherry.

That is the end of the scene in the vineyard; the vintage is over, all is at peace again and the wine growers start a new year of work. The must is stored in the bodegas of the three sherry towns, where the horrible smell of fermentation greets the visitor wherever he walks. The must is the life blood of the bodegas; it is continually examined and checked, as everything depends on it. But that part of the story belongs to the next chapter.

8

The Young Wine

The newly pressed must is sweet, unpleasant and greenish brown. It registers from 10 to 15 degrees Baumé (see Appendix III) of sugar, is viscous, and is slightly denser than water. At this stage it still contains quite substantial amounts of solid matter. The must now goes through the process of *desfangado* – literally, demudding. This can be done in a centrifuge or by letting it rest in a tank for a day before passing it on for fermentation. It allows any earth, pips, bits of skin and so forth to sink to the bottom so that the clear must can be drawn off.

During the first half of the nineteenth century it was quite usual for growers to store the must in their vineyard buildings for the first few months, until fermentation was more or less complete. Then the growers had an alternative idea. During the second half of the nineteenth century the must was impregnated with the fumes of burnt sulphur by means of a most extraordinary machine; this process delayed fermentation for a few hours and gave time for the casks to be brought into Jerez on donkey and bullock carts. Those primitive carts led by dignified, ragged Andalusian peasants, rattling through the streets with the new vintage, were a sight for poets, and they occasionally used to be seen until quite recently. The old sulphuring machines were not a success, though. The fumes gave rise to a number of sulphur compounds including sulphuretted hydrogen, and the fermenting must smelt of rotten eggs; in fact the preservative did more mischief than the sun. Today the onset of fermentation is delayed by using a carefully controlled quantity of sulphur dioxide solution. This is used even when there is no question of moving the casks, as it discourages the rather feeble 'wild yeasts' and enables the 'wine yeasts' to control the fermentation from the very beginning. When grapes are pressed in vineyards with no press-house, it gives a respite for the casks to be taken to the fermentation bodegas in the towns on lorries. It seems a pity that the old carts have been abandoned, but the lorries are undeniably better.

In the past must used sometimes to be fermented in *tinajas* – great earthenware, or more recently, concrete pots, and these are still occasionally found, for instance in Sanlucar. They are also the standard practice in Montilla, where they make the fermentation bodegas look like stage sets for Ali Baba and the Forty Thieves. But they were never widely used in the sherry country, where traditionally must has always been fermented in new oak casks. It is a perfect arrangement, as the must seasons the casks and makes them fit for storing old wines, and they, in turn, feed the must with wood tannin and essential oils that help fermentation and improve the wine. For this purpose it is essential to use good oak. Other woods, such as chestnut and cherry, have been tried, but without success. If the wine is to develop naturally, the casks must be clean and free from bacteria, and only new ones are really reliable. When the staves are shaped in the cooperage they are raised to a high temperature and all the potentially harmful bacteria are destroyed; the casks are then used before they have time to become reinfected. (On one occasion, when old casks that had previously stored a high quality amontillado sherry were used for the vintage, the whole of it was ruined.) The wine gradually permeates the wood and impregnates it with natural colouring and flavour. It is possible to see this quite clearly when a stave from an old cask is cut through. At the same time it leaches out tannin and other compounds from the wood. Wine that is left too long in an immature cask tastes 'woody', and this was always a danger when wine was exported in new casks or casks of unusual size. Before a bodega butt is considered mature enough to use in a fino solera, it should preferably have been used for ten years to avoid any taint of woodiness and to prevent too much tannin leaching into the wine. Old casks are much more expensive than new ones, and when a friend of mine wanted 120 it took him three years to accumulate them. Casks that have been used for shipping wine from Spain to Great Britain are in great demand by the Scottish and United States whisky distillers for maturing their raw spirit.

The fermentation is brought about by yeasts – or, more accurately, by the ferments that are contained within them. These ferments, or enzymes, are protein catalysts which, in different forms, are responsible for many of the chemical reactions that are vital to life. Created by the cells, they are extremely complex substances and are specific in the transformation they will catalyse. Above all, they are completely natural, and so is the fermentation they bring about. Nothing artificial need be added.

The air of the vineyard is laden with yeasts, and they collect in vast numbers on the grape skins to give them their natural 'bloom'. Of the many varieties (others include *Saccharomyces mangini* and *oviformis*), two are of outstanding importance: *Saccharomyces apiculatus*, or 'wild yeast'; and *Saccharomyces cerevisiae* variety *ellipsoideus*, usually abbreviated to *Saccharomyces ellipsoideus*, or 'wine yeast'. The former greatly outnumber the latter, and it is the wild yeasts which start the fermentation; but they are comparatively weak and when the alcohol rises to about 4 per cent they are overcome and die. It is then that the wine yeasts take over. The wild yeasts are also largely inhibited by sulphur dioxide when it is added in solution, and this helps the wine yeasts to take charge at an earlier stage. It also kills many undesirable bacteria and moulds.

Logically this could be carried a stage further: all the ferments could be destroyed and the fermentation then brought about by carefully selected ferments of the best natural strains, specially cultivated for the purpose. This has been done in some wine-growing districts, for instance in Champagne, and the results have been very satisfactory, the general view being that the quality has been brought up to a high level with fewer disappointing wines. There is no likelihood of this being adopted universally for sherry, though, at any rate in the immediate future. Several growers have experimented with pure strains of yeasts which are readily available, but some take the view that the success rate with the traditional fermentation is so high anyhow that there is little to be gained by complicating matters. Others, however, are now using them. Domecq were the first to separate, select and cultivate yeasts which they use to promote the fermentation. They have isolated a true sherry yeast with good fermenting properties that leads to a fine formation of flor. They do not sterilize the must but add a little sulphur dioxide in the traditional way and then seed it with the cultivated yeasts. Cultured yeasts are now also being used by Sandeman, Harvey and Garvey.

Another way of achieving uniformity at high quality is the *pies de cuba* method. Some must that is fermenting well is put into the cask and then unfermented must is added to it. This can be done gradually which helps to keep the temperature down.

After a few hours in the cask, fermentation begins. At the start it is usually very vigorous; in fact it is known as 'tumultuous fermentation'. The temperature rises rapidly and the must froths and bubbles out from the bunghole. To keep losses down to a minimum the casks are only filled to seven-eighths of their maximum capacity and a big earthenware, stainless steel or enamelled funnel, about 45 centimetres wide, is placed in the bunghole to give the must more room to expand. Even so, it often overflows. To get good wine, the temperature is kept as low as possible, and the butts should always be kept out of the sun. An excessive temperature at this stage kills the enzymes that convert the sugars into alcohol, and even if the temperature is allowed to approach this point without actually reaching it, evaporation is increased with a loss of alcohol and desirable aromatic compounds, and harmful bacteria are encouraged.

The sheer vigour of fermentation is usually the problem that the grower has to face. When, on the other hand, a cask will not start fermenting, it is put in the sun. If this does not do the trick, a little must is put in from a cask that is fermenting vigorously.

Tumultuous fermentation is as rapid as it is violent, but when the alcohol rises to about 11 per cent it slows down, and by this stage little or no sugar is left. The ferments can go on working, where there is enough sugar for them to work on, until the alcohol rises to about 16 per cent, but this does not normally arise and strong musts tend to develop into coarse wines. At the end of three or four days the heat and turbulence have died down and a second fermentation begins. Known as the *lenta*, it is much slower than the first; the wine develops steadily for about a fortnight and then more gradually until December or January, when the opaque must suddenly 'falls bright'. It is still immature, but it is wine at last.

At the end of the tumultuous fermentation, practically all the grape sugar has been turned into alcohol, and the reaction can be expressed by a very simple chemical formula:

$$C_6H_{12}O_6 \quad \rightarrow \quad 2C_2H_5OH \quad + \quad 2CO_2$$

glucose　　　　　　ethyl alcohol　　　　carbon dioxide

This simple formula, due to Gay-Lussac, gives a fair enough summary of what happens, but its over-simplification falls laughably short of the truth; and the truth has not yet been fully ascertained. Amerine and Cruess[1] list twelve different reactions and many by-products.

A friend of mine once had to show an efficiency expert from England round a bodega in Jerez. The visitor graciously approved of my friend's sherry, but he was horrified at seeing so much wine being matured in old-fashioned oak butts, and required to know why it was not kept in concrete vats with some oak shavings thrown in to give it the right flavour. There was at least some sense in the inquiry. Vats are invariably used for blending large quantities of sherry and also for storing coarser wines over short periods, but they are not satisfactory for maturing high quality wines. One obvious reason for using oak casks is the fact that they must be properly seasoned before they can be used for shipping wine; fermentation conditions them far better than any other process, and at no cost, so it is obviously efficient in that respect, though this is of less importance than it used to be now that the wine is shipped in bottle. For many years, though, shippers wondered whether the standard butt is really the best size for fermenting must, but none of them was prepared to risk losing part of his vintage by rash experiments. At the end of the Second World War, however, there was a serious shortage of oak and the shippers *had* to experiment. Many thousands of gallons of must were fermented in vats, but the results were not at that time very good. The main difficulty was keeping the temperature down; the kind of fermentation vessels now used, with their accurate temperature control, had not been invented.

More and more must is now being fermented on a large scale. Fermentation is carried out in vast tanks, some of them six metres high, made of fibreglass, reinforced polyester resins or stainless steel, usually of eighty to one hundred butts capacity. Early examples of the first two types were unsatisfactory as very small quantities of chemicals were leached out, and even the minutest trace of a foreign substance will spoil the flavour of a wine. Those problems have now been overcome and the most modern vessels are chemically inert, though stainless steel is generally preferred where cost is no

1 See *The Technology of Wine Making* by M. A. Amerine and W. V. Cruess (Connecticut, 1960). These series of reactions are known as the 'Embden-Meyerhof-Parnas pathway'; and are described in Professor A. H. Rose's *Alcoholic Beverages* (Academic Press, 1977).

object. When used for fermenting they are filled only to about 80 per cent of their capacity, to allow room for frothing and expansion. An advantage of these big tanks is that they can be very carefully monitored, especially with regard to temperature; if the temperature rises excessively from the ideal a spray of water can be turned on, either by hand or automatically by thermostat, pouring down the outside and cooling the tanks very effectively, or else passed through pipes either inside the tanks or circling round them. As a refinement the water may be refrigerated. This technique has been used in many of the leading vineyards of the world, even as far north as Champagne, where heat is not normally a problem. In the southern vineyard areas it has immensely improved the wines, as many were spoiled in the past by being fermented too hot, growing coarse and lacking fragrance. In the sherry country it is probably fair to say that the traditional method is capable of giving as good a wine: the casks are small so that temperature rarely gets out of hand, although there are always a few that do. The large tanks enable the shippers to approximate all their wines to the best and to achieve a greater uniformity, which is a very real advantage to a commercial house specializing in a few major brands, but can correspondingly be a disadvantage to a small, individualistic shipper who wishes to offer a wide choice. The scale of the operation in the big bodegas and the efficiency achieved can be indicated by the fact that Diez-Merito can ferment 12,000 butts in twenty-five days with a labour force of four men; and their plant is by no means the biggest.

The greatest advantage of large-scale fermentation in modern plants is temperature control. This makes a profound difference to the style and quality of the wine. Lower temperatures produce lower rates of fermentation, reduce oxidation and tend to conserve aromatic compounds, but it is essential that temperatures should not be too low, as this distorts the flavour of the wine, suppressing the production of aldehydes. Now that temperatures can be controlled and monitored, a lot of research has been carried out. For first quality finos Harveys have found that 22° to 24°C works best and about 3° higher for olorosos, though others favour higher temperatures; for instance Garveys ferment at 28° to 30°C and Vinicola Hidalgo ferments at 30°C. Some favour temperatures as high as 34°C. As a refinement of the process some shippers, such as Terry, cool the must with a heat exchanger before it goes into the fermentation tanks.

There is, however, still a strong case to be made out for fermenting in individual casks. Valdespino, which is a very traditional house specializing in a very wide range of different, high quality sherries, ferments 80 to 85 per cent in cask, the rest in stainless steel. With most other houses the proportions are the other way round, while some use 100 per cent large-scale fermentation. The advantage of cask fermentation is that each cask develops in its own way, producing a very wide range of styles – though this is by no means absent when large scale-fermentation is used, as the fermented must is put into casks where it develops almost as much individuality. Cask fermentation also provides a very saleable end product in the form of the casks themselves. Whisky distillers need so many that they actually buy new casks and get sherry shippers to ferment wine in them, so that anyone visiting a large fermentation bodega may be surprised to see the names of famous distillers branded on the butt ends.

By the end of September, there is fermenting must in every possible corner of the sherry towns, and you cannot walk through the streets for more than a few minutes without coming across the sickly, vegetable smell of fermentation; it is one of the necessary evils.

The casks of slowly fermenting must are not sealed against the atmosphere but are protected against dirt and dust by wooden stoppers that rest on top and fit loosely into the bungholes, while fermentation tanks have valves that achieve the same effect, so that air can get in quite easily and carbon dioxide, evolved in the course of the fermentation, can get out. They are also left 'on ullage': that is to say, there is an empty space above the wine. Fresh air must be able to circulate freely round the casks to help keep the temperature down, and the carbon dioxide generated by the fermentation needs to be able to escape, so the obvious place to store them would be outside in the open, or in a building with open sides like a Dutch barn. On the other hand, the temperature of fermentation should be kept low, and this calls for the cool atmosphere of a bodega rather than the warm sunshine of an Andalusian autumn. Both methods are quite satisfactory provided the storage patio is well shaded and the bodega has open windows to encourage a good draught with open doors or holes at floor level to let the carbon dioxide escape. Shippers who suffer from lack of space praise the open air, while those with plenty of buildings make use of them. All are unanimous in avoiding exposure to direct sunlight, and more bodegas are being built for maturing must as funds and land become available, so it would appear on balance that this is slightly the better alternative, but there is not much in it when casks are used. The more modern fermentation tanks are of course permanent installations in buildings.

Apart from alcohol, traces of many other organic compounds are formed during fermentation, notably glycerine, higher alcohols, lactic acid, succinic acid and acetaldehyde, with other aldehydes, ketones, organic acids, esters and so on: a great number of compounds, some of which are unidentified and exist only in minute quantities. All of these are sometimes referred to collectively by the trade, with a glorious disregard for accuracy, as 'the ethers'. It is the glycerine that gives a smooth, almost sweet taste to mature oloroso sherry, even when all the sugar has been consumed, and it is the steady development of such compounds that takes place as the wine ages. Like all other irreversible chemical reactions in liquid media, the ageing of wine is accelerated by heat, though an excess of heat destroys the enzymes; moreover, the wine ferments are destroyed more easily than the vinegar ferments, which are then left to do their worst. As a practical compromise, bodegas for storing must are usually less well insulated against heat, and are built with lower roofs than those used for maturing older wines, where a slow rate of development is essential. One shipper recently tried to accelerate the process by alternatively heating and cooling his developing wines, but he did not find it satisfactory. The attempt to hurry the ageing of wine is no new thing. It has been going on ever since the last century, and various other chemical, physical and even electrical methods have been tried. Most of the research has been done in areas where cheap table wines are mass-produced, and no method has yet been devised which can safely be used with high-class wines.

Sherry is a gift of providence. Everything is exactly right: soil, climate, ferments and fruit. But there is a special gift that is more improbable and more astonishing than any of the others, and that is the sherry flor. *Flor* simply means 'flower', and an exotic journalist, who should have been a poet, once wrote that the sherry flor was a small blue flower growing in the vineyards, and was scattered over the grapes at the time of the vintage. It was a beautiful thought, but his poetic licence was unsullied by any vestige of truth. The sherry flor is not a flower at all, but is a rather repulsive-looking film of yeast cells that covers the surface of the must in most of the butts some two months after the vintage, though often it does not appear until the following April or May.

Unlike those which effect fermentation, the yeast cells of the flor function in aerobic phase. There are four of them, all of the genus *Saccharomyces*: *S. beticus*, *S. montuliensis*, *S. cheresiensis* and *S. rouxii*. The first is the strongest and most important, especially on the younger wines, but forms a lower proportion as the wine ages, when that of the second increases. The other two are minor and are not always there, the third being mostly found in Sanlucar.

Some bodegas, such as Williams & Humbert and Vinicola Hidalgo, keep one of two butts of must with glass ends which show the development of flor very clearly, while Gonzalez Byass have one with a small door above the level of the flor, through which it can be seen. The growth of the film is rapid: a month after it first appears, it is already about three millimetres thick. It is almost pure white in colour and is a mass of irregular wrinkles; in fact it looks just like farmhouse cream cheese. It does not taste like that though. If you take a bit out and try it, it tastes bitter, yeasty and very odd. Its arrival is spontaneous and natural; it can very easily be killed but can never be induced to grow naturally on the surface of a wine where it has not appeared of its own accord. Imitators of sherry have taken specimens of flor to South Africa, Australia and California. With great difficulty it has been kept alive and has been induced to grow on the surface of alien wines, but the effect has never been the same. Flor only develops naturally in Spain, in the Jura and, it is said, in the Caucasus. It helps very materially to determine the character of the wine, and Manuel Gonzalez Gordon likened flor in sherry to boldness in children: the weaker they are to begin with, the more virulently does it act. The process of ageing under flor can accurately be described as biological ageing. The flor yeast metabolises some of the components of the wine, principally glycerol. Chemically its effect is to absorb any remaining traces of sugar and to diminish the quantities of glycerine and volatile acids; at the same time it greatly increases esters and aldehydes.

The flor yeasts are quite different from *la fleur*, or *mycoderma vini*, which forms a film on wines of low alcoholic strength that are left exposed to the air, and which is one of the principal enemies of French wine-growers. The Romans spoke of *flos vini*, and the term mycoderma vini was first used by Pasteur in describing his experiments on the Jura wines, which grow a flor not dissimilar from that of sherry. When he wrote his important *Études sur le Vinaigre et sur le Vin*, the term had a less specialized meaning than it has today, and it sounded so dramatic that it caught the imagination of many later writers, some of whom suggested that Jerez enjoyed the privilege of a special kind of mycoderma vini, while others claimed that the yeast was the same but behaved differently in Andalusia. They stuck to their errors with the tenacity of phlogistonists.

The conditions for the growth of flor have been summarized by Fornachon, quoting Marcilla, and by Gonzalez Gordon, quoting Bobadilla. Briefly, they are as follows: the fermentable sugar must all have been used up; the surface of the wine must have free access to the air and must not be stirred or shaken; the temperature should lie between 15° and 21°C; the alcoholic strength should be from 13.5° to 17.5°, preferably between 15° and 15.5°; the sulphur content should be less than 0.018 per cent; and tannin should not exceed 0.01 per cent. The tannin content can be greatly affected by the oak of the casks, so that the insertion of a new stave in a cask in a fino solera can seriously disturb the growth of flor, at least for a short time. As the yeasts are aerobic it is essential that the wine is matured on ullage, so that the casks are not filled to more than 90 per cent of their capacity, giving a good surface for the flor to grow on, and they are never tight-bunged but have loose stoppers that let the air in but keep the dirt out. Other conditions, more recently established, are that the pH should be between 3.3 and 3.4 and that the air should be reasonably humid.

In early spring and autumn, when the vines are in bloom and when the vintage is ready to be gathered, the wine is said to 'flower'; the thickness of the surface film, or *velo*, of flor grows rapidly and attains its purest white colour. If the flowering is a little weak in the odd cask it can be seeded with flor grown for that purpose. There is a charming superstition that the vitality of the wine rejoices at the blossom, but the truth is more prosaic: the temperature of the bodegas at that time happens to be just right. During spring and autumn the velo remains constant in thickness and is light in colour, but it is a living organism: dead cells constantly sink to the bottom and are replaced. During the hottest and coldest months it becomes much thinner, as the dying cells cannot be replaced, and its colour changes to grey. In the coastal towns of Sanlucar and Puerto the climate is more even and hence the flor grows more evenly throughout the year and is much thicker, especially in Sanlucar. The extent that the flor diminishes depends on the variation in temperature and some bodegas are simply no good at all for growing flor sherries. The old fashioned high ones with thick walls are the best. Small differences can matter so much that Javier Hidalgo of Vinicola Hidalgo at Sanlucar has noticed that the flor grows more strongly in butts on the side of the bodegas nearest the sea than in those on the sides nearest the town. And these variations help to account for the difference in style between the flor wines of the three towns, those in Jerez tending more easily to the lustier fino-amontillados.

Butts of wine that are kept apart and are not blended with others generally breed flor for six to eight years, but have been known to do so for as many as fifteen years. As the wine grows older in cask, in the dry atmosphere of the sherry towns, it gradually evaporates, but it loses water more rapidly than alcohol, and if it is not refreshed with younger wine it gets steadily stronger and its flavour increases. At the same time the flor gets thinner and darker, until it eventually sinks to the bottom and disappears altogether when the wine gets too strong and the nutrients have been used up. In the scales of a solera, where the old wine is drawn off at regular intervals and replaced with younger wine, it is possible to continue breeding flor indefinitely, and when a butt has been in position in a solera for fifty or sixty years there is a considerable accumulation of dead cells in the lees.

The sherry flor is a deadly enemy of the *mycoderma aceti*, or vinegar flor, and if any particles of vinegar flor fall into a butt of sherry the two yeasts fight for existence and the stronger wins. If the sherry is breeding healthy flor, the mycoderma accti does not stand a chance; a few butts of must turn into vinegar every year, but once the flor is really established the wine is absolutely safe. In fact, in a well-managed bodega, the number of casks going the wrong way is so few that one or two are turned into vinegar on purpose, to make sure there is enough for the summer salads and the local gazpacho. Neither the good nor the bad yeasts can live without oxygen, and it is largely for this reason that growers in districts where wines are liable to be attacked keep their casks tight-bunged, though this is never necessary in the sherry towns; on the contrary, if a butt of wine with a healthy velo of flor is accidentally tight-bunged and a reasonably free circulation of air is prevented, the chemical action of the flor is radically altered and vinegar can be formed. This can also occur if there is a heavy growth of flor on a shallow vessel of wine, but such a mishap is unlikely save in the laboratory.

I have seen flor growing in a sample bottle of must, and very unpleasant it looked, though the must was perfectly good underneath when it was shaken off. I have been told of the same thing happening to a bottle of delicate fino in England, and it is partly to prevent this that fino sherry exported to foreign countries is almost invariably fortified, though such a growth can also now be avoided by microfiltration.

All the butts used for maturing sherry are made of oak. Other kinds of wood that are more readily available have been tried, especially chestnut, but none has proved satisfactory. I have tried raya sherry that has been matured for nine months in chestnut and have compared it with the same wine matured in oak. The former was much darker, an altogether different and unattractive colour. The wine was not attractive either. It tasted immature while that matured in oak was rounder and had an attractive slightly woody taste. Chestnut gives no character. The size of the cask is important, too. The smaller the cask the quicker the wine matures, but there is also a difference in the way in which it matures. There are many possible explanations: the surface area in contact with the air, in proportion to the volume and depth, is just right when a butt is used, but tends to be too small in a vat; a butt puts exactly the right area of oak in contact with the wine, which becomes 'woody' if a smaller cask is used, and develops less 'character' in a larger cask; it also acts as a very slow selective filter, allowing some constituents of the wine to seep out and evaporate, while air can get in and help with the oxidation. Trillat has demonstrated that when alcohol is stored in wooden casks, the wood tends to influence the oxidation, producing small quantities of acetaldehyde. One of the reasons why oak works so well is that its vegetal fibres can be permeated by water molecules, which evaporate when they get on to the outer surface, but organic molecules cannot get through, so that there is a loss of volume on ageing but an increase in the concentration of the wine. Maturation is a natural process and it is an example of the rule that nature cannot be hurried.

Nature has been very kind to sherry-growers, but such generosity exacts its own price, and sherry is a very perverse wine: until it is fairly mature, no one can tell quite how it will develop. It is utterly exasperating. There are innumerable styles of sherry, and no two butts will turn out exactly alike. One would expect disparity between the wines of various vineyards, or between wines pressed from different types of grapes grown in the same vineyard, or even from similar vines in different areas of the vineyard, but that is only a small part of the story. Even if the must is the same, the oak used to make the casks will never be identical; it may even come from different countries: from Spain, Iran or the USA. The most favoured comes from the USA, usually from New Orleans, though the very best comes from New York. The exact location of the casks in the bodega is also important, as one may be exposed to a continuous draught while another is in a sheltered corner, and the various ferments that settle on the wine may do so in a different order. There is an infinite number of possible variants that may affect the growth and development. If two butts of must, pressed at the same time from the same grapes in the same vineyard, are stored side by side, it is quite possible that one will mature as a delicate, light fino while the other becomes a dark oloroso of the coarsest type. There is no rhyme nor reason about it at all. There is usually a tendency for a given vineyard to produce a majority of wines of a certain class, but it is never more than a marked tendency. There is also the influence of sunning (when it was done) and of pruning, as described in the last chapter, but this produces no more than a strong bias in favour of one or other style of wine. Absolutely anything can happen. In the past the only thing to do was to wait and see, but it is now possible to predict progress by gas chromatography, and young wines are 'educated' to direct them along the path required, by techniques that will be described, so most of the old uncertainty has gone.

After about six months the must starts to show its development, and the *capataz*, or head foreman of the bodega, goes round with his *venencia*, taking samples and putting a chalk mark on each of the casks to indicate the first, rough classification. The capataz in the sherry towns, like the butler in England, belongs to a legendary race, and many are the stories that are told about them. When King Alfonso XII visited Jerez, his host was making a fine display of showing him the best wines, but did not intend to waste his very finest sherry on a mere king. Even so, the King was delighted with what he was given, but the capataz blurted out:

'We have much better than that.'

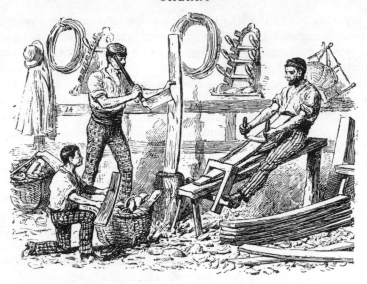

Preparing staves for casks in a nineteenth-century cooperage
(from *Facts About Sherry* by Henry Vizetelly, London, 1876)

'Then you had better keep it,' the King replied, 'for a more important occasion.' *Noblesse oblige*! But the capataz was fully up to standard.

The venencia is a sampling cup that is peculiar to Spain, though Warner Allen in a *History of Wine* pointed out that it is almost identical in shape to the ancient Greek *ephebos*, illustrated on classical pottery, and it could have been handed down throughout the ages. Its name is derived from the word *avenencia*, meaning a 'bargain', as it is used for taking samples when bargaining for the sale of wine. There is a story of a man in Jerez who had a bodega containing some fine old sherries. He wanted to prepare a composite sample to give a general idea of what he had for sale, and the easiest way of doing so was to draw some wine from each cask, using a venencia, and to combine all the samples in a single vessel. Unfortunately he was notoriously mean – far too mean to pay a man to help him – but on his way to the bodega he met a builder he knew and he asked him to come and help. The merchant gave his friend a bowl and told him to follow. Then he filled a glass from the venencia and passed it back to him. Unfortunately the builder was as devoted to sherry as the merchant was to money, and the nature of the work had not been clearly described. The merchant cursed him for being slow and asked for the glass back, so he drained it in one draught. The merchant went from cask to cask, concentrating on what he was doing, and he handed the builder first one glass of wine and then another without so much as glancing at him. His friend, astonished at such unexpected generosity, drank every one of them. Only after twenty glasses was he obliged to call: 'No more for me, Don José, I've had enough.'

Croft-Cooke has aptly likened a venencia to an antique church candle-snuffer. In Jerez it should consist of a black, highly flexible whalebone handle, at one end of which there is a decorative silver hook, while at the other end there is a cylindrical cup made of solid silver and big enough to fill a large Spanish wine glass. In these debased days, however, the cup is often made of stainless steel and the handle is plastic. In Sanlucar, and occasionally in Puerto de Santa Maria, it is made from a single piece of bamboo. A complete section of the cane is left intact between two knots, and this acts as the cup, while the remainder is cut away with the exception of a small segment, about 5 millimetres wide and a metre long, which is used as a handle. The bamboo venencia is undoubtedly the older form.

With the aid of a venencia, samples of wine can be drawn off from beneath the velo of flor without seriously disturbing it. To do this, the venencia is plunged into the wine well beneath the surface and is then drawn out quickly; this disperses the flor over a small area and none of it gets into the cup. The old-fashioned bamboo type is perhaps the better of the two for use with flor wines, as the cup is usually narrower and causes less of a disturbance. This is particularly important with the manzanillas of Sanlucar, and the bamboo venencia is so well established in that town that it is customary to ask for a *caña* of wine rather than a *copa*. After it has been withdrawn from the butt, the handle is swung upwards so that the cup is horizontal, and the wine cascades into the tasting glass that is held ready in the other hand, filling the air with its fragrance. It all sounds very simple, and a good Jerezano can pour the wine with negligent ease into a glass held a metre away, but a lot of skill is needed; if an amateur tries, the wine generally goes on the floor, or flows tidily down his sleeve.

To examine the must, the capataz uses a tasting or dock glass about 12 centimetres high, narrower at the top than at the bottom, and mounted on a short stem; it is only filled to the height of a couple of centimetres, but that is about twice as much as an English public-house schooner contains when full. He holds it by the base, beneath the stem, so that the important part is not fouled with finger marks, and any cloudiness in the must can be seen at once. Nor is the wine warmed by the fingers. When the glass is shaken, it is filled with concentrated fragrance, and the 'nose' tells an experienced taster everything he wants to know. A good must should be 'clean' and 'full'; often it is one without being the other, but it must be both if it is to grow into a first-class wine. In tasting musts and young wines, the palate is useless; they invariably taste thin, acid and nasty; moreover, if any is swallowed it deadens the sense of smell to those that follow. In modern practice the musts are also chemically analysed as some deficiencies can be shown up in this way which would not appear to the taster until after a period of maturation.

At this early stage, the must can only be put into one of four categories, which are distinguished by the following marks:

/ — *una raya*, light and good;
/. — *raya y punto*, slightly less promising;
// — *dos rayas*, musts with less style;
/// — *tres rayas*, or *quema*, coarse or acid.

Every bodega has its own marks for use at each stage of the classification, but the above are typical. There is, of course, a fifth grade: vinegar, marked *Ve*. This is removed hastily to the vinegar store before it gets the chance to infect its neighbours. The *tres rayas* is sent to be distilled. In the old days it was considered to be good going if 60 per cent achieved *una raya*; now, thanks to modern vinification, the avoidance of oxidation, and cleanliness, the figure has risen to 90 per cent.

After this classification the good butts of must are ready to be racked off the lees. The lees consist of bits of skin, stalks, pips, dead yeast cells and any other dense matter that sinks to the bottom. In the front of each cask there is a tight-bunged hole near the bottom that is called the *falsete*. When the wine is racked off, a narrow pipe, or *canuto*, generally made of wild olive wood or mahogany, is driven into the *falsete* and the must flows out. This action is described as *dejar al pique*. After the level has fallen to that of the *falsete*, the cask is gently tilted forwards; this is known as *picar la bota*, and it has to be done very carefully to avoid disturbing the lees. As soon as the jet of wine becomes turbulent, the canuto is stopped up and the cask, containing from 7 to 20 per cent of its original quantity of must, is returned to the horizontal. The lees are poured into open-ended barrels that look like old-fashioned wash tubs, and then into butts, where they remain for a week or two until they have settled. The whole process is then repeated. Afterwards, no clear must remains. According to Dr Walter Charleton's *Two Discourses*, published in 1692, wine should be racked off the lees 'in the wane of the Moon, and fair Weather, the Wind being Northerly', but this practice is not currently followed in Jerez.

The must that separates out when the lees are collected together is known as *claros de lias* and is used in blending sherry for local sale. The lees themselves are either distilled for alcohol or else sold to the chemical industry for making cream of tartar, whichever is more profitable at the time.

After the must has been racked, it is at last called wine, though some shippers go on calling it 'must' until it is two years old, while others, following an old Spanish proverb, say that it has grown into wine by St Andrew's day (30 November).

The wine is now checked for alcoholic strength, which is likely to be between 14° and 16° Gay-Lussac. Any of the first category, that has a good growth of flor, and is likely to develop as a wine of the most delicate style (known as fino) is fortified to about 15.5° Gay-Lussac, if it is deficient in alcohol; such a slight fortification helps to prevent disease without affecting the quality or style. On the other hand, those of the lower categories, which often grown little flor, and which would normally develop as rather heavier wines (known as olorosos) are fortified to about 18° Gay-Lussac. This finally kills any flor that may exist and determines their character once and for all. It is always done after the racking to avoid waste of alcohol in the lees. In this way the shipper can, to some extent, decide what class of wine he is going to make, though he can never increase his supplies of fino by causing flor to grow on wines where it does not appear of its own accord.

Until after the Second World War industrial alcohol could not be used for fortifying, as it often contained impurities which reacted unfavourably with the wine, and its use was illegal, although some undoubtedly *was* used for making bad wine during the sherry boom. But the cheap Spanish table wines, which used to be distilled, are now being exported in enormous quantities, and there is a serious shortage of grape alcohol. Industrial alcohol, on the other hand, is now very pure, and can be used with complete success. For some reason which would defy a chemist or any man of reason, the very mention of industrial alcohol seems to send shudders up and down the spines of the wine trade and governments – particularly in Germany. They get slightly less upset if it be called 'non-grape alcohol', distilled from a fermentation of some kind, such as that of sugar beet, rather than a chemical synthesis; but this again is nonsense as a process of fermentation is generally the cheapest way to produce alcohol. The fact is, though, that prejudice has triumphed over reason. Non-grape alcohol has very rarely been used and this only by mistake in years of shortage, when people have bought what alcohol they could get on assurances that they would not check. Indeed it could only be checked by C_{14} testing, which is a modern innovation, as the alcohol is chemically pure and as good as anything distilled to the purity of absolute alcohol from the grape. And everyone knew that non-grape alcohol was being used. It is used no longer. Prejudice has triumphed utterly, especially in the EEC and all sherry exported is subjected to a C_{14} test. The product used is *destillado*, made by distilling wine, which has to be healthy, and is 95 per cent pure alcohol.

Very strong alcohol is not altogether safe to use for fortification – even if it is distilled from grapes – as it reacts violently with the wine and spoils it. A fifty-fifty mixture of alcohol and mature sherry, known as *mitad y mitad*, *miteado*, or *combinado*, is much safer. Some shippers also add a little mature oloroso sherry to the butts in which the flor has been killed, but not normally more than a gallon in a butt containing 110 gallons. This makes it develop more quickly.

After the wine has been racked off the lees and fortified, it is allowed to rest for a week or two and is then classified for the second time as:

        y — *palma*, a wine breeding flor;
        l — *raya*, a rather fuller wine with no flor;
        ll — *dos rayas*, inclined to be coarse;
        # — *gridiron*, no good at all.

This classification gives a better indication of how it will develop than does the first, but the wine is still its own master and evolves just as it likes – often quite differently from how the capataz expects. At this stage the wine is said to be *sobre tablas* and is generally ready to be added to a criadera, but it may be kept longer for a third classification, especially if there is any doubt about its classification.

Good sherry cannot be cheap because of the losses that occur while it is being matured. By the time of the second classification, 10 per cent of the original must has already been lost: 1 per cent escapes during fermentation or is absorbed by the wooden casks, 1½ per cent evaporates and 7½ per cent, on average, is lost in the lees. Rayas are sometimes stored out of doors under the sun, but this is seldom done nowadays as losses can rise to as much as 30 per cent.

Each cask is matured separately for a time as an *añada*. The term is derived from *año*, meaning 'year' and an añada wine is simply a vintage wine – one that has been kept apart and has not been blended with any other. It seldom remains as an añada for more than two or three years, and usually for much less time, but the way in which sherry is matured will be described in the next chapter. There are, however, exceptional instances in which a wine is allowed to remain as an añada indefinitely. A shipper, for instance, may lay down a butt of good quality must when one of his children is born, and the wine will be fully developed when the child comes of age. In at least two bodegas – those of Williams & Humbert and Gonzalez Byass – there is a complete range of vintage wines going back for many years, and they are very interesting to taste, though of no particular value. That at Gonzalez Byass is descended from the 'piano' of wine mentioned by Vizetelly in 1876.

While the young wine is maturing its development is carefully watched and it is frequently checked for any sign of disease. The most important clue is given by the bouquet, but the wine must also be examined for colour and clarity. This is done in a 'camera obscura', and there is one of these in every bodega: but they are not camera obscuras at all in the popular sense of the word. They look like dovecots, standing on little wooden poles. Each has a candle inside, and when the wine is spun round in the tasting glass against the flame any suspended particles or cloudiness are shown up at once. Very often today an electric candle is used, which looks horribly bogus but works quite well and is less trouble. When there is any doubt, though, a real candle is used for the ultimate test.

Although sherry, owing to its high alcoholic strength, is less prone to disease than are most other wines, there are at least eight diseases that can attack it at this stage, and they can all be identified immediately from the aroma and the appearance of the wine. Each has an established remedy, and the ancient skill of the capataz is now reinforced by modern laboratories, where accurate analysis discloses the extent of the disease and regulates the treatment.

One symptom that is easy to recognize is the smell of vinegar. This may well mean that the wine is *picado* (pricked) or else suffering from *acetificacion*, and actually turning into vinegar owing to the attack of mycoderma aceti. This is most likely to gain a hold when the temperature has been allowed to get too high, and it is very infectious; it is spread to other casks by bodega utensils, and the spores can be carried through the air. If there is the least suspicion of vinegar, all utensils are washed in an aqueous solution of potassium metabisulphate and the infected cask is immediately taken away. The mycoderma aceti oxidizes the alcohol to form acetic acid:

$$C_2H_5OH + 2[O] \rightarrow CH_3COOH + H_2O$$

This reaction can be stopped by adding a good dose of sulphur dioxide solution to kill the vinegar flor and then tight-bunging the casks to exclude air, but infection is now very rare, and the wine is more likely to be put into the vinegar store at once and allowed to go its own way. A mild attack can sometimes be overcome simply by fortifying, but this has to be done with care; if there is a good growth of flor, it will attack the mycoderma aceti and effect a natural cure; to fortify the wine would kill the flor and promote the disease it is intended to cure. The late Don José Pan, of the Misa bodegas, regularly added a little alcohol to the must from his vineyards before fermentation began, and his process gave good results, particularly in very bad vintage years, when the wine is normally deficient in alcohol. He claimed that a small proportion of alcohol added at this stage prevented harmful yeasts and bacteria from gaining a hold and directed the fermentation along the right path. Such a fortification, however, has to be done with very great care, as any excess of alcohol could inhibit fermentation and leave sugar in the must. In general alcohol is only added to protect musts that are exceptionally weak, which is only likely to arise in those rare years of bad weather. The practice is now obsolescent, if not obsolete.

The acidity of wine expressed in terms of tartaric acid should generally be about 5.20 grams per litre, and if it is too low, tartaric acid can be added. Any suspected tendency towards acetic fermentation is examined by measuring the volatile acidity – that is to say, the acid contained in a distillate obtained from the wine. Pure acetic acid boils at 118°C, and therefore distils over quite easily, while the majority of the other acids in the wine remain in the residue. An old wine may safely contain as much as 2 grams per litre, expressed in terms of acetic acid, but anything over 0.80 grams per litre is considered dangerous in a must.

When Walter Charleton wrote his *Two Discourses* in 1692 there were apparently other causes of acidity: 'Among the External are commonly reckoned . . . immoderate Heat, Thunder or the report of Cannons, and the admixture of any exotick body, which will not symbolize or agree . . . especially the flesh of Vipers . . .' He also stated, quite rightly, that lack of alcohol could influence a wine to turn to vinegar, but he added: 'The Spirits of Wine may be Exhausted . . . Suddainly by Lightning; which doth spoil Wine . . . not by Congelation or Fixation of its Spirits . . . but perhaps by Disgregation and putting them to flight . . .' No modern authority would endorse these ancient observations.

In the past there were a number of diseases which had to be carefully monitored, but for all practical purposes these have been abolished by modern vinification and cleanliness. A vinegary smell together with a bitter-sweet taste and lack-lustre appearance could indicate the disease of *mannite*, or *la peste* (plague), caused by a micro-organism that decomposes the sugar into short, rod-like crystals of mannitol, which gather together in great numbers, forming colonies. The remedy was to chill the wine and to add sulphur dioxide.

The biggest nuisance in the Jerez bodegas used to be *scud*, or *nube* (cloudiness), sometimes known as *tornado*, or *vuelta* (turning), or in France, *la tourne*. It showed up as a cloud, rather like steam, suspended in the wine. A similar effect was produced in the hottest and coldest seasons by falling particles of flor, but scud also gave a very unpleasant smell. Unfortunately it was highly infectious and once the bacteria got a hold, they could be killed only by a disinfectant, such as sulphur dioxide.

A fourth disease was *hilo* (oiliness), or *la graisse*. The wine became 'ropey' and viscous; when it was poured out, it looked like oil. This was most common with finos, but was generally only seasonal and cured itself.

Cloudiness can be caused by excessive cold, when cream of tartar comes out of solution and is held in suspension. This happens both in casks, where it is harmless, and in bottles, where it spoils the appearance of the wine but does not affect the bouquet or flavour. Cloudiness in bottle can largely be prevented by refrigeration to a low temperature and then filtering before shipment; this process is being used by practically all of the shippers. A chemical method based on ion exchange can give similar results, but it is illegal in some countries; ultra-cooling (see page 258) is in any event preferred, so this alternative is not used.

In earlier editions of this book I described a bacterial infection caused by *Lactobacillus trichodes* and diseases known as *casse ferrica*, *casse oxidasica* and *casse caprica*. Even then they were very rare indeed and now, with modern oenology, they have, like the others, to all intents and purposes disappeared.

Most vermin and parasites are harmful and mischievous, though there is one that is actually said to be good, and that is the *ácaro*, a mite. It can be seen with the naked eye and lives on the stoppers of certain casks containing high-quality finos; it is claimed that the presence of ácaros is a sure sign the wine is good, as they work in some way to reduce the acidity, but their benevolent disposition has never been verified by scientific experiment, and I think they probably do nothing at all; they are simply blessed with a good taste in wine. They belong to a large and objectionable insect family which includes the cork weevil that is such a menace to those who would lay down vintage port. They are a serious nuisance in some wine districts, and their rather extraordinary way of life has been described in detail by Sannino.

The technicalities of the bodega may be vital to the sherry shipper, but they mean nothing at all to the casual visitor; all he sees are the great buildings, permeated with the aroma of maturing wine; he steps from the bright, hot sunlight of the patio into the huge, dim nave, where everything is quiet and at peace. Richard Ford likened bodegas to cathedrals, and his simile was so good that everyone who has written about sherry after him has used it. There is something rather awe-inspiring about the sight of so much wine. The buildings are enormous and lofty, and the light is very subdued. But, unlike cathedrals, they are all quite modern and most were built during the nineteenth century. Before that time, much less wine was produced and it was sold when it was only a year or two old. After the Napoleonic Wars and the abolition of the Gremio, the great shipping houses began to accumulate large stocks of old wine and regularly exported better and more expensive sherries than ever before. To store them, they built their great bodegas round the periphery of the town. Structurally they are all very similar, with thick walls and high roofs to keep the temperature down; the roofs are often insulated with cork sheet and the walls are made with hollow bricks. Small windows protected with iron grilles are set high up in the walls and are left open all the time to let the air circulate freely, but they are covered with esparto-grass blinds during the day to keep the sun out. The floors are earth, though the passages between the casks are sometimes paved with oak blocks made from the waste material of the cooperage. Brick or stone is rarely found. During the hottest and driest months the floors are sprinkled with water twice or three times a week; it soaks in and evaporates gradually during the next few days, helping to keep the temperature down; it also increases the humidity, and so reduces the rate of evaporation of the wine.

The tall, heavy roofs are supported by rows of square, white-washed columns that help to make bodegas look like cathedrals. The effect is best of all where there is no central row of columns, as in Osborne's beautiful bodega of San José, in Puerto de Santa Maria, which was built in 1837. Some shippers renew their whitewash every year and their bodegas look immaculately clean; others do not bother, and let the cobwebs of ages accumulate; it makes not a scrap of difference to the wine; in fact, one famous shipper told a complaining and hygienic English lady that he would stuff the cobwebs right inside the wine if he thought they would improve it, and gossip says that one of the younger shippers, wishing to give an air of antiquity to his buildings, bought cobwebs by the sackful and draped them from the walls. But if cobwebs do no harm, anything evil-smelling, on which bacteria could develop, must not be allowed anywhere near the wine, and any trace of rotting animal or vegetable remains is scrupulously cleaned up. Some shippers go even further and say that pleasant scents are actually good for the wine; for instance, jasmine is sometimes trained to grow up the walls.

Underground cellars used to be considered not really satisfactory because the circulation of air is not good enough; Domecq's have

SHERRY

one cellar, but it is very airy and could not be built economically today, and Vinicola Hidalgo in Sanlucar have one bodega that is actually below sea level. Gonzalez Byass have a deep, damp dungeon in the garden, which they use for storing vinegar. However, in the 1980s Garvey proved that underground cellars can work by building some large ones between the by-pass and the vineyards. They are very well ventilated.

While the general plan of all the traditional bodegas is similar, each has its own individuality and charm; two (at Williams & Humbert and Harvey) have round columns instead of square ones and these, with the classical symmetry of the buildings, look particularly attractive. There used to be a third at Augustín Blazquez, and when its old bodegas in the town centre were pulled down to be redeveloped for housing (it has moved into new ones at the edge of the town) the building with round pillars was carefully preserved as a community hall. At Harveys the Cámara bodega is lit by chandeliers made from old bottles. Many have beautiful gardens – Harveys, Gonzalez Byass, Williams & Humbert, and Caballero, for instance – while others have enchanting patios, notably Valdespino and Barbadillo. In fact, the sherry towns are delightful places to live in.

Building costs have risen in Spain as they have everywhere else. Nevertheless in the 1960s Ruiz-Mateos built some of the most beautiful bodegas in Jerez and in the 1970s Croft, at Rancho Croft, built a complete range of very fine bodegas in the traditional style to create one of the most impressive establishments of all, since ample land on the edge of the town allowed the buildings to be well spaced apart. A unique and enormous building was put up in the same decade by Domecq's, inspired by the Great Mosque at Cordova, but this is used for the maturation of brandy. The arches receding into the distance give a remarkable visual effect that was even more striking when it was newly erected and before the oak casks were put in. Other traditional bodegas have been built on the edge of the town by Emilio Lustau and by Real Tesoro.

Not surprisingly, though, others have been forced by rising costs – and sometimes through lack of space – to try other methods. Some bodegas are now built on more than one level and Gonzalez Byass has a large, three-storey bodega of concrete construction dating from the 1960s. The Ruiz-Mateos group built a very modern building on the road to Cadiz cunningly designed so that, despite its enormous size, every part has an ample circulation of air, and the roof is insulated by means of a foamed material; it now forms the headquarters of Bodegas Internacionales. Another method of construction for rather smaller buildings is to use a polished aluminium roof. This reflects the sunlight and gives excellent results at low cost, but results tend to fall off if the surface becomes dirty or corroded.

Butts of wine are stored in the bodegas[1] one on top of another, in rows, three or four tiers high; there is even occasionally a fifth tier of small casks. They are kept apart by wooden blocks rammed firmly home and the whole structure is very stable, but each of the butts in the lower tiers must contain plenty of wine, so that the weight is evenly distributed; an empty cask would cause a weakness that could shatter the whole structure. The trouble begins when one of the casks in the middle springs a leak and has to be replaced. The wine it contains may well be worth several hundred pounds, and must be saved, but the neighbouring casks must not be moved, as maturing sherry should be disturbed as little as possible. This is achieved by making a *puente*, or bridge. The wine in the defective cask is siphoned out and the cellarmen lift the casks in the upper tier, using levers, known as *tranquillas*, made of black poplar wood. They need only leave a gap of about an inch, and the casks are kept in place with oak wedges. The one that leaks can then be lifted out, leaving the remainder completely stable. The most skilled part of the work is getting the wedges into the right positions; any error would be extremely dangerous, and the consequent loss could amount to several thousand pounds. When the broken cask is at the end of a tier, those above it are held in position with ropes secured to casks further along, so that the whole structure is securely bound together.

After the wine has been made, its final development rests entirely with providence: there is nothing further to be done, but it must be examined regularly for strength and quality until it is ready for use in a solera or for blending. As before, the capataz puts a chalk mark on each cask to define the style, and the following are typical:

y — *palma*, a fino sherry that is both light and delicate;
$\not{y}$ — *palma cortada*, a rather stouter fino, tending towards amontillado;

[1] The word *bodega*, generally in the plural, is also used loosely to signify a wine shipper's complete establishment.

+ — *palo cortado*, a full-bodied yet delicate wine of particularly good style, not breeding flor;

I — *raya*, a darker and fuller wine, not breeding flor;

II — *dos rayas*, a style similar to the above but coarser and less attractive.

There are, of course, many variants of these signs from one bodega to another, and, in particular, the oloroso sign (ø) is often used in place of the *raya*; when this is done, the *raya* sign is used in place of *dos rayas*. It does not matter in the least which sign is used provided the meaning is clear.

Apart from classifying the wine into its various varieties, there are many additional terms in current use to describe some of the subtle differences that distinguish one wine from another, and most of these have been listed by Manuel Gonzalez Gordon. A wine may be *verde* (green) or *maduro* (mature), depending largely on the ripeness of the grapes at the vintage; it may be *delgado* (thin) or *gordo* (fat), depending on its strength; a wine that is likely to develop well is *firme* (stable), but if it is weak, with a tendency to acid, it is described as *tierno* (tender); it may be *basto* (coarse) or *fino* (fine); *limpio* (clean) or *sucio* (dirty); *bonito* (elegant) or *apestoso* (foul); *blando* (soft) or *duro* (hard); the bouquet may be *lleno* (full) or *vacio* (empty); *punzante* (sharp) or *apagado* (feeble); very commonly a wine is described as having *mayor* or *menor cuerpo* (greater or less body) or as *ligero* (light); it may or may not be *redondo* (round). And there are many other common descriptions; in fact, the list could be endless.

I once counted the marks on two sets of eighty-four butts in two separate bodegas at a famous shipper's; the wine came from Palomino grapes grown in the same vineyard, and was two years old. In the first bodega there were five butts of *palma*, thirty-six of *raya*, and forty-three of *dos rayas*, with no *palo cortado* or *palma cortada* whatsoever, while in the second there were one each of *palo cortado* and *palma cortada*, twenty of *palma*, thirty-two of *raya* and thirty of *dos rayas*. The relative absence of that exquisite wine palo cortado is partly the result of the phylloxera; the old vines gave much more of it. The development is very much of a gamble, especially for the smaller shippers; the larger shippers carry such great stocks of young wine – perhaps as many as 4,000 butts of every vintage – that the differences average out. It was to overcome these differences and to produce a sherry of uniform quality that the solera system was developed.

9

The Wine Matures

===

If a cask of young sherry is left to mature and is not tampered with
in any way, it will gradually become stronger and its character will
steadily develop; it may also evolve subtle distinctions of bouquet
and flavour; or it may even change its style completely. Very often
it will become better than its mark would suggest, as every *capataz*
is a notorious pessimist and never spares the chalk, but he will not
hesitate to up-grade a wine that proves to be good. At the end
of three years most butts will have settled down and the basic
classification will not be changed again, but there are always a few
of indeterminate character that remain a law unto themselves and
which cannot be classified finally for ten years or even longer.

Mature sherry falls into three basic classes: *fino, palo cortado*
and *oloroso*. Each of these has various sub-divisions, depending on
age and quality, and each will be considered separately. This is
complicated by the fact that some of the descriptive words used are
the same as those used in the earlier classifications, but they do not
necessarily have the same meanings. All styles are completely dry,
as the fermentation is complete and the whole of the sugar is used
up. If a sweet sherry is required, it is obtained by blending, at a later
stage, with specially prepared sweetening wines.

Except for certain styles of manzanilla, fino is the lightest and
most delicate of all sherries. It has a delightfully fresh, slightly
piercing and very clean bouquet, is completely dry, and has exactly
the right natural acidity without appearing at all acid to the palate.
It is often described as straw coloured, though the yellow tinge is so
light that it is really more like hay. Its alcoholic strength normally
lies between 15° and 18° Gay-Lussac.

The term *palma* (*f*) is reserved for finos of the highest quality,
with a particularly clean and delicate aroma. As the wine ages it

may become *dos palmas* (⸀), *tres palmas* (⸀) or *cuatro palmas* (⸀), but this classification is purely arbitrary; a shipper may put the dividing line where he likes, so that one shipper's *palma* could be similar to another's *tres palmas*. As standards of comparison, such graduations are better ignored except when referring to wines coming from the same source. The term *palma cortada* is used, as in the classification of musts, to denote a stouter fino tending towards amontillado. A fino of little merit, that lacks delicacy, is known as *entre fino*.

A fino, left as a vintage wine, shows to perfection when it is about six years old. When it grows older in cask, any of three things may happen: it may gain in body and develop a new depth of bouquet, becoming first a fino-amontillado and then an amontillado; it may gradually grow stronger in flavour but retain its fino character, becoming that rarest and most wonderful of wines, an old fino; or it may just grow steadily coarser and nastier. As usual it is a pure gamble, though the dice are loaded in favour of amontillado.

Amontillado is given its name because of its resemblance to wines grown in the district of Montilla, near Cordova. Superficially, the similarity can be striking, though amontillado sherries are more distinguished and have a greater quality of flavour. The term did not come into general use until the beginning of the nineteenth century. The first mention of amontillado is said to be in the books of Pascual Moreno de Mora (the predecessor of Picardo & Cia, at Puerto de Santa Maria), who sold some to an associated house at Cadiz on 11 January 1769. In 1814 he wrote to England about an amontillado being sold to the shippers in Puerto de Santa Maria, and he shipped some to Le Havre in 1812. It was mentioned in England by Henderson in the *Quarterly Journal of Science and Arts* in 1825 and Henry Douglas in his book on Spain published in 1837.

The development from fino is gradual, and the points at which a fino becomes a fino-amontillado, and a fino-amontillado becomes an amontillado, cannot be determined exactly: shippers vary in their optimism. As the fino ages the flor dies away through lack of nutrients, and maturation proceeds by a process of oxidation, similar to that of an oloroso. In other words the maturing process begins as one of biological ageing and proceeds to physico-chemical ageing when it passes from a fino into an amontillado. The characteristic bouquet of an amontillado has been described as 'nutty'; it is certainly deep, and is completely fresh and clean. The colour graduates from the straw colour of an amontillado-fino to the amber of a young amontillado, and then to the dark gold of an old amontillado, while the alcoholic strength may be anything from 16° to upwards of 23° Gay-Lussac, which is attained naturally by very old amontillados that have never been fortified. In the Valdespino bodegas, for instance, there is a cask of fino Inocente that has not been refreshed since 1940. In 1991 it was showing as an exquisite amontillado with an alcoholic strength of 22°.

For a fino to turn into an amontillado takes at least eight years, and thereafter maturation continues steadily. Such a wine is necessarily expensive, and worth the money. As an example, Domecq's Botaina has an equivalent age of about fifteen years. But in producing wines that are commercially attractive it is possible to take a short cut by slightly fortifying a suitable fino and feeding it into an amontillado solera.

To taste through the solera of a fine amontillado is a fascinating experience beginning, as it must, with a fine fino and progressing through the graduations to a mature amontillado and ultimately to a wine of such concentration that it is really too overpowering to be drunk in any quantity. But such a wine may be a gem for blending.

Genuine amontillado is absolutely delectable. Ever since I can remember, I have been drinking wine in England out of bottles labelled 'amontillado'. As a boy, I used to laugh at Edgar Allan Poe for making such a fuss about a cask of commonplace sherry,[1] but it was I who was the fool. Most of the 'amontillado' sold in England contains little or none of the genuine wine; it is just bastardized fino. Some of the better merchants do list genuine amontillados, but only at a high price. Since amontillado has, of necessity, to mature in cask for at least eight years, and preferably far longer, and as only a limited proportion of fino develops into amontillado, it is necessarily expensive. Commercially, amontillado, like all the other styles of sherry, is matured by means of the solera system, rather than as añada wines, but this makes little difference to the price, as

1 See his story 'The Cask of Amontillado' from *Tales of Mystery and Imagination*. Others have chided him for referring to a *pipe* of sherry, but he was not necessarily wrong; in the seventeenth century, sherry was sometimes shipped in pipes, as port is today, but the word 'amontillado' was not used until the third quarter of the eighteenth century, and very little was exported until the middle of the nineteenth. From internal evidence, it would appear that the gruesome event related in the story took place in about 1790, so it is rather a comedy of errors.

the cost of establishing a solera to produce wine of this style is itself prodigious.

Palo cortado is a rare wine that is the delight of sherry drinkers; it is often classed as a style of oloroso, but this seems very unfair to oloroso. It is similar to oloroso in breeding little or no flor, but in other ways it is a law unto itself. It has a deep and subtle bouquet more like amontillado, and it is clean and crisp on the palate, though it is darker in colour. The strength varies from 17° to 23° Gay-Lussac. Since the phylloxera only a very small proportion of the must develops in this style, and a palo cortado solera is excessively difficult to operate. Apart from the problem of finding sufficient young wine of good quality to supply it, bad mismanagement can result in palo cortado debasing itself and turning into oloroso. According to age, it may be classified as *palo cortado* (⊁), *dos cortados* (⚹), *tres cortados* (⚹) or *cuatro cortados* (⚹), but as with palma, the classification is purely arbitrary and varies from one shipper to another. Palo cortado in Spain has long suffered the same indignity as does amontillado in England: most of the palo cortado in the bars of Jerez is nothing of the sort; it is cheap, popular wine of not dissimilar style synthesized out of amontillado and oloroso leftovers. Alas, the same thing is now beginning to happen in Great Britain. The only way to be sure of drinking the real thing is to get one of those wines shipped uncommercially, for the love of it, by an enthusiastic shipper or merchant. In Sanlucar palo cortado is called Jerez cortado.

Oloroso, in Spanish, means 'fragrant'. The name is descriptive, distinguishing these wines from the coarser, less fragrant rayas, though looked at simply as a word, its use may come as a surprise: the virile and piquant aromas of finos and amontillados are much more striking. In its natural state it is completely dry, although it often has a slightly sweet after-taste caused by traces of glycerine produced by the oloroso fermentation. When this characteristic is particularly noticeable, the wine is sometimes distinguished by a special mark, converting the raya into a tick: ✓. It is known as *pata de gallina*, or hen's foot, possibly owing to its nutritive qualities. A young oloroso is just slightly darker than a fino, but as it matures it rapidly grows darker and browner. Oloroso has more vinosity than other styles, and blends well with sweet wines to produce the rich dessert sherries that are so popular in Great Britain and Scandinavia. A mature oloroso is strong in alcohol and would normally register

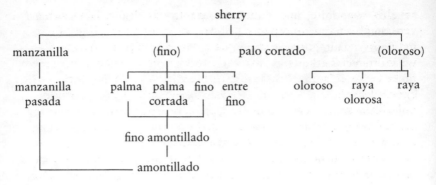

17° Gay-Lussac, while very old wines register over 23°. Olorosos do not grow flor and the process of maturation, known as physico-chemical ageing, is quite different from that of finos.

Rayas are olorosos that lack distinction and quality; they are used in blending the cheaper sherries and are usually stronger than good olorosos of the same age. Wines of intermediate quality are called *rayas olorosas*. Light rayas are sometimes describes as *rayas finas*.

The account given above may be of some guidance, but it is impossible to describe the aroma or flavour of a wine at all accurately; the only thing to do is to taste and to remember, though Manuel Gonzalez Gordon invented a graphic and helpful simile by comparing fino to an almond, amontillado to a hazel nut, and oloroso to a walnut.

If the various styles of wine were represented by a family tree, it would look something like the diagram above.

Manzanilla is made at Sanlucar de Barrameda. It is a complete subject in itself and will be dealt with separately in the next chapter. It is put where it is in the family tree simply because its lightest styles are so very light; but, as will be seen, these are really only the first members of another complete family.

In 1920 Williams & Humbert laid down a butt of must to celebrate the birth of a member of the Humbert family. They laid down another, for a similar reason, in 1922, and in 1924 they decided it would be interesting to put aside a butt of every vintage from the same vineyard: Alamo, in Balbaina. These añada wines only receive the initial small fortification and one light fining with egg whites; they are seldom sampled and are never bottled, but they steadily evaporate, and a minute quantity is drawn out with a venencia from time to time for tasting. As it is out of the question to maintain the quantities in the casks by refreshing them with similar wines, the level gradually falls, and every fifteen years or so they are racked off into smaller casks. To ensure that an adequate surface is exposed to the air, casks in which wine is maturing are normally only filled to 80 per cent of their capacity, and about 5 per cent evaporates every year. It has been estimated that a butt of wine from which nothing was drawn would take about seventy years to evaporate completely, but in practice it looks as if none of the Williams & Humbert añada wines can survive much more thanks to sampling and evaporation; in the meantime, they represent completely natural sherry in all its varieties. They are classified from time to time, and it is interesting to see how they change over the years. For comparison two classifications thirty years apart are shown below: those of 1957 and 1987.

	CLASSIFICATION OF 1957		CLASSIFICATION OF 1987	
	Degrees		Degrees	
	Gay-		Gay-	
Year	Lussac	Classification	Lussac	Classification
1920	22.8	Amontillado Viejo	22.9	Amontillado Viejísimo
1922	21.8	Amontillado Viejo	22.0	Amontillado Viejísimo
1924	21.8	Tres Cortados	22.0	Tres Cortados
1925	21.0	Tres Cortados	21.1	Tres Cortados
1926	21.0	Dos Cortados	21.1	Dos Cortados
1927	21.0	Amontillado	21.1	Amontillado Viejísimo
1928	20.2	Amontillado	20.4	Amontillado Viejísimo
1929	19.8	Oloroso	20.0	Palo Cortado
1930	19.8	Raya Vieja	19.9	Oloroso Viejísimo
1931	18.8	Palma Cortada	19.0	Palma Dos Cortados
1932	18.8	Amontillado	18.9	Amontillado Viejo
1933	18.8	Amontillado	18.9	Oloroso Viejo
1934	18.0	Fino Viejo	18.1	Fino Viejísimo
1935	18.0	Palo Cortado	18.1	Palo Cortado
1936	18.4	Oloroso	18.5	Oloroso Viejo
1937	18.4	Amontillado	18.5	Palo Cortado
1938	18.4	Palo Cortado	18.5	Palo Cortado
1939	18.0	Fino Viejo	18.1	Oloroso
1940	18.0	Oloroso	18.1	Oloroso
1941	17.6	Oloroso	17.6	Oloroso
1942	18.0	Palma	18.1	Amontillado
1943	18.0	Raya Oloroso	19.8	Raya Oloroso
1944	16.4	Palma	16.6	Palma Cortada
1945	17.2	Raya Fina	19.2	Oloroso

Year				
1946	16.7	Amontillado	19.6	Amontillado
1947	16.4	Amontillado	17.9	Oloroso
1948	16.4	Palma Cortada	16.6	Oloroso Ligero
1949	16.0	Palma	16.1	Oloroso
1950	16.0	Raya Fina (?)	17.0	Oloroso
1951	15.2	Oloroso	17.4	Oloroso
1952	15.2	Raya Fina (?)	16.1	Oloroso
1953	15.3	Fino Amontillado	16.5	Palo Cortado
1954	15.1	Fino (?)	15.8	Palma
1955	15.7	Fino (?)	18.0	Oloroso
1956	15.5	Fino (?)	16.5	Oloroso
1957	15.2	Fino (?)	15.8	Fino Amontillado
1958			15.4	Palo Cortado
1959			15.3	Amontillado Fino
1960			15.8	Raya Oloroso
1961			17.8	Palo Cortado
1962			19.0	Raya Oloroso
1963			19.1	Dos Cortados
1964			18.8	Palo Cortado.
1965			19.0	Palo Cortado
1966			18.4	Oloroso
1967			19.5	Oloroso
1968			19.2	Oloroso
1969			18.8	Palo Cortado
1970			18.4	Palo Cortado
1971			19.6	Oloroso
1972			19.8	Oloroso
1973			19.6	Oloroso
1974			22.3	Oloroso
1975			17.1	Oloroso
1976			21.5	Oloroso
1977			22.0	Oloroso
1978			16.8	Oloroso
1979			17.6	Oloroso
1980			17.5	Oloroso
1981			17.4	Palo Cortado
1982			17.7	Palo Cortado
1983			17.7	
1984			17.9	
1985			18.0	
1986			18.0	

As the butts of must preserved as añadas were selected from the best produced by the vineyard each year, there is a far higher proportion of first-class wines, particularly of palo cortado, than would normally be expected, but every style is represented. The character of the wine is determined to a considerable extent by the presence or absence of flor. It has already been described how commercial sherries, if they show a tendency to develop as olorosos, are helped on their way by a fortification that kills the flor. The wines listed above have not been tampered with at all, and one or two of the younger ones occasionally grow flor in substantial quantities despite a distinct leaning towards oloroso, but the rapid increase in strength shown by such wines kills the flor after only four or five years, whereas those developing as finos retain their flor for twice as long, until they eventually develop into amontillados or *finos viejos*. As nothing is done to bias their development, however, the unexpected becomes more probable, and they are definitely hard to classify, particularly when they are young and still growing flor. As they grow older, each gets steadily darker and gains in flavour, but when all of them are displayed side by side in a row, it is seen that there are wide differences between the colours of the wines grown in successive years, depending on how each has developed. The figures also show how they gain in strength as they mature until they reach equilibrium and the strength remains practically steady. Sherry takes about as long as a human being to attain full maturity; while the development then slows down, it never stops entirely. Such is the concentration and excellence of the older wines, that it is hard to classify them at all: they attain an apotheosis that can only be described as 'very old sherry'. Even the 1930 was a memorable wine when it was classified as a humble raya in 1957; by 1965 it was so obviously good that it was reclassified as an *oloroso viejísimo*, and so it remained in 1987. At Domecq's bodega, there is a cask that was once fino and that is well over two hundred years old; it has, of course, been refreshed from time to time with old wine of the same style, but it is now practically black and is so strong in flavour that it cannot be drunk unless blended with a younger wine.

At the moment no vintage sherries are marketed, but customers can always be found for something rare, different and good. Wisdom & Warter started to set aside wine in 1987 to mature as añadas. None is yet old enough for sale but some very interesting bottles could result eventually. Cowper would have us believe that 'Variety's the very spice of life', and it is partly the great variety found in sherry that makes it suitable for drinking at any time and prevents it from ever becoming monotonous. But the shipper is expected to supply his customers year after year with the wines they like, and the quality must never vary. The traditional way of maturing sherry was to keep it in its separate añadas until it was ready for use, but it developed in all its many styles and the shippers could not supply high quality wines in any substantial quantities if the character was to remain unchanged: it is quite easy to blend a wine down to a consistent mediocre standard, but really good wines, especially if they are dry (such as a first-grade delicate fino), need to be shipped in their natural state. If some imaginary and gargantuan shipping house could have a million butts of añada wine steadily maturing, it would probably be able to find sufficient casks of every kind to satisfy all its requirements, but such an arrangement would obviously be out of the question. It was therefore necessary to devise a way of producing identical wines in large quantities without lowering the quality, and the solera system was invented.

It is one of the convenient qualities of sherry that if a reasonably small proportion (perhaps a third) of the contents of a cask of superior old wine is withdrawn, and the void is filled with a slightly younger wine of the same style, the younger wine gradually takes on the quality of the older; after a few months, the wine in the cask will be absolutely indistinguishable from what it was before. It is this that makes the solera system possible.[1]

A solera consists essentially of a number of casks of identical wine of a style which the shipper wishes to prepare as one of his standard products. At intervals throughout the year, a quantity of wine is drawn off and is replaced with younger wine of the same style. The solera is then said to be 'refreshed'. The wine in all the casks is kept on ullage; they are only filled to 90 per cent of their capacity so that there is plenty of air to feed the flor or to oxidize the oloroso, as the case may be. Quite clearly, a solera containing wine with the qualities of an añada wine twenty years old cannot be refreshed with añada wines only a year or two old; the contrast would be too great and the wine would lose its quality. The solera is therefore refreshed with wine that is only slightly younger, drawn from a *criadera*, or nursery. This, in turn, is refreshed with wine drawn from another criadera; there may be eight or nine criaderas in all, until the last contains wine sufficiently young in character to be refreshed with añada wine that may be anything from nine

1 The solera system has been scientically investigated and mathematically analysed. See *Theory and Application of Fractional-Blending Systems* by Baker, Amerine and Roessler, Hilgardia, May 1952.

months to several years old. It can therefore be described as a dynamic system of maturation.

Each of the stages of development, represented by a criadera or by the solera, is called a *scale*; thus there may be five criaderas and the solera, making six scales in all. The word *solera* is also used to denote the whole system and, in the above example, the shipper would talk of his solera when referring to all six scales as a single entity. Such soleras are often given fancy names. As all sherry is matured by means of this system, it is clearly absurd to refer to 'solera sherry' as if it were a distinct style, though the term has been misapplied in this way by a number of merchants, who use it to denote a rich dessert oloroso.

Wine that is carefully matured in a solera never varies in quality. It may well be that one or two 'interesting' wines that would develop in the añada system are lost, but the quality of the wines produced by a solera is not one whit inferior to comparable wines matured as añadas; it may even be better, as some shippers think that the wine is improved by its contact with the oxygen of the air as it is moved from scale to scale; but this is a moot point. Moreover, the sherry towns contain an enormous number of soleras of varying sizes, each of a different style and quality, so there is just as much variety as there was before. The ownership of first-class soleras is the secret of success for a sherry shipper; his whole business depends on their quality and style; they are of incalculable value, and he gives them all the care and attention that is humanly possible.

The above description, however, is necessarily oversimplified, and there are many details to be filled in. The word *solera* has no connection with *sol*, but is derived from the Latin *solum*, or Spanish *suelo*, meaning 'floor', though the word has divaricated considerably from its origin and is used in normal speech to denote an entablature, plinth or lintel. Warner Allen preferred to derive it from *solar*, which can mean a noble house or an ancestral mansion. But that is only one of many meanings; more usually it simply means a plot of land or, as the infinitive of a verb, to make a floor, or even to sole shoes. So we are back to earth again. When used in connection with wine, the specialist meaning has kept far nearer the derivation: a solera is the basis or foundation for making wine. It is not known when the word first came to be used in this way, nor is it known exactly how long the solera system has been operating in its present form. The ability to mature a young wine by blending with an older one has presumably been common knowledge amongst wine growers in the sherry district since very early times, but it was probably not organized into a working system until after the Napoleonic Wars; there is no mention of soleras in the work of Esteban Boutelou, published in 1807, though he does refer to *vinos de manzanilla*, grown at Sanlucar, which can only be matured by the solera system. This confirms the general opinion that soleras originated at Sanlucar in the late eighteenth or early nineteenth century, but the evidence is very slender, as the term *manzanilla* may well have had a different meaning at that time. The solera system is certainly not heard of in the archives at Jerez or Puerto de Santa Maria until much later. In the records of the ancient house of Garvey the words *solera* and *criadera* first appeared in the inventory of 1849, though they were probably in use earlier. Two of the criaderas of amontillado mentioned in that inventory are still working, and Gonzalez Byass have a famous solera of oloroso that was laid down in 1847. When Diego Parada y Barreto wrote his book in 1868, soleras were common, though the old añada system was used more extensively than it is today.

The most obvious and logical way to start a solera would be to buy a large stock of wine of a given vintage and, after all the casks have been matured as añadas, to put aside those of the desired quality for use as a solera. The same thing could be done the following year, the wine being used as the first scale of a criadera, and so on until sufficient scales were available. The expense and difficulty of creating a solera by such a system are obvious. This can be avoided to some extent by collecting wine of the desired style and quality simultaneously from several sources. Moreover, there can be more than a year's gap between the age of the wine in the various scales, but the greater the gap, the more slowly can the wine be shifted from scale to scale.

Clearly, the number of scales and the number of butts in each scale depend on the effective age of the wine and also on the required rate of production. There is nothing magical about the number of scales a solera may have, as approximately the same result can be obtained by having a few scales and drawing very little as by having many scales and moving the wine frequently; this especially applies to amontillados and olorosos, where the shipper may produce a similar wine from an eight-scale solera refreshed with young must or a two-scale solera refreshed with old añada wines. This does not, however, apply to fino, as the flor will only continue to breed if the solera is carefully regulated, and if insufficient fino is drawn, it becomes *seco* and loses its delicacy. It is essential to keep the wine progressing in a fino solera as the young wine brings with it the nutrients that are essential for the well-being of the flor yeasts. Soleras producing manzanilla in Sanlucar have even more scales than have fino soleras, though these are necessarily elaborate; that producing fino San Patricio at Garveys is refreshed from a criadera of seven scales. To prepare wines of greater body, fewer scales are generally required. There are always more scales in a fino solera than in an equivalent amontillado or oloroso solera. As an extreme example, Valdespino's Inocente solera has ten scales.

In the middle of the nineteenth century, when the solera system was coming into general use and was replacing the añada system, the wines were still usually kept as añadas for five or six years. It was found, though, that it was unnecessary to keep them for so long, nor was it desirable, as wines which were that mature had developed too much individuality and could not very readily be absorbed into the criadera. The period for keeping them as añadas was therefore gradually reduced. When the second edition of this book was published it was still generally considered best practice to keep them for two or three years by which time they were old enough to be classified with reasonable certainty. For many years before that, though, some shippers had been keeping their wines as añadas for only about nine months. This has now become normal practice. Experience shows a shipper which vineyards grow the wines he needs for a particular solera, and modern, carefully controlled fermentation techniques have largely cut out the freaks, so that nine months is quite long enough. The use of these younger wines has kept costs down and has not produced any detectable change in the sherries drawn from the soleras. However, some of the traditional shippers still keep their añadas longer – Sandeman, for example, keep finos for one to one and a half years and olorosos for two to two and a half years.

In numbering the scales of a criadera, that next to the solera is number one; this is preceded by number two, and so on, the youngest wine being added to the scale with the highest number. It is instructive to taste samples drawn from successive scales, as the steady development of the wine is at once apparent. If these samples are analysed, it is seen that each scale is stronger in alcohol than that immediately before it; the acidity is also slightly greater, while the proportion of aldehydes and esters rises rapidly.

A wine of very great apparent age can only be produced by an elaborate solera. This is made more difficult to explain by the fact that the last criadera of a solera is not necessarily refreshed with must or with añada wines, but may be refreshed with mature wines prepared in another solera. Thus a solera of oloroso may have fifty butts in each scale – though each successive scale is likely to have one or two butts less than the one immediately before it, to allow for evaporation and loss. This solera would give a pleasant and mature wine; part of its output would be used without any further treatment, but another part would feed the last criadera of a solera of oloroso viejo, containing perhaps twenty butts in each scale. The wine from this second solera would have greater properties of age and would be used for blending expensive dessert sherries, but it might not be old enough for the very finest dessert sherries, and so part of it would be used to refresh the last criadera of yet another solera, producing an oloroso viejísimo; this would probably have only five butts per scale. In some houses such a complex solera would be referred to as a single unit; in others each section would have a different name and would be considered separately. An example is afforded by Sandeman's fabulous solera of oloroso. This is operated in two parts, though wine is drawn off for blending at various stages. The first part consists of ten criaderas and a solera. This is followed by three more criaderas and another solera, making fifteen scales in all. By the seventh criadera of the first section, the wine is already fully mature. The oloroso from the second solera is almost certainly unique.

Wine is usually drawn from a solera once, twice or three times a year, and the amount taken on each occasion may be a very small quantity or as much as 40 per cent. In a typical solera of fino, producing wine of unvarying quality, 30 per cent might be drawn twice a year, though the tendency now is to have more scales and to move the wine faster, for instance by drawing 30 per cent three times a year. On the other hand, a shipper with a prize solera of very old amontillado, palo cortado or oloroso might only draw 5 per cent once a year, so that the quality and age steadily increase. Conversely, some old-established soleras have been ruined by drawing more wine than they could safely supply. When a wine has become very popular, and demand outstrips supply, it is all too easy to succumb to the temptation to increase the *sacas* – to draw off more wine. But this is very short-sighted. One fino sherry, popular in the 1920s, was spoiled in this way and virtually disappeared from the market. The lesson has been learned. For this reason, houses that sell wine as Solera 1066, or some such name, are instantly suspect. In the clubs of Jerez they are accused of using their telephone number or the first number they thought of. Very often, in fact, they use the year the solera was laid down, and at least one excellent wine is sold under such a name, but absolutely anything might have happened to the solera since it was laid down, so the name is meaningless. All the wine in a solera is so mixed up that it is obviously impossible to calculate its age:[1] one can speak of its 'equivalent age' by comparing a solera wine with añada wines of similar development, but such a test is really quite worthless, as añada wines develop in such a haphazard way. Only the quality is important: the age is immaterial.

People often think of a solera as being worked very scientifically with the wine drawn on fixed days every year, but this seldom happens, as the system is remarkably flexible and wide variations are possible provided it is carefully watched. To some extent, the quantity and date of withdrawal are governed by demand, and slightly different quantities may be drawn at different seasons. When working a solera of flor wine, however, it is advisable not to disturb it when it is flowering, and the best times are winter and summer – though, now that the conditions for the growth of flor are more clearly understood than they used to be, and fino soleras are kept in very well insulated bodegas, the difference in the thickness of flor with the seasons is much less than it used to be and the problem of disturbing it is less. The further problem of oxidation of the fino once it has been withdrawn has also been mastered by keeping it out of contact with the air. Domecq, for instance, keep it under nitrogen.

As the yeast cells die they fall into the bottom of the cask and after a time there is a considerable accumulation. Up to a point this is a good thing as they contribute to the flavour of the wine by autolysis, but when it gets too much they can make the wine turbid. The casks in a fino solera have to be cleaned out every twenty-five

1 Though an estimate can be made. See *Theory and Application of Fractional-Blending Systems* by Baker, Amerine and Roessler, already referred to.

years or so, which is done by rotation so that there are always plenty with a substantial amount of lees.

The instruments traditionally used in working the scales of a solera are illustrated on the next page. The wine is siphoned from a cask by means of a *bomba* or *sifon*. One end of this is inserted well below the flor, and the siphon is started by a bodega workman, or *arrumbador*, sucking at the other end; he is said to *llamar*, or call, to the wine. Given sufficient skill, he stops calling just in time to avoid disaster, but occasionally there is a mishap, and he is then said to *coger*, or catch it. If he were working with strong wine, mitad y mitad, or brandy, he could well be asphyxiated, and a glass of very sweet sherry has to be administered at once, to absorb the alcohol and act as an antidote. Once the siphon is working properly, the wine is collected in wooden or enamelled *jarras*, which hold one arroba – the standard measure used in the sherry area; there are thirty arrobas to a shipping butt.[1] Most siphons are fitted with taps, and these can be turned off easily when sufficient wine has been withdrawn. The more primitive sort have to be lifted hastily out of the butts.

The operation of refreshing a solera is known as *rociando*. Wine cannot be poured straight in through a funnel, as this would churn up the lees and would also damage the flor. To overcome this, a *rociador*, or sprinkler, is used, consisting of a slightly curved enamelled pipe, the lower half of which is perforated with small holes; its shape is so adjusted that the fresh wine sprays out gently, as if it were coming from the rose of a watering can, but all the holes are beneath the flor and well above the lees. To introduce the fresh wine even more gently into a butt with a heavy growth of flor, a *garceta* may be used instead of a rociador. This is simply a close-meshed hessian sack, which is gentler, slower and more difficult to use; but it is the only satisfactory instrument for refreshing the manzanilla soleras at Sanlucar, and is also quite often used when working fino soleras in the other sherry towns.

---

1 An arroba can be a measure either of volume or of weight, and the measure varies between different districts of Spain. In Jerez, it is equal to 21 pounds weight of grapes or 3.66 imperial gallons. A standard shipping butt contains approximately 110 gallons, or 30 arrobas, though it is sold as 108 gallons to allow for waste. Bodega butts are larger, and hold 140 gallons; this allows an adequate air space above the wine.

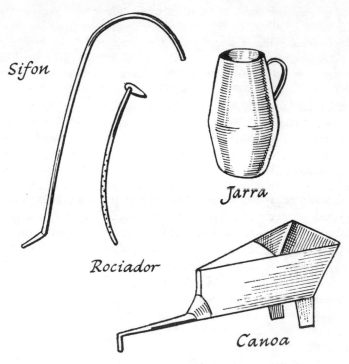

Sifon

Jarra

Rociador

Canoa

The working tools

The fresh wine is poured into the rociador through a *canoa*, or 'canoe' – a gently sloping, boat-shaped funnel that is placed on top of the butt. The canoa is so wide that the jarras can be emptied very quickly with no risk of waste, though sometimes a piece of gauze, or similar obstruction, is fitted into the spout to make the wine flow into the rociador slowly and cause less of a disturbance in the cask. In working the scales of a solera, the capataz does his best to see that the wine from each butt is distributed as evenly as possible amongst those in the next scale. Thus, if five jarras are drawn from one butt, five distinct butts in the next scale would be refreshed with one jarra each. If this were not done, variations might occur in the development of the individual casks of a solera. Individual casks in the soleras are examined regularly and if one fails to come up to scratch it is taken out.

In the 1960s this work, like so many of the bodega tasks, was mechanized. The sifon, the jarra and the canoa were replaced with a pump and plastic hose. Pumps have long been used for moving wine in bulk to blending tanks, and several forms have been perfected which do no harm whatsoever to the wine. Their use for working the scales of the soleras, however, was new. The result is that a *quadrilla* of four workmen could move the wine in seventy butts in the course of a day instead of in thirty, as before, and they went home cheerfully and with a smile instead of being dead tired.

By the 1970s, with higher labour costs and increased demand, this simple degree of mechanization was not enough. Pipelines were installed in the bodegas with terminals where one could be linked into another, so that wine can now quickly be moved from one place to another, wherever it is needed. In some installations pipes pass beneath the ground to link buildings that are some distance apart, and in at least one they pass beneath a public road. All of this does no harm at all provided that everything is kept scrupulously clean. There is inevitably some loss of wine but this is small compared with the saving in labour. But if the distances are too great there can be problems with loss of wine and with keeping the pipes clean. To avoid this Crofts, in its big Rancho, moves wine from one building to another in tanker lorries.

The use of pipelines is, of course, by no means unique to sherry shippers. They have been used with complete success for years in handling delicate table wines, for instance in bottling plants.

The quadrillas are no more, and with their passing, the whole atmosphere of the bodegas has changed. There used to be lots of people who were obviously busy. Now there is emptiness, with an occasional isolated workman operating his machinery.

A popular and erroneous belief held by visitors to the sherry towns is that the scales of a solera are mounted one on top of another, so that wine from the fourth or top tier in the bodega is used to refresh wine in the third tier, but this very seldom occurs in practice. An even and low temperature is vital while the wine is maturing, especially for finos, and the best position is in the bottom two tiers, where the finest finos and amontillados are kept. Olorosos are stored in the third tier, and the fourth tier, when there is one, is used for olorosos and for the sweet and colour wines that are specially prepared for blending. These wines, of course, can also be matured in the lower tiers if there is room for them.

The scales of a solera are often separated; they may be in equivalent tiers at various places in the same bodega, or even in entirely different bodegas a mile or two apart. The different scales of important soleras are often divided between the various buildings to minimize fire risk. One famous shipper keeps corresponding criaderas of his best fino solera in the two lower tiers on opposite sides of a gangway, and makes a point of refreshing the more senior criadera on the left with wine drawn from the more junior on the right, and vice versa, so that any draught or variation in atmosphere that may exist between the two sides will affect all the wine equally. This, perhaps, is carrying things unnecessarily far, but it demonstrates how everything possible is done to maintain the highest quality and standard of uniformity.

There is a requirement that the minimum age of a wine should be three years before it can be shipped. To comply with this a shipper can only sell a third of his stock annually. Most sell less. Owing to the use of the solera system, there is no way in which one can say that a wine is three years old or can put any other precise figure on it; but the panel of tasters at the Consejo Regulador can reliably assess the character and age and can reject a wine that is manifestly immature. The Consejo Regulador also keeps a very close bureaucratic tag on all the movements of wine within the area, maddening the shippers with the pettifogging demands of mounds of paperwork that seem to grow worse yearly. Stocks are also monitored so that the officials can see if the figures do not add up and if wine has therefore manifestly not been matured long enough. One can quite easily see how such figures could be rigged by a dishonest shipper, but in practice the very existence of the solera system, with the need to keep the wine moving regularly through it, helps to ensure that young wine is not sold while the old wine is kept, which in any case would not be economic.

As fino progresses through its solera, the alcoholic strength, which is 15.6° to 16° in the young wine that is fed in, decreases gradually as it progresses through the criadera to a strength of about 14.6° in the solera, while the volatile acidity goes down, as do the proportions of tartaric acid, pyruvic acid, sulphate ions, proteins and glycerol, the yeast feeding on these last two. In the early stages the content of lactic acid goes up, possibly owing to a malolactic fermentation. The dry extract also goes down, largely owing to the reduction in glycerols and proteins. With amontillados the alcohol rises from 14.6° to 18°, and the volatile acidity, potassium, sulphate ions, pyruvic acid, malic acid, lactic acid, proteins, and glycerol and polyphenols go up while the tartaric acid goes down. With oloroso the alcohol rises from 18.2° to 19.6°, the other compounds varying as for amontillado.

10
Manzanilla

Manzanilla is prepared at Sanlucar de Barrameda. The British connection with Sanlucar goes back for many years, long before manzanilla was heard of. There were certainly British merchants there at the beginning of the sixteenth century, and their church of St George was founded in the reign of Henry VIII, when the town was the main port and metropolis of the sherry district; but that story has already been told. Sanlucar is a pleasant little place that still retains traces of the days when it was a vital port. Conquistadors sailed from there to discover new worlds. There are still the great houses of the noble families, and even a royal palace. In the 1950s and 1960s it seemed to be enchantingly asleep, but now all that is changed: the world has found that it likes manzanilla and the town has woken up to what appears, compared with the old days, to be frenzied activity.

In the summer Sanlucar is much cooler than Jerez, and some of the rich Jerezanos have houses there. The people are charming and happy; flamenco is sung and danced spontaneously in the streets, and there is something delightfully informal about it all:

> Señorita Consuelo Osorio de Moscoso, daughter of the duchess of Montemar, and Lady in Waiting to Princess Beatrice de Bourbon-Orleans, has just left ... Sanlucar prison. She had served one month in goal for 'an action prejudicial to the head of the State'.
>
> A year ago, Señorita Osorio sent a cable to Don Juan, claimant to the Spanish throne, in Estoril. She said, 'She hoped to see Don Juan in Madrid when this impostor has left.'
>
> The authorities fined her £570. They declined to accept the argument of her lawyer that she was not referring to General Franco as 'an impostor' but to a claimant to the throne of Spain.

Señorita Osorio refused to pay and in May this year she received notice that she would have to serve one month in gaol. Ex-Queen Elena of Italy was then visiting Princess Beatrice, who informed the authorities that she could not spare her Lady in Waiting and would be glad if they would leave the matter over until the Queen left.

The local judge agreed. One week later the princess informed him that her Lady in Waiting 'is now free to go to gaol'.

The judge sent a written order for Señorita Osorio to report to the prison. She declined to go, however, and insisted that the civil guard should be sent to arrest her.

In the face of this situation the judge announced that he was ill and could deal with no business. The mayor of the town departed on 'urgent business' to Jerez, and it was not until three days later that three civil guards came to arrest her.

At the gaol, she was received by the Governor, who said that he and his family had moved out of their quarters to offer them to Señorita Osorio.

Daily Telegraph, 1947

It could only have happened in Spain, and of all Spain, it would be most likely in Sanlucar.

The town is very ancient, perhaps even older than Cadiz, and the pagan temple of the Morning Star once stood there, hidden in a dense wood. Fragments of old buildings and many ancient coins are still found: the site is now known as *Sanlucar el Viejo*. *Barrameda* is said to be a modern word. Just outside the harbour, there is a hidden reef, or *barra*, that is very dangerous to shipping, and there used to be, on the bank of the river, a convent of the Jeronimite fathers, whose walls served as a landmark to guide pilots past the reef. There was also an enormous pine tree near the convent, called *el pino de la marca*; it was so wide that two men could not span it, but it was blown down in a gale some years ago. Inside the convent was an image of Our Lady, and it was called Santa Maria de Barrame-da, because its divine powers delivered sailors from the reef. Soon the two names were combined and corrupted to give the modern Sanlucar de Barrameda. That is the accepted story, but the following passage from Steven's translation of Mariana's *History of Spain* (1592) would suggest an alternative derivation:

After a siege of 6 months, the Moors raised their camp from

before Xerez, being in want of all necessaries, and fearing lest King Sancho should offer them Battel. After they had pass'd the River Guadalete, rather in the nature of Flight, than a Retreat, one ask'd of the Moorish king the Reason why he sho'd so much Fear, and he answer'd: 'I am the first that rais'd the Family of Bar-ameda to the Regal Dignity; my enemy is descended from above 40 Kings, which in Battle would have been a great Terror to me, and a mighty Incouragement to him.'

So it seems probable that the name is really Moorish.

For many years Sanlucar knew great prosperity and was an important provincial centre. Francisco Pacheco, the master and father-in-law of Velazquez, was born there in 1564. But the fortunes of Sanlucar began to decline when the great Indies trade was diverted to Seville and Cadiz in the seventeenth century, and the shipping business for the wine trade also gradually migrated, first to Puerto de Santa Maria and then likewise to Cadiz. By 1762 J. Hinxman was able to write: 'The town declines daily, and its principal trade is in salt.' By the time George Borrow called there in 1839, on one of his hot-gospelling missions, it had become noted for its thieves, rogues and smugglers. Nevertheless, he actually succeeded in selling prohibited books (Bibles in Spanish and Gitano) in the customs house, of all places. He might well succeed in doing the same sort of thing were he alive today.

Perhaps owing to its antiquity and geographical position, Sanlucar is mentioned in English travel books more frequently than either of the other sherry towns. Henry Swinburne, writing in 1810, described how it was a quiet and pleasant town without much business. But when the arch-disparager Richard Ford went there in 1858, he described it thus:

White and glittering, it is an ill-paved, dull, decaying place; pop. 16,000 . . . San Lucar exists by its wine-trade, and is the mart of the inferior and adulterated vintages which are foisted off in England as sherries. Nota bene, here, at least, drink *manzanilla*, however much it may be eschewed in England, which being, fortunately, not a wine growing country, imports the very best of all others, leaving the inferior for native consumption.

Inevitably, of all British travellers, the most unfortunate was Charles Tovey:

. . . wretched streets of San Lucar. Of paving and pitching there was none. The only pitching was the probability of the vehicle's upsetting and pitching me into the foulest composition that eyes ever saw or nose inhaled. In the centre of the street is an open drain, and the filth is abominable. Pigs wallowed in all directions, and were busy making their meals from the sewage matter. The stomachs of the residents cannot be very fastidious if they eat pork. The lower orders appear very degraded. Beggars, with their perpetual whine, assail you at every step. A poor wretched woman, covered with ulcers, and one-half of her face eaten away with cancer – a child in her arms whose mouth and face were diseased in a similar manner – persecuted me terribly. Her offensive appearance induced me to give more than the usual donation, in order to get rid of her; instead of which it acted as an encouragement to follow me wherever I went, and when I visited a Bodega she waited outside. I took a walk through the Almeida on the banks of the Guadalquivir, and congratulated myself upon my escape; but I was not to see the last of her. She must have made a liberality known to her fraternity, for on my return to the town I found her with about a dozen others, and I was almost mobbed until my friend came to my rescue. There are no police to interfere, and the priests give beggars encouragement . . .

If this account were accurate, one can only say that the town has changed beyond all recognition: nothing but its ancient beauty remains. Its greatest glory, though, is its wine. If one may be permitted, as usual, to digress, Mr Tovey's death in 1888 was as fraught with odd misfortune as was his life. When, in the words of the *Clifton Chronicle*, 'he passed peacefully away . . . at the somewhat patriarchal age of 76 . . . and was gathered in as a shock of corn in due season,' the usual burial arrangements had to be modified: '. . . the body was enclosed in a shell, encased in zinc (it being considered that lead would add too much to the already heavy burden), the outer coffin being of polished oak, with massive brass furniture.' Amongst the many mourners in his funeral procession was E. A. Harvey, and Tovey was sincerely missed, for he was a good man.

The English were not the only visitors to Sanlucar. When the Duchess of Alba retired to her estates there in 1745, following the Duke's death, Goya went to visit her and prepared the twenty-two drawings of the *Sanlucar Sketch-Books*. The tormented passion of these books was to become the inspiration for his *Caprichos*.

Manzanilla is a comparatively modern wine. In the very early days there is evidence that a form of malmsey was grown in Sanlucar; later wines conformed to the normal sherry styles and there was also a red wine called *vino carlón*. Until well into the nineteenth century, much of the sherry prepared there was boiled down to make a dark colouring wine, or *vino de color*, used in blending. It is not known who first found how to prepare manzanilla, nor the exact date, but it probably happened in about 1800. In a list of wines on sale in 1803 manzanilla was not mentioned, though probably some of those listed as *vinos finos de lujo*, or *de luxe* fino wines, were exactly the same thing. Esteban Boutelou wrote of manzanilla in 1807, but the name did not become common in commercial records until after the end of the Peninsular War in 1814. The name first appears in the books of Barbadillo in 1827 and the wine was regularly sold from 1830. For the most part, however, it was sold in cask for local consumption until the coming of the railway in 1877 opened up a bulk trade in the Peninsula. In the middle of the century most of the trade from Sanlucar was still in oloroso and colour wines sold to the shippers of Jerez and Puerto de Santa Maria. They also became good customers for manzanilla, which they used for blending, and direct sales were neglected in their favour. By 1892 the production of manzanilla had become predominant but it was not bottled very extensively until the early years of the present century. It was first introduced into England by Dr J. Gorman, of Puerto de Santa Maria, a physician who abandoned the practice of medicine to spend the latter part of his life in the wine trade. By the 1920s the old trade in colour wines had disappeared.

The origin of the name has been the subject of much learned controversy. The following theories have been suggested: firstly, that it takes its name from the little Andalusian town of Manzanilla, not far from Seville; secondly, that it is derived from *manzana*, meaning 'apple'; thirdly, that there was a vine of the same name; and fourthly, that its flavour resembles that of *manzanilla* – the common camomile. The first theory is popular with tourists but with no one else. The wines made in Manzanilla hardly have even a superficial resemblance to those of Sanlucar, and to derive the name by analogy with that of amontillado is obviously unjustified. The theory owes something to the writings of Charles Davillier, and is now discredited. The second theory is quite often heard in the sherry district, but the bouquet of manzanilla is so unlike the penetrating aroma of an apple that the derivation is too far-fetched to be taken seriously. The third theory, found in the dictionary of Ramón Joaquín Domínguez, can be dismissed at once, as there has never been a vine with a name even remotely similar. The fourth theory is almost certainly the right one, and the resemblance has frequently been remarked upon by those with the right kind of imagination. One wonders whether the name was first used as a jest to describe the newly invented wine. The first reference I have been able to find to it is in a book written by Esteban Boutelou and published in 1807: 'De las uvas blancas aparentes como la *listan*, pisadas en buena disposicion, y expimidas levemente, se obtienen vinos blancos sin el menor viso, que se distinguen constantemente por su olor de *manzanilla*, y por su fragrancia exquisita que tanto aprecian los Gaditanos.' ('From white grapes such as the listan pressed in a good condition and gently you get white wines without the slightest colour, which are firmly distinguished by their aroma of *manzanilla* and by their exquisite fragrance, which is so greatly appreciated by those who live in Cadiz.') The Listan is a synonym for the Palomino. He goes on to refer to *vinos de manzanilla*; and it would appear that the manzanillas we know today date from about that time.

It is as well to utter a warning: in many of the Spanish *pensiones*, if you ask for manzanilla, you are likely to get a cup of camomile tea, which is said to be good for the stomach. Even the aromatic resemblance, however, is unlikely to make it welcome. To add to the confusion, there is also the manzanilla olive, and the story is told of a prominent sherry shipper who sent a small barrel of them, preserved in brine, to one of his customers, for Christmas. A very worried wine buyer telephoned and complained diffidently that his present of manzanilla had been tampered with: the wine tasted strongly of salt and it was full of foreign bodies.

Sanlucar is both distinctly cooler than Jerez – so much so that Jerezanos drive down there after work to avoid the sweltering heat of summer – and also more humid. These differences have a considerable impact on the metabolism of the flor yeasts which grow there in superabundance. There are also several minor differences in viticulture and oenology. For instance, the grapes never were sunned, and excessive concentration is avoided by never pruning short and by picking the grapes early enough for them to have ample acid; but these practices are by no means unique to Sanlucar and are, indeed, becoming normal everywhere. By far the most important difference lies in the way that the soleras are operated.

Manzanilla cannot be made by the añada system: if casks of must are allowed to mature naturally over the years, not one develops as manzanilla, but all grow into the conventional styles of sherry, differing only very slightly from those matured in the other towns. The tendency to develop into a specific class of wine is naturally apparent in about six months, but after the must has been racked off the lees, it is fortified to a lower degree: generally to about 14.5° Gay-Lussac, and never more than 15.5°. After a few more months, musts that have proved suitable are added to the youngest criadera of a solera, and it is from then onwards that the principal differences are found. Instead of moving the wine in the solera every six months or so, it is drawn at intervals of one to three months, though in some soleras the pause may be no more than a fortnight. The quantity taken, however, is very much smaller: usually about three to five jarras, as compared with the ten in a typical sherry solera. Manzanilla soleras have more scales than those producing fino: never fewer than nine, and sometimes as many as fourteen. The casks are also kept emptier, leaving a large surface area in contact with the air, and hence there is a larger area of flor. The soleras look different, too, because the bodega butts are mounted on stone supports, or *bajetes*, instead of wood. Sheets of cork are placed between the casks and the supports to prevent rot.

Manzanilla, of course, is a flor wine, and requires all the care bestowed on finos in the other towns; that is to say, it must be regulated accurately, and the flor must not be disturbed, so a garceta is used for refreshing rather than a rociador. The flor grown by manzanilla looks slightly different from that of fino; it grows more profusely and for a greater length of time in the spring and autumn. If, through mismanagement, it goes away, the consequences are completely disastrous, and there is a saying in Sanlucar that 'a bodega which does not flower is a bodega lost'. Manzanilla has been described as *el vino de la alegria* – 'the wine of joy'; it is as delicate and as temperamental as a woman.

The alcoholic strength of the wine from a healthy solera lies between 15° and 15.5° Gay-Lussac. This is somewhat weaker than fino, but manzanilla seldom deviates from these limits, as any wider variation would put such a delicate wine in danger of disease: a higher strength would reduce or even kill the flor, which gives the wine its natural protection, while a lower strength would make it impoverished and faint-hearted, lacking the balance necessary to fight infection. Until the 1980s it had to be fortified to 18°, even on the Spanish market, to prevent the development of flor in open bottles, but with modern filters all the yeasts can be taken out and it is sold throughout the world at its natural strength. It is also often bottled younger than it used to be as the modern taste is for pale, fresh wines.

The fino form of manzanilla, or *manzanilla fina*, is by no means the only one: all the other principal styles − fino-amontillado, amontillado, and oloroso − have their manzanilla equivalents, which are basically similar to those of sherry, but each of which has something of the sharp, penetrating and aromatic character associated with manzanilla. The fino form, however, is by far the most common and the adjective is invariably left out.

As with fino, when manzanilla fina ages, it loses its flor and gains in strength, first becoming *manzanilla pasada*, which is equivalent to fino-amontillado, and then *manzanilla amontillada*, when the strength may rise to as much as 20.5° Gay-Lussac. These latter wines are prepared by means of successive soleras, each being of greater equivalent age, and the wine in them is moved less often than that in the fina soleras. Palo cortado (called here Jerez cortado) and oloroso are also made in Sanlucar, using the must that shows no tendency to grow flor. The method of preparation is similar to that of the other towns, but the wines are slightly more piquant.

The date of the vintage, and the working of the soleras, are the two principal differences in the making of manzanilla, but there is a third factor that is entirely natural and vitally important: the climate. Sanlucar, like Puerto de Santa Maria, is by the sea, but unlike Puerto, it is bounded on the north by the wide mouth of the Guadalquivir and by the plains of the Marismas, which expose it to northerly winds. The climate could accurately be described as 'bracing' and, probably because it is so near the sea, there are less extremes of temperature than in Jerez. There are far too many mosquitoes, otherwise it would be an ideal place to live in: the climate, in fact, is delightful. It is rather more humid than the other towns, as the water lies very close to the surface of the ground, and a well can be made in some of the vineyards by digging only a few feet down. This does not appear to affect the quality of the grapes very much, as some manzanilla is prepared from grapes grown in the vineyards near Jerez, while some shippers in Jerez own vineyards near Sanlucar, and the must develops into normal sherry when taken to their bodegas. But while the climate is not sufficiently different to affect the vines, the wine is far more susceptible to small changes of atmosphere, and the temperature also influences the growth of flor. Manzanilla can only be prepared in Sanlucar: attempts to make it in the other towns have produced only some strange finos, and when casks of manzanilla are taken to Jerez, or even to Puerto de Santa Maria, they rapidly lose their freshness and delicacy and turn into rather ordinary finos. After only six or seven months they are completely spoilt. For the same reason the wine had the reputation of not travelling well: when shipped to England, it was often blended with fino, fortified and even sweetened. It remained an excellent wine, but it retained only a shadow of its natural elegance. But nowadays the real thing is available in Britain, almost as fresh and as elegant as in Sanlucar. Modern fast transport, bringing the wine in containers or in bottles so that it does not get oxidized on the way, as it used to do when transported in cask, has transformed it.

Rather ruefully, the wine growers of Sanlucar used to refer to their bodegas as the 'store-houses for Jerez'. Most of their wine was taken there, where it was blended for export. To some extent it still is, and a little manzanilla is often included in wines of an entirely different class to add to their fragrance. In the past Sanlucar always suffered first when there was any recession, as the shippers in Jerez avoided buying other people's wine when they could not sell their own. At the turn of the century, when the demand for sherry slumped, many wine growers there were ruined utterly: they had no other markets, and their bodegas were abandoned; their wine, which had become worthless, was left to perish. Nothing at all could save them. The misery was repeated when the German blockade prevented shipments from being made to Great Britain during the Second World War, and a grower with a stock of manzanilla normally worth half a million pounds was left virtually penniless. But happily things are very different now. The leading Sanlucar houses have become shippers in their own right and on a large scale. This drive owed much to the rise of the Rumasa empire, which absorbed one after another of their traditional customers and provided the motive for the development of direct sales. Their style of wine, too, has been becoming increasingly popular and they suffered less than most people from the recent decline in trade. It has become particularly popular in the Netherlands. Much of its gain in popularity is thanks to the efforts of Antonio Barbadillo and, more recently, of Javier Hidalgo.

Perhaps manzanilla is an acquired taste, though it does not take long to acquire. But in the cold, sunless English winter, a full-blooded amontillado or oloroso used to be favoured. With the coming of central heating and a move towards lighter drinks generally, manzanilla has at last come into its own. More now is sold than ever before. Manzanilla is at its best, though, drunk in great draughts under the sun. When a nineteenth-century Earl of Derby was stricken with gout, his doctor forbade rich sherries and ordered him to try manzanilla. His wine merchant supplied a case, but he tried only one bottle. He sent the rest back, with a note that he preferred the gout. Perhaps we should be charitable and suppose that Lord Derby was sent an indifferent example, for manzanilla is so light, and so attractive, that it is almost impossible to drink less than a bottle at a sitting on a hot day. It is a soothing, apparently innocuous wine, but on no account is it a wine to get drunk on: the hangover is appalling and it gives one a stomach-ache that lasts a week. But taken in moderation, it is a joy and a delight, a wine that stirs men to poetry. Manuel Barbadillo wrote a whole book about it, and his lyric *Canción de la Manzanilla* is as enchanting as the wine it acclaims:

> *Manzanilla! Manzanilla!*
> *Cantar de una seguidilla . . .*
> *Revuelos de soleares . . .*
>   *Todo el cante de los mares,*
> *de la sierra . . . y de Sevilla!*
>
> *La caña en alto; la risa;*
> *la ilusión como una brisa,*
> *de verde y oro, en la frente.*
> *Con tu aroma, alegremente,*
> *la vida se immortaliza!*

11

The Final Blend

When the shipper has prepared his wine and matured it in his soleras, his work has only just begun. The most difficult task of all follows: it has to be blended and prepared for export.

Just a few of the completely dry aperitif sherries sold in Great Britain are straight solera wines. These are very good, but the market is limited and they are, of necessity, expensive. Such sherries are an acquired taste: the palate has to be trained to enjoy their austerity and delicacy. All the sweeter aperitif sherries have to be blended, as do the great, rich, dessert olorosos.

The work of blending calls not only for knowledge and experience, but also for a special flair – an intuitive understanding and taste for wine. The great shippers are not only craftsmen, they are artists. Even when the cost does not matter, their work is intensely difficult: they must prepare a completely balanced wine that is old without being bitter, and soft but not cloying. They must also consider the price and prepare a wine their public can afford. Their task is confused by a mass of conflicting aims and limitations.

Every shipper has his standard range of wines. In the past a big shipper may have had thirty or more standard blends available, but this is no longer economically possible. Any shipper starting nowadays would choose to promote only four or five wines on which he could concentrate his efforts. This has been done, for instance, by Crofts. Older-established shippers still have to keep a wider range to satisfy repeat orders, but they are generally trying to cut down. Until the 1960s and 1970s many special blends used to be prepared for merchants throughout the world to sell under their own labels; and this was especially so for the British trade which used to have many small merchants with fine traditions of individuality. But many of the largest shippers decline to supply this trade at all now, save for the very notable exception of Diez-Mérito. For the most part it is left to the smaller, specialist houses.

Few shippers have a wide enough range of soleras to supply all their different blends, nor would they wish to have, as the demand for some styles is very small. It is here that the *almacenistas*, or store-keepers, come to the rescue. Many of these have excellent soleras; they are well known locally, though they seldom sell any wine direct to the public. Shippers generally rely on their own soleras for their greatest and oldest wines, though almacenistas do carry small stocks of these; on the other hand, almacenistas can supply many of the unusual wines that may be required from time to time for blending. Sometimes they contract to sell the whole output of a solera to an individual shipper, year after year, but more often the wine from each solera is divided among a number of people at the highest price the almacenista can get – a service that used to be particularly valuable when there were many smaller houses with limited capital. Before the phylloxera, shippers had less wine of their own and relied on almacenistas to a far greater extent. In recent years shippers' stocks have been increasing and the trade of almacenista has been in the decline. This is perhaps a pity. Large stocks in the hands of almacenistas gave an added degree of flexibility and promoted competition. The late Tom Spencer of William & Humbert, one of the notable figures in the history of the trade, strongly believed in this way of carrying on business and relied on them to a considerable degree. But nowadays, out of a total stock of some 900,000 butts of wine, only about 60,000 are held by almacenistas.

During the nineteenth century, especially in the boom years and the years during which the vineyards were ravaged by oidium, considerable quantities of wine were brought into Jerez and Puerto de Santa Maria from vineyards well outside the normal sherry area, particularly from the hills to the south-west of Seville and from the villages of Manzanilla, La Palma, Villalba, Moguer, Niebla, Chucena and Bollullos de Condado. Some of these were quite good, but most were thin and feeble, and they undoubtedly harmed the reputation of sherry.

In the early years of this century Montilla-Moriles wines were still regarded as falling within the sherry area, and were regularly imported to the sherry towns to be used for making blends, while young wines were used, either alone or in conjunction with young sherries, for feeding soleras there. The Spanish attitude to delimitation, however, has been strict and purist. As the first tentative step, following the decree of 1933 montilla could be brought into the sherry towns only in years when the sherry vintage was exceptionally bad and could then be used only in the cheaper blends. The regulations have now been made even tighter and they cover, of course, other 'foreign' wines, quite apart from montilla. In the proclamation of December 1964 the total exclusion of these wines was envisaged, but in the transitional regulations the Consejo Regulador was empowered to permit musts of the same year from the provinces of Seville, Huelva and Cordova, grown on albariza soils and having a character similar to sherry, to be brought in where the circumstances are exceptional (which would be likely to apply only where the sherry vintage fails) and then only to the extent of 10 per cent of the total sales effected by a given shipper for direct consumption. They have now vanished from the sherry towns, with the exception of a relatively small amount of Pedro Ximenez from Montilla. Huelva has ceased from making its rough olorosos of old and now vinifies its grapes to make cold-fermented, fruity table wines.

Another wine, called *Rota tent*, made in the sherry area, used once to be popular, but unfortunately this is now only of historical interest, as the American forces have absorbed the village of Rota and use it as a naval base. The bodega has disappeared and the wine, although still produced, is not made in commercial quantities. In the seventeenth century red wines from many other districts in Spain were sold in England as 'tent'; it was a generic name derived from *tinto*, meaning coloured, and Rota tent was best known as a communion wine, but it really deserved a better fate, as the miracle of transubstantiation is just as easy with a baser medium. It is reddish-brown in colour, fairly dry, and has a most extraordinary flavour that merits respect rather than affection. It is prepared in a peculiar way from a special black grape, called Tintilla de Rota, that grows in the arena soils near the coast. The grapes are first sunned for two or three weeks and then put in tubs. These are not quite filled, but are covered with esparto-grass mats to prevent too much air or dirt getting in; they are left for about a month and stirred from time to time before being pressed in lagars. The resulting must is fortified with 10 per cent of alcohol, and a little *arrope*, or colour wine, is also added.

Given twenty or thirty years in the wood, tent develops into a wine of surprising quality, and during the 1950s the bodegas of Agustín Blazquez had a small quantity of the 1792 vintage; of course, it had been refreshed with younger wine, but it had exceptional character. I blended some of this old tent with a popular dessert oloroso, and the result was outstanding, but there is so little left anywhere that it will never be used commercially. In the nineteenth century it was occasionally blended with pale wines to add colour to them.

Apart from the various styles of sherry which have already been described, various special wines are prepared which a shipper uses solely for blending.

Six styles of sweet wine are used: *Pedro Ximenez, moscatel, dulce pasa, dulce apagado, dulce de almibar* and *mosto concentrado rectificado*. They are quite different in sweetness, flavour, colour and price; each is appropriate to a different style of sherry. All are essential save for *dulce apagado*, which used to be imported from just outside the sherry area and which can no longer be brought in, and *dulce de almibar*, which has been phased out as a result of EEC regulations.

Pedro Ximenez and moscatel are rich, sweet wines that are almost like liqueurs. They find great favour with the ladies of Andalusia, but are seldom exported except when blended with drier sherries. Both are extremely expensive, particularly Pedro Ximenez (or PX), which is the great traditional sweetening wine of Jerez. It is prepared from the grapes grown on Pedro Ximenez vines, which traditionally were sunned for as long as possible before they were pressed – generally for about two weeks. The grapes are naturally sweet and sometimes attain as much as 16° Baumé on the vine. The sunning makes them sweeter still, the normal figure being about 24°, though as much as 30° is sometimes attained. If such grapes were pressed and fermented in the normal way for sherry, the sweetness of the must would be so great that fermentation would cease before all the natural sugar was used up. In practice, however, an even sweeter wine is needed for blending. To achieve this the wine is vinified as a *mistela*. After pressing, the must is run into 500-litre casks which already contain at least 60 litres of *aguardiente*, or wine spirit, which must be entirely free from impurities. When the cask is full, the must will then register its 24° Baumé and about 8° or 9° Gay-Lussac. Some houses bottle and market this wine, and when they do

THE FINAL BLEND

it is fortified to between 17° and 19°. With the rising cost of labour, however, few growers can afford to sun their grapes for the traditional period, though this is compensated for to some extent by later picking. Correspondingly more brandy is then used to get a sweet enough wine: the more the brandy, the less the fermentation and hence the sweeter the wine. The casks are filled to the top and tightly bunged, so that very little fermentation takes place: only about one degree of sweetness is lost and converted into alcohol. After about four months, the new wine is racked off the lees, and a further dose of aguardiente is then added – generally 18 litres. This raises the strength to 13° Gay-Lussac, but the sweetness is correspondingly diluted and is generally about 21° Baumé. The strength and sweetness, however, vary between quite wide limits, depending on the initial sweetness of the grapes and how much aguardiente the grower chooses to add. These wines are very dark with less nose than one would expect, but they are full of flavour and of a sugary, syrupy sweetness.

Moscatel wine is made in a similar way, using Moscatel grapes, but these are not sunned for quite as long. Most moscatel comes from wines grown on the arena soil near Chipiona, which gives a high yield, and is vinified by the local co-operative there, but the very best vines are grown on the albariza soils in the centre of the sherry triangle. It is an elegant, very dark wine with a very characteristic bouquet and flavour, and very sweet indeed.

Both Pedro Ximenez and moscatel improve with age, and they are generally matured by the solera system, stocks of old Pedro Ximenez being among the most valuable assets of the great shippers.

Pedro Ximenez, however, is gradually becoming extinct. The vine does best in the Montilla-Moriles area and it is there that most of the wine is produced; it is the last wine to be imported legally into the sherry area. Although the vine is grown in the sherry vineyards, it does not do nearly so well there. In recent years sweet wines have been produced by the same method, but using good quality Palomino grapes that have been left to get very ripe and are then sunned until they reach 28° Baumé. These have proved completely satisfactory and are already supplanting Pedro Ximenez.

This new sweetening wine, known as *dulce pasa*, must be distinguished from the *dulce apagado* (quenched sweetness), otherwise known as *dulce recimo* or *mistela*, which used to be made outside the sherry area and the importation of which is now forbidden. It

235

was a cheaper and less distinguished sweetening wine made from grapes grown, for the most part, in Los Palacios, or sometimes from further afield – from Huelva, for instance, or from Montilla. The fact that such wines can no longer be brought in is really another example of the extreme seriousness with which the Spanish are regarding geographical limits. The wines were not much different from those produced in the sherry vineyards and were used in such small quantities that they did not mask the character of the sherry. And a considerable quantity of such wines always was vinified in the main area, but when top-quality Pedro Ximenez could be brought in from Montilla-Moriles, it was regarded as a waste to use first-class grapes which could have been used for making sherry. Such grapes are now used for making the best sweetening wines and this is helped by the increase in the area planted. But cheap dulce generally comes from newly planted vineyards, where the vines are too young to give a good sherry, or from grapes picked at the very end of the vintage, or when the weather has been bad. There is no especial sweetness in the grapes themselves, and the sugar is retained, as when vinifying Pedro Ximenez, by adding aguardiente to the empty casks before they receive the must; but when making a dulce about eighty litres are used instead of sixty. The resulting wine generally has about 9° Baumé of sweetness. The strength naturally depends on the amount of alcohol added, but it is generally fairly high – about 17° Gay-Lussac. Apart from being cheaper to prepare, dulce apagado had the advantage that it was somewhat lighter in colour than wines made from grapes that have been sunned a long time, or which are overripe, and it was therefore suitable for use in wines such as 'medium sherries', which the public expects to be moderate in colour as well as in flavour and in price. The best dulces are very grapey in flavour and quite delicious.

In ancient times wine was often sweetened with honey, but this gave a strong flavour which would utterly spoil the delicacy of sherry. The same problem arises with all the sweet wines mentioned above: each has it own flavour and colour. While this is undoubtedly an advantage when blending rich dessert sherries, it makes them unsuitable for sweetening delicate finos, where they would mask and destroy the flavour of the wine. A similar problem arises in blending some of the popular 'cream' sherries, which need to be sweet but not dark. There is indeed at present a vogue for some that are actually pale, and are so labelled. It was therefore necessary to find a sweetening agent without any noticeable bouquet or flavour of its own; and the first answer was invert sugar. This consists of glucose and laevulose in equal quantities: sugars that are absolutely pure and are identical with those contained in natural grape juice. They sweeten sherry without appreciably altering its flavour or colour.

Before it can be used, the invert sugar is first blended with fino sherry; it is then matured for a time and is allowed to settle down. The resulting wine is called *dulce de almibar*, or *dulce blanco*, and is surprisingly expensive. But added sugar is forbidden by law in some countries, such as Germany, and it has now virtually been phased out owing to EEC regulations – an example of the predominance of German thinking in the Common Market. Instead, *mosto concentrado rectificado*, 'rectified' concentrated must, is now used – must which is concentrated under low pressure so that it boils at 50° to avoid caramelization until it is laden with some 33 per cent sugar. The flavouring elements including proteins and polyphenols are also extracted and it is deionized and is decolourized with activated charcoal. Although the EEC regulations may be sensible in relation to table wines, they are irrelevant to the blending of sherry, where the addition of natural sugars is above reproach.

Very often the natural colour of a blend needs to be augmented, particularly when making a brown or 'Old East India' sherry. This is achieved with *vino de color* which, in its best form, not only adds colour but also enhances the quality and distinction of the blend. To obtain vino de color, a dark syrup is first prepared by concentrating unfermented must over a slow wood fire in a metal cauldron that looks like a Victorian washing copper. The fire is carefully regulated to keep the must simmering very gently, and the surface is skimmed to remove scum, just as if a cook were preparing jam. When it is sufficiently concentrated, the fire is damped down, and the cauldron gradually cools. Altogether it takes from fifteen to twenty hours to prepare, and the result is a sweet, non-alcoholic syrup, called *sancocho* if the must is reduced to one-third of its original volume, or *arrope* if it is reduced to one-fifth. The former has 30° Baumé of sweetness, and the latter about 38°. The depth of colour rises in much the same proportion, and the syrup is as dark as black treacle, though not of the same consistency. To make vino de color, two parts of arrope or sancocho are mixed with one part of unfermented must; a short period of tumultuous fermentation follows, which is succeeded by a very gradual secondary fermentation until the wine falls bright in the new year. This is the very best form of vino de color, and is called *color de macetilla*, or wine of the little mallet, possibly because it was once sold by auction owing to its scarcity and value. It has about 12° Baumé of sweetness with an alcoholic strength of some 9° Gay-Lussac; it is aromatic, dark, and develops an outstanding flavour as it grows old. Good vino de color is often matured in soleras and is very valuable. It has a remarkable and complex flavour, on first impact appearing to be sweet, but it has an astringently dry aftertaste. A cheaper and more common colour wine is prepared by mixing sancocho or arrope with must that has already fermented; this is known as *color remendado*, or patched colour.

Warner Allen (whose classical scholarship I cannot hope to emulate) has pointed out that both sancocho and arrope were well known in the days of the Roman Empire, when there were two wine syrups, called *sapa* and *defrutum*. The former was boiled down to one-half of its original volume and the latter to one-third, corresponding broadly to the two modern products. These syrups are mentioned by Pliny, Columella, Virgil, Varro and Martial, while the Greek comedians of the fifth and fourth centuries BC spoke of boiled-down must as *hepsema*. Although the Romans knew nothing of distillation, they strengthened their wines by adding sapa to the must before fermentation, and also sweetened them with syrups. The art of making these syrups was evidently passed on to the Moors in Spain, whose religion forbade alcohol but who were allowed unfermented grape juice. From the Moors the knowledge came down to the modern Spaniards, and so, in vino de color, we have something very like the classical wines.

Very little colour wine is now used, though, as the current taste is for light wines and brown sherry, which used to be so popular, has now practically disappeared. In the past a little was used for adding colour to young wines fed into oloroso soleras so that the colour wine and the sherry harmonized and matured together.

Yet another series of wines is used in blending the cheaper sherries, namely *claros de turbios*. This is clear wine that separates from the lees – both from the accumulated lees in the bodega butts, and from those obtained when the wine is *fined*, or clarified, after it is blended. These have all the basic characteristics of the wine from which they are obtained: some of the body, and much of the refinement disappears, but the fundamental quality remains, and the claros from first-class sherries are excellent wines in their own right. Some shippers used to fine their wines after they were landed in England. A famous merchant sold wine he obtained from the lees of a great dessert oloroso under another name at a very competitive price. The demand became more than he could meet, and the shippers in Jerez were hard put to it to produce an acceptable substitute at anything like the price.

The lees are first put into casks and are stored for several weeks, when the heavy impurities sink to the bottom and a quantity of clear wine can be decanted off without further treatment; this happens more quickly if the casks are stored in the open, owing to the low night temperatures, which encourage precipitation of the less soluble constituents. The wine obtained at this stage is nearly as good as the original. According to the traditional process, the lees that do not fall clear are then put into closely woven sacks which are piled into open-ended casks. A certain amount of almost clear but rather inferior wine permeates out, which is good enough to be used in very cheap blends for the local bars. The sacks are next put into a simple mechanical press to extract even more wine, but this is only suitable for distillation or for rinsing casks. There is nothing left in the sacks except dry earthy matter, which is useful as fertilizer, or which can be sold to chemical manufacturers for the extraction of tartrates. Today, however, this process is obsolescent. Instead of the sacks, the lees are pumped through a specially constructed lees press which filters them under pressure. The wine comes out perfectly clear and the residue is so solid and earthly that the deposits between the filter elements resemble enormous biscuits – they are just as dry and far harder.

Until the middle of the eighteenth century sherry was prepared from wine that was only a year or two old; it was sweetened and coloured but remained fundamentally thin, feeble and acid, though not weak in alcohol, as it was fortified. At about that time, there was great competition from other strong dessert wines. 'Mountain' wine from Malaga was more popular than sherry, and Portuguese wines were encouraged by low rates of duty arising from the Methuen Treaty of 1703. Partly owing to the restrictive practices of the old vintners' guild, the Gremio, sherry could no longer compete effectively in terms of price, and some shippers began to export better wines that had been matured for several years in the wood, though others sold cheap wines which were so inferior that they brought sherry into disrepute.

The standard shipping butt holds thirty arrobas, and all blends are prepared in multiples of that figure. Sherries shipped at the end of the eighteenth century were made up from something like this:

selected sherry	Ro
aguardiente (spirit)	2@
PX	4@
vino de color	2@

Ro stands for *resto*, being the remainder of the wine not accounted for specifically in the *cabaceo*, or formula; in the above example, it would amount to 22 arrobas. The wine was hardly as good as the very cheapest olorosos shipped at the present time, but it was a big advance on those made previously; it helped the shippers keep the trade at a fairly steady level in face of competition, and started a better class of business that eventually led to the sherry boom in the nineteenth century. Finos and dry aperitif wines were not exported at all until the 1850s, and the first shipments were no drier than modern medium sherries, but they catered for a select market which previously had little use for sherry. Although the mainstay of the trade has always been the sweeter wines, the importance of the market for finos is exemplified by the immense popularity of Tio Pepe; and the market for finos is steadily rising.

The public taste in sherry is a complete enigma: it is forever changing. There was at first little demand for the new, very dry wines, but the sales steadily rose immediately after the Second World War. It was a period of austerity allied with incompetence, when England was one of the last countries in the world to retain sugar rationing and was short of everything sweet. Yet the driest and most austere sherries were all the rage there. Then in the 1950s and 1960s, when sweet things became easy to get, the public delighted in smooth, brown, sweet olorosos, particularly if they were labelled 'Cream'. In the 1980s the tendency was to go for drinks that are light in colour in the totally mistaken belief that they are in some way more innocuous – hence the fashion for lager beer and the lighter coloured whiskies. So it was with sherries, and 'pale creams' became all the rage, with Crofts the market leader. Very dry wines have an unaccountable snob value, but so often, when guests confidently ask for 'the driest there is' and are given just that, they are utterly horrified and sip their wine with expressions more appropriate to one who sucks a lemon. Unsweetened sherries are an acquired taste, but once they are understood, they are enjoyed so much that they are never abandoned. The answer, commercially, is to label a sherry 'dry' but in fact to make it fairly sweet, and this applies particularly to the American market. I once asked a famous shipper why a new wine he had introduced was called 'dry' when, to my own taste, it was utterly ruined by being oversweetened. He replied that it *was* dry: absolutely the driest thing the Americans would drink. And his sales on that continent prove how right he was. That is why most of the finos and amontillados exported are sweetened slightly, though occasionally it is so little that the sweetness can only be detected when they are compared with natural wines; this also applies to a few that are sold in Spain, though the amount of sweetening added there is really minute. It seems a pity to sweeten finos, as they inevitably lose a little of their natural finesse and delicacy, but to leave the matter there would be to over-simplify the problem. Owing to the difference in climate, wines that taste austere in Jerez taste even more austere in the northern countries, and the further north you go, the more you notice it; you can even tell the difference after a journey from London to Edinburgh. One shipper claims that a trace of sweet wine in a fino merely robs it of this excessive austerity, and that his slightly sweetened fino tastes the same in London as the natural wine does in Jerez. There is undoubtedly some truth in this, but for my part I still prefer the natural wine. It is just a matter of personal taste, though, and everyone should judge for himself. Above all, the label is nothing to go by.

These factors must all be borne in mind when preparing a blended sherry that will appeal to the public, and they form the background of an intensely difficult art.

Sweetened wines, however, have a further advantage from the shippers' point of view: because the sweetness masks the subtler distinctions of bouquet and flavour, they are easier to blend. A first-class, unsweetened, straight solera wine is inimitable: it can never be matched perfectly by any other shipper, and when the full output of the solera has been sold, there is no other source of supply. On the other hand, if the wine is even slightly sweetened, it can be imitated exactly, and there is practically no limit to the quantity that can be supplied. A vast number of wines of every class are available, differing only slightly one from another, and there are an infinite number of permutations and combinations that will give a similar result once the subtler distinctions can be ignored. If a sweetened wine is based on a particularly elegant and unusual solera, it may be very difficult to imitate, but it will never be impossible.

In preparing a blend, only one thing is vital: the nose. There is no substitute, and no amount of enthusiasm or industry will be of any avail if the nose is insensitive. All blending is done solely on the bouquet of the wine until the very last stage: when a practically perfect match has been achieved, it is tasted, principally to judge the sweetness. Some years ago, King Umberto II of Italy visited the sherry towns, and was astonished when someone was introduced eulogistically as 'the best nose in the region'. It sounds odd praise, but there could be none higher.

When a shipper wishes to make up a blend, the first thing he must do is to prepare the *cabaceo*. This is done in the tasting-room, taking measured quantities of first one wine and then another in a tall glass, and experimenting until the bouquet and flavour are exactly right. The quantities are then scaled up to give the standard shipping measure of thirty arrobas. Many of the finer blends, relying on the shippers' principal soleras, remain unaltered year after year, but the humbler wines, containing proportions of leftovers, have to be separately blended for every shipment, though the basic ingredients are invariably the same. The blend is prepared by comparison with a sample of the last cabaceo. These samples, or *referencias*, are always kept for several years.

The work is most interesting when a merchant asks for one of his sherries to be matched. Unfortunately merchants often make matters more difficult than they need: I have heard of a sample being sent in a bottle tainted with paraffin, and others are spoilt by the cork not being properly matured in wine. These difficulties are merely incidental; the principal obstacle is the perversity of merchants who ask a shipper to match one of their wines and will tell him neither the price they are willing to pay, nor the quantity they are likely to buy. Sometimes the normal supplier ships the wine at a very low price because he happens to have a surplus of that style, or, if he is a little man, because he simply cannot afford to lose any trade; he may even sell it at a loss to oblige a merchant who is a good customer for his more profitable wines. If a rival blends an identical wine and quotes a fair market price, he is suspected of offering bad value, and all his other wines fall under suspicion. There is always the temptation to blend a wine that is just slightly inferior, and is therefore cheaper. A wise merchant does not change his shippers unnecessarily, and if he has some reason to change, he should put all his cards on the table and ask for the nearest possible match at the price he is willing to pay, or for the best wine of the same style that can be supplied at the price he is already paying, thus improving the quality. A merchant who changes his suppliers in the hope of saving a few pence is a fool. There was a merchant who, shortly after the First World War, used to buy a fine oloroso from a well-known shipper for £150 per butt, which was a high price in those days. After he had been supplied for several years, orders stopped. Ten years later, the same merchant asked the original shipper to match the sample of oloroso at £80 per butt. This was done, and the wine was supplied with the mark that the merchant had previously used for the £150 wine. He visited Jerez and complained that the demand for that particular sherry was nothing like it had been ten years earlier. He had asked seven shippers in succession to match the wine at £10 a butt less than he had been paying before. The difference between any two successive blends was negligible, but the difference between the wine originally supplied at £150 and that supplied at half the cost was vast, and he was retailing it at precisely the same price. He should have known that wine drinkers are not generally stupid.

When an order for a match comes in, the shipper takes the sample into his blending-room, where he keeps bottles of all his standard wines; these may number as many as fifty, some of them drawn from his soleras, some of them blends which he makes up regularly, and others being the special wines used for blending, which have been described above. Helped by his experience, he can sort out those that are required, and sometimes the task is quite simple; on the other hand it may take several days; he may also have to get some unusual style of wine from an almacenista.[1] Even when the match is quite straightforward, the blender does not make it exact; he must estimate the slight change in flavour that invariably occurs following the sea voyage. Sometimes the task is impossible. A friend

---

1 It is even possible to buy an artificial wood flavouring of a chemical nature; as it remains on sale, presumably someone buys it, but I have no idea who, nor why.

told me of a customer who bought a fine sherry which would in 1956 (when I heard the story) have cost £225 per butt, and somehow lost a butt in an obscure corner of his cellar, where it remained for fifty years. When he found it, such wine as was left was superb, and he asked my friend to match it. This was done and the shipper quoted a price of £1,000 per butt for a maximum of two butts. The merchant said the price was absurd, but the shipper could only suggest he went on buying the original wine, from the very same soleras, and kept some of it for fifty years, when he would get what he wanted.

Fino wines in their simplest, greatest and alas most expensive form are straight solera wines with no additions whatsoever, save for a very small fortification with alcohol, and several examples are exported. Others, which are sold in Spain as natural wines, are sweetened slightly for the export markets, although the names are not changed. Most of those sold in Great Britain are blended from good basic wines mixed with cheaper Chiclana finos, or similar wines of less character. A little manzanilla is often added to improve the bouquet, and when manzanilla is exported it is sometimes blended with a little fino, as already described. When a delicate fino or manzanilla is sweetened, dulce de almibar was formerly used, but this has now been replaced by rectified must.

One shipper, Luis Caballero, has introduced a new method for maturing his Puerto Fino. The idea is to keep it as fresh as possible. A mature fino is drawn from the solera. It is then fined and filtered as if for bottling but is put into casks with five arrobas of young wine growing vigorous flor. It continues under the flor until required, when it can be drawn off, ultra-cooled and bottled. He describes it as *solera sobre tablas* and the results are impressive. He claims that it has a greatly enhanced shelf life.

'Medium' sherries are often prepared from very complicated cabaceos that may contain as many as fifteen ingredients, and the quality is governed very largely by the price. The cheapest often have a small proportion of very young wine and claros de turbios; it is the only way that the surprisingly good wines sold at very competitive prices can possibly be produced.

Something has already been said of the extremely dubious use of the word 'amontillado' when applied to cheaper wines for export; these can only contain a limited amount of genuine amontillado, and consist primarily of anything from fino to oloroso. At best, they are fino-amontillado. Here is an actual example of an 'amontillado' blended for a well-known merchant:

Fino Fuerte	Ro
Amontillado Dolores	5@
MZA Puro	2@
Vino Chiclana Fino	7@
Dulce	2½@

Fino Fuerte is a rather powerful and full-bodied solera fino. MZA stands for manzanilla, and Chiclana fino is self-explanatory. The only amontillado in the cabaceo is the Amontillado Dolores, which in fact is not an amontillado at all, but a standard export mark that is available in large quantities; it is made up from several wines of which about half are amontillados. This use of standard blends in preparing special wines is entirely sensible, as it naturally cuts down the work and reduces the price. Carried to its logical conclusion, a special wine for a merchant may consist of nothing more than two or more standard marks blended together, and an example is afforded by a popular 'amontillado' sold by a London merchant. This has the following cabaceo:

Amontillado Dolores	Ro
Oloroso Historico	12@

The Oloroso Historico is a fine dessert wine, with several constituents including some oloroso of great age, so the blend is a medium sherry of rare distinction, but that does not make it an amontillado.

When Vizetelly visited the bodega of Cosens (now disbanded) in 1875, he saw the following blend being made up:

amontillado pasado, 1820	7@
double palma (amontillado), 1869	10@
single palma (fino)	12½@
Pedro Ximenez	½@

It would have been a very pleasant, rather dry sherry, typical of those that are popular today. It is instructive to note that the wines used in that blend were matured by the añada system. The previous year Gonzalez Byass had been able to buy 183 butts of eleven-year-old añada wine from an almacenista.

One of the best respected of the medium sherries is Dry Sack.

This is prepared by a highly sophisticated process. Wine is blended from two three-scale oloroso soleras and one four-scale amontillado solera together with a small quantity of Pedro Ximenez. As a blend it is then passed through another solera of three scales.

All five forms of sweetening wine are used in preparing these medium sherries, depending on the character and colour of the wine.

In preparing top-quality amontillados, palo cortados and olorosos, there is a complication that has not yet been discussed: the oldest wines of these styles are incomparable in aroma and elegance, but they are so highly flavoured that no one can drink them. They are a delight to the nose, but when they enter the mouth, it is overwhelmed and shrivels up. Strong wines have been known to develop in this wonderful but exasperating way throughout the ages, but only in Jerez and Madeira are they at all common. Pliny recorded the historic vintage of ancient Rome as that of the consulship of L. Opimius in 121 BC:

> The year of the consulship of Lucius Opimius; when the tribune Gaius Gracchus was assassinated for stirring up the common people with seditions, was renowned for the excellence of its vintages of all kinds – the weather was so fine and bright (they call it the 'boiling' of the grape) thanks to the power of the sun, in the 633rd year from the birth of the city; and wines of that year still survive, having kept for nearly 200 years, though they have now been reduced to the consistency of honey with a rough flavour, for such in fact is the nature of wines in their old age; and it would not be possible to drink them neat or to counteract them with water, as their over-ripeness predominates even to the point of bitterness, but with a very small admixture they serve as seasoning for improving all other wines.

Thus it is with sherry, save that the viscosity does not greatly increase. When these really old wines are blended with younger ones, their harshness disappears, but all their elegance and maturity shines through, and they irradiate the blend with their goodness. A very small proportion of ancient wine can transform a younger one. If a centenarian oloroso is swirled round a sherry glass and emptied out again, the minute volume that clings to the glass will be enough: when a young oloroso is poured in, its colour darkens, the aroma of the old wine predominates, and the blend has all the character of antiquity. It is thus that the greatest dessert sheries are made: the proportion of old wine need only be small, but its quality must be impeccable. One might have a cabaceo something like this:

Oloroso Viejo	Ro
Oloroso Viejísimo	12@
Oloroso Centenario	½@
PX Viejo	4@

And such a wine would be the climax of a banquet.

The actual blend used for one of the greatest dessert olorosos is as follows:

1st Criadera Oloroso Viejísimo	Ro
Solera Oloroso Viejísimo	8@
Solera PX	4@
Concentrated rectified must	3@
Aguardiente	1@

It is a magnificent wine.

Few wines can hope to be blended with a centenarian sherry, but all must conform to the standards of their shippers, and the standards are generally high. Many excellent sherries are shipped under attractive names that mean nothing in particular, and to mention any of them would be invidious, as they are legion. Some names, however, have definable meanings and the most romantic of all is East India Sherry. Some delicate table wines are ruined by a sea voyage, but stronger wines, such as sherry, are often improved enormously; this has been well known for hundreds of years and is mentioned both by Pliny and by Cervantes. During the eighteenth and nineteenth centuries butts of sherry were often shipped as ballast in sailing boats. Merchants in Bristol used to commission ships to take their wine across the equator and many stories are told of wily old sea-captains who set sail with a cargo of wine and got no further than Lundy Island, where they made merry for a month and then sailed back again. Although the wines are undoubtedly improved by a long sea voyage, there was nothing magical about the equator: the continued rolling perfected the blend and infused the wine with the oxygen that permeated through the staves of the cask, ageing it more rapidly. A similar effect could be produced in this country. Captain Rochfort Scott related how, at the beginning of the nineteenth century, one English industrialist gave premature age to his sherries and madeiras by tying the casks on the swinging beams of two steam-engines in his factory. He thus combined a ship's motion with a tropical climate, and the wine never had to leave the country. After a few weeks' oscillation, he passed them off as East and West India Particular. Alas, the East India Sherries sold today are no longer sent to sea, save for the short journey from Cadiz to England. They are mostly big-bodied wines with some age, though the quality is variable.

Another famous wine of the past, rarely seen today, was *vino de pasto*. In Spain the name was given only to local beverage wines; the sherry was a slightly sweetened, light amontillado that was pleasant enough but undistinguished. Wines of this style were amongst the first of the drier sherries pioneered in Britain by such shippers as Garvey, Pemartin and Gonzalez Byass.

Amorosos are smooth, sweet olorosos that justify their name, which in Spanish means 'loving'. But the name of the wine has nothing to do with *amor*; it is that of a famous vineyard which was noted for such wines. The name is still sometimes used owing to its beauty, though sherries of this style are now more often called 'cream'. There are an enormous number of these cream sherries, and they naturally vary considerably in quality and price, though all but the very cheapest appear to be quite good. The forerunner was Harvey's Bristol Cream, which is still the market-leader. These rich olorosos are prepared from high-class solera wines sweetened, for the most part, with Pedro Ximenez, though the other sweetening wines are also used to prevent the colour from getting too dark, especially nowadays when light coloured wines are fashionable.

A more recent innovation is the invention of pale cream sherry. The pioneer was Crofts Original, which rapidly rose to be market leader. Sweet and easy to drink, pale cream sherries are fashionably light in colour and look as if they are dry. Crofts is a complex blend, containing a substantial amount of fino with some amontillado and oloroso, sweetened by rectified concentrated must. Others are variations on the same theme. Sandeman, for example, use a higher proportion of oloroso.

Brown sherries are blended with solera olorosos and raya wines of all ages, sweetened with Pedro Ximenez and moscatel. It is surprising how much raya can be included in such blends without impairing the flavour. They also generally contain vino de color, and the combination makes them extremely rich. Carried even further, so that the wine consists mostly of sweetness and colour, with only a small proportion of sherry, it becomes 'blended paxarete', which is bought by distillers in Scotland, the USA, South America and the West Indies; they use it to add colour, flavour and smoothness to their cheaper whiskies and rums. The name paxarete, or *pajarete*, is also applied in Jerez to blended colour wines, and is derived from la Torre de Pajarete, between Villamartin and Prado de Rey, in the mountains beyond Arcos de la Frontera, not far from Bornos, where wines of this type used to be made. Some of these were shipped to England, and at least one eighteenth-century wine label was engraved with the name *paxarotta*.

The last stage in preparing a cabeceo is to add colour, if necessary The colour of the wine is compared with standard slides in a tintometer or, in the more up-to-date bodegas, in an electronic colour comparator, and vino de color is added if the blend is not dark enough. Vino de color itself is so dark that samples have to be diluted with nine times their own volume of water before their colour can be compared. On the very rare occasions when the colour of a blend has to be reduced, this can be done by passing it through a powdered-carbon filter; the treatment is most unusual and would normally only be used to satisfy the eccentricity of some merchant, or, very occasionally, to reduce the colour of a 'pale cream' sherry. Mercifully no one has yet thought of deodorizing the wine.

When the cabeceo has finally been determined, the wine is blended. Small quantities may be mixed in casks, but large blends are prepared in vats that generally hold eighty to 125 butts. The wine is generally left in the vats for three or four days; it is then pumped into bodega butts where it remains if possible for a minimum of six months, to settle down thoroughly before shipment. In the days when a multitude of blends was prepared for individual merchants who bought in small quantities, they were shipped by the butt or hogshead, occasionally by the quarter cask (which cost extra) and very occasionally by the tierce, holding a third of a butt. Such casks have to be carefully seasoned. The best way of preparing these is to use them for fermentation, though satisfactory results are also obtained by filling them with steam mixed with ammonia and then storing them for a time full of low-quality wine put aside for this purpose. They are disinfected by burning a piece of sulphur inside on the end of a wire, which is an admirable arrangement except when someone tries to do it with a cask that had stored aguardiente:

Blending sherry for shipment in a nineteenth-century bodega
(from *Facts about Sherry* by Henry Vizetelly, London, 1876)

the explosion is surprisingly loud. Nowadays, however, practically all sherry is bottled at source, and before long it will be 100 per cent. Butts practically ceased from being used some time ago and were replaced by inert, stainless steel cylinders. Plastic containers are often used for paxarete.

When a merchant places regular orders for a special blend with the same shipper year after year, six months' or a year's supply is generally prepared in advance, to be sure of rapid delivery and unvarying quality. It is therefore courteous, to say the least, for a merchant to give a year's notice to a shipper if he intends to discontinue one of his special marks or to find another source of supply. If this is not done, the shipper may be landed with a quantity of ready-blended wine for which he has no market and which has to be sold off as a job lot or else re-blended at considerable trouble and expense.

Shippers likewise prepare their own standard blends well in advance and sometimes have shipping soleras of ready-blended wines, the casks not being kept on ullage. This is becoming the usual practice with sweet sherries that are complicated blends. For instance, as has been mentioned, Williams & Humbert have two criaderas and a solera of blended Dry Sack. On the other hand Domecq have gone back to the former practice of simply leaving the blends in wood for six months to settle down before ultra-cooling. Some merchants, before it became the practice to bottle sherries at source, used to make their own final blends in England, using wine bought from two or three different shippers. This had the advantage that it made them independent of any one supplier, but it was seldom economical unless their requirements were so large that they could not be supplied from a single source. Otherwise, as the integrity of sherry shippers is proverbial, it hardly seems worth while. Until the 1970s many merchants had their own blends constituting a complete range of sherries. Very few do that today. Most sherry today is sold by supermarkets who sell the same wines through many outlets, while wine merchants and off-licences usually sell shippers' blends, though sometimes under their own names. To give a specific example of what has happened, in the late 1960s Wisdom & Warter sold 130 blends; now they sell between twenty and thirty.

Odd experiments in blending have also been tried by publicans, and one of them was quoted in *Poole's Tales* by Charles Tovey. The

SHERRY

narrator, meeting a stranger in a churchyard, recognized him as Burley, the late landlord of an inn near Cambridge.

'You can't deny it, Burley; your wines, of all kinds were destestable – Port, Madeira, Claret, Champagne – '

'There now, sir! to prove how much gentlemen may be mistaken, I assure you, sir, as I'm an honest man, I never had but two sorts of wine in my cellar – Port and Sherry.'

'How! when I myself have tried your Claret, your – '

'Yes, sir – *my* Claret, sir. One is obliged to give gentlemen everything they ask for, sir. Gentlemen who pay their money, sir, have a right to be served with whatever they may please to order, sir – especially the young gentlemen from Cambridge, sir. I'll tell you how it was, sir. I would never have any wines in my house, sir, but Port and Sherry, because *I know them* to be wholesome wines, sir; and this I will say, sir, my Port and Sherry were *the – very – best* I could procure in all England.'

'How, the best?'

'Yes, sir – *at the price I paid for them*. But to explain the thing at once, sir. You must know, sir, that I hadn't been long in business when I discovered that gentlemen know very little about wine; but that if they didn't find some fault or other, they would appear to know much less – always excepting the young gentlemen from Cambridge, sir; *and they are excellent judges!*' (And here again Burley's little eyes twinkled a humorous commentary on the concluding words of his sentence.) 'Well, sir; with respect to my dinner wines, I was always tolerably safe; gentlemen seldom find fault at dinner; so whether it might happen to be Madeira, or pale Sherry, or brown, or – '

'Why, just now you told me you had but two sorts of wine in your cellar!'

'Very true, sir; Port *and* Sherry. But this was my plan, sir. If any one ordered Madeira: – From one bottle of Sherry take two glasses of wine, which replace by two glasses of Brandy, and add thereto a slight squeeze of lemon; and this I found to give general satisfaction, especially to the young gentlemen from Cambridge, sir. But, upon the word of an honest man, I could scarcely get a living profit by my Madeira, sir, for I always used the best Brandy. As to the pale and brown Sherry, sir – a couple of glasses of nice pure water, in place of the same quantity of wine, made what I used to call *my delicate pale* (by the by, a squeeze of lemon added to *that* made a very fair Bucellas, sir – a wine not much called for now, sir); and for my old *brown* sherry a *leetle* burnt sugar was the thing. It looked very much like Sherry that had been twice to East Indies, sir; and, indeed, to my customers who were *very* particular about their wines I used to serve it as such.'

'But, Mr. Burley, wasn't such a proceeding of a character rather – '

Wines prepared for the Spanish market are generally sold at whatever strength they may happen to have after the final blend has been prepared; this varies between wide limits, as shown in the list of añada wines. The weaker sherries prepared for export, however, are generally fortified using mitad y mitad. This is the last stage in the blending.

The practice of fortifying wines goes back to remote antiquity; distillation was probably discovered in China whence it passed to Baghdad and was brought to Spain by the Moors. Wines were fortified originally to stop them turning into vinegar, which was a common calamity before the coming of scientific oenology. Above all, it helped them to 'travel', as the movement and varying temperatures of a journey would easily induce disease in any wine that lacked balance or was weak. At the same time, it coarsened them, to some extent, and masked their delicate flavour. There were frequent complaints, particularly in the nineteenth century, that sherry was over-fortified, but this tendency was encouraged by British merchants, who expected it to be spirituous and strong. Some critics, including Vizetelly and Tovey, suggested that it had to be fortified only because it was badly made, being matured on ullage, as compared with the full casks of France and Germany – a criticism that was manifestly absurd. Quite apart from these considerations, there is, with fino, always the danger that an open bottle will grow flor if it is unfortified, and this was a very real risk in the past, but it has been eliminated by modern filtration which takes out all the yeasts. Fortification also prevents there being any possibility of a secondary fermentation following the addition of fermentable sugars in the blend.

The strength at which sherry has been shipped has varied over the years for three reasons: taxation, cost and, not least, fashion. As can be seen from the table of añada wines on page 207, sherry left entirely to its own devices may be as strong as 23° Gay-Lussac or, if young, may go down to about 15°. Fortifying a wine by adding alcohol obviously adds to the cost and this has recently been emphasized as the entry of Spain into the EEC has resulted in there being a duty on the alcohol used, which has greatly increased the price; but conversely, a strong wine is much easier to ship as nothing will go wrong with it, though now that wine-making is thoroughly understood there is little chance of anything going wrong anyhow. There is a possible risk if it is sweetened, as a weak wine may well start fermenting again. This has actually happened with young sherry shipped as cheaply as possible to the Netherlands. German wine shippers have been facing the problem for years and have been developing their own techniques of sterile bottling, carried out under hospital-like conditions, to avoid it; but the sherry shippers, with their tradition of fortification, were not prepared for it. It was forced upon them partly by differential duties and partly by a wish to ship very cheap wines for new markets. Traditionally sherry has been shipped between 18° and 20° with the very old wine – an almost *de minimis* proportion – being stronger. The way wines are taxed varies greatly from country to country. Some countries, such as Germany and Belgium, have a sliding scale depending on strength, so that every degree counts. In Denmark, in contrast, there is a fixed rate for fortified wines. In the USA there are two duty bands, one between 14° and 21° and the other up to 25°. In Ireland there are three bands: 15–18°, over 18° to 22° and over 22°. In Great Britain the higher duty band begins at 18° so that is the critical point; another range of duty begins at 22°, but this is of little practical interest. Between 80 and 90 per cent of sherries are now shipped below 18° strength, so they are naturally less robust than they used to be.

In the 1950s and 1960s it was usual to ship even fino sherries at 20° to 21° and the minimum strength allowed by the regulations was 17.5°. The regulations were altered following Spain's entry into the EEC and the minimum is now 15.5°. It is now usual to import manzanilla at 15.5°, finos at 16.6° and other wines at 17.5°. There used to be an interesting dodge, seldom practised and much frowned upon, of bringing in the same wine at two different strengths and blending them after the duty had been paid. This has now been forbidden and anyhow would be irrelevant with sherries being imported at lower strength. But it is the existence of the higher duty band at a rather critical strength which largely accounts for the lower-strength sherries that we know today – a lowering of strength that is much encouraged by accountants and marketing executives. Fashion also plays its part, though. There is a tendency throughout the world to move towards lighter styles of drinks generally, brought about by caprice rather than by any aesthetic judgement. This is especially so in the United States. A sherry shipper, then, has to study his markets carefully to know to what extent he needs to fortify and opinions differ widely as to the merits of sheer strength. In my own judgement a fine dessert wine with some age tastes rather emasculated below 20°, but a young fino, which could taste spirity at the old strength, is improved by having less fortification. It has been the practice for many years to fortify those wines for the Spanish market somewhat less than those intended for export.

The idea of importing sherries at low strength is often said to be a new one but it is not. From approximately 1895 to 1925 sherry was largely sold in England at 30° Sikes (to use the contemporary scale), corresponding to about 17° Gay-Lussac, and these were years of disastrous slump. In those days the British public wanted their short drinks to have a 'kick' and sales improved when the strength was increased. Nowadays there is a clear movement towards lighter drinks, and we shall see what we shall see.

To quote some current examples, Tio Pepe – which registers 15.3° in the solera – was fortified to 16.6° for sale in Spain and to 17.8° for sale in the United Kingdom. Since 1991 it has been sold in the United Kingdom at 16.5°. La Ina is being imported at 15.5°. I like them that way. Dry Sack is sold at three different strengths: 17.5° in the EEC, 19.5° outside the EEC and in the Duty Free stores, and 20.5° in the USA. To my own old-fashioned palate the 19.5° version tastes better than the 17.5°, having more vigour and structure. But market forces and duty bands have to be complied with.

Before leaving the various styles of sherry I should mention a liqueur: *ponce*. It is not a sherry at all, but many of the shippers produce their own particular versions and no two are alike. Ponce is blended with sweet sherry, brandy, sugar syrup, vanilla and other flavourings. Some use oranges, others do not. The result is very sweet and flavoursome. Two other variants are authorized and have long been produced in very small quantities: Jerez Quinado, which is a sharp, sherry aperitif flavoured with quinine, and Jerez Aromatizado, which is a fruit-flavoured sherry aperitif.

It has always been the whim of the public that sherry should be 'bright and clear'. In the eighteenth and early nineteenth centuries, when white wines were made less skilfully, it was common to use coloured glasses to hide the particles that floated in suspension; but there is now no excuse for any such imperfections. One sometimes suspects that the public care more about colour than about the bouquet and flavour, and they enjoy demonstrating their sophistry by returning to the merchant (or more probably to the off-licence) any bottle that shows a trace of sediment or cloudiness, even though its flavour may be perfect. They would reject most of my favourite old sherry out of hand. Although shippers may grumble about the excessive attention paid to such a triviality, a completely bright wine undeniably looks more attractive than one that is cloudy, and a successful merchant must pander to the public taste even when it exasperates him.

The technique of clarifying or fining wine by adding something to precipitate the cloudy particles has been practised for centuries. A manuscript of Jac. Pragestus, M.D., in the Sloane collection at the British Museum, dating from the sixteenth or seventeenth century, gives the following instructions:

> Take half a quarter of white starch and about a quarter of fine white sand and a pint of isinglass and a good handful of bay salt fine beaten and the whites of two eggs and beat them with a spoon in a porringer till it will run thin and then overdraw the piece of wine about a gallon and put all the things in together, so beat it up extraordinary well and fill it up, and this will make it perfect wine.

A similar recipe was given by Dr Walter Charleton in his *Two Discourses* (1692), and wines were regularly fined at that time. The technique differs very little today and will be understood by any chemist; apart from wine, it is used regularly in the kitchen, where white of egg is specified for clarifying consommé.

There are two basic types of clarifying agents: animal and mineral. The former contain albuminous substances that are positive colloids and react with tannin and pectic matter, which are negative colloids, to produce small, heavy, insoluble particles that gather any suspended matter as they fall through the wine. Mineral agents are purely physical in their action.

The traditional method employed in Jerez consisted of fining with white of egg followed by a further treatment using Spanish earth. The number of eggs required for a butt of wine might be anything from four to twenty, depending on the style of wine and the extent of the cloudiness, but sixteen was typical. About one and a half gallons of wine were drawn from the butt into a jarra, and the egg whites were put in. The mixture of white of egg and wine was whipped up vigorously with a small broom made of thyme branches, and the prepared finings were poured into the butt, which was stirred with a pole, or *apaleador*. Nowadays the process is essentially the same but commercially produced egg albumen is usually used. The effect of the egg albumen is to gather nearly all the suspended or colloidal particles and to bring them down into the lees; at the same time it reduces the tannin content and the depth of colour.

In the olden days the eggs used to be brought over from Morocco and before the Spanish Civil War lorry-loads came through Gibraltar. The yolks were a perquisite of the capataz, who sold them very profitably to the local restaurants and confectioners. Thereafter the eggs were bought locally. Egg white can also be bought already separated from the yolks and canned; there are forty to a tin.

Occasionally gelatine is used instead of egg white to fine cheap or dense wines; isinglass is also used but is less popular than it was in the past.

After a few days the work of the albumen or gelatine is completed by the use of Spanish earth, or *tierra de vino*. This is a very fine-grained, slate-coloured earth obtained from Lebrija. It is about 90 per cent aluminium silicate. First it is saturated with water to make a paste, which is rolled like pastry to remove any lumps. One kilogram is then put into a jarra and one and a half gallons of wine are poured in slowly, stirring all the time. To obtain better mixing after all the wine has been added, it is poured from one jarra to another, about a dozen times, and is then introduced into the butt. It cannot be poured in directly but has to be added very slowly and is diffused throughout the wine by means of a small metal platform suspended on wire underneath the bunghole. The action of the earth is purely physical; it slowly sinks through the wine like a moving filter, collecting together all the albumen and everything else in its way.

The particles suspended in wine may consist of many things. In their crudest form, they are simply bits of grape skin, though these are never found in sherry owing to the early racking and the use of the solera system. More often the cloudiness is caused by salts such as tartrates; these are most likely to appear straight after blending, and when this happens the wine is fined immediately. But unfortunately fining takes away just a little of the quality and should be done no more than is necessary to make the wine clear. This loss is reduced if the wine is left for three or four weeks on its finings before it is racked off, when the soluble compounds that are temporarily taken into the lees return to the sherry; additional fining in England should be unnecessary if the wine has been carefully made. It should simply be passed through a filter immediately before bottling.

The public taste for wines that throw no sediment is unhappily one of those things that the sherry shippers, in common with wine growers all over the world, just have to live with. One feels some sympathy with the public. Wine that throws no sediment looks better, needs no skill in handling, and can be drunk right to the end of the bottle so that there is no waste. But no wine behaves like that naturally. If there is to be no risk of precipitation, the compounds which might cause it have to be removed or at least modified. This emasculates the wine. Any sherry shipper will agree that untreated wine tastes better. And just occasionally, for discerning and educated customers, they ship some. For the mass market, though, they cannot risk it. The marketing executives have triumphed again!

Even if the wine is clear when it leaves the bodega, there is still danger of its becoming cloudy owing to precipitation of cream of tartar when the temperature gets low, and this is particularly troublesome when sherry is exported to Canada, Scandinavia and Scotland. It is especially tiresome when clear wine has been bottled during the summer and gets cloudy in bottle during the winter. There are various chemical and physical methods for overcoming this, but perhaps the best is intense refrigeration, known as ultra-cooling or *ofique*, which was pioneered by the French and is now in use for nearly all the wines. This brings the precipitation about on purpose by reducing the temperature to a very low level and keeping it there for three to eight days before filtering, but the wine is not frozen. Typically it may be brought to −7° to −8°C for fino and −11°C for cream, but no ice is formed. Practices vary from shipper to shipper, but a useful formula for arriving at the right temperature is to halve the alcoholic strength and take away one. Thus an 18° wine would be ultra-cooled at −8°C. The process can be speeded up by seeding the wine with tartaric crystals. It can then be brought down to −6°C for a minimum of four hours so that the whole process can be completed in twenty-four hours from room temperature and back up again. Some shippers are seeding with four days' cooling preceded by centrifuging and filtering. The thick deposit is then centrifuged and crystals separated for use in the next batch, though crystals cannot be removed from cream sherry because too much colouring matter is entrapped in them. The wine is finally filtered and kept in cool tanks prior to bottling. The method has proved completely successful with dry wines, but not entirely so with blended sherries, which are notoriously perverse and still very occasionally go cloudy. Experiments have been conducted with a new kind of plant to do the job more quickly by a combination of low temperature and ultrasonic vibrations. This process is being used successfully by port shippers. There can be no doubt, though, that ultra-cooling does take some of the quality out of a wine, and shippers tend not to use it on their very best wines – which anyhow are likely to be bought by people who understand wine. For instance, Harveys do not ultra-cool their 1796 range, nor Gonzalez Byass their Apostoles range.

Other treatments that have been used in the past include the addition of very small quantities of meso-tartaric acid. This has been found to act as a stabilizer at any rate for short periods, which is all that is normally necessary.

Oxidation is an enemy of sherry as it is of all wines. While the casks are kept on ullage in the bodega, the velo of flor protects fino sherries from oxidation, and oxygen needs to be present to feed the yeasts, while oxidation is an essential part of the development of oloroso sherries. However, once a fino is deprived of its flor it can oxidize only too quickly and the leading shippers are going to a lot of trouble to keep oxygen out. A satisfactory way of doing this is to keep the wine under a blanket of nitrogen, both in containers and in bottles. It has also been found advantageous to use metal screw caps with plastic linings rather than corks. They do not look nearly so good, but they work.

Finally, before any sherry can be exported a shipping sample is carefully checked for quality by the Estación de Viticultura y Enologia in Jerez. Tests include a Carbon 14 test to see that no industrial alcohol has been used for fortification – a recent requirement brought about by the EEC law and regarded as of especial importance in Germany. Special tests have to be carried out to meet the requirements of certain countries and all samples are tested for volatile acidity. In a typical day about 150 samples are tested and analysed, with a rejection rate of about 3 per cent, a rate that is kept low because the larger shippers are equipped to do their own tests and the smaller ones can ask for a preliminary analysis before making up large quantities for shipment.

Rather as a curiosity, the authorities have been carefully monitoring radioactivity over the years. Expressed as units on the scintillator, in 1962 it was 13; it peaked to double between then and 1965; now that nuclear tests have stopped it has gone down again to 17. I have not been able to extract from the authorities any figures for the years after Chernobyl; but it is to be remembered that the radioactive cloud went north. None of this is dangerous but it is clear that the nuclear powers are capable of bringing about a rapid increase in radioactivity that will manifest itself in all the natural foods we eat or drink. At present, however, natural sources such as cosmic rays and building stones are the major contributors.

Traditionally, wines were shipped to the major importing countries, notably the United Kingdom, in oak butts; these were either returned for further use or sold to whisky distillers, and the wines were bottled at their destination. In 1968 there was an historic happening: Williams & Humbert shipped a tank of 12,012 gallons on the SS *Pacheo*. It was a complete success. Some shippers showed the sceptical distrust that their grandfathers had shown to the bottle, but shipping by tank soon became the general practice for large consignments. However, this is also rapidly becoming obsolete. There is a general move throughout wine-growing countries for bottling at the place of origin, and this is the EEC policy. Most sherry is now bottled in Spain; soon all will be.

12

Into the Glass

The choice of sherries available in Great Britain is not as great as it was when each wine merchant shipped his own blends, but it is still enormous, and anyone should be able to find many that please; but wine drinkers are often very unenterprising. Many of them are principally interested in one or other of the great table wines. They are perplexed by the many styles of sherry, and sometimes never find one that really satisfies them; some, for this reason, avoid sherry altogether. There are so many styles that they must confuse anyone who has not studied them. The final choice depends on the time of day, the weather, and the other wines that are taken with the meal. Above all, it depends on what one happens to fancy. It is not easy to advise anyone. There is only one hard-and-fast rule: judge for yourself and drink what you enjoy.

No one has the right to tell others what they should drink, but that has never prevented people from asking. The only possible answer is that people who drink sherry regularly generally agree about which styles suit certain occasions, and it is as well to try following their example before attempting something original. But one's own taste is all that matters. To be dogmatic is a form of ignorance, and it is often a manifestation of wine snobbery. Other people's views may act as a guide, but they are only opinions, and they should be treated as such.

For those who enjoy a glass of wine and a biscuit in the morning, any style of sherry is suitable, though the majority prefer a dry wine when the weather is hot and a sweeter wine when it is cold. Likewise a wine that tastes too sweet as an aperitif before lunch may be very acceptable before dinner in the cool of the evening. Very dry sherry has an unaccountable snob appeal, but habitual wine drinkers do generally prefer such sherries as aperitifs; others, who wish to appear knowledgeable, ape them, and often drink very dry sherry at the most improbable times. My own preference is certainly for a wine without the least trace of sweetness, save in the depth of winter, when the sugar in a slightly *abocado* sherry is very comforting. Unsweetened sherries of practically every style can be bought quite readily, including unsweetened olorosos, which came on the market in the 1980s. On a hot summer's day before lunch a manzanilla or fino is usually the most pleasing style, but in the cooler seasons an old amontillado or an unsweetened oloroso is often better – a wine that is still completely dry, but which has more body.

In choosing an aperitif sherry, one must obviously consider the table wine that is to follow. A very old amontillado would destroy the flavour of a moselle; it would even overpower most burgundies. Many wine drinkers like to arrange a progression of flavours, leading up to a big white wine, like a burgundy or rhône, with a light manzanilla or fino sherry; but many white wines, like those from the Saar or Loire valleys, are light in themselves and have high acidity so that instead of a progression there is a rather unsatisfactory contrast. Here the contrast with an amontillado, a palo cortado or a dry oloroso is a more satisfactory one; and sherries such as these with the soup provide just the right degree of contrast when champagne is served as an aperitif to be followed by a white table wine as the first or only wine at dinner. Claret can follow a young amontillado or a delicate palo cortado; burgundy can withstand a somewhat older amontillado or an oloroso; a rhône wine could safely follow a comparatively old sherry.

A dessert sherry should generally be more or less sweet: in the British climate, a completely dry wine is seldom appropriate after a meal, though a dry palo cortado or dry oloroso can be delicious after lunch on one of our rare hot summer's days. A wine to be drunk at the end of a meal should have plenty of body, and although I have enjoyed an old amontillado after lunch, palo cortado or oloroso is generally more attractive. Earle Welby was undoubtedly right when he wrote that sherry is far better than port to drink after champagne.

The great Professor Saintsbury suggested a meal with a different sherry for each course, and it is surprising that more people have not tried it. Sherry is generally at its best with food. In Spain, it is taken with a *tapa*. The word means a lid, or cover, and is said to be derived from an old Spanish custom of putting a plate with a morsel of food on top of the sherry glass. Bars in Spain compete with one another to provide good tapas, and the choice includes such things as cheese, prawns, fish, small steaks, tomatoes, olives, potato salad, chips, pâté, fried squid, fancy sausages, egg, meat balls, salt cod, ham and a multitude of specialities. Such tapas should be served more often in Britain; they are delightful in themselves and show the wine off to the best advantage. Perhaps they soon will be, as in 1990 a number of tapas bars suddenly emerged in this country.

Saintsbury suggested as his sherry dinner:

> Manzanilla will carry you nearly through dinner, and others of the lighter class will go all through, though they may not be drinkable in quite such volume. I once even attempted a fully graded *menu* and wine-list with sherry only to fill the latter – a 'sherry dinner' to match the claret feasts often given by lovers of the Gascon wine. It was before I began to keep such documents, and so I am not quite certain of the details. But if I were reconstructing such an entertainment now, and had the wherewithal as I once had, I should arrange it somewhat thus: Manzanilla with oysters; Montilla with soup and fish; an Amontillado with entrées and roast; an Amoroso or some such wine with sweets; and for after dinner, the oldest and brownest of 'old browns' . . .

It would be hard to suggest a better arrangement but one could devise a hundred others equally good.

Fino sherries are particularly good with food. My own favourite working lunch is a large glass of fino sherry with a salad or with more easily portable food such as a slice of quiche or a well-filled sandwich.

While the second edition of this book was in the press I got married and proudly took my wife to the vintage feast in Jerez. Soon after midnight the two of us, walking with a sherry-shipping friend in the *feria*, began to feel the need for dinner. We were passing by a stand where they were spit-roasting chickens, basted with oil and flavoured with the most delicious herbs. I ordered a chicken and a bottle of fino. 'A *whole* bottle, for *three*?' Deborah asked, aghast. But she did not bat an eyelid when I ordered the second. It is, after all, not so very much stronger than many table wines and one drinks more with impunity when well exercised and in the air of Andalusia.

This is no new idea but rather a return of an old custom, for in the nineteenth century lunch was often a simple help-yourself, off-the-sideboard affair, and there were always decanters of sherry and port.

Sherry is a white wine, and the general rules for serving white wines apply. A fino tastes better if it is chilled but not frozen and this is especially so in hot weather; wines of greater body need only be very slightly cool; and dessert sherries are best served at room temperature. On no account should any sherry be warmed.

Sherris-sack was first drunk from silver vessels – and they usually held a man's measure. Then, during the seventeenth century, Venetian glass was introduced into England, and sherry was generally drunk from flute glasses. A wide choice of wine glasses is available today; many of them are aesthetically very beautiful; hardly any are suitable for drinking wine out of, and the so-called 'sherry glasses' are by far the worst of all. One of the most beautiful things about sherry is its deep, penetrating fragrance that prepares the palate to receive the flavour of the wine; the bouquet of a good sherry is so attractive that one can enjoy it without tasting the wine at all. If it is served in a public-house sherry glass, all that is lost, and the beauty of a really good sherry is destroyed. Such a wine needs a big glass with plenty of room for the full fragrance to gather within it. Tulip-shaped wine glasses filled only half-way are very good, but the special tall tasting glasses, known as dock glasses and used in the wine trade, are better still. These are from three to six inches high and gently taper in towards the top; they should only be filled to the height of one inch or so. A smaller version which is very good is the copita, now widely available. But good glasses not only show up the beauty of a wine; they also reveal its faults. There is a saying in Jerez: *solo hay dos clases de vino de Jerez, el bueno y el mejor* – 'there are only two kinds of sherry, the good and the better'. That is largely true, but there are a few sad exceptions, especially in this cut-throat competition of today, and most of these find their way to the public bars, where small glasses are not always out of place. Such glasses also preserve one from the worst features of spurious wines compounded elsewhere.

When Pepys visited Mr Thomas Povy at Lincoln's Inn Fields, he was taken to see the wine cellar: 'where upon several shelves there stood bottles of all sorts of wine, new and old, with labels pasted upon each bottle, and that in order and plenty as I never saw books in a bookseller's shop.' To the modern eye, these bottles would have looked strange and irregular in shape. Instead of corks, they were fitted with glass stoppers sealed over with wax. Although corks had been used as stoppers for amphorae in the first century BC they did not come into general use till the end of the seventeenth century: until then wine was not aged in bottle, and many of the great wines we enjoy today could not have been matured. What happens to sherry after it has been bottled depends very much on its style. A delicate, unsweetened fino begins to deteriorate immediately. There is an excellent fino sherry, widely sold in public houses, that is often abused for being below standard, or for not being as good as it used to be. The brewers buy it in bulk; then they store it in warm warehouses for a year or two; then they send it to the publican, who keeps it for another year or two before he opens it in a bar as hot as a furnace; the bottle is left open for weeks, and then the wine is served in the wrong glasses, and some perspicacious customer complains that it is imperfect. The bottle may or may not then be returned with a stiff letter to the long-suffering shipper. The wine does not stand a chance.

In progressive companies modern stock control limits the time spent in the warehouses. At last we have something to praise accountants for.

A fino is never at its best after more than three months in bottle. Light amontillados also deteriorate and coarsen in bottle, but they do so rather more slowly. Strange things can happen when dry sherries are kept for a long time in bottle. In my own cellar I laid down some fine palo cortado rather more than twenty years ago. For the first three or four years it improved; then it went through a bad patch that lasted for six or seven years. After that it came out on the other side, showing great age and elegance that have (so far) improved annually.

An unsweetened oloroso remains unharmed for several years. If the wine is sweetened, its behaviour is quite different. Fino and light amontillado do not improve but they last far longer and can safely be kept in bottle for two or three years. The development of a medium-quality amontillado in bottle over a long period of years is extremely speculative. Some years ago I inherited three bottles of an identical amontillado that had been in my grandfather's cellar for twenty years. One had absorbed all its sugar and had become a bone dry, very smooth wine of outstanding character, while the other two were dreadful. A really first-class amontillado, palo cortado or oloroso, if it is initially sweetened, develops in bottle and steadily improves. It gradually consumes its sugar, and becomes remarkably smooth while the bouquet and flavour develop to be exceptionally deep and clean. Such wines are said to have 'bottle age'. Given long enough in the bottle, a dessert oloroso becomes absolutely dry, though this may well take fifty or sixty years if it is very sweet to begin with. I have tasted a sherry that had been in bottle for over a hundred years, and it was truly remarkable. One of the finest dessert sherries I remember was a good oloroso my father bought off Innes, Smith & Co. Ltd, of Birmingham, before the war; it was still very sweet thirty years later, but had developed a remarkably mellow flavour. Such wines improve with every year in bottle, and they have long been sought after by wine lovers. They should be kept at least ten years if the quality of bottle age is really to be appreciated.

Owing to their high cost, old bottled sherries are not listed by many merchants, but I have tasted excellent examples from John Harvey & Sons, Christopher & Co., and from Morgan Furze & Co. I was once told by an absent-minded friend that one of these firms had some for sale, but he had forgotten the merchant's name, and the directions he gave me were terribly vague. Needless to say, I went into the wrong shop, and when I asked for old bottled sherry I was told firmly that there was no such thing. I asked again, but more explicitly, and was told there was no such thing as *vintage* sherry. I could only reply that I had some of the 1792 vintage in my own cellar, but that I was not trying to buy any vintage sherry: I wanted old bottled sherry. The fellow behind the counter then informed me that sherry was made on the solera system. He knew: he had been to Jerez. I gave him my usual address there in case he should want to call again, but left his shop in sheer despair. There are very few wine merchants as ignorant as that, but there should not be any. To find one within a stone's throw of Piccadilly was, I hope, an achievement. The shop, mercifully, has since closed.

Once the bottle has been opened, fino sherry gets coarse very quickly: the more delicate the wine, the more noticeable this is. Professor Saintsbury said that he could notice the difference between lunchtime and dinner. A natural fino should be drunk within three days of opening the bottle; anyone who takes longer should buy half-bottles. Alternatively, as soon as a bottle of sherry is opened, half of it can be decanted into a clean half-bottle which, if immediately and tightly corked, preserves it almost as well as if the wine had not been opened at all, as there has been hardly any time for it to become oxidized. Nowadays there are gadgets that help: one of these, the Vac-U-Vin, evacuates the space above the wine, while another, the Winesaver, fills it with inert nitrogen and carbon dioxide; both prevent oxidation. The process of oxidation is also slowed down if the wine is kept at an even, cool temperature, and I have kept an open bottle in the door of a refrigerator for about ten days without very serious deterioration.

The same thing applies to the other styles of sherry provided they are completely dry. Oxidation completely spoils them and since few people could wish to drink these wines chilled, the easiest way of ameliorating it is not available. The more body or sweetness a wine has, the longer it lasts, and, at the opposite end of the scale, a brown sherry can safely be left for a month, even in a decanter. Decanters are far less airtight than corked bottles, and sherry tends to deteriorate more quickly if it has been decanted. This does not generally matter, as a good wine seldom gets the chance to last for more than a day or two, and decanters are very decorative, but they are only really necessary when the wine has been in bottle for two or three years and has thrown a slight deposit.

Strong wines such as sherry and port sometimes attack their corks, which crumble and leak, utterly spoiling them. This can be avoided if the bottles are stored upright, and this is often done in bodega reference rooms, where the wine is only stored for three or four years. If it is kept upright for longer, there is the danger that the cork may get too dry and cease from being airtight. This is why all wine is normally binned horizontally, and sherry is no exception if it is to be laid down for a long time. For sherry to be laid down, it should be corked with long corks of the first quality, like those used for vintage port. Although I have kept sherry that has been corked with short-stopper corks for over twenty years without losing a bottle, the risk of leakage occurring when corks of this kind are used is very considerable and they are to be avoided. Nowadays some people even use metal screw-tops with thin plastic seals inside. This is said to reduce the risk of oxidation and it probably does. It is certainly all right for a fino that is intended to be drunk soon after it is bought, but I have known a good amontillado to become positively nasty after a year or so. Sherry, like other wines, should be stored in a dark place, as light catalyses oxidation. The traditional sherry bottle is made of very dark, almost black glass, and that helps.

There is a dictum of Robert Benchley that 'Drinking makes such fools of people, and the people are such fools to begin with, it's compounding a felony.' A man who drinks fine wine because he enjoys it will never become a drunkard: wine stops being a pleasure long before it becomes a danger. Taken the right way, it is wholly good. During the Great Plague, only Dr Hedges, of all the London doctors, escaped contagion; he drank a few glasses of Sherris-Sack every day, and wrote in his memoirs: 'Such practice not only protected me against contamination, but instilled in me the optimism which my patients so much needed.' There is a legend that many years ago there lived an archbishop of Seville who so far exceeded the decent complement of years laid down in Holy Writ as to reach the age of a hundred and twenty-five. He was a man of regular habits and drank a bottle of sherry with his dinner every day, save when he was feeling at all unwell; then he drank two bottles.

In Castile and the north of Spain sherry is given as a tonic to expectant mothers. When George C. Howell, of New York, examined the ages and habits of the sherry shippers in Jerez, he found that 10 per cent were light or very light drinkers, and the other 90 per cent were heavy drinkers; 10 per cent died before reaching the age of seventy, and the other 90 per cent lived longer; 15 per cent lived to be ninety. If a sherry shipper dies aged less than seventy, his colleagues regard it as a case of infant mortality. Henry Swinburne recorded the curious fact that, 'The earth in the cemeteries of Xeres, has the quality of preserving corpses incorrupted for years and ages.' Some doubt has been cast upon the accuracy of this observation, but if indeed it is true, I am sure the quality of the earth has nothing to do with it: by the time a Jerezano dies, he is safely pickled by eighty years of steady drinking.

When a Jerezano opens a bottle of sherry, he throws a little on the floor before filling his glass. There is a good reason for this, as it gets rid of the wine that may have been corrupted by contact with the cork. But it is also a ritual – a sacrifice to the earth that gave the wine its being. Then he does the really important thing: he drinks the rest of the bottle. But he bears in mind the rule of St Gildas the Wise: 'If any monk through drinking too freely gets thick of speech so that he cannot join in the psalmody, he is to be deprived of his supper.'

APPENDIX I

Spanish Names

———

Readers may be perplexed by the formation of Spanish names. The Spaniard uses the surnames of both parents, putting that of the father first. The two names may or may not be joined by *y*, meaning *and*. Thus if Sr Fernandez married Srita Gomez and they had a son whom they christened Pedro, his full name would be Pedro Fernandez (y) Gomez. In normal speech and informal writing, the second name is generally omitted unless it is necessary for clear identification. Some Spanish names, moreover, are double-barrelled.

A Spanish lady retains her maiden name after marriage but adds her husband's surname. Thus if Ana Lopez married a Sr Castillo, she would become Ana Lopez de Castillo, and would be referred to as Castillo's Señora. If her husband were to die, she would revert to her maiden name, while describing herself as Castillo's widow.

To British ears, the system sounds rather complicated, but it is entirely logical, and may help to explain the formation of some of the names mentioned in the text.

APPENDIX II

The Chemical Effects of Plastering

To investigate the effect of yeso, the Lancet commissioner prepared two specimens of must at the same time and in precisely the same way, save that one was plastered and the other was not. First he analysed the lees and then the must and the following results were obtained:

Analysis of Lees from (1) 'Mosto' with Sulphate of Lime and (2) 'Mosto' without Sulphate of Lime.

	(1) per cent	(2) per cent
Alcohol and water	73.86	77.76
Albuminoids	4.93	3.96
Potassium bitartrate	3.02	6.30
Calcium tartrate	7.38	2.82
Tartaric acid	1.50	0.71
Potassium sulphate	0.62	0.30
Calcium sulphate	0.61	0.34
Gummy matters	8.08	7.78
Potassium phosphate	–	0.03
Total	100.00	100.00

The lees of wine which have been treated previously with sulphate of lime contain a greater proportion of organic matters than the lees of a wine not so treated, consisting of just those matters, such as albuminous bodies, which are likely if retained in the wine to make it susceptible to objectionable changes and deterioration. Again tartrate of lime in lees of previously treated wine occurs largely, but not entirely, in the place of acid tartrate of potassium in the lees of untreated wine, but it will be observed that in the latter tartrate of lime is also an important constituent. The lees of treated wine further contain an increased proportion of free acid.

The analysis of (1) 'Mosto' previously treated with Sulphate of Lime and (2) of 'Mosto' not so treated.

	(1) per cent	(2) per cent
Solid matters	2.16	1.88
Sugar	0.37	0.23
Potassium bitartrate	0.093	0.28
Tartaric acid	0.338	0.21
Acetic acid	0.09	0.05
Mineral matter	0.37	0.23
Potassium sulphate	0.34	0.085
Potassium phosphate	–	0.041
Alcohol by weight	11.62	10.85
Alcohol by volume	14.37	13.43
Proof spirit	25.18	23.54
Alcohol by volatile ether	0.0214	0.0071
Alcohol in volatile ether	0.0382	0.0172
Total alcohol in ethers	0.0596	0.0243

It will be seen that in these important results we have complete confirmation of the view . . . that the changes induced by the addition of sulphate of lime are the formation of sulphate of potassium in the wine, the separation in the lees of tartrate of lime, and the production of free tartaric acid. Thus the potassium acid tartrate in the untreated wine amounts to 0.28 per cent, whereas in the treated wine it is only 0.093 per cent, just one-third the quantity. It is important to note, however, that not all the acid tartrate of potassium has been removed. The quantity of potassium acid tartrate reduced is in proportion to the increase of free tartaric acid. Further, while the untreated wine contains 0.085 per cent of potassium sulphate the treated wine contains 0.34 per cent, or just four times as much.

There is another point of considerable interest brought out in this analytical contrast and that is in regard to the ethers. The fixed ethers may be looked upon as contributing the peculiar flavour of wine and the volatile ethers the aroma. The type of the former is ethyl tartrate and of the latter ethyl acetate. Now although these wines were produced from grapes of the same vintage, were crushed, fermented, and racked at the same time and were of precisely the same age – though that was only a few months – yet there is a great and important difference in the amount of ethers. In the wine treated with sulphate of lime they are more than double in amount that of the wine not so treated.

APPENDIX III

Baumé, Sikes and Gay-Lussac

A good indication of the sugar content of unfermented grape juice is obtained by measuring the specific gravity by means of a hydrometer. This is possible by virtue of the fact that, while the amount of sugar in the must may vary widely from one vintage to another, the other constituents remain substantially constant and do not affect the hydrometer. It is essentially a method of comparison, but it gives the wine-grower all the information he needs. Commercial versions of the Baumé hydrometer are readily available, and they are calibrated by the manufacturers using standard solutions of common salt. 0° is registered by distilled water. 15° is given by 15 parts by weight of salt to 85 of water. A 15° Baumé solution of sugar fermented right out results in 16.4° Gay-Lussac of alcohol. Very roughly each degree Baumé yields a degree of alcohol on fermentation.

Once the must is completely fermented, the specific gravity is largely determined by the proportion of alcohol in solution, and a hydrometer gives an adequate indication of the strength of the wine. Since 1816 the standard instrument used in Britain has been the Sikes hydrometer, which was devised by a customs official. Its method of construction, calibration and use are exactly defined. In Spain and France Gay-Lussac's volume-alcoholometer is used, giving a direct reading of alcohol by volume, and this very reasonable measure is now the standard scale used in the wine trade throughout the world. The graph opposite may be used to compare the two scales.

For some purposes it is customary to refer to alcoholic strength as a proportion of proof spirit. Spirit of proof strength is that which weighs exactly twelve-thirteenths that of an equal measure of distilled water at 51° F (10.5° C). It corresponds to approximately 57 per cent alcohol by volume. 100 British proof gallons are equivalent to 137 American proof gallons.

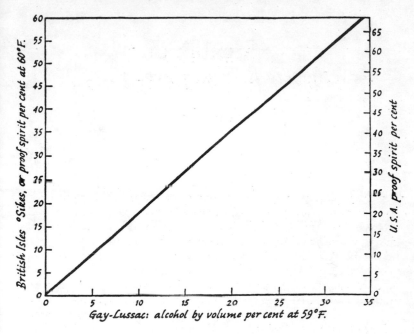

APPENDIX IV

Selected Export Statistics

===

Export statistics (in barrels) for 1774 (following Pan Ferguson):

Haurie	670
Brickdale	561
Isidoro G. Piker	415
Cavezas	213
Romano	164½
Minchacao	158
Roy	138
Herederos de Rizo	79
Tagle	44½
Juan Pedro Haurie	42
Baamonde	15
Abad	9
Joseph Gutierrez	7
Martin Romero	5
Romero	4½
Palmero	2
Demetrio Sunosey (?)	1½
Juan Lacosta	1
Gabriel Franco	1

Export statistics (in arrobas) for the year commencing 1 September 1798. From an old document formerly in the possession of J. M. Rivero.

Juan Haurie y Sobrino	143,461
Jacob Gordon	114,820
Pedro Beigbeder	64,717
Enrique Douvell	37,244
Miguel Brickdale	31,770
Juan Pedro Lacosta y Sobrino	17,036

Martinez y Ca.	10,785
Francisco Antonio de la Tixera (CZ)	4,539
Gaspar Aguado	4,293
Diega Maria de Roy	3,435
Juan Pedro Casaubon	2,805

Export statistics for the year 1856, abstracted from the 1875 catalogue of Duff Gordon & Co., whose wines ranged in price from £35 to £92 per butt – 'credit as usual'. Quantities in butts.

From Jerez		*From Puerto de Santa Maria*	
Gonzalez & Dubosc	3,885	J. W. Burdon	3,507
Pemartin & Co.	3,239	Duff Gordon & Co.	3,036
P. Garvey	3,144	Mously & Co.	2,154
P. Domecq	3,033	Diaz, Merello & Co.	2,056
S. de al Sierra	2,536	Widow X. Harmony & Co.	1,995
M. Misa	2,047	M. M. de Mora	1,746
F. G. Cosens	1,864	M. & F. Tosar	1,417
Paul & Dastis	1,433	V. M. de la Portilla	1,046
Ysasi & Co.	1,079	B. Vergara	938
P. Biegbeder & Co.	1,013	J. M. Pico	927
D. de Goni	1,001	M. Gastelu Yriarte	820
F. Victor & Co.	915	S. Campbell & Co.	698
Bermudez & Co.	795	F. W. Cosens	686
Lacosta & Capdepon	755	Nephews of P. Harmony	584
P. L. Villegas	670	F. Morgan & Co.	431
M. Pareja	626	M.G. Bustamente	340
P. A. Rivero & Sons	484	W. Rudolph	335
Villacreces, Costello	422	Gorman & Co.	296
J. A. de Agreda	403	Widow Victoria & Sons	238
F. Paul	303	A. Delgado & Son	213
J. Gordon	265	Hamilton & Thorby	191
M. Ponce de Leon	241	W. Oldham	185
Six shippers under 100	254	Nine shippers under 100	365

Finally it is instructive to include a list for 1874, at the height of the boom, to see the number of shippers who came – and went. The quantities are given in arrobas; fractions have been eliminated against individual names, but totals are exact.

From Jerez		*From Puerto de Santa Maria*	
Sres Gonzalez Byass y Cia	196,468	D. Federico Rudolf	67,496
D. Manuel Misa	127,841	Sres Vda de X Harmony y	
D. Pedro Domecq	94,344	Cia	51,985

APPENDIX

Sres D. Federico Guillermo Cosens y Cia	92,549	Sres Duff Gordon	51,904
Sres Garvey y Cia	82,736	Sres Gonzalez Byass y Cia	43,045
Sres Wisdom & Warter	71,960	D. Manuel Moreno de Mora	41,903
Sres Mackenzie y Cia	60,999	Sres D. Federico G. Cosens y Cia	37,023
D. Julian Pemartin	56,158		
D. Bartolome Vergara	48,468	D. Juan Guillermo Burdon	30,097
Sres Heyward Wilson y Cia	48,047	Sres M. & F. Tosar	27,295
Sres Noble y Malvido	46,516	D. Vicente Merello	26,402
Sres Matthiesen Furlong y Cia	42,454	Sres M. Lassaletta y Cia	24,800
D. Juan Haurie Sobrinos	37,756	D. Carlos S. Campbell y Cia	24,763
D. Ricardo Davies	36,580	D. Ramon Jimenez Davila	18,105
Sres D. Guillermo Woellwath y Cia	31,658	Sres Stallard y Smith	14,283
		D. Manuel Castelu e Iriarte	14,282
D. Jose C. Gordon	22,336	Sres J. Jimenez y Cia	13,738
Sres Ysasi y Cia	21,334	D. Jose Maria Pico	12,269
Sres Alexander Webber y Cia	21,255	Sres M. Sancho y Ahuja	11,621
		Sra Vda de Vitoria e Hijos	10,365
D. Adolfo Capdepon	21,149	D. Guillermo H. Hughes	7,845
D. Diego de Agreda	20,376	D. A. Rovello	7,816
D. Jose Pemartin	16,256	Sres Morgan Brothers	6,440
Sres Polak Hermanos y Cia	15,775	D. Francisco Heald	6,424
Sres R. Parada y Cia	14,541	D. W. de Loma	6,103
D. J. J. V. Vegas	14,074	D. Jorge Garrard	5,325
Sres Cramp Suter y Cia	13,425	Sres de Alberti Hermanos	5,224
Sres Steenackers Hermanos	12,039	D. Luis Chorro	4,943
Sres Joanico Hermanos	11,502	Sres Horedaros de Micon	4,051
Sres R. y F. Romero	11,494	D. Juan Antonio Martinez	2,837
Sres R. C. Chartres y Cia	10,031	D. Jorge Thuillier	945
Sres Duque de San Lorenzo y Marques de la Mesa	9,728	Sres Lorenz Arms & Sohne	860
D. Damian de Goñi	9,371	Sres Loma y Gomez	822
Sres Smith Flude y Cia	9,158	Sres Wm. Wilders y Cia	320
Sres McShane y Cia	7,842	Sres B. Costello y Cia	285
Sra Viuda de Paul	6,560	Sres Kinloch y Cia	105
Sres Keppel Hesselink e hijos	6,513		
D. Manuel de Elejalde y Coma	3,553		581,717
Sres Gordon Beigbeder e hijo	3,316		
Sres Toms y Cia	3,285		
Sres D. Guillermo Phesey y Cia	3,221		

D. John Barnett	2,985
D. Pedro A. Rivero hijos	2,888
Sres Kruger & Borrett	2,273
Sres D. Edmund Brace y Cia	2,170
D. Jorge Garrard	1,988
Sres Santarelli Hermanos	1,416
Sres Herran y Cia	1,365
Sres Almeida y Cia	1,042
Sres Mambrino y Cia	390
D. Manuel Francisco Paul	150
D. Rafael de la Cueva	90
D. Serafin Alvarez	50
Sres W. P. Thompson	45
	1,379,501

APPENDIX V

Making of Casks in the Bodega

In all bodegas the visible heads of casks are marked in white with various hieroglyphics which give certain information about the wine. Information of only temporary interest is written on in white chalk, but if it is of lasting importance it is stencilled on in white paint.

Soleras and criaderas, of course, are never moved, and the information is stencilled on them in full, but only on the first and last casks in the row. A white arrow → is added pointing in the direction of the other casks to which the same information applies; if there is more than one row, there are additional arrows pointing to the other rows: $>$ or $\lessgtr$

Criaderas, soleras and blends usually have special or fancy names. Other wines are often marked, where appropriate, with the name of the vineyard, or with the initials of the vineyard owner or those of the almacenista from whom the wine was bought. Añada wines are marked with the last two digits of the year of the vintage.

Each cask bears the symbol 1/23, or 1/50, or 1/5, etc. This means that it is one of 23, or 50, or 5, etc., casks of the identical wine. If there is only one cask of a particular wine, the word '*sola*' is used instead.

Wherever figures such as 21/3, or 7/10 are written in chalk after another word or words, these denote the day and month when the wine was submitted to a certain operation such as fining, fortification, etc.

The more important signs used in classifying sherry have already been listed in Chapter 8. There are many additional signs used to describe the various tasks of the bodega, and these are chalked on the butt ends to show that the wine has been fined, or fortified, or is defective in some way, etc. Signs are available to give any likely information, but these vary slightly from one shipper to another, and a detailed list is beyond the scope of this book.

APPENDIX VI

Climatic Statistics

Comparing the number of days of rain with the total rainfall will show what anyone who has lived in Jerez has experienced: there are few, indeterminate, cloudy days; it is usually sunny or else raining cats and dogs. The years of maximum and minimum rainfall are included to give an idea of the wide variations from year to year. Wind statistics have been excluded owing to the difficulty of producing a summary of reasonable length that makes sense: but it must be remembered that the temperature and strength of wind make a material difference to the development of the grapes as well as to the comfort of living there. There are two other statistics that should be mentioned. The days of frost average three in December, five in January, two in February and a half in April. In the other months there is none. The meteorological station is more exposed than the town of Jerez, as the statistics taken in the garden of Williams & Humbert show far fewer, a typical number being two in January. But these are not days of frost at all as such things are understood in northern Europe. The thermometer just touches zero or presumes to go a little below it for an hour or two in the middle of the night. Highest temperatures are also of interest. The temperature rises to above 30°C on 22.5 days in July, 26 days in August and 14 days in September. August can feel very hot indeed.

CLIMATIC STATISTICS

The following statistics, averaged over a number of years, were supplied by the local meteorological office.

Month	Temperature			Humidity
	Average	Maximum	Minimum	%
January	11°	15.88°	5.92°	84
February	11.2°	17.03°	6.57°	85.33
March	13.68°	18.96°	8.11°	74.6
April	16.62°	21.75°	9.6°	68.53
May	19.3°	26.3°	12.3°	40.7
June	23°	29.2°	18.1°	59.7
July	25.5°	32.7°	16.9°	59
August	25.5°	32.9°	17.1°	60
September	23.18°	30.05°	16.01°	68
October	19.31°	25.48°	13.09°	71.28
November	13.61°	19.86°	9.03°	79.9
December	12.82°	16.69°	6.19°	85.1

Month	Rain			
	Total (mm)	No. of days	Record max. (mm)	Record min. (mm)
January	96.41	12.5	1970:337.1	1968, 1957:13
February	79.53	12.36	1969:201	1957:0.5
March	120.19	10.08	1960:193.6	1966:0.7
April	54.68	8.0	1971:187.6	1965:1.3
May	48.1	6.6	1959:157.9	1954:0.1
June	18.2	4.2	1970:93.2	1956:0
July	0	0	1964:2	
August	7.0	1	1952:53	
September	21.9	6	1954:25	1956, 1964:3
October	75.7	8.8	1960:259	1964:0.3
November	96.29	10.28	1961:440.5	1971:32
December	104.16	11	1963:369.4	1956:9.8

APPENDIX VII

Stocks of Maturing Sherry as at 1 September 1978

Jerez shippers   2,996,800 hectolitres
Puerto de Santa Maria shippers   499,600 hectolitres
Sanlucar shippers   637,300 hectolitres

           Total   4,133,700 hectolitres

Jerez almacenistas   142,400 hectolitres
Puerto de Santa Maria almacenistas   38,600 hectolitres
Sanlucar almacenistas   173,200 hectolitres

           Total   354,200 hectolitres

Overall total: 4,487,900 hectolitres.

Glossary

===

ABOCADO: slightly sweetened.

ACHICAR: literally, 'to lessen'. A verb used when the quality of wine in a solera is diminished by drawing excessive quantities.

AFUERA: wine made from grapes grown on albariza soil; areas of such soil.

AGUAPIE: the second pie pressing.

AGUARDIENTE: grape spirit.

ALBARIZA: the name given to the best soil in which sherry vines are grown. It is white in colour and contains a high proportion of calcium.

ALBILLO CASTELLANO: the name of a vine.

ALMACENISTA: a man who has a bodega where he holds wines for sale to shippers.

ALMIBAR: a solution of invert sugar formerly used, when mixed with wine, for sweetening paler sherries.

ALMIJAR: the yard outside the vineyard building where the grapes are dried before being pressed.

ALMIZCATE: the space between two bodega buildings.

AMONTILLADO: a style of wine obtained when fino sherry is aged for a long time in the wood. It resembles wines formerly prepared only in Montilla.

AMOROSO: term used chiefly in England for a type of light and not very dry oloroso sherry.

AMPELOGRAPHY: the comparative study of the vine.

AÑADA: unblended wine made only from grapes of a particular year.

AÑINA: the fourth, in order of merit, of the four leading districts round Jerez whose soil is albariza.

APALEADOR: stick used for stirring wine during fining.

ARANZADA: the measure of area used in the vineyards. One aranzada = 0.475 hectare or 1.1737 acres.

ARENA: the third, in order of merit, of the three types of soil in which sherry vines are grown: red in colour and sandy.

ARROBA: either a measure of grapes by weight, equivalent to about 25.4 English pounds, or a measure of wine by volume, equivalent in Jerez to about 3.66 imperial gallons. The exact measure varies in different parts of Spain.

ARROPE: a syrup obtained by simmering must down to one-fifth of its original volume.

ARRUMBADOR: bodega workman.

BALBAINA: the third, in order of merit, of the four leading districts round Jerez whose soil is albariza.

BARRO: the second, in order of merit, of the three types of soil in which sherry vines are grown.

BARRIL DEL GASTO: a barrel of cheap wine kept for workers to drink in the bodega.

BASTO: adjective applied to wine, meaning 'coarse'.

BIENTEVEO: a temporary look-out post erected in a vineyard near the time of the vintage.

BOCOY: an unusually shaped butt of varying size but generally containing about 40 arrobas – that is, about 146½ imperial gallons.

BODEGA: a large overground warehouse in which sherry is stored: also applied (generally in the plural) to the whole establishment of a sherry shipper or almacenista.

BOMBA: siphon used in bodegas.

BOSADOR: funnel inserted into the bung of a barrel into which the must can rise during the tumultuous fermentation.

BOTA: butt.

BOTA CHICA: a shipping butt containing 30 arrobas or about 110 imperial gallons. On arrival at destination it will, after evaporation, contain only about 108 imperial gallons.

BOTA BODEGUERA: an old butt which, through age, has lost its shape and whose contents are doubtful.

BOTA DE EMBARQUE: shipping butt: another name for a bota chica.

BOTA DE RECIBO: standard-sized butt (31 arrobas or about 111.63 imperial gallons) used locally for measuring and receiving wine.

BOTA GORDA: bodega butt, that is storage butt containing 36 to 40 arrobas (132 to 146 imperial gallons).

CABACEO: a blend of wine.

CABEZUELA: second sedimentation of musts.

CAMERA (OBSCURA): a wooden structure with a candle inside for testing the brightness of wines.

CANOA: a wedge-shaped funnel used for filling casks.

CANASTA: cane basket used in the vineyards.

CAÑOCAZO: the name of a vine.

CANUTO: short wooden pipe with a cork which is inserted in the bunghole in the head of a cask, when it is desired to draw wine from that cask.

CAPATAZ: foreman of a bodega.

CARRASCAL: the second, in order of merit, of the four leading districts round Jerez whose soil is albariza.

CASCO: a cask.

CASSE: a generic term for various forms of wine disease.

CEPA: a vine.

CLAROS: a bright wine.

CLAROS DE LIAS: clear wine obtained from the lees of must.

CLAROS DE TURBIOS: clear wines obtained by putting turbois through linen bags or, nowadays, filters.

COLOR, VINO DE: wine used for deepening the colour of blends.

CORREDOR: broker, who buys and sells wine.

CRIADERA: a series of butts which are never moved and from which periodically wine is drawn to refresh a solera or another criadera, an equal quantity of wine being replaced, drawn from another criadera or from stocks of añada wine.

CRUJIA: the broad, central transverse aisle in a bodega building.

CUARTO (BOTA): quarter cask (¼ butt).

CUARTILLO: a measure of wine by volume: 1/32 arroba.

DESFANGADO: literally, 'demudding': the separation of must from heavy impurities before fermentation.

DULCE, VINO: a sweet wine.

DULCE APAGADO: a form of sweet wine obtained by adding alcohol to unfermented must. Formerly made outside the sherry area.

DULCE PASA: a sweet wine made as a dulce apagado from Palomino grapes grown in the sherry area.

EMBOTELLADO: the bottling department of a shipper's bodega.

ENOLOGY: modern spelling of oenology – the science of wine making.

ENTRE FINO: a fino wine that lacks distinction.

ENYESADO: the addition of yeso (gypsum) to the must.

ESCALAS: the scales of a solera.

ESCRITORIO: office.

ESPALDERAS: the structure of wires used for supporting vines in vineyards.

ESPIRRAQUE: third pie pressing used in small vineyards.

FINO: pale, delicate wine in which flor has bred freely.

FLOR: film of yeast cells growing on the surface of some classes of sherry.

GARCETA: closely woven sack used to slow down wine flowing into a cask.

GAZPACHO: an Andalusian soup made with garlic and vinegar.

HECHO: literally 'made', but it is a term applied to wine that is fully mature.

HILO: oiliness: a disease of young wines.

HOGSHEAD: cask holding 54 gallons.

INJERTA: grafting.

JARRA: a wooden jar bound with iron, or a metal jar used for transferring wine from one cask to another and containing approximately three-quarters of an arroba.

JEREZ CORTADO: the name given to palo cortado produced in Sanlucar de Barrameda.

LADRONCILLO: metal pipe used for transferring wine from cask to cask.

LAGAR: wooden wine press.

LEVANTE: hot, seasonal easterly wind peculiar to southern Spain.

LIAS: the lees of must.

LISTAN: another name for the Palomino grape.

MANTUO CASTELLANO: the name of one of the vines growing in the sherry area.

MANZANILLA: a distinctive style of sherry prepared at Sanlucar de Barrameda.

MACHARNUDO: the first, in order of merit, of the four leading districts round Jerez whose soil is albariza.

MADRE: the 'mother' of wine, that collects at the bottom of casks and is left undisturbed when working a solera.

MAJUELO: wine pressed from grapes grown on young vines.

MANNITE: a disease of sherry in which mannitol is formed.

MARC: grape residues after the complete pressing.

MARCO REAL: square pattern used in planting out vineyards.

MARQUISTA: a merchant who exports wines under his own marks but who has no separate bodegas.

MEDIA (BOTA): a hogshead (= ½ butt).

MITAD Y MITAD (MITEADO): a fifty-fifty mixture of alcohol and mature sherry, used for fortifying.

MONTILLA-MORILES: a wine-growing district in the hills near Cordova.

MOSCATEL: a sweet wine made from Moscatel grapes.

MOSTO: must: the juice of grapes. It ceases being must and becomes wine as soon as the fermentation is complete. Some growers enjoy drinking this very young wine but it is never sold. In the sherry country, however, the term *mosto* is used more loosely, both before and after fermentation and until the wine has been racked from the lees.

MYCODERMA ACETI: a living ferment that tends to turn wine into vinegar.

NUBE: cloudiness: a disease of wine.

OCTAVO: an octave (⅛ butt).

OENOLOGY: the science of wine making.

OFIQUE: a method of refrigeration to prevent wine from going cloudy.

OIDIUM: a fungoid parasite of the vine.

OLOROSO: wine in which either there has never been much flor or in which growth of flor has been stopped by the addition of spirit: a dark and full wine.

PAGO: a distinct, named vineyard.

PALMA: a high quality fino.

PALMA CORTADA: a rather stouter fino tending towards amontillado.

PALO: literally a stick but applied in bodegas to a piece of iron with attached brush used in fining wine.

PALO CORTADO: a rather full-bodied sherry of particularly good style.

PALOMINO: the most popular vine for preparing sherry.

PASADO: a wine that has developed with age.

PATA DE GALLINA: literally, 'hen's foot'; a style of oloroso which is dry but tastes slightly sweet owing to the presence of natural glycerine.

PAXARETE: sweet wine partly consisting of Pedro Ximenez used for sweetening blends of sherry and for colouring whisky.

PEDRO XIMENEZ: the name of the vine producing the grape which, when dried and pressed, makes the best sweet wine.

PERRUNO: the name of a vine.

PESO: an old-fashioned measure of value sometimes used in buying and selling wine and in calculating the value of stock. One peso is equal to 3.75 pesetas and there are 15 reales in a peso.

PHYLLOXERA: the 'vine louse'; a destructive insect parasite of the vine.

PIE: a method of pressing grape residues following the first pressing in the lagar.

PISADOR: one of the men who tread the grapes in the wine-presses at the vintage.

PONIENTE: a cool, humid wind that often blows in the sherry country.

PRENSA: the hydraulic pressing of the grape residues.

PRENZAS: wine made from the third pressing at the vintage by means of hydraulic presses.

PULPITO: a form of mechanical wine press.

PX: short expression for Pedro Ximenez.

QUADRILLA: a team of four arrumbadores.

RACIMO: a bunch of grapes.

RAYA: a term used in classifying must. Also a coarse form of oloroso.

RAYA OLOROSA: a light raya.

REAL: an old-fashioned measure of value but one still sometimes used in buying and selling wine and in calculating the value of stock. One real equals 25 centimos or a quarter of a peseta. There are 15 reales in a peso.

REDONDO: adjective applied to wine, meaning 'round', or well balanced.

REFERENCIA: a sample of a blend retained by the shipper.

ROCIADOR: perforated pipe used in refreshing casks of wine.

ROCIAR: to refresh a cask of wine; to fill it from another cask.

ROCÍO: process of running the scales of a solera.

RUEDO: an aisle along the length of a bodega building.

SACAR: to draw off wine from a cask either for shipment, or to refresh another cask.

SANCOCHO: a syrup obtained by simmering must until it is one-third of its original volume.

SECO: dry.

SIFON: siphon used for drawing wine from a cask.

SOBRE TABLA: literally 'on the board'. Wines that have been racked clear of the lees but have not been blended with other wines.

SOLEO: the sunning of the grapes.

SOLERA: a series of butts which are never moved and from which wine is periodically drawn, whereupon the solera is refreshed with an equal quantity of wine from a criadera. Also used loosely to describe the complete unit, consisting of the solera itself and all its criaderas.

TENT: a style of wine made at Rota.

TIERRA DE ANAFAS: albariza soil.

TIERRA BLANCA: albariza soil.

TIERRA DE LEBRIJA: Spanish earth used for fining wine.

TIERRA DE VINO: Spanish earth used for fining wine.

TINAJA: earthenware jug used in bodegas; in the country a large earthenware jar used for storing and, in Montilla, for fermenting wine.

TINETA: a wooden carrier in which grapes at the vintage are carried in from the vineyards to be pressed.

TIRADOR: one of the men who work the wooden screw press used in the second pressing of the grapes.

TONEL: a very large storage cask containing, two, three, four or more butts.

TONELERO: cooper.

TOSCA: albariza soil.

TRESBOLILLO: diagonal pattern used in planting out vineyards.

TURBIOS: the lees of wine, as opposed to lias, the lees of must.

ULLAGE: empty space in wine cask.

UVA: grape.

VELO: surface film of flor.

VENDIMIA: vintage.

VENENCIA: an instrument consisting of a small silver cup on the end of a long whalebone handle used for drawing small quantities of wine from casks for tasting; also made sometimes of a split bamboo.

VID: vine.

VIDUEÑO: wine made from grapes other than Palamino, and grown on albariza soil.

VIEJO: old.

VIEJISIMO: very old.

VIÑA: vineyard.

VINO DE PASTO: in Spain a pale, cheap table wine for general drinking; in England a medium sherry blended as an aperitif.

VINO DE XERES: sherry.

YESO: gypsum (calcium sulphate), a small quantity of which is sprinkled on grapes before they are pressed.

ZAPATOS DE PISAR: cowhide nail-studded boots used in the pressing of the grapes.

Sources and Bibliography

Calendar of State Papers, State Papers (Spain), manuscript papers (including Roos's Narrative), and consular reports in the Public Record Office.
Papers in the Manuscript Room of the British Library.
Old papers, manuscripts, prepared abstracts and early printed books in the private library of the late Don José de Soto y Molina, of Jerez.
The private letter-books and early records of Duff Gordon & Co., Garvey, S. A., J. M. Rivero, S. A., Williams & Humbert, Ltd and Wisdom & Warter Ltd.
Walter Gilbey's *Travelling Journal*, 1874.

PUBLISHED WORKS

Abela, Eduardo, *Los Vinos Españoles en la Exposición Universal de Chicago*. Madrid, 1893
Allen, H. Warner, *Sherry*. London, 1933
 – *Number Three Saint James's Street*. London, 1950
 – *A Contemplation of Wine*. London, 1951
 – *Port and Sherry*. London, 1952
 – *A History of Wine*. London, 1961
Alvarez-Batista, M. A., and E. Garcia-Maiquez, 'Componentes Aromaticas de la Fermentacion Alcoholica de Jerez'. Microbiol. Españ., 1984
Amerine, M. A., Ph.D., and Cruess, W. V., Ph.D., *The Technology of Wine Making*. Connecticut, 1960
Anon., *A Iovrnall, and Relation of the action . . . upon the Coast of Spaine*, 1625. London, 1626
 – *Pasquil's Palinodia, and his Progresse to the Taverne*. London, 1634
 – *Memorial Ajustado . . . entre Don Juan Aurie y . . . los Diputados del Gremio de Vinateria*. Spanish, 18th C
 – *Memoria Presentada a la Real Sociedad Economica de Amigoes del Pais de Jerez de la Frontera . . .* Jerez, 1857
 – *International Exhibition, 1862: Reports by the Juries*. London, 1863

– *Exposición Nacional Vinicola de 1877: Catalogo General*. Madrid, 1877
– *Account of Spain*. London, 1703
Arlott, John, 'At the Sign of the Bat and Ball' (in *Compleat Imbiber I*). London, 1956
Badell Roig, L., 'Vides Europeos . . . Estudio de las Sinonimas.' Barcelona, 1951
Baker, G. A., M. A. Amerine and E. B. Roessler, 'Theory and Application of Fractional-Blending Systems.' California, 1952
Barbadillo, Antonio P., *Historia de las Bodegas Barbadillo*. Sanlucar de Barrameda, 1989
Barbadillo, Manuel, *El Vino de la Alegria*. Jerez, 1951
Barry, Sir Edward, Bart., *Observations – on the Wines of the Ancients*. London, 1775
Barton, Nicholas, *The Lost Rivers of London*. London, 1962
Berry, C. W., *Viniana*. London, 1934
– *In Search of Wine*. London, 1935
Birch, Thomas, *The Court and Times of Charles I*. London, 1848
Blasco Ibañez, V. (tr. I. Goldberg), *La Bodega*. London, 1923
Boutelou, Esteban, *Memoria sobre el Cultivo de la Vid en Sanlucar de Barrameda y Xerez de la Frontera*. Madrid, 1807
Briggs, Asa, *Wine for Sale*. London, 1985
Brown, Georgius and Francisco Hohenbergius, *Civitatis Orbis Terrarum*. Cologne, 1572
Brown, Ivor, *Say the Word*. London, 1947
Bryant, Sir Arthur, *Samuel Pepys, the Saviour of the Navy*. London, 1938
Buckton, G. B., *A Monograph of British Aphids*, Vol. IV. London, 1882
Busby, James, *Journal of a Recent Visit to the Principal Vineyards of Spain and France*. London, 1834
Campbell, Ian Maxwell, *Wayward Tendrils of the Vine*. London, 1948
C(osens), F. W., *Sherryana*. London, 1886
Carr, Sir John, *Descriptive Travels in . . . Spain . . . in . . . 1809*. London, 1811
Casa-Domecq, Marques de, *Memoria Sobre el Estado del Negocio de Vinos de Jerez de la Frontera*, 3rd ed. Madrid, 1923
Castellet, Buenaventura, *Enología Española*. Barcelona, 1865
Charleton, Walt., M. D., *Two Discourses Delivered to the Royal Society*, 3rd ed. London, 1692
Charleston, R. J., 'Early English Drinking Glasses' (in *Compleat Imbiber I*). London, 1956
Chiarlone, Dr Quintin, *Tratado sobre el Cultivo de la Vid*. Madrid, 1856
Christian, Russell, *Sherry*. London, 1881

Columella, Lucius Junius Moderatus (tr. H. B. Ash, E. S. Forster and E. H. Heffner), *On Agriculture*. London, 1954, 1960

Connell-Smith, Gordon, *Forerunners of Drake*. London, 1954

Consejo Regulador, *Los Vinos de Jerez. Jerez-Xérès-Sherry*. Jerez, n.d.

Cortés y Morales, Balbino, *Tratado Teorico y Practico de Vinificación*. Madrid, 1866

Cortina, Juan, *Cartas Escritas por Joaquin Portillo a Don Bruno Perez*. Jerez, 19th C

Crawford, Anne, *A History of the Vintners' Company*. London, 1977

Croft, Pauline, *The Spanish Company*. London, 1973

Croft-Cooke, Rupert, *Sherry*. London, 1955

de las Cuevas, Jesus, *Nuevas Paginas sobre la Viña y el Vino de Jerez*. Jerez, 1952

de las Cuevas, José, *Biographia del Vino de Jerez*. Jerez, 1949

– *Historia del Brandy de Jerez*. Jerez, 1952

Cunningham, W., D. D., *The Growth of English Industry and Commerce*, 4th ed. Cambridge, 1905

Dalton, Charles, *Life and Times of General Sir Edward Cecil, Viscount Wimbledon*. London, 1885

Darwin, Sir Francis Sacheverell, *Travels in Spain*. Cambridge, 1927

Denman, James L., *Wine: The Advantages of Pure and Natural Wine*, London, 1865

– *Wine and Its Counterfeits*. London, 1876

– *Wine and Its Adulterations*. London, 1867

– *The Vine and Its Fruit*. London, 1866

Domecq, María del Santísimo, *Una Dama Según el Corazón de Dios*. Madrid, 1949

Domecq Williams, Beltrán, 'Dry Residue in Sherry Wines.'

– 'State of the Art on a Very Special Fermentation Product.' 1989.

– 'Ageing of Sherry under Flor.' Oxford, 1982

– paper: *Ageing of Sherry under Flor*. Oxford, 1982

Douglas, Henry, *Spain*. London, 1837

Ebn-el-Awam (ed. Claudio Boutelou), *Libro de Agricultura*. Seville, 1878

Encyclopaedia Britannica.

'English Officer', *The Last Month in Spain, or Wretched Travelling through a Wretched Country*. London, 1816

Fernald, H. T. and Shepard, H. H., *Applied Entomology*, 5th ed. London, 1955

Fernandez de Bobadilla, G., *Viniferas Jerezanas*. Madrid, 1956

Fernandez Formentani, Antonio, *Costumbres y Leyes de Antaño*. Jerez, 1890

Forbes, R. J., *Studies in Ancient Technology*, Vol. III. Leiden, 1955

Ford, Richard, F. S. A., *A Handbook for Travellers in Spain*, 3rd ed. London, 1855
– *Gatherings from Spain*. London, 1861
Fornachon, J. C. M., *Studies on the Sherry Flor*. Adelaide, 1953
Francis, A. D., *The Wine Trade*. London, 1972
Froude, J. A., *History of England*, Vol. I. London, 1862
Frumkin, Lionel, *The Science and Technique of Wine*. London, 1965
Garcia de la Leña, Cecilio, *Disertacion en Recomendacion del Famoso Vino Malegueño Pero Ximen*. Malaga, 1792
Garcia del Barrio Ambrosy, Isidro, *La Tierra del Vino de Jerez*. Jerez de la Frontera, 1979
Garcia de Luján, Alberto, *El No Cultivi de la Viño*. Sevilla, 1988
– 'Patologia de la Vid'. *Agricultura*, Nov. 1989
Garcia de Luján, Alberto and Miguel Lara Benitez, *El Portainjerto de Vid 13–5 Evex*. Madrid, 1990
Garcia de Luján, Alberto, Belén Puertas Garcia and Miguel Lara Benitez, *Variedades de Vid en Andalucia*. Sevilla, 1990
Garcia de Luján, Alberto, A. Garrido, and J. M. Bustillo, *Influenceia de la Sequia en el Comportamiento de Diverse Portainjertos de Vid*. Puerto Réal, 1982
– *Comportamiento de Nuevos Portainjertos de Vid en Terrenos Calizos*. Puerto Réal, 1982
Garcia de Luján, Alberto, M. Gil and M. A. Rodriguez, *Nuevos Resultados de los Ensayos de Disinfeccion de Seulos en la Lucha Contra la Vivasis de la Vid*. Puerto Réal, 1982
Garcia de Luján, Alberto and M. Gil Monreal, *Aspectos de la Seleccion de Viniferas en Zona del Jerez*. Puerto Réal, 1982
– *Sobre la Distribucion del Sisteima Radicular de la Vid*. Madrid, 1982
Garcia de Luján, Alberto, Jeronimo Sorano and Miguel Lara, *Tipos de la Variedad de Vid Palomino*. Jerez, 1990
Gardiner, S. R., *History of England, 1624–1628*. London, 1875
Gee, Walter Mallock ('Don Pedro Verdad'), *From Vineyard to Decanter*. London, 19th C
Goethe, H., *Handbuch der Ampelographia*. Berlin, 1887
Gonzalez Byass & Co., Ltd., *Old Sherry, 1835–1935*. London, 1935
Gonzalez Gordon, Manuel Ma., *Jerez-Xeres-Scheris*, 3rd ed. Jerez, 1970
– *Sherry*, London, 1972
– *Sherry, The Noble Wine*. London, 1990
Goyot, Dr Jules (tr. L. Marie), *Culture of the Vine and Wine Making*. Melbourne, 1865
Gutierrez, Bartolomé, *Historia . . . de Xerez de la Frontera*. Jerez, 1886
Halley, Ned, *Sandeman: Two Hundred Years of Port and Sherry*. London, 1990

SOURCES AND BIBLIOGRAPHY

Hann, George E., *Some Notes on the Technical Study and Handling of Wines*. London

Hare, Augustus, *The Story of My Life*, Vol. 2. London, 1896

Harrison, Godfrey, *Bristol Cream*. London, 1955

Hartley, Joseph, *The Wholesale and Retail Wine and Spirit Merchant's Companion*. London, 1839

Henderson, Al., *The History of Ancient and Modern Wines*. London, 1824

Hernandez Robredo, Leopoldo, *La Filoxera y la Vid Americana*. Logroño, 1908

Hesiod (tr. Dorothea Wender), *Works and Days*. London, 1973

Hewett, J. T., F.R.S., *The Chemistry of Wine Making*. London, 1928

Hidalgo, L., A. Garcia de Luján and I. Benitez Gidon, 'Etat actuel de la sélection clonale et du matériel de multiplacion de la Vigne en Espagne.' *Bulletin de l'O.I.V.*, 1985

Hinxman, J., *New Account of the Inhabitants, Trade and Government of Spain*. London, 1762

Hole, Edwyn, *Andalus*. London, 1958

Holweck, Rt Rev. F. G., *Biographical Dictionary of the Saints*. St Louis, 1924

Howell, George C., *The Case of Whiskey*. Altadena, 1928

Howell, James, *Familiar Letters*. London, 1713

Hutton, Edward, *The Cities of Spain*. London, 1906

Hyams, Edward, *The Grape Vine in England*. London, 1949

Imms, A. D., *A General Text-book of Entomology*, 5th ed. London, 1942

Johnson, Hugh, *The Story of Wine*. London, 1989

Kay, Billy and Cailean Maclean, *Knee Deep in Claret*. Edinburgh, 1983

The Lancet, 'Report on Sherry.' London, 29 October 1898

Leon, Diaz, J., *Siluetas Jerezanas*. Jerez, 1898

Livy (tr. C. Edmonds), *The History of Rome*, Book XXVIII. London, 1850

Lomax, D. W., *The Reconquest of Spain*. London, 1978

Longfield, Ada K., *Anglo-Irish Trade in the Sixteenth Century*. London, 1929

Loomis, Albert, J., S. J., 'Religion and Elizabethan Commerce with Spain.' *The Catholic Historical Review*, 1965

de Madrazo, Pedro, *Sevilla y Cadiz*. Barcelona, 1884

Maillet, Pierre, 'Le Phylloxéra de la Vigne.' *Revue de Zoologie Agricole et Appliquée*, 1957

Marcilla Arrazola Juan, *Tratado Practico de Viticultura y Enología Españolas*. Madrid, 1949

Mariana, Juan, *Historiae de Rebus Hispaniae* (Book XXV). Toledo, 1592

– (tr. Captain John Stevens), *General History of Spain*. London, 1699

Martial, *Epigrams* (in Bohn's Classical Library)
Martial, Marcus Valerius, *Epigrammata*. London, 1822
de Medina y Mesa, Pedro, *Libro de Grandezas y Cosas Memorables de España*. Alcala, 1548
de Mesa Ginete, Francisco, *Historia Sagrada y Politica de . . . Jerez de la Frontera*. Jerez, 1888
Mey, Wim, *Sherry*. The Netherlands, 1988
Milward, R. J., *The Battle of Barrosa*. 1958
Ministerio de Agricultura, *Reglamento de la Denominacion de Origin Jerez-Xeres-Sherry y de su Consejo Regulador*
Morewood, Samuel, *History of Inebriating Liquors*. Dublin, 1838
Mountfort, Guy, *Portrait of a Wilderness*. London, 1958
Muñoz y Gomez, Agustín, *Noticia Histórica de las Calles y Plazas de Xerez de la Frontera*. Jerez, 1903
Ordish, George, *The Great Wine Blight*. London, 1972
Pan Ferguson, Manuel, *La Vendimia y sus Problemas en el Siglo XVIII*. Jerez, 1952
Parada y Barreto, Diego, *Noticias sobre la Historia . . . del Comercio Vinatero de Jerez de la Frontera*. Jerez, 1868
– *Hombres Ilustres de la Ciudad de Jerez de la Frontera*. Jerez, 1875
Peecke, Richard, *Three to One*. London, 1625
Peman Medina, Cesar, *Las Polillas y la Pudrición de la Uva*. Madrid, 1962
Pemartín, Julian, *Diccionario del Vino de Jerez*. Barcelona, 1965
Perold, A. I., *A Treatise on Viticulture*. London, 1927
Persons, Robert, S. J., *Annals of the English College, Seville* (in Publications of the Catholic Record Society, Vol. XIV). London, 1914
Pliny (tr. Rackham, H.), *Natural History*. London, 1945
Portillo, D. J., *Noches Jerezanas*. Jerez, 1839
Pragestus, Jac., M. D., *How to Make . . . Spanish Wine Fine*. Sloane MS., British Museum.
Prothero, R. E., *Letters and Journals of Byron*. London, 1898
Pudney, John, 'The Tippling World' (in *Compleat Imbiber I*). London, 1956
Quirós Carrasco, José María, *Unas Notas . . . sobre . . . Yeso*. Jerez, 1958
Rainbird, George, *Sherry and the Wines of Spain*. London, 1966
Rallon, Estéban, *Historia de Xerez de la Frontera*. Jerez, 1891
Ray, Cyril (ed.), *The Compleat Imbiber I*. London, 1956
Read, Jan, *The Wines of Spain*. London, 1982
– *Sherry and the Sherry Bodegas*. London, 1988
Redding, Cyrus, *A History and Description of Modern Wines*. London, 1860

Richardson, Pelham, *Notes on the Wine Duty Question and Mr. Shaw's Pamphlet*. London, 1851

Roos, L. (tr. Dubois, R. and Wilkinson, W. P.), *Wine-Making in Hot Climates*. Melbourne, 1900

Rose, A. H., *Alcoholic Beverages*. London, 1977

de Roxas Clemente y Rubio, *Ensayo sobre las Variedades de la Vid*. Madrid, 1807

Ruiz Castro, Aurelio, 'Principales Plagas de Viñedo y sus Tratamientos.' *Annuario de la Vid 1946–7*. Madrid, 1947

Saintsbury, George, *Notes on a Cellar-Book*. London, 1920

Sancho de Sopranis, Hipolito, *Historia Social de Jerez de la Frontera*. Jerez, 1959

– *Documentos para la Historia del Vino de Jerez*. Jerez, 1959

Sandeman, Geo. G. Sons & Co., Ltd., *Port and Sherry*. London, n.d.

Sannino, Dr F. Antonio, *Tratado de Enología*, 2nd ed. Buenos Aires, 1948

Schulten, Adolf. *Tartessos*. Madrid, 1924

Scott, Capt. C. Rochfort, *Excursions in the Mountains of Ronda and Granada*. London, 1838

Seltman, Charles, *Wine in the Ancient World*. London, 1957

Shaw, Thos. Geo., *The Wine Trade and Its History*, 2nd ed. London, 1864

– *Wine, the Vine and the Cellar*, 2nd ed. London, 1864

Simon, André L., *History of the Wine Trade*. London, 1906

– *Bottlescrew Days*. London, 1926

– *Vintagewise*. London, 1945

– *Bibliotheca Gastronomica*. London, 1953

– *The Star Chamber Dinner Accounts*, London, 1959

Sitwell, Sir George, *Letters of the Sitwells and Sacheverells*. Scarborough, 1900

de Soto y Molina, José, *Cosas Notables Ocurridas en Xerez de la Frontera desde 1647 a 1729*. Jerez

Stonor, R. J., *Stonor*. Newport, 1951

Stoye, J. W., *English Travellers Abroad, 1604–1667*. London, 1952

Strong, Dr John, *Glasgow and its Clubs*. Glasgow, 1857

Sugden, John, *Sir Francis Drake*, London, 1990

Swinburne, Henry, *Picturesque Tour through Spain*. London, 1810

Tarapha, Francisco, *De Origine Ac Rebus Gestis*. Antwerp, 1553

Thompson, W., *Practical Treatise on the Grape Vine*, 7th ed. Edinburgh, 1871

Thorpe, Sir Edward, F.R.S., *Alcoholometric Tables*. London, 1915

Thudichum, J. L. W. and Dupré, A., *A Treatise on the Origin, Nature and Varieties of Wine*. London, 1872

Thudichum, J. L. W., *On Wines, their Production, Treatment and Use*. London, 1873
– *A Treatise on Wines*. London, 1894
Tovey, Charles, *British and Foreign Spirits*. London, 1864
– *Wine and Wine Countries*. London, 1877
– *Wine Revelations*. London, 1883
Twiss, Richard, F.R.S., *Travels Through Spain and Portugal*. London, 1775
Uden, Grant, *Drake at Cadiz*. London, 1969
Unwin, Tim, *Wine and the Vine*. London, 1991
de Uztariz, Geronymo (tr. Kippax, John), *The Theory and Practice of Commerce and Maritime Affairs*. London, 1751
Venner, Thomas, *Via Recta ad Vitam Longam*. London, 1622
Viala, P. and Ravaz, L. (tr. Dubois, R. and Wilkinson, W. P.), *American Vines*. Melbourne, 1901
Viala, P. and Vermorel, V., *Traité Général de Viticulture et Ampelographie*. Paris, 1901
Vidal-Barraquer Marfa, José Ma., 'Los Portainjertos en el Viñedo.' *Analas de la Escuela de Peritos Agrícolas*, Vol. XI. Barcelona, 1952
Viljoen, H. G., *Ruskin's Scottish Heritage*. Urbana, 1956
Vizetelly, Henry, *The Wines of the World, Characterized and Classed*. London, 1875
– *Facts about Sherry*. London, 1876
Waugh, Alec, *Merchants of Wine*. London, 1957
Westney, R., *The Wine and Spirit Dealer's . . . Vade-Mecum*. London, 1817
Wheatley, Dennis, *The Seven Ages of Justerini's*. London, 1949
Wheatley, H. B., F.S.A., *The Diary of Samuel Pepys*. London, 1905
Williams, Neville, *Contraband Cargoes*. London, 1959
– *Wine and Food Quarterly* (various numbers)
Wyndham, Richard, *Sherry – from Grape to Glass*. London, 1950(?)
Xandri Tagueña, José Ma., and Gomez Navarro, Modesto, *Anuario de la Vid*. Spain, 1946–7
Yates, John W. D., *A Manual of Recent and Existing Commerce*. London, 1872

Index

Abad, 110
abonado, 141
ácaro, 196
Account of Spain, 34
acetaldehyde, 182, 186
acetic acid, 194
acidity, determination of, 195
  volatile, 195
Actas Capitulares, 13
adulteration, 91–6
ageing of wines, 182 *et seq*, 203, 247
  artificial, 248
agostado, 137
aguapie, 165, 169
aguardiente, 234, 235, 236
Aguera, Señor, 68
Ahold, 108
Alamo, 206
Alba, Duchess of,
albariza, *see* soil
albero, *see* soil
Alcazar, 2, 9
alcohol, grape, 178
  industrial, 191–2
aleopathy, 147
Alfonso VII, King, 11
Alfonso X, King (Alfonso the Sage), 10,
  11–12
Alfonso XII, King, 90, 187
Alfonso XIII, King, 101
Alhambra, 9
Ali Baba, 176
Alicante, 89
Allen, H. Warner, 20, 48, 188, 211,
  238
Allied Breweries, 49, 104
almacenistas, 65, 103, 232
almijar, 159

Al-Motamid, 10
alomado, 139
aluminium silicate, 257
Amadeo, King, 90
Amerine, Prof., M.A., 179
amontillado, 3, 125, 203 *et seq*, 245,
  236, 265
  alcoholic strength of, 219
  blending of, *see* blending
  development of, 203–4
  name of, 203
amoroso, *see* sherry
Andalusia, 1, 4, 8, 15, 34, 50–1, 64
Andalusia Company, 19, 22
Angel, Maria del Rosario, 66–7
Añina, 125
Anita, 46
añada wines, *see* sherry
apaleador, 257
appellation contrôlée, 102
Aragonese sherry, 93
Arcos de la Frontera, 8
Arcos, Duke of, 20
arena, *see* soil
Aristotle, 5
Armada, 25 *et seq*
arroba, 216, 240, 242
arrope, *see* colour wines
arrumbador, 216
Australia, 86, 183
Avery, John, 45
Ayamonte, 16, 20

Babycham, 48
Bacchanalian Sessions, 34
bajetes, 227
Baker, G. A., 210
Balao, Rafael, 110

Balbaina, 125
bandits, 130–1
Bank, 46
Barbadillo
  Antonio, 106, 230
  house of, 108, 111, 118, 225
  Manuel de, 230
Barnett, Augustus, 105
barro, *see* soil
bastardes, 18
Barrosa, battle of, 51
barrosa, 123
Bat and Ball, The, 35
Batten, Sir W., 32
Baumé, 175, 235
Bayona, Conde de, 43
beer, 5
Belgium, 254
Benchley, Robert, 268
Benetton, 109
Berbers, 8
Berges, Carmen, 66
Bernal y Ponce, Lorenzo, 166
Betjeman, John, 118
Bertola, 104, 108
bienteveos, 128
bina, 139
Black Hand Movement, 98
Blasco Ibañez, Vicente, 98
Blazquez, Agustín, 111, 198, 234
blending, 135, 209–11, 231–60
  amontillado, 244, 246
  brown sherries, 238, 248
  'cream' sherries, 236, 240, 248
  dessert sherries, 236, 262
  fino, 245
  manzanilla, 229
  matching, 242–4
  'medium' sherries, 244, 246
  montilla moriles, 232–3
  'nose', 242
  oloroso, 245, 246
  pale cream, 240, 248
  pale cortado, 246
  sweet wine, 234
  old wines, 246–7
Bobadilla, Don Gonzalo Fernandez de,
  108, 123, 184
bodegas, 34, 39, 182, 218
  buildings, 42, 66, 196–9
  in vineyards, 130
Bodegas, Calle, 14

Bodegas Internacionales, 42, 43, 104,
  108, 111, 199
Bodenham, Roger, 12, 22
Böhl de Faber, John Nicholas, 64–5
  Aurora, 65
  Cecilia, 64
Boleyn, Anne, 19
Bollullos de Condado, 232
Bols, 108
bomba, 216–17
Bonaparte, Joseph, 52
Bordeaux Mixture, 142, 149
Borrow, George, 223
'bottle age', 265–6
Boutelou, Esteban, 212, 225
Brackenburg, consul, 75
brandy, 77, 116, 118
Breton, Nicholas, 22
Brickdale, John, 37
Bristol, 46, 247
  'Bristol Cream', 46, 48, 248
  'Bristol Milk', 45, 46, 47–8
  British Medical Journal, 91
Brotherhood of St George, 19
Brown, George Massiot, 45
Bucellas, 46
Buck, Walter, J., 82–3
bullring, at Puerto, 65
Burdon, John Williams, 65–6
butt, *see* casks
Byass, Robert Blake, 68, 69
Byron, Lord, 51

cabaceo, 242, 249
Caballero de los Olivos, Don Diego,
  149
Caballero, Fernan, 64
Caballero, Luis, 66, 110, 244
Cabeza de Aranda, Don Antonio, 38
Cabeza de Vaca, Alvar Nuñez, 15
Cabeza y Zarco, 38, 51
Cadiz, 4, 5, 11, 24–5, 26, 29, 31, 33,
  37, 50, 96
  abortive expedition against, 29–30
  British consul in, 73, 75
Caere, 8
Calcavella, 46
calcium in soil, 123, 140, 147
California, 183
Calle Larga, 2
camera obscura, 193
Campbell & Co., 63
Campbell, Ian Maxwell, 99

Campbell, Roy, 61
canastas, 158
Canham, Mr, 33
canoa, 217
canuto, 190
capataz, 60, 187–9, 202
Capdepon, Adolf, 63
carbon 14 test, 192
Carlos III, King, 66
Carr, Sir John, 51
Carrascal, 125
Carthaginians, 6
Cartuja, 14
Casa-Domecq, Marqués de, 98
casks, bodega butts, 187
  butts, size of, 15, 186
  classification marks on, 187,
    199–200
  early reference to, 15
  for fermentation, 176–8, 181
  for maturing wine, 179, 182, 185–6,
    193, 207
  pipes, 25
  replacement when broken, 199
  seasoning of, 176, 249
  shipping, 240, 260
  storage in bodegas, 199
Casino Nacional, 84
casse blanca, 173
  cuprica, 196
  ferrica, 196
  oxidasica, 196
Castellar de la Frontera, 12
Castile, 12
Castile, King of, 17
Castillo de San Filipe, Marques del, 69
castra, 141
Catherine of Aragon,
Catholic kings, 11
Cato, 5
Caucasus, 5
cavabien, 138
Cecil, Edward, 29
cellars, in bodegas, 197–8
cenizo, see oidium
centrifuge, in grape pressing, 169–70
Ceritium, 7
Cervantes, 247
Cette, 86
Chamberlain, Sir T., 24
Champagne, 177, 180
champagne, 262
chaplain to the British colony, 100–1

Chantrey, John, 34
Chapman, Abel, 82
Charles I, 29
Charles V, 133
Charleton, Walter, M. D., 88, 170–1,
    195
Charterhouse Monastery, the, 14
Chaucer, Geoffrey, 16, 118
Chesterton, G. K., 97
Chiclana de la Frontera, 73, 125, 127,
    129
  wines from, 244
Chipiona, 14, 20, 22, 127–8, 129, 235
cholera, 63
Cholmondeley, Lord, 41
chlorophyll, 156
chlorosis, 147
Christian reconquest of Jerez, 11
Christie's, 98
Christopher & Co., 266
Chucena, 232
Civil War, 111, 131
Clarence, Duke of, 15
clarifying wine, 256–9
claros de lias, 191
  de turbios, 238–9
classification, see sherry
climate, 2–3, 125–7, 136, 228–9
clonal selection, 132
cloudiness in sherry, 195–6, 256–9
cobwebs, 197
Coll, Enrique, 83
color de macetilla, 238
  remendado, 238
colour wines, 225, 237–8, 241
  arrope, 237
  sancocho, 237
Columbus, Christopher, 15
Columella, 5, 134–5, 238
combinado, see mitad y mitad
Connell-Smith, Gordon, 20
Consejo Regulador, 102, 117, 127,
    128, 138, 144, 174, 219, 233
Constancia bodega, 68, 69
Constantinople, fall of, 13
co-operatives, 128
coopers, 15
Copas, Las, 168–9
copper sulphate, 142
Cordova, 9
corks, 265, 267
Cortes de la Frontera, 12
Cosens, F. G., 63

INDEX

Cosens, F. W., 63
Coto Doñana, 1
Covadonga, 11
Cowper, William 209
'cream' sherries, 236, 240, 248
criadera, 210 et seq
Croft, John, 106
Croft & Co., Ltd, 106–7, 111, 198
Croft-Cooke, Rupert, 20, 189
Crofts, Sir James, 22
Cromwell, Oliver, 32
Cross, Mr. Justice, 87
Cruess, W. V., 179
Cuesta, Luis de la, 66
Cuevas, José de las, 134
Cuprosan, 142, 149
custom duties, 18, 254
cuytes, 18
CZ, 38

Daily Telegraph, 221–2
Darwin, Sir Francis, 50
date wine, 5
Davillier, Charles, 226
defrutum, 238
delimitation, 233
Delage, family, 37, 110
de la Riva, house of, 42, 111
Democritus of Abdera, 5
Denman, James L., 93
Denmark, 254
Derby, Earl of, 230
desbraga, 140
deserpia, 138, 139
desfangado, 175
destillado, 192
development of sherry, in bottle, 265–8
    in cask, 186–7, 207
dextrose, 156
Diaz, Leon, 83
Diaz, Morales, 104
Dickens, Charles, 86–7
Diestro, 104, 108
Diez Hermanos, 77, 108
Diez Merito, 104, 232
diseases of sherry, 132, 193 et seq
Diwan of Principe Marwan, 10–11
Djemdet-Nast period, 5
Domecq, bodegas, 7, 198
    family of, 39, 61
    house of, 37, 111
    Lembeye, Pedro, 52–4, 57 et seq, 131

Adela, 58
Juan Pedro, 60–1
Juan y Hijos, 59
Domínques, Ramón Joaquín, 226
Domitian, 7
Don Ziolo, 108
Douglas, Henry, 203
Drake, Sir Francis, 24–5
'Dry Sack', 23, 108, 246, 251
Dubosc, Juan, 68
Duff, Sir James, 40–1, 44
Duff Gordon, Cosmo, 65
    house of, 57, 65
    Sir William, 53–5
Duke of Wellington, 44
dulce, see sweet wines
Dupré, August, 92
Duty bands, 254

East India Sherry, 237, 247–8
Ebn-el-Awam, 11
Edward I, King, 41
Edward III, King, 15
Edward VII, King, 97, 101
Edwards, Peeter, 26
E.E.C., 116, 237, 260
Egypt, 5
El Christo, 70
El Idrisi, 10
Elizabeth I, Queen, 22, 24, 25
El Maestro, 70
Engelbach, Edward, 78–9, 80
England, early trade with, 15–16, 17, 37
English early merchants, 13, 17 et seq.
    pirates, 13, 24–5, 29
Enrique III, King, 13
Enrique, IV, King, 12
Equizabel, Marcos, 108
eriophyes vitis, 151
espalderas, 138, 144
esparto grass mats, 161
espirraque, 165
Estacion de Viticultura, 123, 140, 259
Estevez, Señor, 62; José, 110
Estridge, William, 21
Esvique, Juan, 19
evaporation of wine, 186, 197, 206–7
excommunication of insects, 149
export trade, early, 13, 15, 18 et seq, 63, 72, 128

falsete, 190

INDEX

Falstaff, 27, 87, 94, 171
Farrell, James, 53
Ferguson, Diego, 169
fermentation, 175 *et seq*, 213
    lenta, 178
    temperature control in, 180
    tumultuous, 178
Fernandez Gao Hermanos, 83
Fernandez y Gonzalez, José Maria, 83
Ferrier, Capt. David, 38
fertilization, 141
Fiennes, Colonel, 46
filtration, 253, 258
Financiera Rumasa, *see* Rumasa
fining, 257–9
fino, 3, 125–6, 191, 202 *et seq*, 213, 263
    alcoholic strength of, 219, 254
    blending of, *see* blending
fino-amontillado, 203, 206
Fino San Patricio, 41
Fitch, Dr Asa, 152
Fixera, Francisco Antonio de la, 38
Fleetwood, Mr, 51
Fletcher, John, 26
floors, sprinkling with water, 197
flor, 182 *et seq*, 189, 203, 213, 227–8, 259
Flying Inn, The, 97
Ford, Richard, 6, 16, 60–1, 196, 223
Fornachon, J. C. M., 184
fortification, 191–2, 253–5
Fortnum & Mason, 79
Foster, John Cary, 82
Fuller's *History*, 46
fumigation, 142
fungoid parasites, 142–3, 148
Furlong, Charles Harman, 75, 82

galley slaves, 26, 29
Galsworthy, John, 99
garceta, 216, 227
Garcia de Angulo, José R., 173
Garcia Lorca, Federico, 61
Gardiner-Brown, Elizabeth, 38
Garvey, house of, 41, 104, 106, 108, 111, 198
    Patrick, 41, 60
    William, 41–2, 50, 59, 80
gas chromotography, 187
Gaunt's House, 45
Gay-Lussac, 178, 191, 204, 235
Gee, Walter Mallock, 94

gelatine, 257
Genesis, 4
Geraldino y Croquer, Tomás, 35
German touts, 90
Germany, 89, 254
Gibalbin, 106, 169
Gilbey, W. & A., Ltd, 107
Gilbey, Walter, 69
Giralda tower, 9
Gladstone's licensing policy, 80, 90
Gisper, Don Mariano, 42
glasses for sherry, 264
glucometer, 158, 161
glucose, 156
glycerine (glycerol), 182
Goethe, H., 133
golpe lleno, 139
Gonzalez
    & Dubosc, 68
    Angel, Manuel Maria, 67 *et seq*
    Byass & Co., Ltd, 66, 67, 68, 71, 107, 109, 111, 138, 169, 183, 198
    Gordon, Manuel Maria, 183, 184, 200, 206
    Rodriguez, Don José Antonio, 66
Gooden, James, 44
Gordon & Co.,
    Alexander, 110
    Arthur, 37
    C. P., 37, 51, 75–6
    family, 37
Gordon, Murphy & Co., 53–4
Gorman & Co., 63
Gorman, Dr J., 225
Goths, 8–9
Goya, 224
grafting, 140–1
Graham-Dunlop, A., 73, 88
Granada, reconquest of, 11, 12
Grand Metropolitan Hotels, 107
Grand National Club, 84
grapes, chemistry of, 156–7
    for eating, 120
    picking, 158
    sugar from, *see* sugar
    sunning of, 159, 161, 234–5
    varieties of, *see* vines
Great Britain, trade with, 35
Greek wine, 5
Greeks, 5
Gremio, 36–7, 40, 197
gridiron, 192
grocers, 90

Guadelete, battle of, 8
    river, 14
Guadalquivir, River, 2, 17, 22
Guerrero, 110
guild of wine growers, see Gremio
Gutierrez, Bartolome, 25
gypsies, 157
gypsum, 91, 164, 170–3

Hamburg, 85, 86
Hamilcar, 6
Hampton Court, 155
Hannibal, 6
Harmony
    nephews of P., 63
    bodegas, 65
    widow, 63
Harpers Wine & Spirit Gazette, 117
Harryson, Jefferye, 26
Harvey,
    Charles, 47
    E. A., 224
    Jack, 48
    John, 47
    John & Sons Ltd, 42, 45, 48, 72,
        103, 105 et seq, 108, 110, 111,
        198
    Thomas, 47
Hartley, Joseph, 88
Hasdrubal, 6
Hassall, Dr A. H., 173
Haurie,
    Juan, 37, 39–41, 57, 59, 83
    Juan Carlos, 52–3, 57, 59–60
    Juan y Sobrinos, 40
Hawkins, John, 24
Hedges, Dr, 268
Hehner, O., 173
Heijn, Albert, 108
helicopters, 142
Henry VIII, King, 18 et seq.
hepsema, 238
herbicides, 146
Heresbachius, Conrad, 41
Herrera, Alonso de, 131
Herrick, Robert, 22
Hertford, Marquis of, 41
Hesiod, 161
Hidalgo,
    Emilio Martin, 77
    Javier, 156, 185, 230
hilo, 195
Hinxman, J., 223

Hiram-Walker, 111
Hodgson, Francis, 51
Hombres Illustres de Jerez de la
    Frontera, 25
honey, 236
hoopoe, 157
Howell, George C., 268
Howell, James, 123
Huelva, 16, 73
Hughes, Ted, 118
Humbert, Amy, 77
    Arthur, 78–9
    C. F., 78–9
hunger, year of, 52
Hutton, Edward, 31

Iberians, ancient, 7
Ibn Abd al-Mun'im al Himyari, 10
Idrisi, see El Idrisi
Imperial Pemartin, 82
injerta, 140
injerta de yema, 141
Innes, Smith & Co., Ltd, 266
Inquisition, 20, 21 et seq.
insects, 143, 149 et seq.
Instituto Nacional de Investigaciones
    Agrarias (INAO), 140
International Distillers and Vintners
    Ltd, 107
iron compounds, 143, 148
irrigation, 126–7
Irving, Washington, 64
Isabella II, Queen, 69–70, 78
isinglass, 257
Ivison, 110
Ivison, Fletcher, 63

Jamaica, 33
James I, King, 28, 118
Jam-Sheed, 4
jarra, 216–17
jauria, 60
Jerez de la Frontera, 1–3, 10, 26, 50,
    60–2, 90, 120, 129
    archives of, 15, 23, 25
    arms of, 11
    climate of, 136
    destruction of, 11
    Muy Noble y Muy Leal Ciudad, 12
    names of, 3, 6, 8, 9, 31
    origin of, 4
    reconquest, 11
    siege of, 12

suffix *de la Frontera*, 12
walls of, 7, 120
Jerez Aromatizado, 256
Jerez Quinado, 255
Jerez Superior, 127, 144
Jerez-Xérès-Sherry, 102
Jews, explusion of, 14
Jimena de la Frontera, 12
Jimenez, Don Pedro, 134
Joel, consul, 96–7
Johnson, Dr, 23
Jonson, Ben, 22, 118
Juan I, King, 12
Jusuf, 12

Kelly, Michael, 88
King, Alderman, 20
Kyle, Mr, 148

Lacave, family of, 37
house of, 104, 108
Lacoste, family of, 37
lactic acid, 182
laevulose, 156
lagar, 162
Lancaster, Diana, 58
Lancet, The, 95, 172
Lebrija, 73, 127, 129
lees, 190–1, 238–9
Lembeye, Pedro, 40
Lepe, 16
levantar varas, 144
Levante, the, 4, 13, 84, 124, 126
Libyan wine, 5
lime, 142
Lisbon, 46
Livy, 6
Lomeni's Crusher, 166
Lonergan & White, 41
Los Palacios, 133
Los Tercios, 125
Lustau bodega, 7
Lustau, Emilio, 37, 66, 110, 117, 121, 199

Mackenzie & Co., 72, 83, 106, 110
Madeira, 46, 61, 64
Magellan, Ferninand, 15
Mahomet II, 13
Malaga, 33
sack, 23
wine from, 36, 89, 239
Malbrank, Francis, 33

malic acid, 156
malmsey, 5
mannite, 195
manzanilla, 3, 115, 125, 143, 189, 202, 206, 221–30, 263 *et seq*
alcoholic strength of, 227
name of, 225, 244
preparation of, 227
styles of, 228
travelling properties, 229
manzanilla olives, 226
Manzanilla, village of, 225
Manzanilla-Sanlúcar de Barrameda, 102, 221
Mappa Mundi, 10
marc, 165
Marcharnudo, 125
Marcilla, 184
marco real, 138–9
Mariana, Juan, 222
Marismas, 1, 228
Marlowe, Christopher, 22, 28
Martial, 5, 7, 238
Martinez, Eloy, 155
Mary, Bloody, 24
Mary, Queen of Scots, 25
Matthiesen, Furlong & Co., 82–3
maturation, 187 *et seq*, 204
in bottle, 265–6
Mayflower, The, 29
mead, 5, 7
mechanical harvesting, 159
Meddus, Dr, 31
Medinaceli family, 66
Medina Group, 108, 110–11
Medina Sidonia, Dukes of, 17–18, 26, 36
Melgarejo, Juan, 25
Melson, William, 24
Merula, Georgius, 134
Mesopotamia, 5
Methuen Treaty, 35, 239
mice, inebriate, 71–2
Middleton, Thomas, 22
mildew, 134, 142, 148
mill hopper, 166
Ministry of Food, 47–8
Misa, house of, 42, 104, 108
Manuel, 43, 77
mistela, 234
mitad y mitad, 192, 253
miteado, *see* mitad y mitad
Moguer, 232

monasteries, and viticulture, 14
Monemvasia, 6
Montepío de San Gines, 118
Montilla wine, 127, 263
Montilla-Moriles, 87, 116, 133, 232, 235
Montpensier, Duque de, 78
Moors, 11, 17
  conquest by, 9, 120
  prohibition of wine, 10
Morena de Mora, Pascual, 203
Morgan, F., & Co., 275
Moron de la Frontera, 12
moscatel, see sweet wines, vines
Moseley bodegas, 69
mosquito verde, 149–51
mosto, 156
Mountain (wine), 36, 46, 239
Mountfort, Guy, 82, 121
Muillet, Professor Pierre, 152
Mundy, Peter, 29
Murphy, Colonel, 53
Murphy, Patrick, 39
muscatel, see sweet wines, vines (moscatel)
must, 147, 156, 162 et seq, 174, 175 et seq, 187, 190–1
  classification of, see sherry
  rectified concentrated, see sweet wines
mycoderma aceti, 185, 194
  vini, 183

Napoleon, 52
Napoleonic Wars, see Peninsular War
Nelson, Lord, 56
Netherlands, 112–15
Nicholson, E. M., 121
Niebla, 232
Noah, 4
no cultivo, 146
no labreo, 146
nube, 195

oak, for casks, 176, 186
oidium, 72, 142, 148, 152
old bottled sherries, 266
Oldham, W., 63
oloroso, 125–6, 182, 191, 202 et seq, 247, 262 et seq
  alcoholic strength of, 205–6, 220
O'Neale, 39, 110
  bodega, 7, 39

Oporto, 106
Ordish, George, 152
Orlidge, James, 45
Osborne, Conde de, 65
  house of, 109, 111, 197; see also Duff Gordon
  Thomas, 41, 65
Osorio de Moscoso, Consuelo, 221–2
Oste, John, 20
Ostrych, William, 18, 19, 21
Otaolaurruchi, 104, 108
oxidation, 156–7, 168, 186, 203, 259
  avoiding in bottle, 267

Pacheco, Francisco, 223
pagos, 125
pajuela, 149
palma, 192, 199
palma cortado sherry, 199
palo cortado, 141, 200, 202, 205 et seq, 265
  development of, 205
Palomino Fernán Yáñes, 131
Palomino y Vergara, 40, 104, 108
Palomino vine, see vines
Pan, Don José, 194
Pando, 79
Parada y Barreto, Diego Ignacio, 25, 125, 131, 212
Pardoner's Tale, The, 16
Paez, Luis, 108
Park, Gordon, 90
Parsons, Robert, 22
Parte Arroyo solera, 69
Pasquil's Palinodia, 22, 170
Pasteur, Louis, 152, 183
pata de gallina, 205
paxarete, 249
peasant rebellions, 81, 98
pectin, 156
Pedro Ximenez vine, see vines, wine; see sweet wines
Peecke, Richard, 30–1
Pemartin, family of, 37
  house of, 44, 104, 108
  Julian, 61, 80–2
Peninsular War, 44, 50–2, 197
Pepys, Samuel, 32, 33, 264–5
Perez de Guzman, Alonso, 17
Perpignan, 86
Perry, William, 45–7
Persepolis, 4

Pery, Thomas, 20
peste, la, 195
pests, see insects
Philip V, King, 35
Phayre & Bradley, 106
Phillips, Thomas, 56
Phoenicians, 4, 5, 6
photosynthesis, 156
phylloxera, 85, 98, 128, 131, 140, 149
   et seq
  treatments for, 155, 232
Picardo y Cia, 203
Pickering, Henry, 37
pie, 164–5
pies de cuba, 177
pipes, see casks
pisador, 162–4
Pius V, Pope, 25
Plague of London, 268
Planchon, M. J. E., 152
plastering, 91, 92; see also gypsum
Platt, Sir Hugh, 141
Pliny, 135, 170, 238, 246
Plymouth, 15
poda, 142
Poe, Edgar Allan, 204
polychrosis botrana, 151
pomace, 169
ponce, 255
Poniente, 126
port, 44, 262
Portillo, D. J., 25, 172
Portrait of a Wilderness, 121
potassium, 172, 194
potassium sulphate elimination, 173
Povy, Thomas, 264
Praeterita, 57, 94
prensa, 165
presses,
  history of, 162–5
  horse-driven, 166
  hydraulic, 166, 168
  mechanical, 165–7
  pneumatic, 168
  screw, 164
pressing boots, 162–3
pressing by foot, 162–4
pressing, continuous, 169–70
pressing rooms, 162–3
pressing, temperature during, 162–4
Price Waterhouse, 114, 117
Prince Regent, 41
Probus, 7

Protectorate, the, 31
pruning, 141, 142–3
pseudococcus citris, 151
Puerto de Santa Maria, 2, 3, 10, 26,
   34–5, 66, 127, 129
Puerto Fino, 244
Puerto Real, 7, 63, 127, 129
pulgón, 73, 149–60
Punch, 75
Punic War, 6
Puntal, capture of, 29
Pye, Henry James, 118
Pyrenees, 9

Quebec, 89
Quiros Carrasco, José Maria, 173

racking off, 190–1
radioactivity, 260
railways, 74
rainfall; see climate
Raleigh, Sir Walter, 22
Randolph, Thomas, 31
Ravenna Cathedral, 155
raya, cask markings, 190, 192, 200
  sherries, 206
Réal Tesoro, 110
Recceswinth, 8
recogida, 144
rectified must, 237, 244
referencias, 242
refreshing solera (rociando), 185, 210,
  216
  mechanization of, 218
refrigeration, 258
Reina Victoria, 46
Reneger, John, 21
repaso, 139
Revueltas Carrillo y Montel, Don
   Francisco, 172
riparia, 140
Rivero, 110
  J. M., 38, 101
  Don Pedro Augustin, 58
rociador, 216–17, 227
Roderick, King, 8
Roger II, King of Sicily, 10
Rome, export of wine to, 7
  rule of, 6–7
Rooke, Sir George, 35
Roos's narrative, 28
Rota, 20, 35, 127, 129
  tent, 20, 104, 233–4

Roxas Clemente, 134
Rudolph, W., 63
Ruiz Hermanos, A. R., 104
Ruiz-Mateos, 105, 198
    José-Maria, 103–4
Ruiz-Mateos, Zoilo, 103, 104
Rumasa, 104, 107–9, 112, 128, 229
rumney, 14
Rupert, Prince, 46
Ruskin, John, 55 *et seq*, 94
    John James, 53 *et seq*
    Telford & Domecq, 54, 59
Russell, James, 45
Russia, 74

Sacas, 214–15
saccharomyces, 183
Sachs, P. J., 134
sack, 15, 22, 23 *et seq*, 27–8, 31, 34
Sacristia, La, 68
St Dionysius, the feast of, 11
St George's Church, Sanlucar, 18, 19, 33, 37
St Gildas, the Wise, 268
St Matthew, feast of, 157
Saintsbury, Professor George, 97, 262–3
Salamanca, battle of, 51
Salvation Army, 97
sámago, 149
Sanchez, Juan, 59, 61
sancocho; *see* colour wine
Sandeman, 111
    David, 44, 45
    George, 43–5
    George Glas, 45
    George G. Sons & Co. Ltd, 44, 80–3
Sandeman's Bodega Grande, 101
Sandeman palace, 99–100
Sanlucar de Barrameda, 1, 2, 3, 7, 15, 17–18, 24, 26, 33, 34, 38, 127, 129, 221 *et seq*
    name of, 222–3
    Sketch-Books, 225
    soleras, 227–9
    wines of, 225; *see also* manzanilla
San Miguel, church of, 2
Sannino, Dr F. Antonio, 196
Santa Barbara, 155
sapa, 238
Saracens, *see* Moors
Sauterne, 90
scale, in solera, 211 *et seq*, 217–19

Scheres, 8
Scotland, 35
Scott, Capt. Rochfort, 63, 248
screw caps, 267
scud, 195
Šeriš, 9, 10
Seagrams, 45
sediment, 258
Seritium, 8
Seville, 9, 10, 11, 22, 28, 268
    wines from, 232
Shakespeare, 22, 27, 171
Sheridan, Richard, 88
sherry,
    adulteration of, *see* adulteration
    amontillado, *see* amontillado
    amoroso, 248, 263
    añada, 147, 193, 206
    añada system, 210–13
    Australian, 86–7, 127
    brown, 262–3, 238, 248
    classification of, 190, 192–3, 199–200, 202 *et seq*, 206
    cream, 240
    development of, *see* development
    East India, 237, 247–8
    fakes and imitations, 73, 85 *et seq*
    fashions in, 240–1, 254–5
    fino, *see* fino
    flor, *see* flor
    French, 86–7
    Hamburg, 86
    keeping qualities, 265–7
    name of, 33–4
    oloroso, *see* oloroso
    palo cortado, *see* palo cortado
    paxarete, 249
    price of, 73, 94, 115, 117
    shipments to UK, 15
    'solera', 46, 247, 260
    South African, 86–7
    strength of, 254–5
    with meals, 261–3
sherry dinner, 263
sherry parties, 102
Sherry Shippers' Association, 101
Sherryana, 85
Shiel, Bernard, 63
    family of, 41
    R., 63
shipping, 34, 247–9
Shiraz, 6
Showerings, 48, 104, 106

Siemens, Peter, 133
Sierra, Simeon, 69
sifon, 216–17
Sitwell, George, 20
Sixtus V, Pope, 25
slump, 96, 229
smuggling, 223
snobbery, 261
snuff, 41
soil, albariza, 120, 122 et seq, 134,
    135, 140, 147, 235
  albero, 122
  arena, 120, 124, 135
  barro, 120, 124, 135
  solera system, 185, 210, et seq
  history of, 212–13
  for manzanilla, 213
  name of, 211
  shipping, 211, 247
  tools used in working, 216–17
'solera' sherry, 244
Soto, Luis de, 30, 109
  Victorina de, 67
Soto y Molina, Don José de, 63
Soult, Marshal, 51, 52
South Africa, 2, 86, 183
Spanish earth, 257
sparganothis pilleriana, 151
Spencer, Tom, 232
Spenser, Edmund, 22
spraying, 142
stalking machines, 166–7
Star Chamber, Court of, 22
Stephenson, George, 74
Stonor, Henry, 38
storks, 2
Strabo, 5
Strachey, John, 47
strikes, 118, 158
Strong, Dr John, 35
succinic acid, 182
sugar in or from grapes, 148, 156
sugar invert, 237
sulphur, 175, 194
sulphuric acid, 91
Summerskill, Dr Edith, 47
sunning, see grapes
supermarkets, 110, 117
Suter, George W., 62, 63
sweet wines, 234 et seq, 240–2
  for blending, 234
  dulce apagado, 235, 236
  dulce de almibar, 237, 244

dulce pasa, 235
moscatel, 234–5
rectified concentrated musts, 237,
    244
  Pedro Ximenez, 116, 234–5, 248
Swinburne, Henry, 268

tajón, 123
tanks, for fermentation, 179–80
Tales of the Alhambra, 64
Tangier, evacuation of, 33
Tarik Ben Zeyad, 8
tannin, 156, 162, 184
tapas, 117, 262–3
tartar, cream of, 172, 173
tartaric acid, 156, 172, 173
  meso-, 259
Tartessus, 4
taxes, 13, 254
Teher-e-Kooshon, 5
Telford, Henry, 54
temperature, atmospheric; see climate
    during vinification, 180
tent, 20; see Rota tent
Terry, family and firm of, 66, 83, 108
Theophrastus of Eresos, 5
Theopompos, 4
'thirsty thunderbolt, the', 62
Thompson, Thomas, 33
Thomson, J. G. & Co., Ltd, 33
Thomson, W., 152
Thudichum, Dr. J. L. W., 91–3, 96,
    172
tierra blanca, de anafas, de vino, 122,
    257
Tilden, Thompson & Croft, 106
Times, The, 85, 91, 93, 95
tinajas, 176
tinetas, 158
Tio Mateo, 108
Tio Pepe, 71, 240
tiradores, 165
Toledo, 9
Tom's Coffee House, 44
tosca, 122
Tovey, Charles, 4, 84, 88, 223–4,
    252–3
towers in vineyards, 130
tractors, 137
trade marks, 45; infringement of, 59
Trafalgar, battle of, 56
Trebujena, 1, 73, 127, 129
tresbolillo, 138–9

Trillat, 186
Trocadero mole, 74
Trollope, Antony, 96
Tryana, 20
Tucker, Mr, 148
Tunnicliffe, Dr F. W., 96
Turner, Dick, 97

ullage, 181, 184, 210
ultra cooling, 196, 259
ultrasonic vibration, 259
Umberto II, King of Italy, 242
uncinula necator, see oidium
Union de Exportadores de Jerez, 104
United Dutch, 108
Urch, Ann, 47
    Thomas, 47
U.S.A., 15, 254
uvas de cuelga, 135

valderrama, 104, 108
Valdespino, Antonio, 34
    house of, 45, 181
Vandalusia, 8
Vandals, 8, 13
Van Horn, Mr, 43
Varela, 104, 108
Varro, 5, 238
Vasey, Mr, 95
Vaslin Press, 168
vats, 179, 249
Velazquez, 223
venencia, 187–9
Venice, 13
Verdad, Don Pedro, 94
Vergara & Dickinson family, 40
Vergara and Gordon, 104, 108
Victoria, Queen, 97, 99
Victoria Eugenia, Queen, 46
Victoria Wine, 94
Vidal-Barraquer, Professor José Ma.,
    152
Villalba, 232
Viña Tula, 130
Viñarvey, 106
Vine Products, 87
vines, age of, 155
    Alban, 131
    Albillo Castellano, 134
    Albuelis, 135
    American, 140
    Beba, 135, 155
    Black Hamburg, 155

Calgalon, 134
Cañacazo, 134, 135, 136
clonal selection of, 132, 147, 174
crossings, 140
diseases of, 132, 137, 147 et seq
Gabriela, 135
Horgazuela, 131
Listan, 131
louse, see phylloxera
Mantuo Castillano, 135
Mantuo de Pila, 135
Mantuo de Rey, 135
Mollar Blanco, 134
Mollar Negro, 135
Moscatel Gordo Blanco, 131, 135,
    136, 161
Palomina, 131, 235
Palomino, 35, 131 et seq, 149, 161
Palomino, clones, 132, 133
Palomino de Jerez, 131, 136
Pedro Ximenez, 131, 133 et seq, 136,
    161
Perruno, 135
Temprana, 131
wild, 5
vinegar, 185, 190, 194
vineyards, 120 et seq
    area 5 of, 125, 128–9
    cultivation, 147
    guarding of, 128
    houses in, 130–1
    labours in, 137 et seq
    location of, 125
    mechanization of, 138, 145
    order for destruction, 114–16
    patterns for planting, 138–9
    yield of, 174
    see also soil
Vinicola Hidalgo, 42–3, 198
vino carlón, 225
vino de color; see colour wines
vino de pasto, 248
vinos de romania; see rumney
vintage, failure of, 98, 136
    gathering of, 157–9
    time of, 157–8
    wines, see sherry, añada
    years, 207–8; see also sherry, añada
Vintners' Guild of Jerez; see Gremio
Virgil, 238
Visigoths, 8
viteus vitifolii, 152
Vizetelly, Henry, 92, 94–5, 130, 245

INDEX

Waddington, Dean, 88
Wake, James, 20
Walden, Lord Howard de, 98
Ward, Phillipa, 34
War of the Spanish Succession, 35
Warden, The, 96, 264
Warter, Joseph, 75, 77–9, 80
Watneys, 107
weeding, *see* vineyards, labours in
weeds, 145, 147
Welby, Earle, 262
Wellington, Duke of, 44, 108
Westwood, Mr, 152
Williams, Alexander, 77, 80, 83
   Carl, 102
Williams & Humbert Ltd, 77, 79, 103,
   104, 108, 111, 198, 206–8
Willmes press, 168
Wilson, Dr, 63
   James, 59
Wimbledon, Viscount, 29

wine, origin of, 4–5
Wine Trade Club, London, 43
Wine Trade Review, 90
wines from outlying districts, 128
Wisdom & Warter Ltd, 63, 75, 77,
   109, 209

Xenophon, 5
Xeque, 23
Xera, 4
xerampelus vitifolii, 152

yeasts, 175 *et seq*, 182
yema, mosto de, 165, 169
yeso 170–3; *see* gypsum
Young Pretender, 37
Ysasi family and bodegas, 75

zapatos de pisar, *see* pressing boots
Zola, Émile, 94
Zona, 127, 144

Faber Books on Wine
SERIES EDITOR: Julian Jeffs

―――――

Other titles in the series are available from your usual bookseller or, in case of difficulty, use this order form to order direct from Faber and Faber.

Please send me the following:

	ISBN prefix 0–571		qty	total
Bordeaux, David Peppercorn				
pbk	13654–0	£14.99	＿＿	＿＿＿
French Country Wines, Rosemary George				
hbk	13894–2	£14.99	＿＿	＿＿＿
pbk	15311–9	£8.99	＿＿	＿＿＿
German Wines, Ian Jamieson				
hbk	14154–4	£17.99	＿＿	＿＿＿
pbk	14155–2	£8.99	＿＿	＿＿＿
Italian Wines, Philip Dallas				
pbk	15179–5	£7.99	＿＿	＿＿＿
Port, George Robertson				
hbk	16541–9	£14.99	＿＿	＿＿＿
pbk	16542–7	£8.99	＿＿	＿＿＿
The Wines of Australia, Oliver Mayo				
hbk	16395–5	£15.99	＿＿	＿＿＿
pbk	16396–3	£7.99	＿＿	＿＿＿
The Wines of Greece, Miles Lambert-Gócs				
hbk	15387–9	£14.99	＿＿	＿＿＿
pbk	15388–7	£7.99	＿＿	＿＿＿
The Wines of the Rhône, John Livingstone-Learmonth				
hbk	15111–6	£25.00	＿＿	＿＿＿
pbk	14622–8	£14.99	＿＿	＿＿＿

Please enter total value here   £ ＿＿＿

Add 15% for p & p   £ ＿＿＿

Total   £ ＿＿＿

Methods of Payment
By cheque, made payable to Faber and Faber Ltd, or by credit card. Please add 15% of total order value to cover postage and packing, and allow up to 28 days for delivery.

Payment by Cheque
I enclose a cheque in the sum of £ _____

Payment by Credit Card
Please debit my Access/Visa (delete as appropriate)

Card No ☐☐☐☐☐☐☐☐☐☐☐☐☐☐☐☐

Expiry date of card _____

Signed _____ Date _____

Name _____

Address _____

_____

_____ Postcode _____

Please allow up to 28 days for delivery.

Send to: Orders Department, Faber and Faber Ltd, Burnt Mill, Elizabeth Way, Harlow, Essex CM20 2HX
(Telephone 0279 417134/Fax 0279 417366)